The IRA

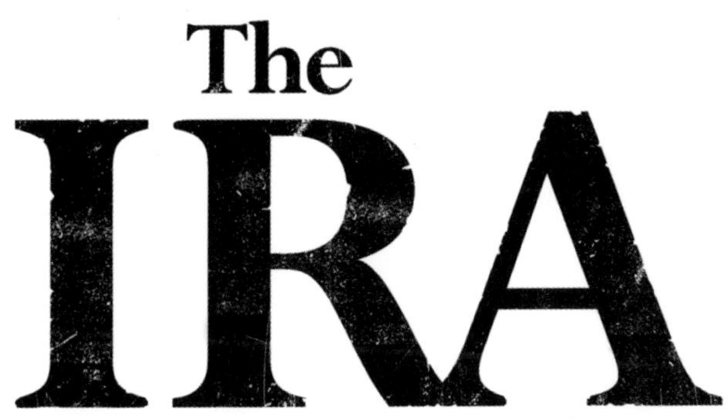

A DOCUMENTARY HISTORY 1916–2005

The IRA

A DOCUMENTARY HISTORY 1916–2005

Brian Hanley

Gill & Macmillan

Gill & Macmillan
Hume Avenue, Park West, Dublin 12
www.gillmacmillanbooks.ie

978 07171 68316

Index compiled by Grainne Farren
Design by Burns Design
Print origination by Burns Design
Printed in Poland

This book is typeset in Sabon and Trade Gothic.

The paper used in this book comes from the wood pulp of managed forests. For every tree felled, at least one tree is planted, thereby renewing natural resources.

A CIP catalogue record for this book is available from the British Library.

5 4 3 2 1

CONTENTS

Michael Collins, former IRA adjutant general, in the uniform of commander in chief of the Free State army, shortly before his departure for Cork in August 1922. COURTESY OF THE NATIONAL MUSEUM OF IRELAND

ACKNOWLEDGMENTS

This book would not have been possible without the assistance and generosity of many archivists, librarians and their institutions. Seamus Helferty at University College Dublin Archives Department, repository of the most important collections on the IRA, was, as always, exceptionally helpful. A very gracious thanks to him and the staff at UCD. Gerry Kavanagh and his colleagues, Glen Dunne and Bernie Metcalfe, at the National Library of Ireland, went beyond the call of duty to assist me. I would also like to thank Maura Kennedy at the Dublin City Library & Archive, Caitriona Crowe at the National Archives of Ireland and Conor McNamara and Colette O'Daly at the National Library's Manuscripts Department for their assistance. I wish to thank Lar Joye, Curator of the marvellous 'Soldiers and Chiefs' exhibition at the National Museum of Ireland, Collins Barracks for his help. Thanks to Finbarr Connolly at the National Museum for help with images.Thanks also to Martin Spain at *An Phoblacht/Republican News* for permission to republish material from AP/RN. I am also grateful to the Workers' Party for permission to use photographs from their collections.

I also wish to thank Dave Browne, Seán Curry, Mary McMillen, Scott Millar, Eamon Melaugh, Seamus Murphy, Kya Richards, Peter Rigney, Mick Ryan, Ciaran Swan, Maurice Twomey Jr and Padraig Yeates for their generosity with images.

In the time spent working on this book I was lucky enough to be employed in the History Department at St Patrick's College, Drumcondra, and would like to express my gratitude to my colleagues there. I also wish to thank the students who have taken my courses at NUI Maynooth, Queen's University, Belfast, Trinity College, Dublin and St Patrick's.

I also must thank Fergal Tobin of Gill & Macmillan for his enthusiasm for this project and Alison Walsh for her careful editing.

A special note of thanks to Michael MacEvilly, a republican and scholar who was of great assistance to me when I worked on my PhD ten years ago, as he was to dozens of researchers over the years. Sadly, Michael passed away in 2009.

As ever, my greatest gratitude is to Órla.

INTRODUCTION

The Irish Republican Army (IRA) has been a constant factor in Irish life since 1916. The initials alone provoke a range of reactions in Irish people. Many, particularly in the Republic, identify with what they see as the 'Old IRA', but shun association with the IRA of the modern era. Both the Republic's major political parties, Fianna Fáil and Fine Gael, see themselves as having inherited the mantle of the struggle for independence during 1919-21, exemplified in their holding of annual commemorations of Michael Collins and Liam Lynch. Meanwhile, the modern republican movement and the Sinn Féin party see themselves as the rightful heirs of the IRA of 1919-21 (though this is also contested by their rivals). For some republicans the modern IRA is the same organisation that fought the British from 1919-21 and resisted the Free State from 1922-23, and is still pursuing Ireland's unfinished revolution. Others object strongly to any such link, claiming that the situation that pertained in 1919 was vastly different to that in later decades. (Ulster Unionist opinion, in contrast, is more straightforward, as they have never felt affection for the IRA in any of its guises.)

But what did the IRA actually say at various stages of its history? How were its arguments presented to members and supporters and did its key positions change over time?

The politics of the IRA, the make-up of its membership and its numerical strength has differed greatly over the years, as has the public's awareness of the organisation. For many people it is perceived as a primarily northern organisation. But for most of the IRA's history it was much stronger in what is now the Republic of Ireland than in Northern Ireland. Much of the language we now associate with the IRA dates from the modern era. In Ken Loach's *The Wind That Shakes The Barley* (2006) IRA volunteers discuss why they are fighting 'the Brits'. But there were no 'Brits' in 1921: the term dates from the 1970s. Similarly, when republican bandsmen shouted 'up the 'RA' as the coffins of ten men hanged in Mountjoy during the War of Independence passed Dublin's GPO in October 2001, they were using a term for the IRA that did not exist when those men were executed in 1921.

In the past eight years I have taught courses on the history of the IRA in several universities. While there is always interest in these courses, I have found that students are often unaware of, or genuinely surprised by, aspects of the IRA's history. Many are shocked by the brutality of the Civil War: others by the tactics used by the IRA from 1919-21. The conflicts of the 1940s and even the Border campaign of 1956-62 are often unknown. For a great many people the IRA disappears in 1923 and reemerges in 1969, which leaves out important developments in the history of parties like Fianna Fáil and Clann na Poblachta, the Workers' Party and Sinn Féin.

I hope that the documents presented here will illustrate some of these complexities. This book is not a definitive history of the IRA, nor a complete study of it in any era. For my commentaries I have drawn heavily on general histories of the organisation, on memoirs of activists, the Bureau of Military History interviews, and recent studies of the revolutionary period. I hope the documents, leaflets, posters and newspapers speak for themselves. The bibliography will provide a guide for those who wish to explore further. The internal documentation is weighted heavily towards the 1920s and 1930s for the simple reason that very few modern IRA documents are available. It is to be hoped that this, too, will change in the future and we will be able to add further to our knowledge of one of the most enduring revolutionary organisations in the world.

Brian Hanley

August 2010

IRA bomb factory, Cavan, 1921 COURTESY OF THE NATIONAL MUSEUM OF IRELAND

Chapter 1

WAR OF INDEPENDENCE

P. O. Box 5141.

Head Quarters, Fenian Brotherhood,

706 BROADWAY,

NEW YORK, JANUARY 15TH, 1867.

CIRCULAR.

The following Regulation for the Uniform of the Commissioned Officers of the IRISH REPUBLICAN ARMY, is published for the information and guidance of all concerned, and will be strictly adhered to.

COAT.

All Officers shall wear a FROCK COAT of DARK GREEN CLOTH, the skirt to extend two-thirds of the distance from the top of the hip to the bend in the knee; single breasted for Captains and Lieutenants, and double breasted for all other grades.

1. *For a Major General.*—Two rows of buttons on the breast, nine in each row, placed by threes; the distance between each row 6 inches at the top, and 3½ inches at the bottom; stand up collar, cuffs three inches deep; the COLLAR and CUFFS to be Dark Blue VELVET; lining of the coat to be dark color. The collar and cuffs to be trimmed with gold lace.

2. *For a Brigadier General.*—The same as for a Major General, except that there will be only eight buttons in each row, on the breast, placed in pairs.

3. *For a Colonel, Lieut. Colonel and Major.*—The same as for a Major General, except that there will be only seven buttons in each row, placed at equal distances. The collar and cuffs to be of dark blue cloth, and trimmed with gold lace.

4. *For a Captain, First and Second Lieutenants.*—The same as for a Colonel, except that there will be only one row of nine buttons on the breast, placed at equal distances.

TROWSERS.

1. *For General Officers, and Officers of the General Staff.*—To be of BLACK CLOTH, with a GOLD CORD three-sixteenths of an inch in diameter, down the outer seam.

2. *For all Regimental Officers.*—DARK BLUE CLOTH, with a WELT down the outer seam of Light Green, three-sixteenths of an inch in diameter.

HAT.

BLACK: width of brim 3¼ inches—height of crown 6¼ inches, bound with black silk ¾ inch wide; (army pattern). For general officers GOLD CORD with acorn ends, all other officers, GREEN SILK CORD with tassel ends. The brim of the hat to be looped up on the right side and fastened with an ornament representing the shamrock; three black feathers for general officers, and two for all other officers; a gold embroidered wreath in front encircling the letters I. R. A. on black ground.

FORAGE CAP.

Commissioned Officers, *may* at their pleasure wear Forage Caps, in the field, (army pattern) with the distinctive ornament of the corps and regiment in front.

SHOULDER STRAPS.

For General Officers and Officers of the General Staff, of dark blue ground, 4 inches long by 1½ inches wide, with two rows of bullion around the edge, for all other officers one row of bullion: the ground of all other officers' shoulder straps, to be Green for Infantry, Yellow for Cavalry, and Red for Artillery, with the following ornaments to designate rank, to be placed in centre of the strap, viz:

FOR A MAJOR GENERAL, Two Sunbursts in Silver.
" " BRIGADIER GENERAL, One Sunburst in Silver.
" " COLONEL, Phœnix in Silver.
" " LIEUTENANT COLONEL, Shamrock Leaf in Silver.
" " MAJOR, Shamrock Leaf in Gold.
" " CAPTAIN, Two Bars in Gold.
" " FIRST LIEUTENANT, One Bar in Gold.
" " SECOND " Plain.
" " SURGEONS and ASS'T SURGEONS, black ground with ornaments as above according to their assimulated rank.

SASH.

For GENERAL OFFICERS AND OFFICERS OF THE GENERAL STAFF, COLONELS, LT. COLONELS, MAJORS AND SURGEONS to be of Green Silk, all other officers to wear no sash.

SPURS.

For all Mounted Officers, Yellow Metal, or Gilt.

GLOVES.

For all General or Mounted Officers to be Buff Leather Gauntletts, for all others Buff or White Gloves.

SWORD BELT,

For all officers, a Waist Belt two inches wide to be worn over the sash, of Black Plain, or Patent Leather, with Slings and Swivels, and brass plate in front. All officers to wear appropriate swords, in accordance with their rank, and arm of service.

BUTTONS.

For General and General Staff Officers, Gilt, Convex, large size, ⅞ of an inch in diameter, with I. R. A. in raised letters. For all other Officers, Gilt, ¾ of an inch in diameter, with letters I. R. A. encircled by a wreath.

REMARKS.

Shoulder Straps, Buttons, Cap Ornaments, Belts, Belt Plates and Sashes will be furnished from these Head Quarters at cost prices by sending orders, which in all cases must be attended by the Cash.

By command of

PRESIDENT WM. R. ROBERTS.

S. P. SPEAR,

Adj[illegible] [illegible] War, F. B.

It is the IRA of 1919-21 that maintains the greatest grip on our historical imagination in Ireland. Michael Collins is perhaps the best-known figure in modern Irish history, while the memoirs of IRA leaders like Tom Barry and Dan Breen still sell steadily. Hundreds of places remember with pride the details of an ambush or the activities of a local flying column during the War of Independence. But the extent of the fighting, the regional variations in the IRA's campaign and the tactics the organisation embraced at this time are less well known.

Many date the beginning of war to January 1919, but the conflict was the outcome of a period of radicalisation since 1912, including the Dublin Lockout, the Home Rule crisis, the Great War and of course, the Easter Rising. After 1919 there was a marked variation in the level of violence in different areas, but the conflict was escalating in the months before the Truce in July 1921. Over 2,000 people were killed in Ireland between 1919-21.

The roots of modern Irish revolutionary organisations lie in the Irish Republican Brotherhood, or the Fenians, founded during the 1850s by veterans of the failed 1848 rebellion. James Stephens and John O'Mahony were among those Irish exiled to Paris in the rebellion's aftermath. They mixed with revolutionaries from across Europe and were particularly influenced by the forms of secret organisation favoured by French and Italian radicals. They were influenced, too, by the Europeans' internationalist politics, with Stephens claiming that he 'would fight for an abstract principle of right in defence of any country; and were England a republic battling for human freedom on the one hand, and Ireland leagued with despots on the other, I should, unhesitatingly, take up arms against my native land'.

Stephens returned to Ireland by 1856, while O'Mahony moved on to New York. In the U.S. O'Mahony set about forming a new republican organisation that would fund and arm a revolution in Ireland. Stephens, meanwhile, began uniting the various secret societies and factions in Ireland into one organisation. On 17 March 1858, Stephens and his associates took an oath to make Ireland an 'independent democratic republic'. Initially their organisation had no name, a principle borrowed from continental secret societies, but in time it became the Irish Republican Brotherhood (IRB).

The new organisation adopted a cell structure, or 'circles', small groups of members, bound by elaborate rules and regulations. Stephens' new 'circles' spread throughout the country, propelled by the promise of Irish-American money and forces to aid an Irish rising. But whilst the movement was very successful in recruiting young men in Ireland and America during the 1860s, it was also bedevilled by splits and infiltration on both sides of the Atlantic.

Facing page: Fenian Brotherhood Circular, 1867 COURTESY OF THE NATIONAL LIBRARY OF IRELAND

In May 1866, a band of 800 Fenians, many of them recently demobilised following the American Civil War, under a banner emblazoned with the slogan 'Irish Republican Army', attempted an invasion of Canada, hoping to strike at Britain through one of its imperial possessions and perhaps spark off an Anglo-American conflict. This and similar Fenian efforts in North America came to naught, as did an attempted rebellion in Ireland during 1867. Nonetheless, the Fenians were to prove a major influence on other movements such as the Land League, the Gaelic Athletic Association and the Gaelic League; the Fenians would also organise a bombing campaign in England during the 1880s and as the IRB, had a key role in the revitalisation of republican politics in Ireland in the early 1900s.

ÓGLAIGH NA HÉIREANN – THE IRISH VOLUNTEERS

On 1 November 1913, Eoin MacNeill, Vice-President of the Gaelic League and Professor of History at University College Dublin, published an article entitled 'The North Began' in the Gaelic League journal, *An Claidheamh Soluis*. The article advocated the formation of a militia to be modelled on the Ulster Volunteer Force (UVF), which had been formed on 31 January 1913. The UVF's foundation formed part of a campaign by Irish Unionists to prevent limited self-government, or 'Home Rule', being instituted by the British government.

As a result of the article MacNeill was approached by a group of IRB members who asked that he take the lead in forming this volunteer force. The IRB had already made some moves towards military preparations, believing armed conflict was more likely since the formation of the UVF, but they were aware of the importance of having the broader support that a 'respectable' figure like MacNeill could bring. The Irish Volunteers were founded at a public meeting, attended by several thousand, in Dublin's Rotunda on 25 November 1913.

Many observers presumed that the purpose of the Volunteers would be to combat the UVF. In contrast MacNeill personally believed that the formation of the UVF had been a positive step and that they might overthrow the old leadership of Unionism and even join forces with their nationalist counterparts. Most Irish Volunteers, however, declared themselves prepared to fight to defend self-government, or in the case of the more radical, for independence itself.

The Volunteers were not the only armed force active in Dublin: during late 1913, the Irish Citizen Army had been founded to protect striking workers during the Dublin Lockout. By 1914, the ICA had developed into a trade-union militia, perhaps 300 strong, which included women among its membership.

The IRB, which had about 1,500 members in 1912, was the driving force behind the local organisation of the Volunteers. It remained a small force, poorly armed and led by a committee dominated by IRB members. The Ulster Volunteers, in contrast, numbered about 85,000 men, were led by retired British Army officers and after successful gunrunning at Larne in April 1914, were armed with 25,000 rifles.

This situation changed in May 1914, when John Redmond, leader of the Home Rule movement, whose goal was to ensure self-government for Ireland by parliamentary means, made a decision to take over the Volunteers (thereby neutralising them as a threat and bringing them under his control). He urged his supporters to join the Volunteers and by July 1914, 150,000 men were enrolled, while IRB members were now outnumbered in the Volunteer leadership.

Óglaiġ na hÉireann
Irish Volunteers.

A
PUBLIC MEETING
For the formation of IRISH VOLUNTEERS
and the enrolment of men,
WILL BE HELD IN THE
LARGE CONCERT HALL,
ROTUNDA,
ON
TUESDAY, NOV. 25
At 8 p.m.

EOIN MacNEILL, B.A., will preside

All able-bodied Irishmen will be
eligible for enrolment.

GOD SAVE IRELAND.

CURTIS, PRINTER, 12 TEMPLE LANE, DUBLIN.

COURTESY OF THE NATIONAL LIBRARY OF IRELAND

In late July of that year, 1,500 Mauser rifles were imported through Howth on the *Asgard,* skippered by Erskine Childers, to aid the Volunteer efforts to arm themselves: however, unlike at Larne, when the UVF had been unimpeded, the authorities tried to prevent the Volunteers arming themselves and four people were killed by British soldiers in central Dublin. War had now broken out in Europe and Redmond, after unsuccessfully suggesting that the Volunteers be entrusted with the defence of Ireland, in September 1914 called on the Volunteers to fight 'where ever the firing line extends'; in other words, to join the British war effort. The IRB-influenced minority in the Volunteers refused and expelled Redmond's supporters from the organisation, retaining the Irish Volunteer title. The Volunteers now numbered only 10,000 nationwide, although they had a strong base in Dublin. Eoin MacNeill believed that the force would be defensive, only fighting if the British attempted to introduce conscription. IRB militants in the Volunteers, however, began to plan an uprising, to happen before the War ended. This planning led to the Rising of Easter 1916, when a minority of the Volunteers took up arms, proclaimed a republic, and were defeated after a week of fighting in Dublin city centre. Over 400 people were killed during the Rising and several of its key leaders executed in its aftermath.

THE IRISH REPUBLICAN ARMY, 1916

The term 'IRA' had been used as early as 1866. However, from 1913-1916, the Irish Volunteers or 'the Volunteers' was the common translation of the title 'Óglaigh na hÉireann'. At the start of the 1916 Easter Rising, Pádraig Pearse was appointed commandant general of the republican forces, comprising the Irish Volunteers and the Irish Citizen Army, which then became the Irish Republican Army (members of Cumann na mBan, Fianna Éireann and the Hibernian Rifles also took part in the Rising). This commemorative mass card from 1917 lists several of the executed 1916 leaders by their 'IRA' ranks. Labour leader Thomas Johnson also used the phrase 'Irish Republican Army' in an article in *Irish Opinion* during February 1918, but the term only seems to have acquired more popular usage during 1920: 'Irish Volunteers' was still used on General Headquarters staff material until 1921.

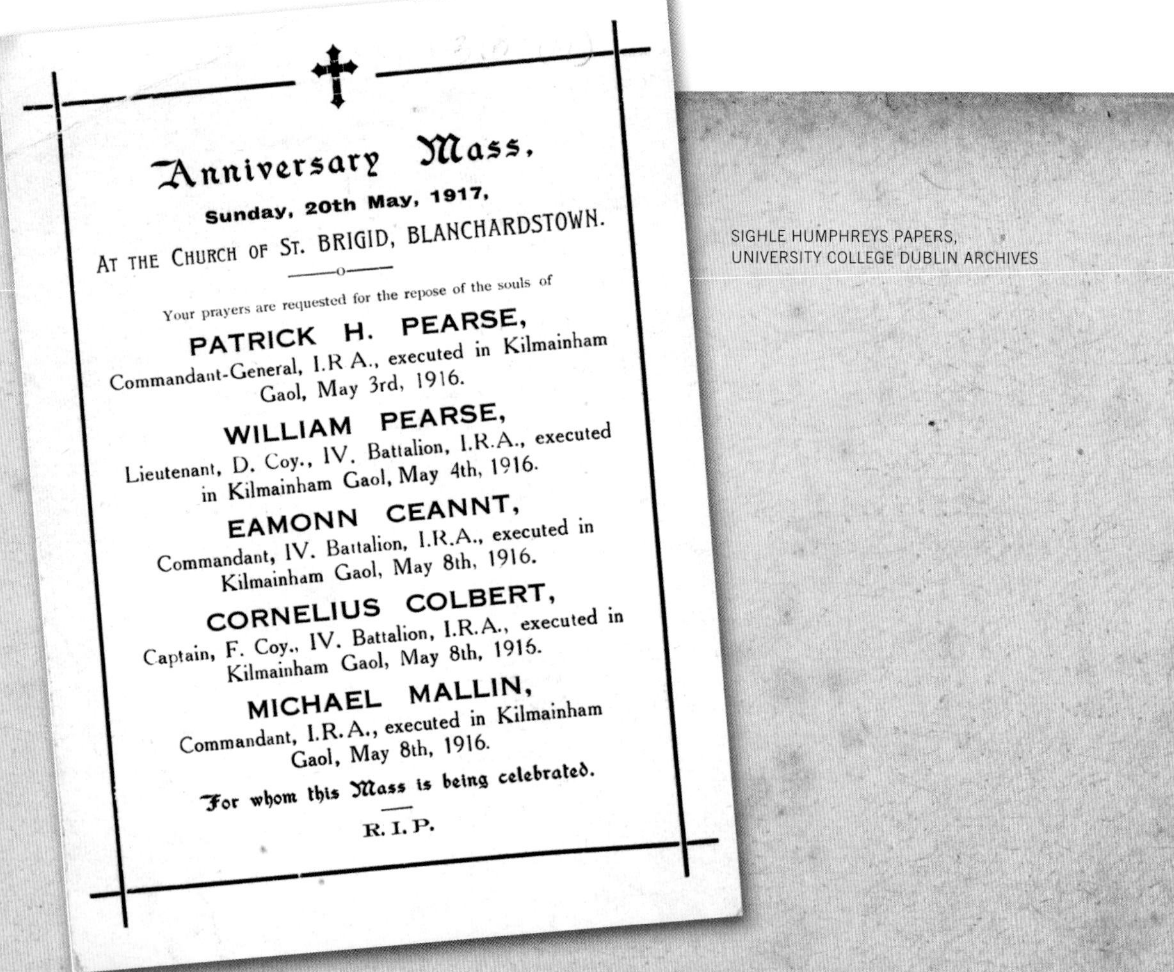

Anniversary Mass.

Sunday, 20th May, 1917,

AT THE CHURCH OF ST. BRIGID, BLANCHARDSTOWN.

Your prayers are requested for the repose of the souls of

PATRICK H. PEARSE,
Commandant-General, I.R A., executed in Kilmainham Gaol, May 3rd, 1916.

WILLIAM PEARSE,
Lieutenant, D. Coy., IV. Battalion, I.R.A., executed in Kilmainham Gaol, May 4th, 1916.

EAMONN CEANNT,
Commandant, IV. Battalion, I.R.A., executed in Kilmainham Gaol, May 8th, 1916.

CORNELIUS COLBERT,
Captain, F. Coy., IV. Battalion, I.R.A., executed in Kilmainham Gaol, May 8th, 1916.

MICHAEL MALLIN,
Commandant, I.R.A., executed in Kilmainham Gaol, May 8th, 1916.

For whom this Mass is being celebrated.

R. I. P.

SIGHLE HUMPHREYS PAPERS,
UNIVERSITY COLLEGE DUBLIN ARCHIVES

NA FIANNA ÉIREANN

The republican scouting organisation, often described as the youth wing of the IRA, Na Fianna Éireann was founded in August 1909, predating the Irish Volunteers by four years. The Fianna was an important training ground for many of those who later became prominent in the 1916 Rising and War of Independence, such as Seán Heuston, Con Colbert and Liam Mellows. Among those involved in the organisation were Bulmer Hobson, of the IRB (who had been involved with a youth hurling league of the same name in Belfast some years previously), Countess Markievicz, Helena Moloney and Seán McGarry. The organisers were conscious of the success of the British Scout movement, founded by Baden-Powell and wished to cut across its development in Ireland. The organisation was open to boys of 8-18 years of age. Pádraig Pearse described the Fianna's role as to, '. . . train the boys of Ireland to fight

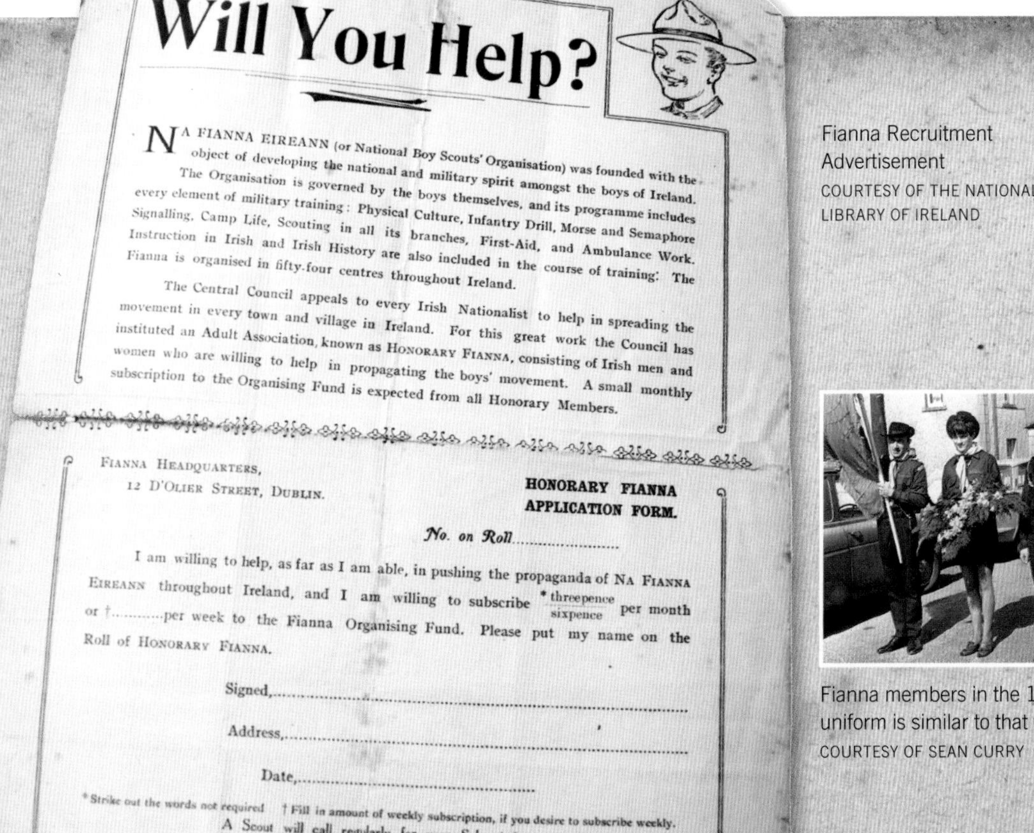

Will You Help?

NA FIANNA EIREANN (or National Boy Scouts' Organisation) was founded with the object of developing the national and military spirit amongst the boys of Ireland. The Organisation is governed by the boys themselves, and its programme includes every element of military training: Physical Culture, Infantry Drill, Morse and Semaphore Signalling, Camp Life, Scouting in all its branches, First-Aid, and Ambulance Work. Instruction in Irish and Irish History are also included in the course of training. The Fianna is organised in fifty-four centres throughout Ireland.

The Central Council appeals to every Irish Nationalist to help in spreading the movement in every town and village in Ireland. For this great work the Council has instituted an Adult Association, known as HONORARY FIANNA, consisting of Irish men and women who are willing to help in propagating the boys' movement. A small monthly subscription to the Organising Fund is expected from all Honorary Members.

FIANNA HEADQUARTERS,
12 D'OLIER STREET, DUBLIN.

HONORARY FIANNA APPLICATION FORM.

No. on Roll..........................

I am willing to help, as far as I am able, in pushing the propaganda of NA FIANNA EIREANN throughout Ireland, and I am willing to subscribe * threepence / sixpence per month or †...........per week to the Fianna Organising Fund. Please put my name on the Roll of HONORARY FIANNA.

Signed,..

Address,..

Date,..

* Strike out the words not required † Fill in amount of weekly subscription, if you desire to subscribe weekly.

A Scout will call regularly for your Subscription.

Fianna Recruitment Advertisement
COURTESY OF THE NATIONAL LIBRARY OF IRELAND

Fianna members in the 1960s: the uniform is similar to that worn in 1920.
COURTESY OF SEAN CURRY

Ireland's battles when they are men'. The Fianna were involved in the Howth gunrunning operation and in the Easter Rising, in which 15-year-old member Seán Healy was killed. They reorganised during 1917 and expanded along with the Volunteers. They were involved in many clashes during this period: a Fianna boy is alleged to have struck a blow with a hurley which caused the death of Detective Inspector Mills of the Dublin Metropolitan Police in early 1917.

CUMANN NA MBAN

Cumann na mBan, the republican women's organisation, was founded in Dublin during April 1914 to provide assistance to the Irish Volunteers. While its members learned first aid, stretcher-bearing and field-signalling, a great deal of its work was in fund-raising, though there was some limited arms training.

Cumann na mBan was not the first republican women's organisation: many of its founders had been members of Inghinidhe na hÉireann, (Daughters of Erin) founded in 1900 to organise opposition to the visit of Queen Victoria to Ireland. Comprised generally of radical nationalists, Cumann na mBan sided with the section of the Irish Volunteers who rejected John Redmond and the Home Rule movement in September 1914. Its members took part in the Easter Rising, working as couriers, nurses and scouts.

While female members of the Irish Citizen Army routinely carried arms, Cumann na mBan were not generally seen as combatants. Nevertheless, they were present in almost every area

Recruitment poster for Cumann na mBan
COURTESY OF THE NATIONAL LIBRARY OF IRELAND

of the fighting. Cumann na mBan expanded in the post-Rising period, with members active in prisoner-support campaigns and in Sinn Féin's election efforts. By 1918, police estimated the organisation had nearly 4,000 members, though the real figure may have been larger.

Some of its members, such as Countess Markievicz, were prominent politically (in her case in several organisations) but most were ordinary activists. During the War of Independence the organisation helped with propaganda, carried messages, arms and ammunition and played an active part in the Dáil's local administration. As in 1916, its members were not seen as combatants and relatively few women (26) were jailed by the authorities. Nevertheless, several women, some of them members of Cumann na mBan, such as Lily Merrin and Josephine Brown, were an important part of the IRA's intelligence network. In February 1922, Cumann na mBan members voted 419 to 63 against the Treaty and the organisation played an active role in the Civil War. Over 400 women (not all in Cumann na mBan) were jailed, and evidence suggests some took part in fighting. (A small Pro-Treaty women's organisation, Cumann na Saoirse, also existed).

AN T-OGLACH

An t-Oglach (alternately *An tÓglác*) was first published on 15 August 1918. Because of the rapid expansion of the Volunteers during the conscription crisis of 1918 (when the British government attempted to introduce compulsory military service in Ireland), it was decided to publish a secret Volunteer paper. Piaras Béaslaí, IRA Director of Publicity, was appointed editor. A four-page sheet, to be sold at two pence a copy, was printed at the Gaelic Press in Dublin's Liffey Street and distributed through commanders of Volunteer units. Each issue contained an editorial, brief reports of Volunteer activities and training notes written by J.J. 'Ginger' O'Connell. *An tÓglác* was published bi-monthly under conditions of increasing difficulty as the authorities clamped down during 1919. After Béaslaí was arrested, Ernest Blythe acted as editor for a period. A room at the rear of a tobacconist's shop in Aungier Street was now used as the print shop for the paper, under the direction of the IRA's Dublin commander, Dick McKee. As well as being a manual for the IRA *An tÓglác* was also used for propaganda purposes and copies of it were sought by the international press.

'RUTHLESS WARFARE'

In October 1918, *An tÓglác* published an article demanding that there be 'ruthless warfare' against those enforcing conscription on Ireland. The article's author was Ernest Blythe, an Antrim-born Protestant who had been a member of the IRB since 1906. Blythe had been an organiser for the Irish Volunteers during 1915 and was jailed in Britain for much of 1916. By 1918, he was a member of the Sinn Féin party. Blythe argued against any lingering hope that passive resistance (the desired policy of many in the broader nationalist movement) would succeed and urged that anyone, civilian or soldier, involved in enforcing conscription, 'be killed without delay'. His language reflects the radicalisation of the Volunteers during 1918 and the key role that the threat of conscription played in the movement's development. Almost every account by veterans in the Bureau of Military History notes the excitement that the threat of conscription provoked; it was in early 1918 that many young Volunteers thought the fight would begin.

In Co. Kerry, for example, in Lixnaw, the Volunteers grew in number from 84 to 260 men during the crisis; in Duagh, from 50 to 200, in Newtownsands from 20 to 150. In Ballylongford and Glenfask, 'virtually every' able-bodied man joined the organisation. Nationwide membership of the Irish Volunteers reached 100,000 in the spring of 1918. Local training efforts were often aided by Volunteers who were ex-British soldiers or War veterans (Cork's Tom Barry was one of a number of ex-serviceman who would play important roles in the IRA from 1919-21).

It was also during this period that the Volunteers attempted to arm themselves. Local units began to collect shotguns from supporters or stole them if necessary. Buying or stealing rifles from soldiers was another tactic; one Volunteer claimed that his unit could get more than enough rifles from drunken soldiers. In other cases soldiers gave weapons out of sympathy; in Ennis three soldiers gave their rifles to the Volunteers after hearing Countess Markievicz speak. But the Volunteers in general remained woefully ill equipped. In Mallow during 1918, a total of 120 men had access to 50 shotguns but only one rifle. Hence the order from their headquarters to raid the police, who were stationed in every small town and village in Ireland and had modern weaponry. In Bantry in September 1918, local Volunteers captured a rifle and revolver from a police patrol. The outnumbered police were simply let go. This situation occurred on numerous occasions well into 1919 and many Volunteers were content to take weapons rather than harm the police themselves. There was no instruction or order from the leadership of the Volunteers to attack soldiers or policemen — but inevitably this activity led to clashes and casualties. In Bantry during the autumn of 1918, there were two failed ambushes on British soldiers.

Facing page: *An tÓglác*, 14 October 1918 COURTESY OF THE NATIONAL LIBRARY OF IRELAND

13

An tÓglác

OFFICIAL ORGAN OF THE IRISH VOLUNTEERS.

VOL. I. No. 4] 14th October 1918. [PRICE TWOPENCE.

"RUTHLESS WARFARE."

[The following article by a leading Volunteer at present in prison emphasises essential points in connection with the Conscription threat].

THE definite military preparations for resisting Conscription are being well looked after; but there must always remain something to be done in the matter of bringing public opinion up to the right pitch of desperate determination and keeping it there. It would be desirable, for instance, to eliminate all talk and all thought of passive resistance. Because passive resistance means in effect no resistance at all. And talk of passive resistance is simply an invitation to the Government to come on. To anyone who will consider the matter for a moment so much must be evident. If in any particular area there were to be nothing but passive resistance, it would mean that there, at any rate, the Government could go on without having to face any casualty list of killed and wounded. It would mean, moreover, that no reinforcements of troops would be required from England or Flanders, that in fact the police, having no armed opposition to fear would, without military assistance, be able in the course of a few weeks to get all the men required. Thus the Government, without any considerable delay, without having lost a man, without any diversion of large forces or any expenditure of ammunition would have laid their hands on all the men they wanted.

Nothing would remain to be done but to reduce to submission as many as possible of the captives. We know that the men who were taken from Frongoch, and who afterwards put up a passive resistance fight had a devilish tough experience. But we may be certain that what they endured would be only a pic-nic in comparison with the treatment that would be meted out in case of passive resistance *en masse* by Irish conscripts. The brutality would be unbounded, and there is little doubt that many would be sent to France and the firing squad would be brought frequently into requisition.

If a man is taken alive after doing his best in the fight, then he may do what he can in the way of passive resistance; but a policy of passive resistance alone would mean that the Government without loss and with comparatively little trouble would be able to seize practically all the men they chose up to the limits of the population. Our active military resistance is the only thing that will tell, and any plans or theories or doubts tending to distract the minds of the people from the policy of fierce and ruthless fighting ought to be severely discouraged.

Once the struggle begins we should realise that it is more and worse than war. For war is the combat of one armed force with another. A conscription campaign would be an unprovoked onslaught by an army upon a civilian population, which would be given no choice but between murder on the spot and massacre after an interval. If England decides on this atrocity, then we, on our part, must decide that in our resistance we shall acknowledge no limit and no scruple. We must recognise that anyone, civilian or soldier, who assists directly or by connivance in this crime against us, merits no more consideration than a wild beast and should be killed without mercy or hesitation as opportunity offers. To prevent our people being divided, to prevent men being seduced by certain exemption if they will surrender, or promises of home service duty if they will attest or by similar treacherous devices of the enemy, we must from the first insist upon a clean cut amongst the population of Ireland. Any man who knowingly and willingly does anything to facilitate the working of the machinery of conscription, must be dealt with exactly as if he were an enemy soldier. Thus the man who serves on an exemption tribunal, the doctor who treats soldiers or examines conscripts, the man who voluntarily surrenders when called for, the man who in any shape or form applies for exemption, the man who drives a police-car or assists in the transport of army supplies, all these having assisted the enemy must be shot or otherwise destroyed with the

Ultimately, conscription was not introduced but during 1919, some of the Volunteers would begin to use the methods that many of their comrades initally balked at. Blythe had contended that violent resistance to conscription was justified because it would save lives in the long run, and it is worth noting that perhaps 35,000 Irish men died in the Great War, far more than would die at the hands of the IRA or their adversaries in twentieth-century Ireland.

(Blythe supported the Treaty in 1921 and was minister for Finance from 1923 to 1932. During 1934, he hailed the Blueshirt movement as the 'authentic successors' to the men of 1916-21. He was also sympathetic to the fascist Ailtirí na hAiséirghe movement during the 1940s.)

'BOYCOTT RIC', 1920

Dáil Éireann, the revolutionary parliament established in January 1919 after Sinn Fein's victory over the Home Rule Party in the general election of 1918, called for a boycott of the Royal Irish Constabulary (RIC). The idea of a boycott, rather than outright attacks, appealed to those in the movement, like Sinn Féin president Eamon de Valera, and the party's founder Arthur Griffith, who were wary of escalating violence. The first recorded killings of police, at Soloheadbeg, Co. Tipperary, on 22 January 1919 (coincidentally on the day the Dáil first met), had caused much shock and were not authorised by the republican leadership, but were carried out by local leaders Seán Treacy and Dan Breen. Many felt that a campaign of killing policemen would not be tolerated by ordinary nationalists. But by the time the notice was issued, in June 1920, the IRA had killed nearly 60 policemen and attacks on isolated and abandoned police barracks had culminated in an offensive which saw over 300 barrack houses destroyed.

As a result of the IRA's campaign, the RIC had been reinforced during March 1920 with new recruits, largely ex-servicemen from Britain, who were soon nicknamed 'Black and Tans'. This notice, from the mid-Tipperary brigade, followed reprisals (frequent by mid 1920) carried out by crown forces in Tipperary and warned civilians of the consequences of contact with the police. During July more police reinforcements would arrive, in the shape of the Auxiliaries, mainly ex-military officers. Many policemen were locals, but others had been recruited elsewhere, and not only in Britain: Australians, Canadians and New Zealanders served with the RIC. Over 500 policemen were killed between 1916-21 in Ireland.

OGLAIGH NA h-EIREANN.

County Tipperary,
June 21st, 1920.

DEAR SIR,

Volunteer Headquarters have issued the following General Order:—

Boycott of R.I.C.—Volunteers shall have no intercourse with the R.I.C., and shall stimulate and support in every way the boycott of this force ordered by the Dail.

Those persons who associate with the R.I.C. shall be subjected to the same boycott, and the fact of their association with and toleration of this infamous force shall be kept public in every possible way. Definite lists of such persons in the area of his command shall be prepared and retained by each Company, Battalion and Brigade Commander.

In accordance with this order, and in consequence of their conduct in their searches, raids, arrests, assaults, robberies, and damage to public and private property, and of their firing into the houses of people in Thurles, Toomevara, Kilcommon, and elsewhere, and their smashing up and burning of Creameries, and in consequence of the murders by them in Thurles and the Ragg, **all** connection with the police will be cut off from this date.

Business people must take their choice of the custom of their neighbours or the cowardly ruffians of the R.I.C. A sensible business man will be able to judge which pays the best in the long run. Every house dealing with the police will be watched from this out. Employers and their workmen are now forbidden to sell or deliver to police, whether living in barracks or in lodgings or private houses, goods of any description, and no house in future can be let to a policeman.

By Order,

COMPETENT MILITARY AUTHORITY,
MID-TIPPERARY BRIGADE.

1920

Our Prisoners

You have heard of the sufferings of Irishmen in gaols in Ireland:

Do you know that anxiety about the welfare of their dependents at home adds to their sufferings!

You can ease their anxiety in this matter by coming to the assistance of the Republican Prisoners' Dependents' Fund.

One way by which you can assist is by attending the

Great Football Contest,

Wexford v. Tipperary

AT CROKE PARK,

ON

Sunday, April 6th.

1919

WILL YOU COME!

'OUR PRISONERS', 1919

One way of mobilising popular support for republican prisoners (and of raising money) was to utilise republican connections with the Gaelic Athletic Association. In many areas during the War of Independence the GAA played an important part in defying the authorities and in bolstering republican support. Many Volunteers were hurlers or footballers and there was a connection between local units and particular clubs, but the IRA also contained a substantial number of soccer and rugby players, as well

Top: Call to boycott RIC COURTESY OF THE NATIONAL LIBRARY OF IRELAND

Right: COURTESY OF THE NATIONAL LIBRARY OF IRELAND

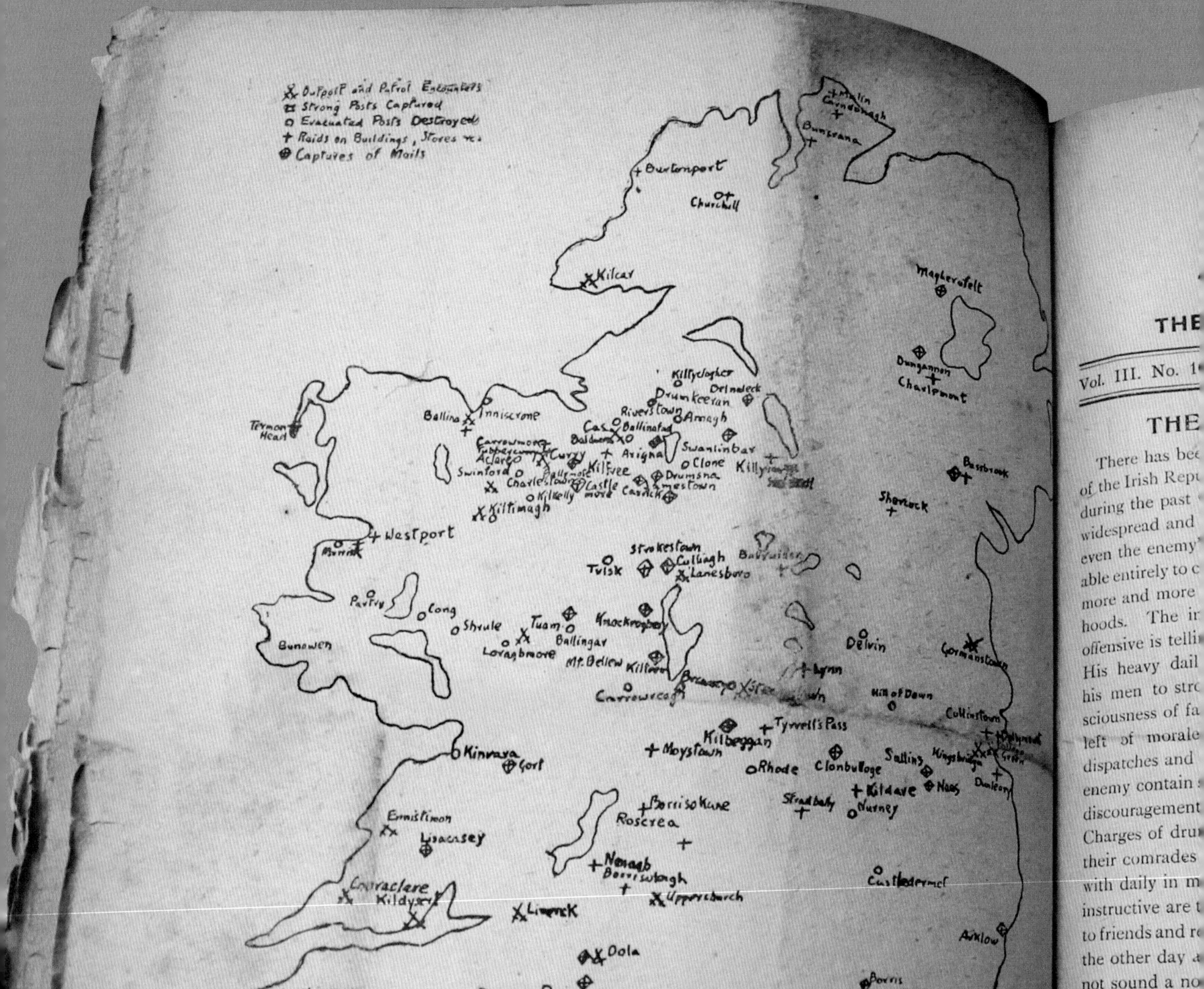

WAR MAP

(Second Half of July 1920.)

War Map, 1920

COURTESY OF THE NATIONAL LIBRARY OF IRELAND

as those who had no interest in sports at all. The organisation was committed in theory to a Gaelic Ireland but the majority of its propaganda, and almost all its internal correspondence, was written in English.

WAR MAP

In March 1920 *An t-Óglác*, while praising IRA activity in Munster, complained that '. . . in other parts of the country things are still very unsatisfactory. It gives no credit to the Volunteers in these districts that they should leave the gallant men of the south to bear all the brunt of the enemies [sic] activities and thus help make the military problems much simpler for the enemy'.

It was very apparent that levels of IRA activity differed greatly from area to area and one of the reasons for the publication of the 'War Map' on the facing page was to stimulate activity in 'quiet areas'. Much IRA activity was concerned with road trenching, (digging large trenches in roads), which hampered the use of motor vehicles by the British and also provided opportunities for ambushes. Raiding the mails, stealing letters and gathering intelligence by reading through them was also widespread: several spies were identified in this way. Cutting telegraph and telephone wires was another important activity. These operations caused a high level of disruption but they were not the stuff of the later legends built around the 'flying columns' and ambushes. In reality, for much of the time, many volunteers did not see action. Even where ambushes were organised, they often failed to result in a sighting of the enemy or were aborted.

The 'flying columns' were intially the result of local initiative, when small groups of men were forced to go on the run and act independently, rather than the result of direction from General Headquarters. They did become more formalised during 1921, but results differed from place to place. The willingness of a local officer to sanction raids for arms, or to plan and lead ambushes, was an important factor in the success or failure of a flying column. In many areas volunteers lacked confidence or were understandably fearful of retribution on their localities. The presence of a Tom Barry, a Séan Moylan (both Cork) or a Dinny Lacey (Tipperary), i.e. a determined officer, seems to have been crucial. In Longford, for example, IRA activity greatly decreased after Seán MacEoin was captured and Seán Connolly killed in early 1921. When MacEoin was captured Liam Lynch commented, 'Cork will have to fight alone now', showing the high regard in which MacEoin was held (and the feeling among the Cork IRA that they were leading the struggle).

There was also the thorny question of national leadership of the IRA. Did control of the Volunteers rest ultimately with the Dáil, through its Minister for Defence,

Cathal Brugha, or with GHQ, especially Richard Mulcahy and Michael Collins, or were local commanders much more important? The Dáil was slow to endorse IRA activity: the first killings were carried out without any reference to it. There was also enduring rivalry between the secret IRB, in which Collins and Mulcahy were leading figures and which had reorganised, too, after 1916, and Brugha, who was suspicious of the 'Brotherhood'. The IRA's deputy chief of staff, Austin Stack, was closer to Brugha than to Mulcahy. Eamon de Valera had become president of the Volunteers and Sinn Féin in 1917, but he had little role in the armed campaign and was in the United States for much of 1920.

While the British alleged that the IRA was a 'murder gang' who depended on fear and intimidation to get its way, republicans pointed to Sinn Féin's triumph at the 1918 general election. They had won 73 seats against six for the Home Rule party and 26 for the Unionists. This was a clear endorsement of Sinn Féin's demand for self-determination, but voters had not been asked to support an armed campaign. In 1920, however, Sinn Féin, in close cooperation with Labour, won the majority of seats on local urban and rural councils, a clearer indication of popular support in the midst of the campaign. In 1921, Sinn Féin again swept the boards in another national poll.

The Volunteers found a political role in setting up Dáil courts and administering local police work, which some saw as equally important in undermining British rule. Not all the violence in Ireland at this time was linked to the republican campaign. There were widespread strikes and workplace occupations, many of which were primarily economic in cause. Some strike activity was linked to the republican effort: the British forces were severely impeded by a railway strike during 1920, for instance. Some of the IRA's actions in the west have also been linked to land agitation, which was so widespread it was described as the 'last Land War'.

DEATH PENALTY

The killing of its own members or ex-members by the IRA has been a recurring feature of the organisation's history. The strictures applying to this are laid out in this order from April 1921. Very few people willingly admit to treachery and governments are slow to release details about their agents: in many instances it is simply impossible to know how many of the people killed by the IRA for spying, were, in fact, informers. In the cases of most of the people killed as spies from the 1920s until the twenty-first century, their families and friends have strongly denied the allegations. It is also an aspect of the IRA's practice that is far from romantic and is therefore little dwelt on.

Facing page: HUMPHREYS PAPERS, UCD ARCHIVES

Óglaiġ na h-Éireann
Árd-oifig, Át Cliat.

THE IRISH VOLUNTEERS
GENERAL HEADQUARTERS, DUBLIN.

NEW SERIES 1920. NO. 17

GENERAL ORDERS.

2nd. April, 1921.

DEATH PENALTY

The penalty of death shall not be inflicted on any member of the I.R.A. without written covering authority from General Headquarters Staff.

The following are offences for which the death penalty may be imposed on members of the Army.

1. Knowingly conveying information to the enemy.
2. Disclosing to unauthorised persons particulars of plans of operations.
3. The treacherous surrender to the enemy or destruction of arms or War material.
4. Grave insubordination on active operation duty, involving danger to others and to the success of the operation.

In all such cases the written proceedings of the relative Court Martial shall be promptly forwarded to the Adjutant General.

BY ORDER

ADJUTANT GENERAL.

'WOMEN SPIES'

Relatively few women were killed deliberately by either side between 1919-21. IRA General Orders expressly ruled out the killing of female spies. However, some alleged women informers were killed. In early 1921, the Cork IRA suffered a number of serious losses. Mrs Mary Lindsay, an elderly Protestant, was suspected of giving information that led to the killing and capture of several IRA volunteers. She was held for several weeks and then she and her butler, James Clark, were killed and their bodies hidden (their remains were never found). In April 1921, Kitty Carroll, a 40-year-old single woman, was taken from her home in Aughnamena, Co. Monaghan and shot dead by the IRA, because she had informed the police about illicit distilling in her district. There have been recurring allegations that the IRA was more likely to kill 'spies' if they were ex-soldiers, Protestants or marginal figures, such as tramps, rather than 'respectable' members of the nationalist community.

16

1920 (New Series).

General Orders.—No. 13.

WOMEN SPIES.

Where there is evidence that a woman is a spy or is doing petty spy work, the Bde. Comdt. whose area is involved will set up a court of inquiry to examine the evidence against her. If the court finds her guilty of the charge, she shall then be advised accordingly, and, except in the case of an Irishwoman, be ordered to leave the country within seven days. It shall be intimated to her that only consideration of her sex prevents the infliction of the statutory punishment of death. A formal public statement of the fact of the conviction shall be issued in poster or leaflet form or both, according to the local circumstances, as a warning and a preventative. Ordinarily, it is not proposed to deport Irishwomen, it being hoped that the bringing of publicity on the actions of such will neutralise them. In dangerous and insistant cases of this kind, however, full particulars should be placed before G.H.Q. and instructions sought.

By order.

Adjutant-General.

TAN WAR OPERATIONS

By the spring of 1921, the War of Independence was entering its bloodiest phase. Late winter had seen Bloody Sunday in Dublin, when 31 people had been killed, both British and Irish, and the Kilmichael ambush in Cork, where an IRA column, led by Tom Barry, wiped out a force of 17 RIC auxiliaries. This had been followed by the burning of the centre of Cork city by Crown forces. In December 1920, Cork, Kerry, Limerick and Tipperary were placed under martial law and in January 1921, the rest of Munster was included.

Both sides were suffering heavy casualties: 203 policemen were killed from January to July, while 48 British soldiers were killed during May and June 1921. The IRA was also displaying increasing ruthlessness: in May, they killed a

70-year old ex-soldier called Mick Sullivan near Rathmore, Co. Kerry and used his body to lure Crown forces into the area. They then ambushed and killed eight policemen. In late May, a landmine in a culvert killed several British soldiers (members of a regimental band) and wounded over twenty others near Youghal, Co. Cork.

But there were also serious setbacks for republicans, In Clonmult, Co. Cork on 20 February 1921, twelve IRA members were killed, their worst losses of the War; this followed the killing of six IRA men at Dripsey and Mallow a month before and the execution of a further seven men who had been captured by Crown forces in these incidents; six IRA men were killed in a failed ambush attempt at Kilmeena, Co. Mayo and six more died at Selton Hill, Leitrim (including Longford's Seán Connolly) during March. Nearly 100 members of the Dublin Brigade were captured after the attack on the Customs House during May (though the IRA presented the attack both publicly and internally as a success).

OPERATIONS REPORTS, 1921

The reports which follow give an indication of the type of activity the war entailed. They vary in intensity and ruthlessness from area to area and the information (regarding casualties for instance) is not always accurate. Accounts written after the heat of battle were often imprecise.

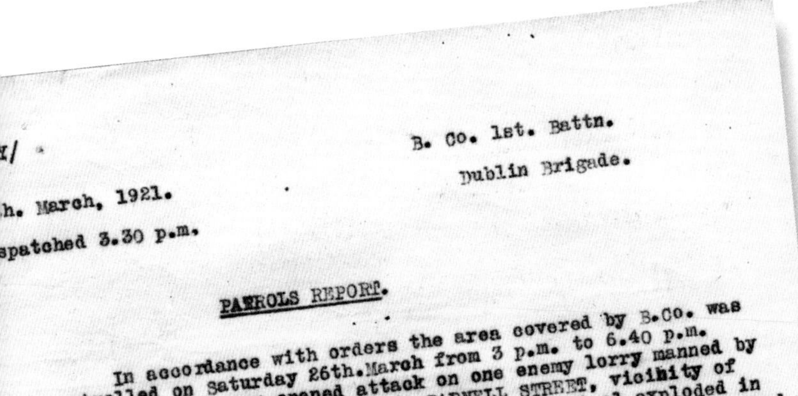

B. Co. 1st. Battn.
Dublin Brigade.

h. March, 1921.
spatched 3.30 p.m.

PATROLS REPORT.

In accordance with orders the area covered by B.Co. was patrolled on Saturday 26th.March from 3 p.m. to 6.40 p.m. Patrol NO.2.-8 men opened attack on one enemy lorry manned by about 16 armed men all told, in PARNELL STREET, vicinity of Moore Street. The first bomb fired by our patrol exploded in enemy lorry. They returned with rifle fire and fire was opened by out patrol to compel enemy to halt. The enemy driver was wounded but speeded up lorry. Our patrol succeeded in getting two more bombs into car both of which exploded and must have accounted for many casualities. We had no casualities here.

Patrol NO.3-8 men, NO.4-10 men were in O'Connell St. and fire was opened on the retreating lorry, about 7 or 8 of the enemy only were visible, one of which received a revolver wound and jumped from the lorry.

NO.3 patrol was despatched outside CO. area to Marlborough St. to cut off retreat of another enemy lorry containing 8 of the enemy armed with rifles in Findlater Place. This lorry was attacked by NO.4 patrol from O'Connell St. end. NO.4 patrol was then attacked by another enemy lorry which came from direction of Nelson's Pillar. NO.4 was ordered to retire to Marlborough St via Parnell St. The two patrols 3 and 4 then attacked the lorry in Findlater's place the intention being to capture the lorry there and hold Findlater's Place as a position for attack on enemy reinforcements arriving in O'Connell St. This we were unable to do owing to three of our bombs failing to explode and enemy reinforcements arriving, our forces retired leaving 5 or possibly 6 of the enemy wounded. We had one of our men slightly wounded. None of our forces were captured.

Details of our ammunition expended are not yet compiled.

Our other patrols met with no enemy forces.

(Signed) O.C. B.1.

This Dublin report illustrates the nature of guerilla war in the capital.

HUMPHREYS PAPERS, UCD ARCHIVES

COPY

AMBUSH REPORT AT BALLYFERMOTT

5 men A.S.U.

Time 1.30 p.m.

O/C NO.4. Sec. A.S.U.

Date 30/3/21.

DISPOSAL OF MEN: Shown on sketch attached to report.

INFORMATION RE ENEMY: On information I received that a cycling patrol of R.I.C. consisting of 4 men left Chapelizod Barracks 3 times a week and patrolled the roads around Ballyfermott. I sent a cyclist to patrol and watch Chapelizod Barracks. On the 30th.inst. he reported to me at 11.30 the patrol had left Chapelizod Barracks. I sent O/C NO.4. Sec. and four men to point shown on sketch. Each man had a .45 revolver but a very poor supply of ammunition. They had no grenades. At 1.30 the cycling patrol was observed going west along the canal. At this time my men were concealed in the ruins of an old house midway between the canal and the railway line. When the R.I.C. patrol reached the canal bridge they turned and proceeded north. The O/C then ordered the wall to be lined in extended formation. This was done. When the patrol advanced fire was opened on them. One policeman ran away; two were shot off their bicycles, the Sergt. attempted to fight but was shot dead. The O/C's reason for not capturing the arms was because he thought the escaped constable would take up a position and would be able to snipe them if they appeared on the road. He had to consider he had but little ammunition, as two men had emptied all they had got. I agreed with him on this statement as I considered he had done well under the circumstances.

RESULT: Good.

AMMUNITION EXPENDED: 30 rounds .45 Revolver Ammunition.

CASUALITIES: One Sergt. killed, one Head constable and constable badly wounded.
Our casualities were nil.

(Signed) O.C. A.S.U.

Time sent 12.3 0 p.m. Date 31/3/21.
How sent : By dispatch.

This report details an ambush on a police patrol at Chapelizod. Volunteers had been watching the patrol's movements for some time.

HUMPHREYS PAPERS, UCD ARCHIVES

PATROL REPORT.

Time 7-40 p.m. Date 20-5-'21.

Procedure.
At 7-35 p.m. the patrol were ordered to take up positions at various corners in Bolton St.
Disposal of Men.
2 men at Bolton Parade, one bomb, one ·45, 2 men at Bolton Court two ·45s, 2 men at Kings Inn St., one bomb, one ·45, 2 men at Farnhall St. one bomb, one ·45.
Information re Enemy.
One tender of Black and Tans came from the direction of Dorset St. through Bolton St. towards the North Dublin Union.
Information re Own Men.
At this time (7-40 p.m.) only two men had got into their positions in Bolton Parade. On observing the tender one man opened fire with his bomb which exploded over the tender.
Result.
One Black and Tan rolled off the car.
Ammunition Expended.
One bomb, one round of ·45.
Casualties.
Enemy one known badly wounded. Our own casualties - Nil.
Remarks.
No fire returned by Enemy who picked up their wounded man and continued their way.
The Men were told off as follows; one bomb one revolver at Farnhall St One bomb one revolver at Bolton Parade, twoo revolvers at Bolton Court one revolver at Kings Inn St.
The lines of retreat were as follows: Men at Farnhall St. to retreat to end of street and get to Henrietta St. across Henrietta Lane leading into Dominick St. Men in Bolton parade to retreat into Kings Inn St. thence into Parnell St. Men in Bolton Court to retreat across waste ground into Cherry Lane. Men in Kings Inn St. to retreat into lane leading into Dominick St.
Only two men had taken up positions at Bolton court, the remainder of positions were not manned in time when the tender passed along Bolton St. going in the direction of the North Dublin Union.

Signed, Coy. Q.M.

PATROL REPORT.

Time 2-30. Date May 22nd, 1921.

Procedure.
To execute Enemy Spy.
Information re Enemy.
Information from 1st Lieut. and Coy. I.O. Leslie Fraser, No. 9 Blackhall Parade. Ex-soldier.
Result.
Execution took place at above time at the Corner of Brunswick St N. outside Walshe's Public House.
Ammunition Expended Six rounds of 450
Casualties men returned safely. No casualties.
Remarks The execution was quick the men behaved very coolly.

Signed, Adjutant, D. Coy. 1st Battn

Leslie Fraser, the 24-year old ex-soldier accused of being a spy, had been drinking in 'Walshe's' (sic) pub before he was shot.

HUMPHREYS PAPERS, UCD ARCHIVES

BRIGADE HEADQUARTERS,

DUNGARVON.

11th April, 1921.

To C/S G.H.Q.

REPORT OF ACTIVITIES AT KILMACTHOMAS night of 5th.

On the night of the 5th nine men were detauled off to hold up the 10-30 p.m. Rosslare Express at KILMACTHOMAS. Two minutes before train was due, one of the men held up signalman and ordered him to put signals against train which pulled up on entering the platform. There were sixteen unarmed troops on train, no officer.

The soldiers were taken off train and their equipment seized.

Signed,

BRIGADE COMMANDANT.

Despite the upsurge in killing by both sides, on this occasion the IRA simply let the unarmed soldiers they had captured go.

HUMPHREYS PAPERS, UCD ARCHIVES

COPY/ NORTH WEXFORD BRIGADE,

16.6.21.

Report of Attempted Ambush at Bunclody:

Date of Ambush: June 5th. 1921.

Time it Began: 8 o'c. a.m.

Time it Ended: 8.5. a.m.

Place of Ambush: On the road from R.I.C.Barracks, Bunclody to R.C. Church.

By whom carried out: 5 men from NO.1.Battn. North Wexford Brigade.

Position of our Men: 5 men were placed behind a high wall (14ft.) on roadside, and the wall was about 4 ft. on the inside. The men were placed 5 yds. apart. The 5th. man acted as scout. He had view of the road but not of the Barracks. Distance between Ambush Party and Barracks 400 yds.

Equipment of Men: 4 shot-guns, 4 revolvers and 2 bombs.

Information re Enemy: 4 police in charge of a Sergt. were observed coming to Mass in the middle of a group of women and children. Our troops let the party through as they could not possibly fire without killing women and children. Just then our men were surprised from behind by a patrol of at least 12 police, who called on them to surrender. One of our men fired 2 shots into the nearest of the enemy and he fell prone, the remainder of the enemy sought shelter and opened fire on our men, fire being also opened by the 4 police on the road. Our troops made good their escape suffering no casualities. The police in the wood behind were armed with rifles. The party going to Mass were armed with revolvers and a bomb each as you will see by the enclosed circular.

Remarks: Before the party left barracks for Mass, the other patrol left by another route for the wood which is situated behind our troops' position. This was the first Sunday that this Patrol entered the wood. They did so as a result of a circular received from their Divisional H.Q., a copy of which I enclose.

Expenditure of Ammunition: 2 rounds of Buckshot and a bomb.

Result: One R.I.C. killed or wounded.

(Signed) Brig. Adj.

Wex. North.

Date 16.6.21.

In Bunclody, the IRA were reluctant to fire on police for fear of hitting women and children.

HUMPHREYS PAPERS, UCD ARCHIVES

Here, in Tipperary, three captured British officers are shot by the IRA in retaliation for the execution of IRA prisoners.

HUMPHREYS PAPERS, UCD ARCHIVES

COPY/

HEADQUARTERS TIPPERARY NO. 3 BRIGADE.

25/6/'21.

Further to report on Capture and Execution of Three Enemy Officers dated 22/6/'21:

While the chase was in progress, the enemy were observed to take articles from their pockets and throw them away. On searching the fields subsequently three ·320 automatics (loaded) were discovered, as well as a pocket book and some papers of no importance; a velour hat and walking sticks. Apparently the Officers were due back to barracks at a certain hour, as a search party with machine gun and bloodhound came through the fields some hours later

Signed,

Brigade Adjutant.

COPY OF NOTE SENT TO O/C TROOPS, FETHARD:

TO:

OGLAIGH na h-EIREANN

Major King, D.S.O.

20/6/'21.

1 The undermentioned Officers were executed at 4 a.m. June 20th.

Lt. Glossop.
Lt. Bettridge.
2nd Lt. Toogood.

2. We are reluctant to carry out such executions but until such time as the British Government cease from executing our Prisoners of War this will re-occur.

3. The Officers upheld the best traditions of their Regiments and died as soldiers should.

4. I have been asked to forward enclosed parcels. Will you. plese, see that they are forwarded to their relations.

HEADQUARTERS TIPPERARY NO. 3 BRIGADE.

22nd June. 1921.

REPORT ON CAPTURE AND EXECUTION OF THREE MILITARY OFFICERS:

At about 4-0 p.m. on Sunday, 19/6/821, a party of four of our men were on their way to reconnoitre an ambush position on the ---- road. Going through the fields they observed three young men in civilian attire standing at a gap in a fence, viewing the country around, ~~xxxxxxxxxxx~~ They appeared to be strangers. Approaching closer, under cover, our men called on them to halt and put up their hands. (Only one of our men was armed with a rifle and Bandolier) On hearing the command "Halt" the strangers seemed surprised and endeavoured to take cover. Our party then separated to encircle them. Seeing two unarmed men , as they thought, closing in on them the strangers picked up some stones and advanced to meet us. A rifle at the ready was the last thing they expected to see, on sight of which they turned tail and fled. An exciting chase ensued, lasting ½ an hour, a few warning shots accelerating the speed of the pursued. Taking steady aim, Vol. H ___ brought one of them to earth with a bullet in the thigh, The others then put up their hands. First aid was rendered. I then questioned them --- They were three enemy officers from Fethard: Lieut. Glossop, R.F.A.; Lieut. Bettridge, R.F.A.: 2nd Lieut. Toogood, 1st Lincolns. I had them blindfolded and conveyed to ~~division~~ the wounded Officer being carried. The O/C 2nd Southern/ Division being in the area was acquainted within the hour.

Prisoners were well treated whilst in our charge and were executed at dawn the following morning.

One of our men rushing after the pursued, waving a bandolier and calling on them to halt, No doubt, hearing such fierce yells, the strangers thought a horde of armed men were at their heels, and their chagrined faces were a study when they found they had surrend-ered to single armed man!

Appended is copy of note sent O/C Troops, Fethard.

Signed,

Bde. Adjutant.

The Limerick IRA was active both in the county and the city; in the case of the city attack, the presence of young women did deter the IRA.

HUMPHREYS PAPERS, UCD ARCHIVES

MID LIMERICK BRIGADE HEADQUARTERS.

21/4/'21.

To: A/G G.H.Q. Dublin.

Hereunder is report regarding the late Fedamore attack. Delay in submitting is due to present enemy activity here.

Fourteen armed men operated, viz. 6 riflemen, 5 revolver men, and 3 shot gun men. There was one house which was frequented by members of the R.I.C. The shot gun men and revolver men approached the house at dark and the riflemen were in aposition to play upon the barrack. The instructions were, that the police be attacked leaving the house and that the riflemen open a simultaneous attack on the barrack to keep the occupants in.

Towards midnight three R.I.C. came outside looking for their bikes, a bomb was fired at them at 7 yds. range and the shot gun men and revolver men also fired at same range. There were seven shot gun shots discharged and about 15 revolver rounds, one man fell and the two others rushed into the house groaning. A fourth R.I.C. man was apparently wounded through the door. The man on the groun was finished off.

Immediately that the three men were fired upon the riflemen opened fire on the barrack. After a few minutes there was a fulisade of bullets from the barrack. The barrack commanded our position and the Verey Lights made us quite visible.

The Brigade O/C was in charge.

Two police bikes were commandeered on the occasion.

Signed,

Adjutant Mid Limerick.

MID LIMERICK BRIGADE.

HEADQUARTERS.

6/5/ '21

About 9-30 on Saturday last four police were observed talking tow two girls At the corner of Mary St. Four revolver men and 2 bombers were standing to not far distant and came on the scene. The two bombs and about half a dozen revolver shots were fired into the party and all were thrown on the ground, a further patrol of 8 riflemen were coming in the direction of the scene and our men had to decamp. The four police and girls were wounded and there was much enemy firing in the vicinity subsequently which is now under curfew at 7-0 p.m. The 7-0 p.m. Curfew which was imposed on the Carey's Head area after the late attack has since been relaxed.

Signed,

Adjutant Mid Limerick.

COPY/ Cork NO.2 Brigade.

Diary of Activities for Month of May 1921.

May.	Battn.	Scene of operations.	
3	1.	Millstreet.	A party of men from the local Coy. entered the Rly. station and burned two waggons of stores and war material consigned to the local Auxies. This Battn. sniped two enemy round-up parties during the month.
30	2.	Abbeyfeale	Battn. A.S.Unit took up positions in town and waited all day for police patrol. The patrol did not turn up.
	3.		NO REPORT.
15	4.	Banteer	R.I.C. constable fires at - he escaped.
	4.	do	Four men entered local station and seized a quantity of whiskey and other stuffs consigned to local police barracks
23	4.		Seven men of A.S.U. took up a position on BANTEER-MILLSTREET road and sniped 4 lorries of Auxies, travelling from MILLSTREET to BANTEER. The Auxies returned the fire with Machine Guns and fired off a large amount of stuff. The snipers retreated after about 20 mins. having wounded three of the enemy
25	5.	Mourneabbey	Six men held up MALLOW-CORK train. No enemy goods on same.
31		Two Pothouse	Two men waiting for despatch rider from BUTTEVANT. No result.
7		L'B'town	Seven men held up MALLOW-NEWMARKET goods train, seized and destroyed enemy stores valued at £500
23	6	Kildorrery	Two snipers were posted on the main road through area to snipe enemy lorries. Nothing turned up.
8		Mitchelstown	Trip wires erected on roads likely to be traversed by enemy patrols. No result.
		"	Two snipers took up positions on the main road to Ballyporeen to shipe enemy lorrie No result as there was no enemy traffic through area.

-2-

May	Battn.	Scene of Operations.	
		Ballindangan	Three snipers were out several days during week end. Got nothing to do.
11		Glanworth	Glanworth and Ballyhooley Coys. tore up Rly. line between Ballyhooley & Fermoy.
11	6	Glanworth	Four men entered village to get a shot at the military stationed there. They were too late as the military had been called back to barracks.
		Kilavullen	The local Coy. tore up 120 yds. Rly line and tried to blow up an important Bridge on the line but failed.
20			Four men entered local station and captured 3 days rations consigned to military at Castletownroche.
2		Doneraile	Three men held up the mails and captured all R.I.C. correspondence.
16	7	Rathcormac	Sixteen men armed with rifles lay in ambush every night for an enemy patrol. No result.
7112		Conna	Ten men held up roads from Fermoy to Tallow for sniping operations. No result.
14		Rathcormac	Two riflemen and six shot-gin men entered Rathcormac at 7.30 p.m. to get some police. No result.
17		Rathcormac	One man sniped police barrack.
20		"	Six riflemen and six shot-gun men entered Rathcormac looking for police. No result.
25		Araglen	Eighteen men lay in ambush for enemy squad. No result as the enemy went back another route.

In addition all Battalions were engaged during the month in trenching roads and destroying bridges with the result that practically all roads leading through the Brigade Area are blocked.

Above and facing page:

Even with the upsurge in violence many IRA operations still centred on road trenching and mail raids, and many planned actions did not occur, as this Cork report illustrates.

HUMPHREYS PAPERS, UCD ARCHIVES

In this attack near Gort, Co. Galway, District Inspector Cecil Blake and his wife (who was pregnant) were killed. In later accounts of the ambush at Ballyturin House some claimed that Mrs Blake had actually taken part in the gun battle: the IRA's report would seem to rule this out.

HUMPHREYS PAPERS, UCD ARCHIVES

H.Q? C Coy. 6th Batt.

EAST CLARE BRIGADE.

1. It was reported to me by the Officers of the Gort Batt. area that D.I. Blake visited Ballyturin House almost every Sunday evening.

2. I went ~~xx~~ there on the 15th May with eight men armed with 5 rifles two shot-guns and two revolvers.

3. We took up position at the Gate House, some of the m[illegible] men were put in the Shrubbery to cut off the enemy's retreat.

4. We waited there from 2-30 until 7-45 p.m.

5. D.I. Blake, Capt. Cornwallis, Lieut. M! Creevy and two ladies drove up to the gate in a Ford touring car, Capt. Cornwallis got out to open the gate.

6. I called on them to put up their hands instead of putting up their hands, they drew their revolvers and fired at us. The ladies refused to leave, we did our best not to hit them, but one of them was killed as well as the three officers.

7. We took what arms and correspondence they had and dismantled the car.

8. I sent a note to Mr. Baggot by his herdsman telling him if there were any reprisals by the enemy, that we would burn his house.

9. I then blew two blasts of a whistle to call in four scouts we had out, when those came in, we retreated in military formation.

10. Our scouts could view the roads for 1½ miles from their positions, which were near our position.

Signed,

Captain.

The IRA in the west was increasingly active by 1921: this report contains a familiar complaint about lack of ammunition available to units and reports about violence against civilians by Crown forces.

HUMPHREYS PAPERS, UCD ARCHIVES

COPY/-

MAYO WEST BRIGADE.
4th. April, 1921.

Enemy have been very active for the past 4 months in this Brigade. Westport Battalion area has been the chief scope for their activities and it would in present conditions be quite impossible to estimate accurately the total No. of raids (fruitless) carried out by them. Newport Battn. area was paid a great amount of attention by the enemy also, Louisburgh next, and Castlebar has escaped most lightly of all.

Six cases of shootings by armed men()soldiers) over the heads of Volunteers occurred in Westport. Three or four in Louisburgh.

On different dates 7 masked and armed men tortured civilians ~~and~~ Westport and Newport Battns. leaving some of the civilians in a very precarious state. Seven cases of this kind occurred in each of Westport and Newport districts. Undoubtedly they were forces of the Crown.

On Tuesday 22nd.March, Brigade Comdt. accompanied by Battn.Comdt. Westport Battn. and Capt. A Coy. Westport Battn. were inspecting or about to do so an ambush point at Cushlough. They encountered a patrol of 4 cyclists R.I.C. at Carrickkennedy within a mile or so from Cushlough or Drummin Bks. They engaged the patrol, and the R.I.C. later after an exchange of shots surrendered, the four being wounded, two it was considered fatally. One the Sergt. has since succumbed. Three revolvers, two fills each with a shot gun and two egg bombs were captured. Reprisals for which we were in no way prepared were carried on an extensive scale in the district in which the ambush occurred and in Westport town. Several houses were burned, furniture and articles of value in other houses were destroyed.

This Brigade could warry on a vigorous, extensive, harrassing campaign if assured of a weekly supply of .303 ammunition. Presently the amount of .303 we have must be used cautiously to return an amount at least equal to that expended.

Would you place this matter before the Staff and let us have an answer in due course.

A Flying Column has been formed in Westport Battn. It is on an operation basis and is moving about the Battn. near points where the enemy gather or move about.

Flying Columns are being formed in 1st. and 2nd. Battn. areas also. 4th, Battn. is scarce in fighting men. Battn. Staff with one Capt. being only reliable men.

(Signed) Brigade Adj.

HEADQUARTERS LEITRIM BRIGADE.

18/4/'21.

To: The Adjutant General.

This is my diary ~~fos-the~~ of operations for the past month.

A convicted spy was shot, he was one of those who informed on those fellows who were shot in Sorvagh.

Four times in succession we had ~~tried~~ attempted to get a patrol, tried Ballinamore twice, succeeded on the 16th . Got a Black and Tan on the street in the evening, he was finished, so when he was taken to the barrack andther B & T rushed ~~out~~ for the door and said he would have blood for blood an R.I.C. held him back, the result was that both wounded each other, they were removed to Dublin and the remains of the B & T taken to Carrick-on-Shannon, so at present they are in a disturbed state. We expect a large force of military.

I do not belive it is much use cutting the roads.

Signed,

O/C Leitrim Brigade.

Leitrim was another area much more active in 1921 than it had been previously. This report mentions the shooting of a spy. The authorities claimed that 73 people had been shot by the IRA for spying between January and April 1921. But the IRA stated that some of those shot and left with notes pinned to their bodies proclaiming them victims of the IRA were actually killed by Crown forces. The Black and Tan 'got' in Ballinamore was Wilfred Jones, a former soldier from London, who was walking with his girlfriend when shot.

HUMPHREYS PAPERS, UCD ARCHIVES

HEADQUARTERS LONGFORD BRIGADE.

28/4/'21.

To: Adjutant General.

Eight of our men of No. 1. Flying Squad carried out an ambush at Clonfin on yesterday. They attacked a cycling patrol which left Granard in the morning and went to Ballinalee. On the return journey the boys met them at the scene of the Clonfin battle ground and got 2 dead and four wounded. This they declare is accurate.

A most peculiar feature of the attack was the si lence of the enemy rifles only about four or six shots were fired from them. Reinforcements arrived from Granard in quite a short time, but all the boys got away unhurt.

I have also to report that 3 or 4 of the enemy were wounded in removing a flag off the house where at one time I resided and where all my furniture was stored. Some weeks ago I destroyed the rifle range one night. This is situated about 1½ miles outside Longford, as a reprisal my furniture was partially destroyed the following night I placed a Republican flag out of the Chimney with Grenade attached. On going up for same one or two were badly got and also some more on the ground.

Signed, O/C.

North Longford had been the area of strongest IRA activity in the midlands. This report dates from after the capture of the area's commander, Seán MacEoin. However, O/C Tom Reddington reports successfully carrying out a booby-trap attack on the police by rigging a tricolour flag at his former home and luring them there.

HUMPHREYS PAPERS, UCD ARCHIVES

HEADQUARTERS BELFAST BRIGADE.

15th May, 1921.

The following is detailed report of Activities during month of April:

4th inst. bombing party. On the morning of date a military Guard at back of Ulster Club in Rosemary St. was attacked by an Active Service Unit from 1st Batt.. Two bombs were thrown one of which failed to explode. None of the enemy were injured. The other bomb displaced one of the sandbags behind which the sentry was entrenched.

10th inst. Military hold up. On the morning of date a party of men from B Coy. 1st Batt. held up two armed military Foot Police, in Donegal St., and deprived them of their service revolvers, ammunition and other equipment. Following this one of the men engaged was arrested, having been identified by Post Office boy and afterwards by military. This man was also identified by military sentry as having taken part in the bombing at Rosemary St. He was not engaged in this operation, but has been sentenced to 15 years penal servitude on both charges.

12th inst. Enemy M.T. lorries attacked. On this date three enemy transport lorries were engaged in removing flour from Messrs. Hughes Dickson's Mills in Diris St. and were held up by a party of D Coy. 1st Batt. Owing to the proximity of the Police Barrack and alarm being raised the men had only time to destroy one engine by smashing it.

23rd inst. Shooting of Auxiliaries. Acting on information received a small Active Servic Unit from 1st Batt. consisting of 8 men, were detailed to locate some Auxiliaries who had arrived in town that morning. They succeeded in killing two of them in Donegal Place in or about 9-0 p.m. As a sequence to this operation the brothers Duffin, Clonard Gardens, were murdered by a party of 6 men whom we believe are attached to Springfield Road Barrack. One of the brothers was Coy. Q.M., B. Coy. 1st Batt.

15th-16th. Raiding Party. A plain clothes party covering the Auxiliaries, opened fire on our men to which they replied. A man and woman were injured by this fire. On this night a party of 12 men from C.Coy. 2nd Batt. proceeded to Dunmurry for the purpose of intercepting Belfast Goods in motor lorries. It was necessary to break into very small parties in order to move through this very hostile area. Two groups of four men each were detected and surrounded by large patrols of A and B Class Specials. In such circumstances there was no opportunity of resisting arrest

Comments. The increase of activities in the Brigade has been fruitful

-2-

fruitful in increasing morale, and eagerness amongst the men for active work and I believe that our succeeding reports will shew greater results. A considerable number of Company Officers and other effectives have been arrested recently, hampering Company work to some extent, but we hope to have all the Companies in thorough working order. The strength of the Brigade has been increased this month, being 530 as compared to 502 for last month.

Signed,

Comdt.

The Belfast report illustrates some aspects of the conflict in that city. An ASU, or Active Service Unit, led by Roger McCorley and Seamus Woods, killed two Auxiliaries on 23 April. Later that night, two republicans, Dan and Pat Duffin, were shot dead at their home in Clonard Gardens. The IRA suspected that a squad of policemen from Springfield Road barracks, led by District Inspector Ferris, were the killers. They shot and wounded Ferris some weeks later. The tit-for-tat cycle continued. By July 1921, sectarian sniping, bomb attacks and inter-communal rioting were on the rise again, a situation that the IRA did not face elswhere. Reports from 1920 indicate that many veteran IRA members were uneasy about being cast in the role of 'defenders' of the Catholic community, and complained about the type of volunteer attracted by sectarian conflict. Belfast IRA man Seamus McKenna stated that, 'About two-thirds of these recruits joined for sectarian reasons only, to fight defensively or offensively against the Orange gangs. Few of them had any conception of Irish-Ireland principles.'

'THE SQUAD'

Although Richard Mulcahy was IRA Chief of Staff, Michael Collins, IRA Director of Intelligence and Adjutant General (along with his public role in Sinn Féin), is the figure most closely associated with the War of Independence. In his intelligence-gathering role, Collins had a network of informants, including policemen and civil servants, who allowed him access to the intelligence files in Dublin Castle. Collins was also President of the Irish Republican Brotherhood, and utilised this network along with his numerous other connections.

During 1919, Collins established a handpicked unit, composed of IRB members in Dublin, who were later christened 'The Squad' or more colourfully, the 'Twelve Apostles'. The purpose of the unit (whose members were informed that they could be publicly disowned by the republican movement, if neccessary, to avoid connection to its activities), was to neutralise Dublin Castle's intelligence network by assassinating its key operatives. In July 1919, Detective Sergeant Patrick Smyth was shot and fatally wounded in Drumcondra; by the year's end, three more detectives had been killed. During January 1920, the assistant commissioner of the Dublin Metropolitian Police was killed and in March, magistrate Alan Bell, who had been investigating the IRA's finances, was shot dead in Dublin.

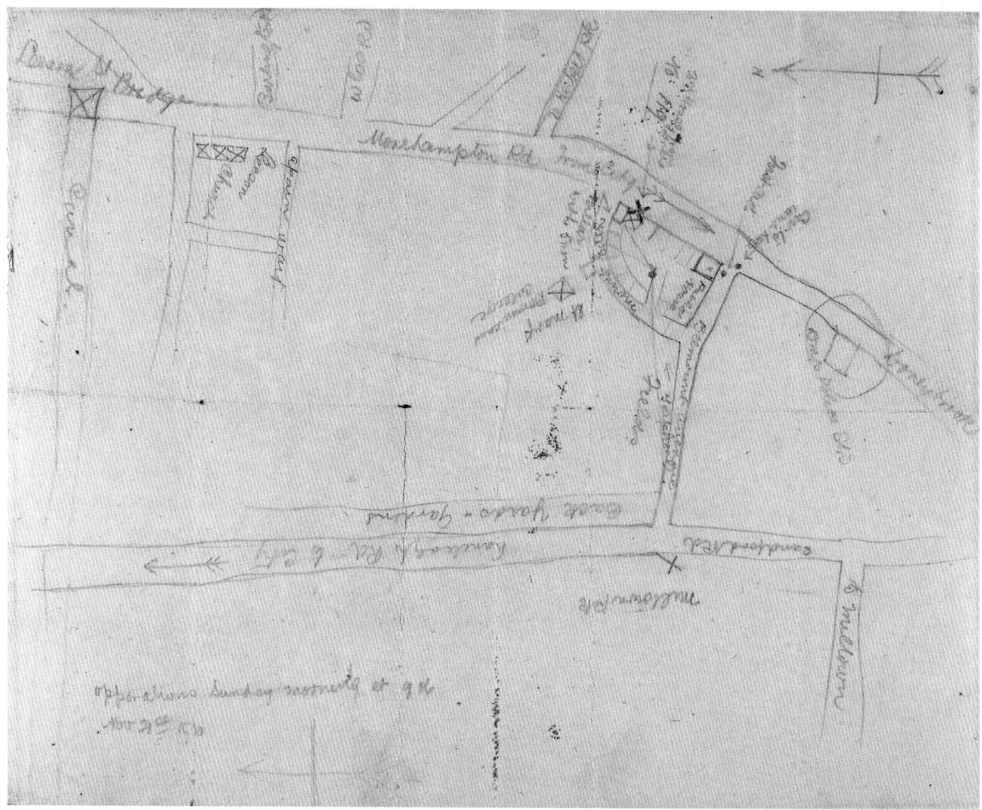

Most of the IRA's targets on Bloody Sunday were based on the south side of the city. At 117 Morehampton Road Captain Donald McClean and his landlord Thomas Smith were shot dead. This map was used by the IRA to locate targets on that day. COURTESY OF THE NATIONAL MUSEUM OF IRELAND

The Squad's most famous operation, undertaken in conjunction with the Dublin IRA, took place on 21 November 1920, when twelve suspected British intelligence officers were killed and several others wounded in a series of raids on lodging houses and hotels. (Two Auxiliaries who happened on an IRA unit were also killed). Later that day in retaliation police raided a football match at Croke Park and opened fire on the crowd, killing fourteen people. On this day, 'Bloody Sunday', the IRA's Dublin commander Dick McKee, along with Peadar Clancy and Conor Clune, was also murdered in Dublin Castle.

In late 1920, members of the Dublin IRA were called to a meeting and addressed by Oscar Traynor on the need to form an Active Service Unit. Men carrying handguns and grenades would operate on a flexible basis and be prepared to ambush police and soldiers when the opportunity presented itself. Frank Flood was a young member of the ASU who was executed along with three of his comrades in March 1921. They had been captured after an abortive ambush near Dublin's North Circular Road. Though nobody was killed in the ambush, the men were convicted of treason.

Twenty-four republicans were executed during the War of Independence, the first being Kevin Barry in November 1920. The Truce, in July 1921, saved the lives of several of those awaiting execution, including Seán McEoin. After the IRA attack on

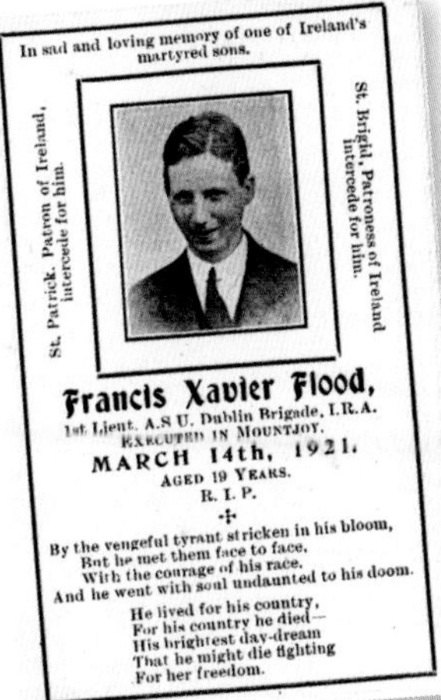

In sad and loving memory of one of Ireland's martyred sons.

St. Patrick. Patron of Ireland, intercede for him.

St. Brigid, Patroness of Ireland intercede for him.

Francis Xavier Flood,
1st Lieut. A.S U. Dublin Brigade, I.R.A.
EXECUTED IN MOUNTJOY.
MARCH 14th, 1921.
AGED 19 YEARS.
R. I. P.

By the vengeful tyrant stricken in his bloom,
But he met them face to face,
With the courage of his race,
And he went with soul undaunted to his doom.

He lived for his country,
For his country he died—
His brightest day-dream
That he might die fighting
For her freedom.

the Customs House in May 1921, during which the building was set on fire, and many IRA members were captured, the Dublin ASU was merged with The Squad to form the 'Dublin Guard'. Frank Flood's body remained buried in Mountjoy, along with nine others until it was reinterred in Glasnevin Cemetary in October 2001.

HUMPHREYS PAPERS, UCD ARCHIVES

TRUCE, 1921

This first issue of *An tÓglác* after the truce of 11 July 1921, which ended the War, expresses confidence that the IRA is in a strong position, noting that the army had been operating more effectively than ever in the lead up to the truce. It warns that, '. . . the guns are silent — but they remain in the hands of the Irish Volunteers'. It also refers to the conflict as the 'War of Independence'.

Unbeknownst to most activists, contacts between the Volunteer leadership and the British had been taking place since the winter of 1920. While violence had reached a new level during 1921 it was unclear which side was 'winning' at the time of the truce. Mulcahy and Collins would later argue that the shortage of arms and ammunition had reached a critical level and that British intelligence was regaining the upper hand in Dublin and elsewhere. At the time of the truce 4,500 IRA Volunteers

An t-Óglác

THE OFFICIAL ORGAN OF THE IRISH VOLUNTEERS.

Vol. III. No. 18.] JULY 22, 1921. [Price Twopence.

THE ROAD OF FREEDOM

Nothing has yet happened which should cause the Irish Republican Army to relax its vigilances. Now as always the soldiers of Ireland stand ready to guard the nation's honour and the rights and liberties of the Irish people. As long as it lasts the truce will be rigidly observed by the officers and men of the Irish Republican Army and no provocative acts or words will be indulged in at this crisis in our country's history. The war was not our seeking; and no persons will welcome the dawn of peace more heartily than the fighting men of Ireland; for they know that there can only be peace where there is freedom. The soldiers of the Irish Republic are not a apart. They are not a band of men who delight in warfare for its own sake. They are simply the armed manhood of the nation, at one with the people of Ireland, flesh of their flesh and bone of their bone sharing the hopes, desires and sufferings of their fellow-countrymen. Their fight has been on behalf of the whole people of Ireland, in defence of the nation to protect what the nation holds dear, to advance the cause to which the nation has given their lives to the struggle and whenever our own noble old Ireland requires them they will spring to her defence again as ready as ever to resist foreign aggression, whoever the aggressor.

The President of theIrish Republic in an important proclamation has warned the people of Ireland against undue confidence. To the soldiers of the Army of Ireland that warning is unnecessary, for they know that they are soldiers and remain soldiers still whatever political contingencies may arise. The organisation, discipline and efficiency of the Irish Republican Army must be maintained unimpaired during the suspension of hostilities. A truce is not a peace; we desire peace as we desire freedom and know that one cannot come without the other. The perfect loyalty with which the truce has been observed throughout Ireland is a splendid proof to the whole world of the perfect discipline of our Army. Right up to the stroke of noon on Monday, July 11th the guerilla warfare raged and never at any period in the War of Independence have our forces shown more widespread activity nor operated more effectively. Not a shot has been fired since noon. The guns are silent—but they remain in the hands of the Irish Volunteers. From the military point of view we remain exactly where we were; we have lost no advantage. From the points of view other than military our position is stronger than ever before.

Now as in the past the strength and efficiency of the Irish Republican remains the keynote of the Irish situation. This is because the Army *is* the Irish nation. It is the will of the whole people to be free expressed in concrete form by the voluntary arming and drilling of the young men of the people. Whether the road to Freedom still untravelled by us be long and steep and rocky, or whether what is left of the road be short and smooth, the soldiers of the Irish Republican Army are ready to march on it again when needed with the same cheerful courage and calm discipline as in the past

A THRILLING ESCAPE

The following is a report received from a Company officer by the O.C. of Cork No. 3 Brigade:—

On the evening of the 17 June at 8 P.M. I was lying in the centre of a field at Castleview. One man was with me, when the military surprised us, and called on us to put up our hands. We immediately jumped to our feet, I drew my Peter the Painter with which I was armed and fired three shots in quick succession at military who were then quickly approaching us. We then took cover as also did the military. While I was in cover I saw some military who were not in cover and fired two shots at them. I then retreated under

(Continued on page 4)

COURTESY OF THE NATIONAL LIBRARY OF IRELAND

were in jail or interned. There was also undoubtedly widespread war weariness, with over 2,000 people killed since 1919. Therefore, the announcement of a truce was very popular with the population at large.

But the news that hostilities were to end came like a bolt from the blue to many of the IRA's local units. Killing had continued right up to the final minutes of the war. There was confusion and some resentment that there had been no consultation about the decision. Ernie O'Malley, then Commander of the 2nd Southern Division, asked, 'Why had the truce been ordered? We were gaining ground, each day strengthened us and weakened our enemy; then why was it necessary to put a stop to hostilities?' A Monaghan IRA volunteer remembered, 'To say that we were jubilant would be untrue. It was more bewilderment'. Another officer described his men's response as a 'mixture of satisfaction and disappointment — disappointment that the possible end had come before we had achieved anything worthwhile, and joy in the hope that we would now have a chance of getting properly armed and meeting the Tans on level terms.'

During the 18 weeks between the truce and the signing of the Anglo-Irish Treaty in December, the ranks of the IRA swelled dramatically, with many expecting a return to hostilities rather than a peace settlement. Some estimates put active strength in July 1921 at as low as 3-5,000 men, but this increased to 72,000 volunteers by December. The aforementioned Monaghan officer lamented that, 'Men who been under orders, total abstainers, both from liquor and ladies, were now being fêted and treated in pubs and were talking to gossipy girls . . . morale was lowered, the men had gone soft'. But despite the resentment felt by some at the 'Trucileers' (as new recruits were contemptuously labelled) the IRA leadership wanted to expand and were pleased at the opportunity to train and re-arm. Over August and September recruits were drilled and given instruction in battle tactics, while intelligence gathering and arms procurement continued. Despite the Truce, sporadic clashes still took place. In Belfast, especially, the violence was worse between July and December 1921 than anything that had gone before.

REORGANISATION

The IRA attempted to professionalise its training regime during 1921, issuing a number of manuals for officers. This engineering manual belonged to Ernie O'Malley, one of the best known IRA commanders of the war. A medical student in Dublin during the Easter Rising, O'Malley joined the Irish Volunteers in its aftermath. He was involved in Volunteer reorganisation throughout Ireland during 1918-1919 and was active in several engagements during 1920. Captured late that year, he escaped from Kilmainham Jail in February 1921 and took command of the IRA's 2nd Southern Division. He opposed the Treaty and was a member of the force that took over the Four Courts in Dublin during early 1922, challenging the authority of the fledgling Free State. When the Four Courts occupiers were forced to surrender, he managed to escape and became part of the anti-Treaty IRA leadership. He was assistant Chief of Staff of the IRA during the early stages of the Civil War until he was captured and wounded in a bloody shoot-out in Dublin during November 1922. O'Malley's accounts of this period, *On Another Man's Wound* and *The Singing Flame*, remain classics.

PRIVATE AND CONFIDENTIAL.

Óglaiġ na h-Éireann.

Engineering Handbook

(No. 1).

IRISH ARMY

OFFICIAL PUBLICATIONS.

Ernie O'Malley's training manual

COURTESY OF THE NATIONAL LIBRARY OF IRELAND

'OUR LATEST ALLY'

One of the original Thompson guns shipped to Ireland in 1921

COURTESY OF THE NATIONAL MUSEUM OF IRELAND

During July 1921, *An tÓglác* announced that the IRA had acquired Thompson sub-machine guns. The gun was originally developed in 1919. The IRA was among the first organisations to recognise its potential and during 1921, Harry Boland (a key member of the IRB) purchased 653 guns on their behalf at a cost of $132,634. Three samples were sent to Dublin and tested during May that year. The guns were then used in an ambush on a British troop train in Drumcondra on 16 June, in which three soldiers were wounded. The IRA had high hopes for the weapon but had very few to hand. In fact, the majority of the weapons they had purchased did not reach Ireland until many years later. During June, U.S. officials seized 495 Thompsons on board the *East Side* at Hoboken, New Jersey, ironically on the same day that they were first used in combat in Dublin. Less than a hundred were imported into Ireland during the autumn and winter of 1921: they were used by both sides in the Civil War. In 1925, the impounded guns from the *East Side* were released into the control of Clan na Gael (the main Irish republican organisation in the U.S.) but the majority of these were not shipped to Ireland until the late 1930s. Although many of the guns were captured, some weapons from the original shipment were still in use in the early 1970s.

A well-armed Active Service Unit of the IRA in Connemara, 1921. ERNIE O'MALLEY PAPERS, UCD ARCHIVES

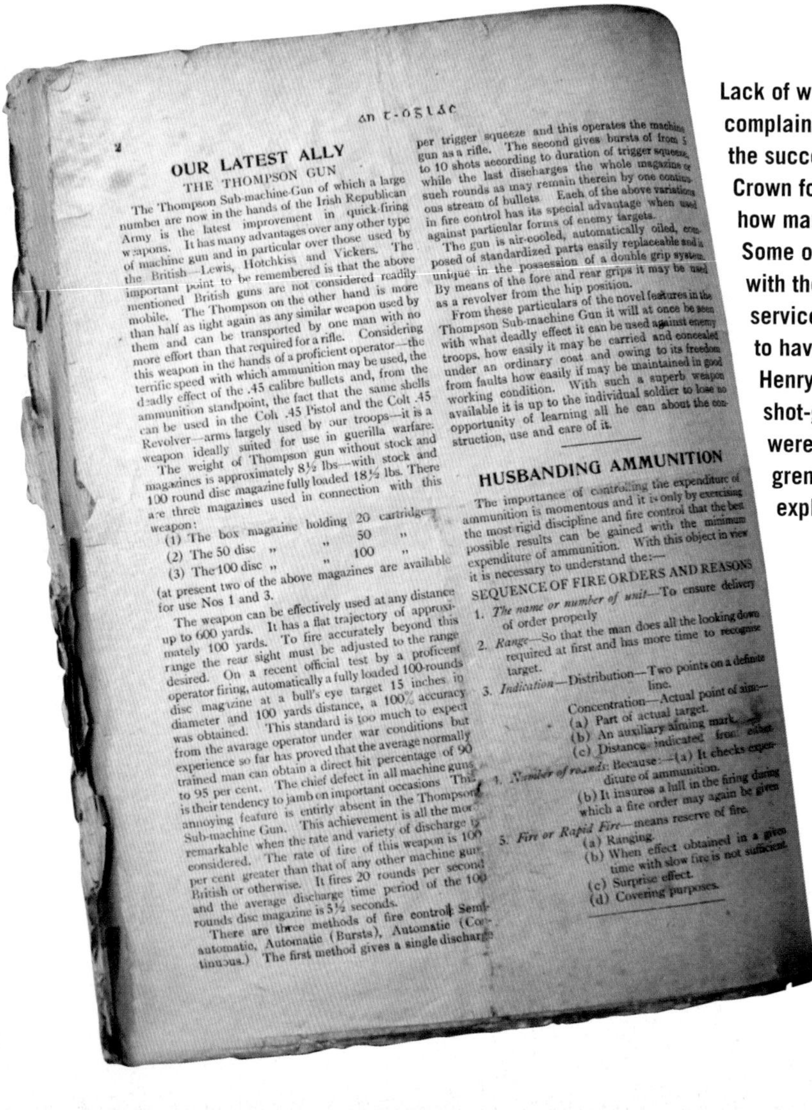

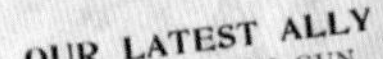

an t-óglác

2

OUR LATEST ALLY

THE THOMPSON GUN

The Thompson Sub-machine-Gun of which a large number are now in the hands of the Irish Republican Army is the latest improvement in quick-firing weapons. It has many advantages over any other type of machine gun and in particular over those used by the British—Lewis, Hotchkiss and Vickers. The important point to be remembered is that the above mentioned British guns are not considered readily mobile. The Thompson on the other hand is more than half as light again as any similar weapon used by them and can be transported by one man with no more effort than that required for a rifle. Considering this weapon in the hands of a proficient operator—the terrific speed with which ammunition may be used, the deadly effect of the .45 calibre bullets and, from the ammunition standpoint, the fact that the same shells can be used in the Colt .45 Pistol and the Colt .45 Revolver—arms largely used by our troops—it is a weapon ideally suited for use in guerilla warfare.

The weight of Thompson gun without stock and magazines is approximately 8½ lbs—with stock and 100 round disc magazine fully loaded 18½ lbs. There are three magazines used in connection with this weapon:

(1) The box magazine holding 20 cartridges
(2) The 50 disc " " 50 "
(3) The 100 disc " " 100 "

(at present two of the above magazines are available for use Nos 1 and 3.

The weapon can be effectively used at any distance up to 600 yards. It has a flat trajectory of approximately 100 yards. To fire accurately beyond this range the rear sight must be adjusted to the range desired. On a recent official test by a proficent operator firing, automatically a fully loaded 100-rounds disc magazine at a bull's eye target 15 inches in diameter and 100 yards distance, a 100% accuracy was obtained. This standard is too much to expect from the avarage operator under war conditions but experience so far has proved that the average normally trained man can obtain a direct hit percentage of 90 to 95 per cent. The chief defect in all machine guns is their tendency to jamb on important occasions This annoying feature is entirly absent in the Thompson Sub-machine Gun. This achievement is all the more remarkable when the rate and variety of discharge is considered. The rate of fire of this weapon is 100 per cent greater than that of any other machine gun, British or otherwise. It fires 20 rounds per second and the average discharge time period of the 100 rounds disc magazine is 5½ seconds.

There are three methods of fire control: Semi-automatic, Automatic (Bursts), Automatic (Continuous.) The first method gives a single discharge per trigger squeeze and this operates the machine gun as a rifle. The second gives bursts of from 5 to 10 shots according to duration of trigger squeeze, while the last discharges the whole magazine or such rounds as may remain therein by one continuous stream of bullets. Each of the above variations in fire control has its special advantage when used against particular forms of enemy targets.

The gun is air-cooled, automatically oiled, composed of standardized parts easily replaceable and is unique in the possession of a double grip system. By means of the fore and rear grips it may be used as a revolver from the hip position.

From these particulars of the novel features in the Thompson Sub-machine Gun it will at once be seen with what deadly effect it can be used against enemy troops, how easily it may be carried and concealed under an ordinary coat and owing to its freedom from faults how easily if may be maintained in good working condition. With such a superb weapon available it is up to the individual soldier to lose no opportunity of learning all he can about the construction, use and care of it.

HUSBANDING AMMUNITION

The importance of controlling the expenditure of ammunition is momentous and it is only by exercising the most rigid discipline and fire control that the best possible results can be gained with the minimum expenditure of ammunition. With this object in view it is necessary to understand the:—

SEQUENCE OF FIRE ORDERS AND REASONS

1. *The name or number of unit*—To ensure delivery of order properly
2. *Range*—So that the man does all the looking down required at first and has more time to recognise target.
3. *Indication*—Distribution—Two points on a definite line.
   Concentration—Actual point of aim—
   (a) Part of actual target.
   (b) An auxiliary aiming mark
   (c) Distance indicated from either
4. *Number of rounds*: Because:—(a) It checks expenditure of ammunition.
   (b) It insures a lull in the firing during which a fire order may again be given
5. *Fire or Rapid Fire*—means reserve of fire.
   (a) Ranging.
   (b) When effect obtained in a given time with slow fire is not sufficient.
   (c) Surprise effect.
   (d) Covering purposes.

Lack of weapons was a major complaint made by local units and the success or failure of attacks on Crown forces was often judged on how many weapons were secured. Some of these men are armed with the modern Lee Enfield .303 service rifle, while others seem to have older Mauser or Martini-Henry rifles. Throughout the war shot-guns were widely used as were a variety of handguns, grenades and improvised explosives.

Chapter 2

GREEN AGAINST GREEN

On 6 December 1921, an Irish delegation, which included Michael Collins, signed a treaty that allowed for a measure of independence for 26 counties of Ireland (partition from the remaining six counties was already in place since 1920). The deal allowed for a greater degree of self-government than Home Rule, but fell far short of the Republic that activists believed had been established at Easter 1916. The scene was set for a bitter split between those who supported the Treaty and those who were opposed to it. Those in the IRA who opposed the Treaty considered that they were defending the Republic of 1916 and were the only ones entitled to the name 'Irish Republican Army': all variants of the modern IRA are descended from those who rejected the Treaty. The resulting Civil War saw at least 1,000 people killed in less than a year.

LIAM LYNCH

From Limerick, Liam Lynch had joined the Volunteers in Fermoy during 1917 and in September 1919, led an attack on regular British troops in the town (one of the first

Officers of the First Southern Division of the IRA, April 1922. Front row, fourth from left is Liam Lynch. Lynch became anti-Treaty IRA chief of staff in March 1922. On Lynch's left is Florrie O'Donoghue, on his right Liam Deasy, Seán Moylan and John Joe Rice. O'MALLEY PAPERS, UCD ARCHIVES

of the War of Independence) in which in he was wounded. In September 1920, his men briefly captured the British Lancers barracks in Mallow and took substantial arms and ammuntion from its stores. In March 1921, he was appointed commander of the First Southern Division of the IRA.

CIVIL WAR

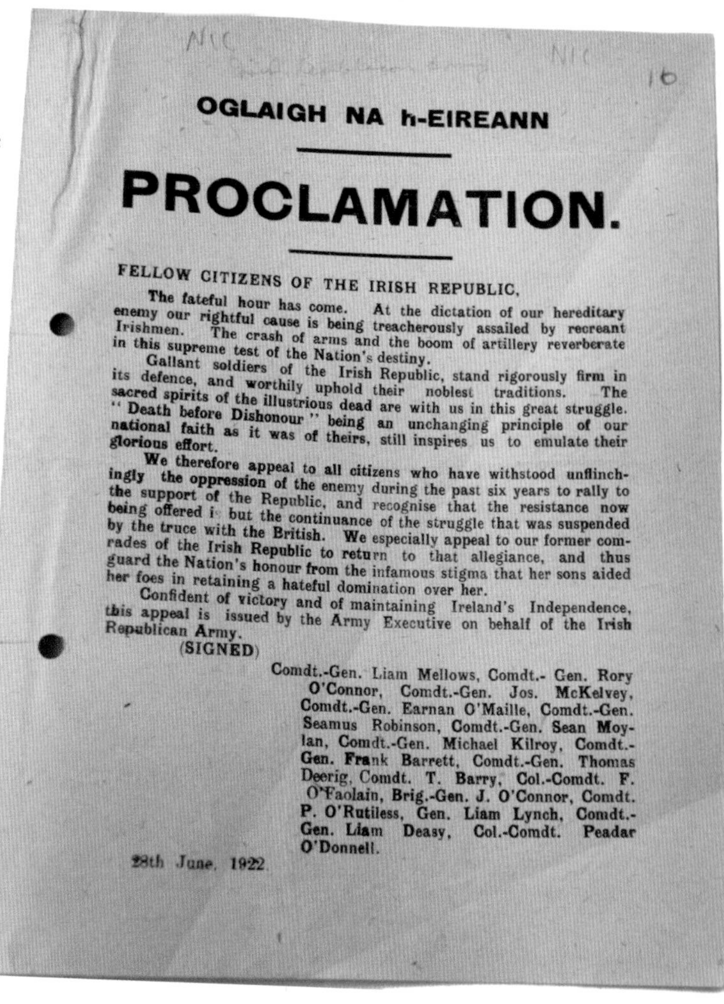

OGLAIGH NA h-EIREANN

PROCLAMATION.

FELLOW CITIZENS OF THE IRISH REPUBLIC,

The fateful hour has come. At the dictation of our hereditary enemy our rightful cause is being treacherously assailed by recreant Irishmen. The crash of arms and the boom of artillery reverberate in this supreme test of the Nation's destiny.

Gallant soldiers of the Irish Republic, stand rigorously firm in its defence, and worthily uphold their noblest traditions. The sacred spirits of the illustrious dead are with us in this great struggle. "Death before Dishonour" being an unchanging principle of our national faith as it was of theirs, still inspires us to emulate their glorious effort.

We therefore appeal to all citizens who have withstood unflinchingly the oppression of the enemy during the past six years to rally to the support of the Republic, and recognise that the resistance now being offered is but the continuance of the struggle that was suspended by the truce with the British. We especially appeal to our former comrades of the Irish Republic to return to that allegiance, and thus guard the Nation's honour from the infamous stigma that her sons aided her foes in retaining a hateful domination over her.

Confident of victory and of maintaining Ireland's Independence, this appeal is issued by the Army Executive on behalf of the Irish Republican Army.

(SIGNED)

Comdt.-Gen. Liam Mellows, Comdt.- Gen. Rory O'Connor, Comdt.-Gen. Jos. McKelvey, Comdt.-Gen. Earnan O'Maille, Comdt.-Gen. Seamus Robinson, Comdt.-Gen. Sean Moylan, Comdt.-Gen. Michael Kilroy, Comdt.-Gen. Frank Barrett, Comdt.-Gen. Thomas Deerig, Comdt. T. Barry, Col.-Comdt. F. O'Faolain, Brig.-Gen. J. O'Connor, Comdt. P. O'Rutiless, Gen. Liam Lynch, Comdt.-Gen. Liam Deasy, Col.-Comdt. Peadar O'Donnell.

28th June, 1922

COURTESY OF THE NATIONAL LIBRARY OF IRELAND

The period after the signing of the Anglo-Irish Treaty in December 1921 was one of confusion for the IRA. Large sections of the organisation instinctively rejected the Treaty, while the Dáil voted narrowly (by 64-57) to accept it. By spring 1922, it was clear a majority of the IRA was against, but by no means agreed on what course to take. Some were in favour of overthrowing the provisional government (led by W. T. Cosgrave) and effectively acting as a military dictatorship; others wanted an attack on British forces to restart the war and hopefully reunite the republican forces. Leading figures such as Liam Lynch still sought to avoid conflict.

As the IRA split, there were stand-offs and clashes between pro- and anti-Treaty factions, almost leading to outright fighting in Limerick. During April 1922, sections of the anti-Treaty IRA seized several buildings in Dublin, including the Four Courts. A general election in May saw a popular mandate for accepting the Treaty (though republicans pointed out that it was fought under a threat of 'immediate and terrible war' with Britain if the electorate chose to reject the ageement). By June, the British government was placing pressure on the new Dublin government, which included Michael Collins, to force the IRA from its strongholds.

On 22 June, two IRB members assassinated Sir Henry Wilson in London: the British government blamed the anti-Treatyites and threatened that unless Collins moved against the Four Courts garrison, they would use British forces to do the job. On 27 June, the new National (or Free State) army began shelling the Four Courts, with artillary pieces borrowed from the British army. The Civil War had begun. The Four Courts garrison appealed to the public to support them on 28 June but within a few days they had been forced to surrender. Some IRA officers felt that sitting waiting for the attack had been a poor strategy and that a determined offensive would have broken the new State. Of the signatories to this appeal, Mellows, O'Connor, McKelvey and Lynch would not survive the war.

IRISH REPUBLICAN ARMY

FIELD GENERAL HEADQUARTERS.

24th August, 1922.

Dept. C/S
Ref. G/O 4.

GENERAL ORDER No. 4.

TO:
O/Cs All Divisions.

DISCIPLINE

It has become necessary to remind all ranks of the Army of the vital necessity of maintaining and restoring Discipline. Some isolated cases have come to my notice which would indicate a certain looseness in some ca ses in this respect, and the danger is that unless these cases are dealt with in the initial stages they may become more wide spread. I am satisfied these acts to which exception is taken are not those of the men who have come through the past trying years, for they are too well aware of the value of strict discipline which more than anything else carried us through the War with England. It is to be feared they are being committed by men who use their positions in the Army to revenge petty spites and jealousies and even perhaps with the intention of bringing the Army into disrepute.

In the future cases of drunkness, boisterous conduct while under the influence of drink, interference with or attempts to intimidate or terrorise the civil population will be severely dealt with, and any members of the Army guilty of these or similarly grave offences will be dismissed the Army, and notification of such dismissals circulated throughout the different Units of the Command.

Needless interference with the Civil Population is especially deprecated, as their good-will and co-operation are very necessary to our success.

The strictest discipline must be observed on the part of men on whole-time Active Service, and such men who in any way mis-behave themselves must be immediately removed from A/S Units.

I appeal to all ranks to maintain, and to insist on the maintenance of the strictes, Discipline, and to uphold the high ideals and traditions of the Irish Republican Army for which such glorious sacrifices have been made and for which so man y loyal comrades gave their lives. Let us not dishonor their memories, or the Cause for which the Army stands, but preserve the same attitude and splendid Discipline as in the past, and which is so necessary and must be insisted on until our objects are achieved and the Republic firmly and securely established.

This Order will be circulated and read to all Units on Parade.

Signed ADJUTANT GENERAL for CHIEF OF STAFF.

DISCIPLINE

Throughout the spring and summer of 1922 there were recurring complaints about the behaviour of the IRA. Goods were requisitioned, homes taken over for billets and robberies carried out amid the general confusion during the build-up to Civil War. On 24 August, the anti-Treaty IRA leadership moved to enforce discipline within its ranks, recognising that the activities of some of its volunteers had alienated public support. For their part, the Free State Army faced some of the same problems and there were also cases of their soldiers carrying out robberies. Nevertheless, the IRA's behaviour during the summer of 1922 probably did push many towards backing the government.

MOSS TWOMEY PAPERS, UCD ARCHIVES

GENERAL RICHARD MULCAHY

Brilliant Strategist of Easter Week

— AND —

CHIEF OF STAFF IN THE BLACK AND TAN WAR

"Every dark hour that Michael Collins met since 1916 served but to steel that bright strength of his and temper his gay bravery.

"You are left each inheritors of that strength and of that bravery.

"To each of you falls that unfinished work."

Extract from General Mulcahy's message to the Army, on the morning of Michael Collins' death.

General Richard Mulcahy first came into prominence in 1916, when he was second-in-command to the late Thomas Ashe in Nth. Dublin. During that historic week he performed the most brilliant feat accomplished by the Irish Volunteers in the Rising. With twenty-seven men he engaged at Ashbourne eighty-five R.I.C., and after an engagement lasting several hours, he killed or captured the lot. Commandant Ashe, with the chivalry which distinguished his brief career, gave the credit for the engagement to his junior who had unquestionably earned it.

Following that brilliant achievement, General Mulcahy rose rapidly in the ranks of the Volunteers. He was Chief of Staff during the Black-and-Tan period, and to him, with Michael Collins, the success in sustaining the armed struggle against the British forces was mainly due.

Hypocrites who never fought for their country or faced the Black and Tans are calling Dick Mulcahy a "Traitor" to-day. Remember, they called Michael Collins a Traitor too!

Printed by the Powell Press, 22 Parliament Street, Dublin. Irish Paper.

FREE STATE AND BRITISH ALLIES

General Macready is at the offices of the Provisional Government directing the campaign against the Irish Republican Army.

They have sent an ultimatum to the Four Courts giving them two hours to clear out before bringing their biggest guns on to them

Artillery for this purpose is supplied to the Free State Army by the British, and British Army instructors are assisting in manning these big guns.

WHAT DO YOU THINK OF THAT?

PROPAGANDA WAR

Anti-Treaty propaganda often accused the Free State Army as being composed of ex-British-Army servicemen or those who had not fought between 1919-21. By mid 1922, ex-British soldiers *were* being recruited to bolster the national army. By the Civil War's end, the army had over 50,000 men in its ranks. But both sides contained many 'Trucileers' (men who had joined the IRA only after the Truce). The anti-Treaty side's allegations that the Free State forces relied heavily on British military aid were nearer the mark: during the Civil War the British supplied 11,000 rifles, 80 machine guns, four-and-a-half million rounds of ammunition, eight 18-pounder guns, a dozen armoured cars and hundreds of vehicles to the Free State.

While the majority of the IRA in 1922 had opposed the Treaty, the military credentials of those who took the pro-Treaty side were vital in countering the accusation that they were traitors to Ireland. Mulcahy and Collins were able to draw on a reservoir of support across the IRA. Collins used the IRB network very effectively to win support for the Treaty, often suggesting that it would enable republicans to gain a breathing space while they prepared for the next round of action.

Top: FRANK AIKEN PAPERS, UCD ARCHIVES

Bottom: COURTESY OF THE NATIONAL MUSEUM OF IRELAND

Among those local commanders who supported this position were Longford IRA leader Seán MacEoin, Monaghan's Eoin O'Duffy and Clare's Michael Brennan, along with the majority of 'The Squad'. Tipperary-born Dan Hogan (whose brother Michael had been killed on Bloody Sunday in Croke Park) Brigade Commandant of the Monaghan IRA, was another prominent pro-Treatyite.

Hardened Belfast IRA men such as Roger McCorley also supported the Treaty, as, in fact, did most of the IRA in that city, and over 600 Belfast men enlisted in the Free State Army during 1922. This was partly because Collins had continued to encourage IRA activities in Ulster during the Truce period, culminating in a joint offensive by both pro- and anti-Treaty factions during May 1922. Supplied with weapons from the pro-Treaty forces, republicans had carried out a wave of attacks across the new Northern Irish state. The offensive was ultimately crushed, severely weakening the IRA in the new Six Counties. Nonetheless, the rhetoric from pro-Treaty IRA leaders on partition was often very militant. During a rally in Armagh in September 1921, Eoin O'Duffy warned that if the Unionists '. . . decided they were against Ireland . . . we would have to take appropriate action. They would have to put on the screw, the boycott. They would have to tighten the screw and if necessary, we would have to use the lead against them'. Rhetoric like this seems to have convinced some northern IRA members that the pro-Treaty side would continue to support them.

CIVIL WAR FIGHTING, JULY 1922

At the outset of the Civil War, the anti-Treaty IRA numbered over 13,000 volunteers, while the Free State Army had only 8,000 men enlisted. Nevertheless, the early stages of the war went very well for the Free State. The pro-Treatyites took control of Dublin fairly quickly and by early August most towns had been cleared of anti-Treaty forces. There was fighting in Tipperary and Co. Limerick (with some local, if short-lived successes for the IRA) but by 10 August, Cork was occupied by Free State troops after landings from the sea. Only 59 National Army soldiers had been killed and they had taken as many as 2,000 prisoners. Collins was reporting that the 'military problem' was now confined to parts of Munster. An extract from Tipperary IRA commander Seán Gaynor's report spells out some of the problems facing his men, particularly a lack of enthusiasm for fighting in the first place. He also notes how clerical condemnation was affecting his men's morale, a view which prefigured the Catholic hierarchy's condemnation of the anti-Treaty IRA's campaign as 'murder before God'. During the summer of 1922, the majority of the Anti-Treaty leadership seem to have favoured a strategy of containment rather than an all-out offensive against the state.

...ving to Lorrha discovered that a column operating in
...2, Bde, area had been disbanded. This had a serious
...e morale of the column and several of the men were
...ing to be disbanded also with the result that the trouble spread
the other columns. On Saturday 22nd. inst, eight men deserted from
Column in Cloughjordan. The remainder had to be disbanded on Sunday
23rd. Two columns were disbanded in Lorrha on Saturday 22nd, inst.
and a report reached me to that effect on Sunday 23rd. to column I
was with at Ballynaclough near Nenagh. This is the only column now
remaining and as it contains only twelve men (the remainder having
been captured in Roscrea action) and as they are also more or less
disaffected by the action of the others, I have decided to return them
to their Units pending the re-organisation of at least one good column.

Every man in this are as disheartened and it will be extremely difficult
to get any further work done. The reasons for this are:-

(1) The absolute hostility of the people towards our men, and the
continued abuses they receive from the civil population.
(2) Scarcity of food.
(3) The feeling that in this fight they are out against their own and
that the destruction that is being done is to the loss of our own people.
even our best men have no heart to fight and will not fight against
the F/State troops if they can avoid it. The pronouncements of the
Clergy are hacing a very serious effect on ourmen, and in many cases
the refusal to give them absolution is turning men from our ranks.

In general the situation in the Division is pretty hopeless and I fear
it will be a considerable time before any effective work is done in
the area.

(signed) Sean Gaynor.

Div. Adjt.

To A/G.
For your information
for C/S
29/7/22

Sean Gaynor's report
TWOMEY PAPERS, UCD ARCHIVES

While the IRA in Dublin had been badly beaten during July 1922, Assistant Chief of Staff Ernie O'Malley was keen to reorganise action in the city. He asked that contact be made with the Irish Citizen Army and a small group led by James Connolly's son, Roddy. The ICA had been maintained by veterans, such as Richard McCormack, from the 1916 period and had carried out some activities in support of the IRA during 1919-21. Roddy Connolly had taken part in the 1916 Rising as a teenager: by 1922, he was a leading member of the fledgling Communist Party of Ireland, having visited Moscow and met Lenin in 1921. The communists took part in some of the fighting in Dublin after the shelling of the Four Courts. While militarily insignificant, Connolly's group's ideas did influence the thinking of some anti-Treatyites, notably Liam Mellows. Mellows suggested, in a series of communications from jail during the autumn of 1922, that republicans could not win back popular support unless they embraced social agitation.

TO O/C 1st. Southern Division.

A Chara,

On last night an arrangement was come to by our staff (on Comdt. Fordes orders) to attack Free State troops stationed in Patrickswell. At 2.o'clock this morning our column proceeded to that village and an assault was made. After fighting for a short time the Comdt. decided to rush the enemy positions, this was done with the entire success, our men pulling the enemy out of the houses and securing their rifles and equipment. In the course of operations Capt. Meaney was fatally wounded and two others slightly wounded, viz. Lieut Doran and Vol. Shannon.

When the prisoners were being removed by lorry, a party of Free State troops, numbering 150 ambushed our men at a place called Hickey's Cross. A stiff engagement ensued, resulting in a loss of two men to us, who were taken prisoners, and one (wounded) to the enemy who was taken prisoner by us. Our troops displayed conspicuous bravery in both engagements. The entire number of prisoners taken was forty, but seven escaped during ambush. Thirty five rifles and 800 rds. .303 also fell into our hands. We are almost held up for Petrol and would ask you to send on some by returning lorry.

Is Mise

for O/C Forde.

IRISH REPUBLICAN ARMY.

Field Head Quarters,
3rd. Southern Division.
BIRR.

To:-

O/C Operations,
F.G.H.Q. Fermoy.

6/9/22.

Synopsis of operations in Tipp. No.I. Bde.

I. Capture of Patrol in Nenagh - 8 men and I Officer. 8 Rifles and I Webley

2. Held Nenagh for 24 hours scarcely any expenditure of amm. Casualties on F.S. side-- One Officer killed (Capt. Byrne) and 2 men wounded.

3. Got two deserters from Nenagh bringing with them 2 Rifles and 200 rds. ammunition (.303) These were Co. Kerry men.

4. O'Briens Bridge Barrack captured (acting in conjunction with Limerick Column)

5. Captured 6 men on their way from Limerick to Dublin after Limk. battle. Five of these men were F.S. Army- one a Transport Lieutenant- They were evidently after looting Limerick City- having upwards of £50 worth of draperies mostly lady's stuff in their possession and 2 Ford Cars.- cars and stuff confiscated till owners are found. Unable to detain Prisoners longer than one week- then released.

6. Portumna Bridge sniped inter mittently.

7. Nenagh Barracks sniped 3 Times without the desired effect- of getting out Troops.

These reports show that the IRA had some initial success in Limerick and Tipperary.
TWOMEY PAPERS, UCD ARCHIVES

IRISH REPUBLICAN ARMY.

Dept. Adjt.

Ref. 1A-9

Your Ref. 25-A

FIELD HEADQUARTERS
NORTHERN AND EASTERN COMMAND

July 26, 1922.

TO:
A/C.S.

7pm.

1. I am using 39, and 86 for appointments at 11 a.m. each morning. I note the other addresses. I think communications office ought to be working definitely tomorrow.

2. I shall send you copies of all forms issued. Casualties forms have been issued, and forms for machine gunners, etc., are ready. I am issuing a General Instruction about commandeering, also on drink, and forms for lists of prisoners, and details of commandeering.

3. I am trying to get this completed and shall send it in as soon as possible.

4. I am arranging to get the widest publicity for the censorship regulations. I am doing my best to get Propaganda working. I had a meeting last night, and found things were very bad. "War News" is the only thing they are capable of turning out. They do not care to eliminate the leading article, but I shall try and make it a bulletin for war news, as soon as I have arranged that all war news shall be collected at a depot and then passed through a censor's hands. I am trying to get stuff printed in Britain. Very little can be done until machinery is got. There is too much stuff available, but no way of printing it.
I am meeting C. na mB. D/Propaganda tomorrow.

5.6.7. Am issuing necessary orders.

8. I interviewed O/C Citizen Army today. He is not in touch with O/C Dublin, but I am communicating him. His name is McCormack. His address for communications is 57 Church Street. Shall see Connolly later re Red Army. His address is 42 Nth. Frederick Street. He lives at 22 St. Patrick's Road, Drumcondra.

9. The I.C.A. consists of 200 men, divided into North City and South City sections. They have 20 PP's, 4 P.b's, and 80 other weapons, mostly .45 calibre. There are three officers in jail and about seven men. I have instructed him to appoint a Vice Comdt., Adjt., and Q.M., also to send me lists of men on railways, ships, and in the printing trade. The girls who work with him will be put in touch with Cumann na mBan. I have asked him to send information regarding petrol. I am now asking O/C Dublin to arrange to co-operate with him in a definite way. If you have any ideas you could send them to O/C Dublin.

10. I shall send you tomorrow draft orders 5, 6 and 7 for correction, and copies of Orders 1, 2, 3 and 4, already issued.

Adjutant

The IRA makes contact with the ICA, July 1922

HUMPHREYS PAPERS, UCD ARCHIVES

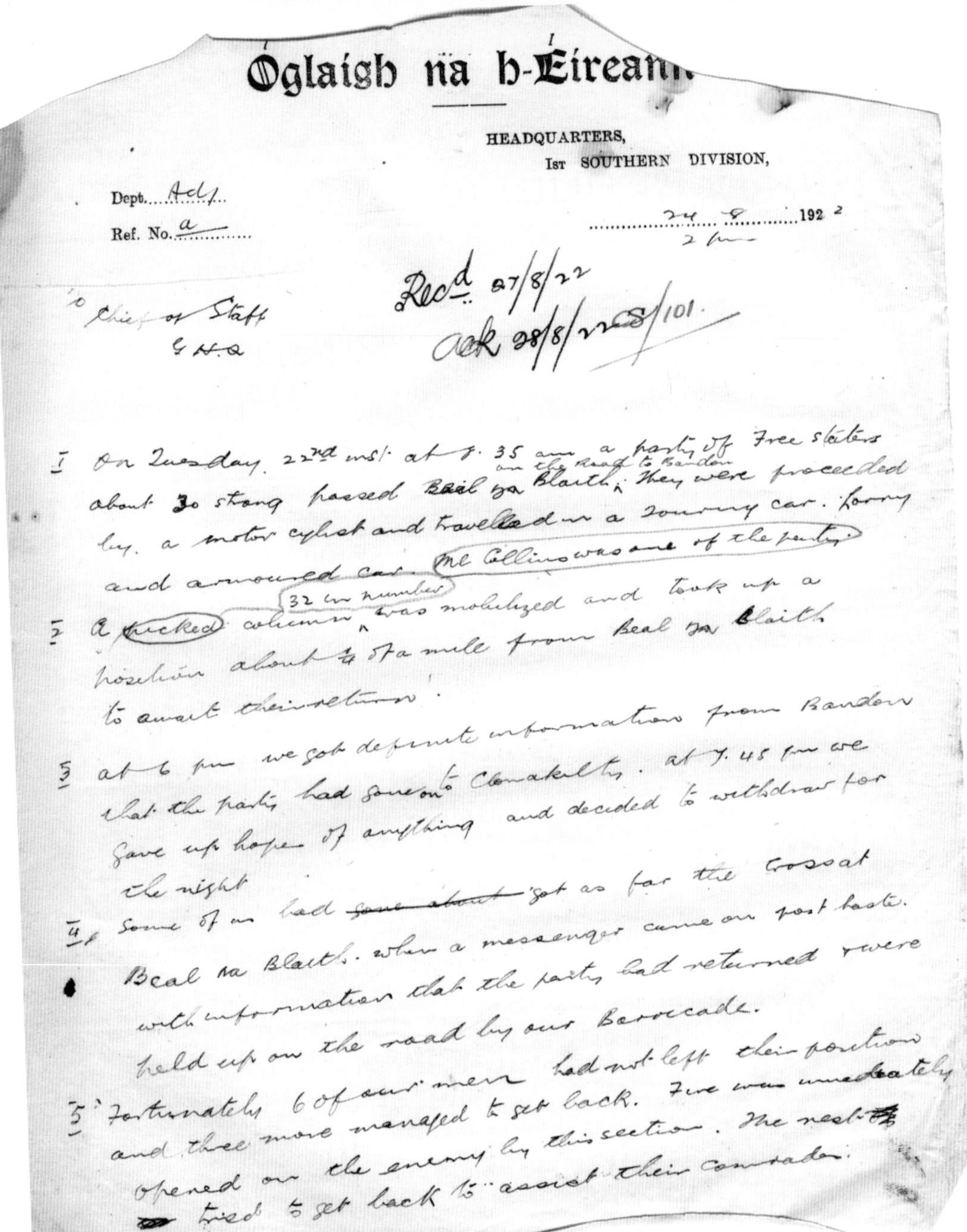

Óglaigh na h-Éireann

HEADQUARTERS,
1st SOUTHERN DIVISION,

Dept. Adj.
Ref. No. a

24 8 1922
2 pm

Recd 27/8/22
ack 28/8/22 S/101.

To Chief of Staff
GHQ

1 On Tuesday 22nd inst. at 7.35 am a party of Free Staters about 30 strong passed Beal na Blath on the road to Bandon. They were preceded by a motor cyclist and travelled in a touring car. Lorry and armoured car. M. Collins was one of the party.

2 A picked column 32 in number was mobilized and took up a position about ¼ of a mile from Beal na Blath to await their return.

3 at 6 pm we got definite information from Bandon that the party had gone on to Clonakilty. at 7.45 pm we gave up hope of anything and decided to withdraw for the night.

4 Some of us had ~~gone about~~ got as far the Cross at Beal na Blath. when a messenger came on post haste with information that the party had returned & were held up on the road by our Barricade.

5 Fortunately 6 of our men had not left their position and three more managed to get back. Fire was immediately opened on the enemy by this section. The rest tried to get back to assist their comrades.

TWOMEY PAPERS, UCD ARCHIVES

BÉAL NA MBLÁTH

The war claimed many casualties, among them prominent members of both sides in the conflict. Cathal Brugha was killed during the early fighting in Dublin; Harry Boland died after being shot by Free State troops on 1 August, while Arthur Griffith died of a brain haemorrhage on 12 August. But Michael Collins, killed in an ambush at Béal na mBláth, between Bandon and Macroom, on 22 August 1922, was the highest-profile casualty of the Civil War.

Óglaigh na h-Éirea

HEADQUARTERS,
1st SOUTHERN DIVISION,

Dept. Adj
Ref. No. ....
....192

but were never in a position during the engagement to render any real assistance.

6 The firing was terrific. the enemy relied chiefly on his machine guns. Now and again you could hear the crack of a rifle from our little party, who never budged one inch from their position

7 The engagement lasted one hour. the enemy managed to remove the barricade, our men were to far away to cover this point with their fire. They beat a retreat, leaving the motor cycle behind, towards Cork. our men continuing to fire on them.

8 I have since learned that Ml. Collins was shot dead during the engagement. Our casualties were nil.

9 The greatest praise is due to the 9 men who stuck to their positions under such a heavy fire. They claimed to have wounded at least three more of the enemy.

10 The enemy used explosive bullets in what ever little rifle firing they indulged in.

11 During the Journey Ml Collins travelled in the touring car and made himself very prominent.

Adj

TWOMEY PAPERS, UCD ARCHIVES

Collins had embarked on a tour of his Cork constituency on 20 August. The war seemed to be going well, with the anti-Treatyites on the retreat everywhere. (Rumours abounded after his death that he had been intending to meet anti-Treaty leaders to bring about a ceasefire.) According to this report from the Cork IRA, Collins' convoy, which included an armoured car, had been spotted by IRA members on the morning of the 22nd on its way to Bandon. Plans were made to ambush the convoy if it returned by the same route. A party of 30 IRA men took up position, but by evening it looked as if the convoy was not returning and at 7.45 p.m. the ambush party began to withdraw, leaving only a few members behind.

However, the convoy did return and some IRA members who were still at the ambush point opened fire. In the ensuing battle, in which the IRA were very much out-gunned, according to their officers, they performed well.

The IRA's report is matter of fact: 'I have since learned that Ml. Collins was shot dead during the engagement. Our casualties were nil . . . the greatest praise is due to the 9 men who stuck to their positions under such a heavy fire . . . During the journey Ml. Collins travelled in the touring car and made himself very prominent.' The circumstances of Collin's death would inspire many conspiracy theories but the IRA's report makes it seem relatively straightforward.

EXECUTIONS

On 24 November 1922, Erskine Childers was executed for being in possession of 'arms': the arms in question being a pistol given to him by Michael Collins. Childers was a veteran of the Boer War, a British civil servant, a sailor and successful author who became a supporter of Home Rule. Radicalised by the failure of the British establishment to challenge Unionist oposition to Irish self-government, he helped organise the smuggling of weapons for the Irish Volunteers on board his yacht, the *Asgard* in July 1914. And even though he worked for British Naval intelligence during the Great War, by 1919 he had become sympathetic to Irish republicanism, opposing conscription and coming to Ireland to work for Sinn Féin. He helped edit the *Irish Bulletin*, the Dáil Eireann newsheet and in February 1921 (after the arrest of Desmond FitzGerald) became director of Dáil propaganda. In May 1921, he was elected TD for Wicklow. He was close to de Valera and opposed the Treaty: during the Dáil debates he was described as a 'damned Englishman' by Arthur Griffith. Childers was relentlessly vilified in the pro-Treaty press as the mastermind behind all IRA activity. His time in the intelligence services during the Great War was used to brand him a spy. Kevin O'Higgins, in particular, seemed to prepare the ground for the execution in a number of his speeches during the winter of 1922. This edition of *Poblacht na h-Eireann* (dated the 'Seventh Year of the Republic' i.e. since 1916) defends Childers' record and warns that he is being targeted by his enemies for death.

Prior to Childers' execution, four members of the IRA, James Fisher, Peter Cassidy, Richard Twohig and John Gaffney, had already been shot on 17 November. Another three IRA members were executed in late November. The IRA responded by threatening to kill all members of the Dáil who had voted for the Public Safety Act, of 28 September 1922, which allowed such executions. On 7 December, members of

POBLACHT NA h-EIREANN

WAR NEWS No. 94

Friday, 17th November, 1922 | Seventh Year of the Republic | Price Twopence

O'HIGGINS PREPARES THE GROUND

The anticipations which he voiced at the time of the arrest of Staff-Captain Erskine Childers are being only too speedily justified as the Army announcement in this issue, and in our "Stop Press" Edition of yesterday, shows. The ghoulish joy of Winston Churchill is finding its ready echo amongst his Irish slaves, who are losing no time in accepting his murderous hints, and getting their Secret Courts to work. This valiant worker and fearless soldier of the Irish Republic is to be thrown to the English wolves by the cowards who wavered where he stood firm and the recreants who foreswore their allegiance when he kept his faith.

The Army statement says truly that the decision of the "Court" in this case is a foregone conçlusion. How could it be otherwise? Read below the words of Kevin O'Higgins, Colonial office "Minister for Home Affairs" spoken on September 27th last in the Kildare Street "Parliament," during his speech supporting Mulcahy's motion for the setting up of these very Courts. In it he pours out his slanderous spite on one specific man—Erskine Childers—who was at that moment in arms for the Republic which O'Higgins had sold for a portfolio. Could any sane person think for a moment that this man could have the remotest chance of a fair trial from a Court constituted by such a "Minister" and supported by such pleas?

Read what O'Higgin's said:—

"I do know that the able Englishman who is leading those who are opposed to this Government has his eye quite definitely on one objective, and that that is the complete breakdown of the economic and social fabric and the state of affairs; that this thing that is trying so hard to be an Irish nation will go down in chaos, anarchy and futility. For his programme is a negative programme, a purely destructive programme, and it will be victory to him and his peculiar mind if he prevents the Government coming into existence under the terms of the Treaty signed in London last December. He has no constructive programme, and so he keeps steadily, callously and ghoulishly on his career of striking at the heart of this nation, striking deadly, or what he hopes are deadly, blows at the economic life of this nation.

MR. W. A DAVIN: On a point of information, may I ask to whom you are referring?

MINISTER FOR HOME AFFAIRS. I am now referring to the Englishman, Erskine Childers. I trust the Deputy didn't think my words were capable of being applied to anyone else."

STOP PRESS

Let the people of Ireland take note of these definitely ascertained and authenticated facts:—

William Cosgrave came back from his visits to the British Government Offices in London at the end of last week with definite instructions that

1. MISS MARY MacSWINEY WAS TO BE ALLOWED TO DIE.

2. ERSKINE CHILDERS AND ERNEST O'MAILLE WERE TO BE EXECUTED.

ERSKINE CHILDERS

TO BE TRIED FOR HIS LIFE TO-DAY

By British Orders

We are authoritatively informed that Staff Captain Erskine Childers, I.R.A. is this morning to be tried for his life by one of the illegal Courts, set up by the British-appointed Junta calling itself the "Provisional Government" for the subversion of the Irish Republic.

The following letter from the Headquarters of the Irish Republican Army was sent to the Dublin daily papers on Wednesday night but was suppressed by that "Government":—

IRISH REPUBLICAN ARMY
GENERAL HEADQUARTERS
November 15th, 1922

Erskine Childers is to be tried for his life on Friday. The verdict is assured beforehand because he is being tried by members of an Army fighting to destroy the Irish Republic which he has fought to maintain, and because you, by your vile propaganda, have loaded the dice against him. You have stated or insinuated that he is an Englishman inspired by hatred of Ireland and anxious to accomplish her destruction. You have stated he is in the pay of England and anxious to ruin this country. English members themselves have refuted this, and only this week, Winston Churchill has shown that the English are howling for his blood, and Churchill's Irish henchmen are preparing to give him the draught.

Erskine Childers is no more an Englishman than was Padraig Pearse or Thomas Davis. Since 1914 he has been labouring and suffering in the cause of Ireland. His services to the nation are too numerous to be set out here. Suffice it to say that in 1918 he threw to the winds a promising career in England and returned to Ireland to place his fortune and his life at the disposal of the Irish nation. His merciless exposure of the brutal regime carried on by the British here helped in a very great measure to unmask England before the world.

His crime is that he has remained constant when others were false, that he refused to break his solemn oath to the Republic, and when the existence of that Republic was threatened by former comrades, with English guns in their hands, he did not flinch but stood true to the faith that was in him.

The soldiers of the Irish Republic have in this resumed war kept to the high tradition that characterised them in 1919, 1920 and 1921. They have not maltreated, not to speak of murdered, any prisoners, and this despite the most intense provocation on the part of the forces opposed to them.

These little men, who fancy with their Imperial masters that murder, executions and torture can defeat the Irish nation, will learn their mistake. Let us hope, for the honour of the Irish nation that they will learn it before they add this crime to the long list of others they have perpetrated.

If Erskine Childers dies at their hands, he will have died in the cause of Tone and Padraig Pearse, and his judges and his executioners will have acted in the cause of Castlereagh and Maxwell, and they should know that they cannot do these things with impunity.

TWOMEY PAPERS UCD ARCHIVES

the IRA shot dead Seán Hales, a Cork TD (and former IRA commander). The following day, on 8 December, four men held since the Four Courts siege, Rory O'Connor, Liam Mellows, Joseph McKelvey and Richard Barrett, were executed in Mountjoy, by order of the cabinet. They were shot purely as a reprisal: there was no legal basis for their execution.

During January 1923, another 32 men were executed. By the end of the Civil War the Free State had executed 77 men, 53 more than the British had from 1920-21. A total of 11,480 republicans were also jailed under the Public Safety Acts of 1922 and 1923, again, far greater numbers than those jailed between 1919-21.

THE IRA RETALIATES

In early November 1922, Liam Lynch complained that while the IRA had attempted to remain committed to the 'Rules of Warfare', the Free State was using every means in its power to crush them. His new orders show a radicalisation in IRA attitudes, with a willingness to embrace more ruthless tactics.

However, while Lynch considered that his men were fighting with one hand tied behind their backs, the Free State believed that it was fighting for its survival.

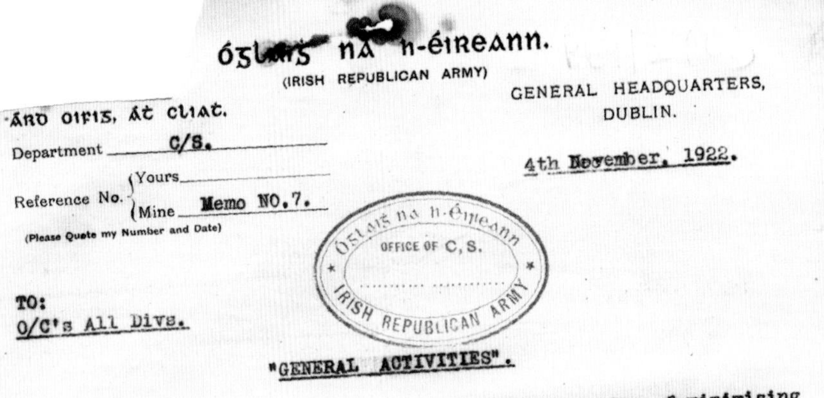

Óglaigh na h-Éireann.
(IRISH REPUBLICAN ARMY)

Ard Oifig, Át Cliat.
GENERAL HEADQUARTERS,
DUBLIN.

Department C/S.

4th November, 1922.

Reference No. (Yours ______ / Mine Memo NO.7.)
(Please Quote my Number and Date)

Óglaigh na h-Éireann
OFFICE OF C, S.
IRISH REPUBLICAN ARMY

TO:
O/C's All Divs.

"GENERAL ACTIVITIES".

1. While due allowance must be made for Press campaign of minimising and concealing our activities it is clear that for some weeks past progress has not been maintained at a regular and satisfactory pace on some areas. This state of affairs must be remedied at once. All O/Cs must realise their responsibilities and affectively answer the latest acts of the enemy by increasing activities and extending the scope of their operations. Recent General Orders explain the policy to be pursued. This policy must be extended to all areas to secure intensified action.

2. Enemy activity has increased during the same period. The Provisional Government of Southern Irelandhas embarked on a ruthless campaign of extermination and it is quite evident that they intend carrying this through to the last ditch. All their efforts are now concentrated on making a success of the terrorist tactics which failed the English in 1920-21. The F.S. Leaders have developed a most callous and bloodthirsty outlook and are prepared to go to any length to destroy the REPUBLIC.

3. Hitherto we have honourably stood by the Rules of War. We have met the enemy in open warfare, pitting our weak arm against his strong one and our armed forces against the resources of the British Empire. We have not adopted against him the same tactics adopted against the British. We have allowed his spies to operate, his officials to organise, his "Parliament" to meet, his Civic Guard to be set up, his agents to denounce us, his finances to pour in unchecked. The newspapers are full with stories of his gala parties

Left and facing page:
By 1923, the IRA was targeting politicians and their property. The cycle of violence produced by state repression can be seen clearly in these orders. During February an IRA raid on the home of Minister for Home Affairs, Kevin O'Higgins, saw his father shot dead, while the young son of James McGarry TD burned to death during an attack on their home.
TWOMEY PAPERS, UCD ARCHIVES

Public safety leglislation allowing for trial by miltary court and execution for a wide variety of offences had been introduced in late September, while rigid censorship of the press was enforced. During the Civil War period the newspapers were not allowed to use the term 'IRA', instead labelling the Anti-Treatyites 'Irregulars'. When criticised by the Labour Party in the Dáil, General Mulcahy explained that allowing official executions might prevent his troops from carrying out unofficial killings (which had already occurred in Dublin during August). Lynch's orders mark a decision to fight the government with tactics smiliar to those used against the British.

-2-

...s while our Volunteers are dragged out and shot
in secret. His salaried supporters have been allowed to go unchecked
while our prisoners have been tortured and murdered in the most devilish fashion. This state of affairs will now end and all efforts will
be concentrated on making the enemy realise that no matter what the
cost may be no Government but that of the REPUBLIC will ever function
in Ireland.

4. Activities on our side have been hitherto restricted to larger
operations of guerilla warfare. In order to effectively protect our
forces and reduce the enemy rapidly the field of operations will be
considerably widened. Harrassing tactics must be continually adopted to weaken enemy morale. Sniping and ambushing enemy parties,
attacking posts, destroying enemy communications and supplies -
these must be pushed forward. Enemy resources must be systematically
attacked and destroyed. His supplies must be cut off. Civilian
support and assistance including Labour in or out of Barracks, must
be prevented from reaching him. His active supporters who openly
stand for murder of our prisoners must be punished. Social intercourse must be forbidden to him. His Courts, his Income, his
machinery of Government must be ruthlessly destroyed. His officials
must be prevented from functioning and every agency employed to
cripple his administration. Firm action must be taken against
newspapers and correspondents who are largely responsible for the
present state of affairs, unless they immediately change their tactics
Stern action must be taken against spies and so-called Defence Committees. Free State Administrative posts, printing places, Tax Offices
and meeting places must be raided and contents removed and destroyed if necessary.

5. The maintenance of discipline is the first duty of Officers and they
will take special care to see that no matter what tactics the enemy
descend to the honour of the I.R.A. shall be preserved inviolate.

6. To be duplicated to Bde and Bn O/C's and transmitted to O/C'S all
Units.

Liam Lynch
CHIEF OF STAFF.

DIRTY WAR IN DUBLIN

In late March 1923, the press reported that a body had been found in Dublin's Clondalkin. Here, an IRA officer identifies the man as one of its officers, Robert Bondfield, a UCD dental student. The Criminal Investigation Department (CID) set up by Michael Collins, with Joe McGrath as Director General, based at Oriel House, Westland Row, was blamed for this and many other killings. Witnesses had seen

H. Q. Dn 1 Bde
3/4/23

To A/G.

Re attached Press Cutting —

Bondfield was acting O/C IV. He was arrested by C.I.D. on Thursday evening last and his body was discovered on Friday evening at Clondalkin.
He had only recently escaped from Portobello.

[illegible]

To D/P

The murder gang appear to be very active in the city at present. What about a 'Special' Bulletin on this. Surely the Church is not going to stand for this kind of campaign. I suppose the two unfortunate lads found at Cabra Rd. is more of their work.

[illegible] for A/G

Noted D/P

Bondfield being picked up by men who had formed an escort for W.T. Cosgrave and Joe McGrath at various events. As the letter points out, two more bodies were found, in Cabra, on Tuesday 3 April 1923. These turned out to be those of Christopher Breslin and Joseph Kernan, both IRA members.

Similar killings of IRA men had been taking place since the autumn of 1922. In one incident three Fianna Éireann members, 17-year-old Edwin Hughes, 17-year-old Brendan Holohan and 16-year-old Joseph Rogers, all from Drumcondra, were arrested posting up anti-Treaty posters on Friday 6 October. Their bodies were found the next day in a quarry near the Red Cow, Clondalkin.

The most famous victim of this dirty war was Noel Lemass, brother of Sean Lemass, who was captured in July 1923 (after the IRA ceasefire) and killed and his body later dumped in the Dublin mountains. Harry McEntee, another Dublin IRA officer, was abducted in late July and found shot dead in early August 1923.

early at work repairing the line.

SHOT AT CLONDALKIN.

YOUNG MAN'S BODY FOUND ON A FARM.

The dead body of a young man was discovered on Saturday afternoon on the farm of Mr. John Dowling, Newlands Villa, Clondalkin, near Dublin.

The young man had been shot through the head, apparently at close range. There was nothing on the body to identify it. The appearance of the remains would indicate that they had been lying for many hours at the spot where they were found.

The body was discovered by a man employed on a farm adjoining that of Mr. Dowling. Residents in the district state that at about seven o'clock on Friday evening shots were heard from the direction in which the body has been found, but little notice was taken of the firing at the time.

The Civic Guards at Rathcoole had the body removed to the Carnegie Library, Clondalkin, and circulated a description of it.

The body has been identified by Mr. John Bonfield, of 103 Moyne road, Rathmines, as that of his son.

An inquest will be held at Clondalkin at 12 o'clock to-day.

Facing page: IRA report on the death of Robert Bondfield

Right: a newspaper report of the murder

TWOMEY PAPERS, UCD ARCHIVES

FUR

Anti-Treaty IRA members in Dublin's Grafton Street, June 1922

COURTESY OF THE NATIONAL MUSEUM OF IRELAND

KERRY, 1923

Kerry saw some of the worst atrocities of the Civil War. General Paddy O'Daly, Commander of the Free State Army in the county, later remarked that, 'Nobody asked me to bring my kid gloves to Kerry and I didn't take them'. O'Daly was not a 'Trucileer'. He had joined the IRB in 1907, was a veteran of the 1916 Rising and had been a leading member of Michael Collins' 'Squad'. In January 1920, he fired the fatal shot that killed William Redmond, Assistant Commissioner of the Dublin Metropolitan Police, and later took command of the Dublin Guard, an amalgamation of The Squad and the Dublin Active Service Unit.

PEACE ?

Over the Mangled Remains of 12 more I. R. Soldiers ?

A TOTAL OF TWENTY BRUTAL MURDERS of Unarmeu Republicans in KERRY——and still the Fight Goes On. The Colonial Forces Must have gone mad to Massacre the Cream of Kerry's Bravest. The Tans Never committed a deed so foul as THIS. LATEST BUTCHERY by Their Green-Coated SUCCESSORS; BUT—

NEVER

WILL ROPES, BOMBS, MINES, AND MACHINE GUNS KILL THE REPUBLIC! Step aside Cowards, Renegades—on with the War! The blood of our Soldier Comrades CRIES TO HEAVEN! NEVER Can there be Peace with the Sir Michael Dyer's of the F. S. Army! PEACE TALK IS ENDED

No Peace with England's Hirelings!

IRA leaflet responding to the deaths of several members TWOMEY PAPERS, UCD ARCHIVES

O'Daly found in Kerry that there was wider popular support for the anti-Treatyites than elsewhere. He also faced sustained pressure from the IRA, with over 60 of his troops killed in the county. In retaliation, Free State soldiers engaged in routine excesses, including the beating of prisoners and the shootings of men who had surrendered, but the worst incidents came in the spring of 1923. In early March, five soldiers were blown up after being lured to a trap mine at Knocknagoshel. O'Daly then announced a new policy of forcing IRA prisoners to clear road barricades, which may have been rigged with similar booby-traps. Within a week, 17 prisoners had been killed by mines, at Ballyseedy, Countess Bridge and Caherciveen.

The Free State Army claimed these deaths came as a result of anti-Treaty explosives: however, one man, Stephen Fuller, had actually survived the Ballyseedy explosion. He recounted how he and fellow prisoners had been beaten, then tied to a barricade and fired on before a mine was exploded among them. A Military Court of Enquiry exonerated the Free State troops but knowledge of the massacres was soon widespread.

DEFEAT

In most areas the anti-Treaty IRA was beaten by the spring of 1923. However, Lynch seemed determined to fight on. On 10 April, he was killed while being pursued by

BRIGADE HEADQUARTERS DUBLIN. 1.

Summary of Operations for fortnight ending 21st. April 1923.

Battn. 1. 8/4/23.
Attack on CLONTARF RAILWAY STATION with bombs and revolvers. Two bombs exploded having been flung through the windows. Revolver fire was also opened on the enemy troops who replied. The enemy had five or six casualties.

" 8/4/23.
Senator Moran's house was bombed simultaneously with attack on CLONTARF RAILWAY STATION. The object was to cover retreat of men on Railway Station job, as this house was reported to be guarded by C.I.D.

" 13/4/23.
Two Delivery Vans destroyed by fire – one the property of BROWN THOMAS & CO., the other THOMS'.

" 14/4/23.
One Delivery Van the property of TODD BURNS & CO. destroyed.

" 16/4/23.
One Van belonging to TODD BURNS destroyed.

" 17/4/23.
One Delivery Van the property of "FREEMAN'S JOURNAL" destroyed

" 17/4/23.
Party of men raided Orchard Confectionery shop in DORSET ST. This place was reported as being enemy "touts" call-office. Nothing found.

" 17/4/23.
Same party went to raid 81, DORSET ST. for same purpose. Only one man was armed. In a tussle a civilian that was in the shop succeeded in taking gun from this man and shot Vol. Tierney dead.

" 18/4/23.
COLLINS BARRACKS attacked. Two grenades were thrown, both failed to explode. Fire was then opened on the sentries with revolvers.

Battn. 2. 9/4/23.
Two motor cycles with side cars containing nine bags of mails taken at FINGLAS BRIDGE.

By 1923, the anti-Treaty campaign in Dublin was reduced to sabotage and sporadic attacks, as can be seen from this report. Newspapers and businesses seen as supporting the government were attacked. IRA volunteer James Tierney from Buckingham Street was killed when a civilian disarmed and shot him on one of these raids.

TWOMEY PAPERS, UCD ARCHIVES

troops on the Knockmealdown Mountains. At the first meeting of the IRA leadership after Lynch's death, Frank Aiken was appointed IRA Chief of Staff. From Camlough in Co. Armagh, Aiken had been involved in the Irish Volunteers since 1913. He was active as commander of the 4th Northern Division during the War of Independence, his area covering parts of Louth, Armagh, Antrim and Tyrone.

Aiken had been slow to resume armed activity during the summer of 1922, maintaining a somewhat neutral positon until he felt that the Free State Army's actions against his men forced his hand. His division was responsible for killing six Protestants during June 1922, however, in reprisal for attacks on Catholics. At the executive meeting on 20 April, several proposals to end the conflict were put forward. What seems clear is that none of the IRA's leaders thought victory was possible. Feelers were put out through go-betweens aimed at securing a peace agreement, but the Free State government was adamant that only surrender would be accepted.

Below and facing page: IRA executive meeting
AIKEN PAPERS, UCD ARCHIVES

2

VOTING: Against: Liam Pilkington, Sean Hyde, B. Quirke, S. Dowling, F. Aiken, T. Ruane, T. Sullivan, S. MacSwiney, S. O'Mara, - 9.

For: T. Barry, T. Crofts - 2.

Did not Vote: P. J. Ruttledge- 1.

8. Recommendation to Government and Army Council to carry on war if F.S. "Government" did not accept our peace terms was not passed, numbers being equally divided for and against.

VOTING FOR: L. Pilkington, B. Quirke, F. Aiken, S. MacSwiney, P.J. Ruttledge, T. Ruane, - 6.

AGAINST: S. Hyde, S. Dowling, T. Barry, T. Sullivan, T. Crofts, S. O'Mara. - 6.

9. On being questioned by the Chairman if majority rule would be accepted as a rule of order of the Free State "Government" accepted 1. and 2. in above resolution: all members with one exception assented. 11 for. The exception T. Ruane would not express his opinion.

10. The Chief of Staff was instructed to summon next meeting when he, or the majority of the Executive, considered it necessary.

(Signed) FRANK AIKEN.

(Date) 11th. July, 1923.

ARMY EXECUTIVE

Minutes of adjourned meeting (from 26th. March, 1923) held on April 20th. 1923.

1. **ROLL CALL:**

Present: Liam Pilkington, Sean Hyde, B. Quirke, S. Dowling, F. Aiken, T. Barry, T. Ruane, T. Sullivan, Sean McSwiney, T. Crofts, P.J. Ruttledge, S. O'Mara.

Absent M. Cremin (Away in England on Army business)
A. de Staic (captured, substitute resigned)
Frank Barrett (captured, substitute killed)
Humphrey Murphy (sick)

2. At commencement of meeting T. Ruane, P.J. Ruttledge and Sean Dowling had not arrived. It was decided to go on with the business and if they came before meeting ended to take their votes on all resolutions or decisions. They came later and below are the decisions arrived at and resolutions passed.

3. The Chairman explained that it was impossible to hold meeting on the 10th. as arranged on adjournment, owing to the Chief of Staff being killed and the intense enemy activity preventing members coming together.

4. Frank Aiken, D.C/S. was unanimously elected Chief of Staff on being proposed by Tom Barry and seconded by Sean MacSwiney.

5. It was proposed by Sean MacSwiney and seconded by B. Quirke and unanimously decided, to appoint an Army Council consisting of three members. Comdt. Gen. Pilkington, Frank Aiken C/S., and Comdt. Gen. Barry were elected members of the Army Council. Sean Hyde, A.C/S. and Sean MacSwiney Q.M. Cork No.1. Brigade substitutes.

6. The following resolution proposed by Frank Aikem and seconded by Sean MacSwiney was passed:

> "We empower the Government and Army Council to make peace "with F.S. "Government" on the following basis:
>
> 1. The sovereignty of the Irish Nation and the integrity of its territory are inalienable.
>
> 2. That any instrument purporting to the contrary is, to the extent of its violation of above principle, null and void."

Voting: **For:** Liam Pilkington, Sean Hyde, B. Quirke, S. Dowling, F. Aikem, T. O'Sullivan, S. MacSwiney, P.J. Ruttledge, Sean O'Mara, - 9.

Against: T. Ruane, T. Crofts. - 2.

Did not vote: T. Barry. - 1.

The following amendment proposed by T. Barry and seconded by Tom Crofts to above resolution was defeated:

> "In view of the position of the Army that we direct the "Government and Army Council to call off all armed resistance "against the F.S. "Government" and F.S. Forces".

Voting/

Óglaiġ na h-Éireann.
(IRISH REPUBLICAN ARMY)

Árd Oifig, Át Cliat.

GENERAL HEADQUARTERS,
DUBLIN

Dept :—

Ref. No. Order of the Day. May 24th, 1923.

To:
All Ranks
From the President.

SOLDIERS OF LIBERTY - LEGION OF THE REARGUARD:

The Republic can no longer be defended successfully byyour arms. Further sacrifices on your part would now be vain and continuance of the struggle in arms unwise in the national interest. Military victory must be allowed to rest for the moment with those who have destroyed the Republic. Other means must be sought to safeguard the nation's right.

Do not let sorrow overwhelm you. Your efforts and the sacrifices of your dead comrades in this forlorn hope will surely bear fruit.. You have saved the nation's honour and kept open the road to Independence. Laying aside your arms now is an act of patriotism as exalted and pure as your valour in taking them up.

Seven years of x intense efforts have exhausted our people. Their sacrifices and their sorrows have been many. If they have turned away and have not given you the active support which alone could bring you victory in this last year, it is because they are weary and need a rest. Give them a little time and you will yet see them recover and rally again to the standard. They will then quickly discover who have been selfless and who selfish - who have spoken truth and who falsehood. When they are ready, you will be, and your place will be once more as of old with the x vanguard.

The sufferings which you must now face unarmed, you will bear in a manner worthy of men who were ready to give their lives for their cause. The thought that you have still to suffer for your devotion will lighten your present sorrow and what you endure will keep you in communion with your dead comrades who gave their lives,and all these lives promised, for Ireland.

May God guard every one of you and give to our country in all times of need sons who will love her as dearly and devotedly as you.

EAMON de VALERA.

TWOMEY PAPERS, UCD ARCHIVES

'SOLDIERS OF LIBERTY', MAY 1923

Aiken eventually secured agreement with the IRA leadership that its men would be ordered to cease fighting. De Valera, as President of Sinn Féin, issued a message to the 'Legion of the Rearguard' telling them that the Republic could 'no longer be defended successfully by your arms' and stating that, 'victory must be allowed rest for the moment' with their enemies. There was no suggestion that the IRA was to accept the Free State. There would be another day. Yet the situation was bleak. According to the record of the IRA's dead, *The Last Post*, over 400 republicans were killed in the 1922-23 period. Over 11,000 men and women were still in prison and the violence had not ended, despite the ceasefire of 28 May 1923. Significantly for de Valera, despite defeat and widespread resentment at the destruction of the war, Sinn Féin still won 44 seats in the August 1923 general election. There was clearly a base for anti-Treaty republicanism.

Chapter 3

LEGION OF THE REARGUARD

Despite its defeat in the Civil War, the IRA remained a significant force in Ireland over the next decade. It helped give birth to the Fianna Fáil party in 1926, and assisted that party in general elections during 1932 and 1933. It also developed radical left-wing policies that saw it take action during strikes and land disputes and establish links with the Soviet Union. Tension over these developments would lead to a split in 1934 and to the formation of the Republican Congress. The era would also see clashes with the Blueshirts and attempts to reach across sectarian lines in Northern Ireland.

THE IRA, 1923-24

Despite the ceasefire, the IRA had no intention of going out of business. It was still determined to overthrow the Free State. During 1923, the army was reorganised as it sought to deal with the new situation.

The Cork commander Tom Barry left the organisation after it rejected his suggestion that it destroy its arms and equipment (what would later be called 'decommissioning'). Barry did not rejoin the IRA until 1932. Sinn Féin President Eamon de Valera (regarded as President of the Republic by the IRA) was arrested during the general election campaign in August 1923, and replaced by IRA Adjutant General P.J. Ruttledge. Then, during October, there was a mass hunger strike by republican

(D)

Chief of Staff Report
Meeting Held August 10t

1. When I was elected Chief of Staff on 20t
Adjutant General (Tom Derrig) had been wounde
days previously, the Q.M.G. (Joe O'Connor) had
and Comdt. Moss Twomey of the C/S. department
When I arrived at General Headquarters I appoi
Acting A/General and Liam P. Acting Q.M.G.

I issued "Suspension of Offensive" Order
the Government and Army Council on the 27th. A
28th. April, 1923 I issued General Order No.19.
to be prepared for the resumption of offensive.
with Comdt. Gen. Moylan, Director of Purchases
regarding artillery and found that none could b
had £50,000 before the middle of Summer.

2. The "Cease Fire - Dump Arms" Order was issu
instruction of the Government and Army Council,
to take effect on or before 28th. May 1923.

On the 23rd. June 1923 I received a documen
T.C. O/C. 1st. Southern Division and T. O'S. O/C
threatening to appeal directly to men if somethi
immediately to secure immunity from arrest, etc.
General Order No. 20. on the 24th. June 1923 poi
man who attempted to usurp the powers of the prop
the Army would be severely dealt with.

3. Tom Barry, at meeting of Government and Army
30th. 1923 recommended the destruction of arms.
by all others present.

Arrangements were made at this meeting of the
Army Council (June 30th) to give financial assista
for men on the run, to look after disabled Volunte
dependents of Volunteers who were killed. An Empl
Scheme was also approved of, which was sent out to
afterwards with instructions to have Employment Co
each Battn. area.

4. In the beginning of July 1923 prisoners in Tin
and Dundalk Jail asked for leave to Hungerstrike.
matter before the Executive Meeting of 11th/12th. J
unanimously decided that hungerstriking was a matte

At this Executive meeting it was decided to do
to prevent emigration. As a result of decisions of
Orders No. 21, 22, and 23, regarding emigration, pen
Volunteers found guilty of Robbery, and ages for rec
sent out. Circulars were also sent out pointing ou
that it was their duty to help in re-organisation of
Fianna.

5. When the President was arrested on August 15th.
A/General became Acting President. Early in October
as A/General.

6. After the elections the enemy offensive to treat
individuals and as criminals began. The Mountjoy pris
the worst as they were subjected to very brutal treatm
decided to go on Hungerstrike. When we heard that the
commenced in Mountjoy I issued an Order of the Day to
to do their best to arouse indignation among the peopl
treatment of our prisoners and to get public meetings
release. When the strike was about thirty days in pr
men were very weak the enemy tried to get the Kilmainha
to undertake to advocate the surrender of arms, but the

The

The Kilmainham hungerstrikers decided to call off the strike a few
days afterwards and their representatives went round all the jails and
camps and got all who were on hungerstrike to come off simultaneously
with them. Some of our people believed the strike to be a failure
and that the Government or General Headquarters should have called it
off. Neiterh the Government or General Headquarters had power to
order any man on or off hungerstrike, and even if they had I believe
the best course was to let the prisoners go on with it or call it
off themselves. I believe this strike was a success/from a national
point of view . The deaths of Dinny Barry and Andy O'Sullivan
clinched the victory the prisoners won the materialism Imperialism
and selfishness that was sweeping the country. Even the bitter
enemies of our country have great respect for the faith and endurance
of the Volunteers who hungerstruck even for a few days.

7.
Watters letter November 1923: I.R.B. tried to approach us through
Watters, Belfast during the hungerstrike. In instructed O/C. 4th.
Northern Division to see Watters and tell him that I would not meet
him and find out what he had to say. He wanted men to attend an
I.R.B. Conference with the object of getting rid of oath, etc.With
A.P's permission I addressed a letter to O/C. 4th. Northern Division
which I instructed him to forward to Watters refusing to attend hole
in corner conferences with men who recognised foreign authority and
who carried on a war of extermination against Republicans. This
ended the matter.

8. When prisoners began to be released the A/General got down to
insisting on reports and all General Headquarters Staff started to
inspect Divisions. By January 1st. 1924 all Divisions and
Independent Brigades had been inspected. Comdt. M.T., who had been
appointed Inspection Officer, inspected 3rd. Southern Division in
December, 1923, 3rd. Western Division and all Brigades in January,
4th. Northern Division and all Brigades in January, 1st. Southern
Division and all Brigades in March, 2nd. Southern Division and all
Units, together with Limerick in May and June, 1st. Western Division
in July. Since December I attended Divisional Councils in 1st.
Southern Division, 2nd. Southern (twice) 3rd. Southern, 3rd. and
4th. Western , Midland, 4th. Northern, Limerick and Dublin 1. Brigade.
A/G. attended Dublin 2. Bde., 4th. Western Division, 2nd. Western
4th. Northern, 3rd. Eastern, 1st. Western and Limerick.

A.C/S. attended 2nd. Western and Midland in December 1923. Comdt.
K. attended 3rd. Eastern Division in December 1923. Comdt. MacBride
inspected Derry City Battn. Tyrone and Belfast Brigade.

Staffs were fixed up in all units inspected. Routine orders were
issued regarding linking up of prisoners and examination of their fit-
ness to be Volunteers, but it was generally found that these Orders were
not carried out as they should until Divisions were inspected in detail.

9. Donegal Area: Owing to the fact that a suitable Officer could not
be found to take charge, the old 1st. Northern Division is now working
as two Brigades and one Independent Battn. (Derry City) under 3rd.
Western Division.

The old 2nd. Northern Division is now Tyrone Brigade.

The old 3rd. Northern Brigade is now Belfast Brigade.

Limerick County is now working as an Independent Command - O/C.
having rank of Brigadier. G.H.Q. has decided to set up as soon as
possible a Division having Headquarters in Limerick, which will include
Clare, Limerick and North Tipp. Brigade, and to put the Galway
Brigades into 2nd. Western Division. It is proposed also to make
changes in 2nd. Western Division, 3rd. Southern and Dublin 2. Brigade.

10. Free State Mutiny: The mutineers tried to get in touch with
General Headquarters in order to get our co-operation for a coup d'etat.
We pretended at first that their feelers did not reach us; but, when
we/

Above, facing page and following spread: In this 1924 report, Frank Aiken explains the problems faced by the IRA in the year after Civil War ended.
AIKEN PAPERS, UCD ARCHIVES

3

we got an invitation to attend a meeting of theirs at which they said they would prove to us that they could capture all Free State posts, we replied, verbally, with A.President's permission, that we would want some more proof of their sincerity than their talk before we would think of touching them. We pointed out that the prisoners, for whose capture they were responsible, were still in jail. I issued a circular to all ranks as to the attitude to be adopted towards them. The Volunteers all over took up what we consider was the proper attitude: that is, if the Mutineers were going to smash the Free State we would not put any obstacles in their way, but we were not going to rely on them or their help to do it.

11. Q.M.G. When Andy Cooney was released in June 1924 the A.Q.M.G resigned and A.C. was appointed Q.M.G. on July 1st. 1924.

11. Leabhair na hAiseirghe: A small group of Republicans have procured the services of Art O'Murnahan, an artist who has a genius for Celtic Art. He is at present working on designs for a Memorial Book in which will be inscribed the names of all those who died for the Republic. I met the Secretary of the Committee and promised that I would do all I could to get Volunteers to help in procuring funds to keep the artist working full-time. At present they have no funds and work must stop if some money is not forthcoming. A/G. is collecting names of all casualties for this Book.

12. 4th. Western Resolutions: Some Officers of the 4th. Western Divisional Staff have been pressing for a Convention since 28th. February 1924, on the grounds that the Executive is illegal as it was not elected at annual convention. I pointed out that annual Convention was impossible, but they declare that it can safely be held These Officers also want Division listsof Executive meetings sent to Divisions. I pointed out that all that concerned Divisions once a decision was arrived at by Executive was to put that decision into effect.

13. Republican Defence Corps: This Corps was organised in May 1924 in Dublin by released Officers in order, as they said, to keep Army intact. I tried to meet them after formation but failed. Owing to a misunderstanding a few of the Corps seized arms belonging to Q.M.G. in June last. I got O/C. Dublin 1. Bde. to arrange a meeting for me with some of them. I met three of them on the 28th. June 1924, and pointed out to them that even if they had legitimate grievances that this was the wrong way to get them redressed. They had some grievances and I listened to them. After a long discussion I pointed out to them that most of the grievances under which they laboured arose partly from their own fault. They agreed. I appealed to them for co-operation and discipline. They agreed to promise to behave as disciplined soldiers while they remained Volunteers in the I.R.A. They gave me a signed statement to this effect on behalf of the Defence Corps. I ordered them to disband the Corps on July 12th. 1924. Since then I have not heard from them. I understand a few members do not agree to disband it. I also ordered them to return the seized arms, which they did.

14. Commission on Regulations and Organisation: For some time past G.H.Q. Staff has decided to get out a definite set of regulations regarding discipline and Courts Martials. A Commission has been appointed for that purpose and will make recommendations to G.H.Q. as soon as possible. A Commission on Organisation could not have been set up to any purpose until after this Executive Meeting.

I suggest that this Executive should discuss the organisation of Army and say definitely whether name of Units and ranks of the Officers commanding Units are to be based on sizes of areas or on numbers. For the work before us I believe they should be based on numbers as far as possible.

Regarding discipline I suggest that Executive should lay down as a broad general rule that any Volunteer found guilty of conduct likely to bring discredit on the Army should be dismissed and not

allowed/

prisoners (including women) in several jails across the Free State. Two men, Denis Barry and Andrew O'Sullivan, died and the strike ended in confusion (though Aiken claims here that it was successful).

By mid 1924, while 600 IRA members remained in Free State jails, most had been released. Aiken reported attempts by members of the Irish Republican Brotherhood and disillusioned members of the Free State army to make contact with the IRA. During March 1924, there was an abortive 'army mutiny', the roots of which lay in opposition to moves to reduce the national army's numbers and the belief that the Free State was no longer pursuing Michael Collins' anti-partition policies. The mutineers seemed to have offered the IRA an opportunity to overthrow the government.

During the mutiny a British soldier was shot dead by gunmen in national army uniforms at Cobh; perhaps in an attempt to draw the British into conflict and reunite republicans once again. But the IRA did not trust the mutineers, among whom were men who were implicated in some of the worst atrocities against republicans during the Civil War.

4

allowed to return until he gives clear evidence of good behaviour in future.

Another vital point for Executive to discuss is the manner in which some of our men take upon themselves so lightly the powers of peace and war. It should be definitely laid down that any Volunteer who attempts to usurp the powers of proper Army authorities is guilty of treason and liable to execution. Every Volunteer should be supposed to be bound in honour and by regulation to get leave from proper authorities before doing anything which is a departure from the orders and regulations laid down for his guidance.

On the whole I think the Army is in a healthy state with the exception of a few Brigades here and there and Dublin 1. Brigade. These Brigades, especially Dublin 1., are improving very fast at present time. I believe the time is opportune for re-organising Army on the lines most suitable to the work which we may have to do and disciplining and training it to do it well.

Chief of Staff

August 9th. 1924

7

are now coming into the open as political die-hards with ex-District Inspector Nixon as their leader. This is the man who was the ring-leader in the Belfast pogroms. I believe he has a bigger pull with the R.U.C. and with all-classes of the Specials than the present Northern "Government". The irreconcilables of these two forces, and they constitute the majority, swear by him. If he should get in power there is little doubt that another reign of terror will ensue. At present the Nationalists in the Six Counties are keeping quiet - satisfied that they are allowed to live. From the meagre data in my possession I should say that the vast majority of them look upon the satisfactory solution of the Boundary Question as the most that could possibly be achieved. They regard Republicans as attempting the impossible and as a menace to their peace. They are also of opinion that the Free State "Government" has let them down over the Boundary question. The majority of them I should say about one-third - are behind the Republic, but they must of necessity keep their opinions to themselves.- they are twice as many as six months ago. I believe that if an attempt were made by Sinn Fein to come into the open in the Six Counties the Republican Movement would leap forward by leaps and bounds. Certainly some effort should be made at the next election to nominate Republican candidates, otherwise it will be impossible to make any progress with army organisation.

The military organisation, defences and equipment in Ulster are much more perfect than in the Free State . Apart from the British garrison and R.U.C. almost every non-Catholic adult man is a trained soldier.- There can be little doubt that detailed plans on the most modern lines for offensive and defensive tactics on the borders are fully worked out.

D/Intelligence.

August 9th. 1924

Ulster IRA inspection report, 1924

TWOMEY PAPERS, UCD ARCHIVES

ULSTER

The vast majority of the post-Civil-War IRA were southerners (there were just over 600 IRA volunteers in the Six Counties in 1924 out of a total of 14,500). In Northern Ireland by the late 1920s, republican commemorations were routinely banned, the sale of republician newspapers prohibited and those wearing Easter lilies at risk of being arrested. Republicans released from jail were sometimes deported to the Free State. The pre-war UVF remained armed, thanks to the recruitment of thousands of veterans into the Special Constabulary (the best known of which were the B-Specials). This inspection report expresses the reality that republicans were a minority in the Six Counties and that nationalists regarded them as likely to bring down trouble on their heads. Instead they hoped that the Boundary Commission (set up to reexamine the border between North and South) would rule in their favour. But there was also some optimism: a claim that one-third of northern nationalists were quietly republican supporters.

The fear of repression is evident here in the warnings about the growing influence of Detective Inspector John W. Nixon. Nixon was widely regarded as having been the leader of a death squad during the Belfast violence and of being responsible for the notorious murder of Catholic publican Owen McMahon and his sons in March 1922. Nixon was dismissed from the RUC in early 1924 and by the time this report was written had become an alderman on Belfast Corporation. He remained active in Loyalist politics until his death in 1949.

Over the next decade, the focus of the IRA remained very much on overthrowing the Free State and membership of the IRA in the North remained small: by 1930 there were just 12 members in Derry, 17 in Antrim and 177 in Belfast.

'GHOSTS'

During the late 1920s, Cumann na mBan was small in membership (with perhaps 50 activists in Dublin) but it had an impact beyond its numbers. Among the organisation's initiatives was a series of posters and leaflets issued by 'Ghosts': during 1928, IRA volunteer Con Healy had been sentenced to five years in jail. A poster bearing the names of the jurors in his case was distributed across Dublin stating that 'death' would be their fate in many countries. During January 1929 one of the jurors in the Healy case, John White, was shot and wounded at his home. White was relatively lucky: in February 1929, Albert Armstrong, who had given evidence against IRA members who removed a Union Jack from his workplace, was shot dead.

93

TO IRISH CITIZENS

"Break The Connection With The British Empire"

The Irish Republican Army are Striving to-day as Tone strove in another generation to free Ireland from British rule.

This can only be achieved by overthrowing the two British imposed governments in Ireland to-day.

The enemies of Ireland are imprisoning the men and women who are carrying out the only practical programme to attain freedom.

Unfortunately some of Dublin's degenerate and slavish citizens assist them in this work. Last month the following:-

John White, Nevada, 23 Ashdale Road, Terenure.	Jeweller.
John Breen, 72 Moyne Road, Ranelagh, ...	Book Shop Proprietor
Wm. J. Green, 14 Ashfield Avenue, Ranelagh, ...	Clerk.
John B. Loughridge, Frankford House, Clonskea, ...	Accountant.
Albert McCready, 1a McCowan's Terrace, Ranelagh.	Clerk
Robert Hugh Pollock, 48 Shelbourne Road, Ballsbridge,	Gent.
Ml. Nugent, 145/146 James' Street, ...	Grocer
Randolph Moore, 2 Havelock Square, ...	Clerk
Wm. O'Mahony, 44 Carysfort Avenue, Blackrock. ...	Traveller
Francis Bray, 12 Charleston Avenue, Rathmines. ...	Clerk.
Vincent Corcoran, Blanchardstown, ...	Farmer
Philip Rodgers, 58 Belgrave Square, Rathmines. ...	Gent.

helped Carrigan and the infamous "Judge" Sullivan to send the Irish Patriot

CON HEALY

To Penal Servitude for five years. These men are Traitors to their Country.

DEATH WOULD BE THEIR FATE IN ANY FREE COUNTRY OF THE WORLD

Issued by "Ghosts"

Leaflet naming jurors in the case of IRA man Con Healy
THE NATIONAL LIBRARY OF IRELAND

'Ghosts' continued to appear in the 1930s. The key figure in their distribution was Sighle Humphreys, Director of Publicity for Cumann na mBan since 1926. Humphreys was the niece of Michael Joseph O'Rahilly ('The O'Rahilly') who had been killed during the 1916 Rising. She joined Cumann na mBan in 1919 and worked as a courier in Kerry during the war. She was active on the anti-Treaty side and had fired on troops when Ernie O'Malley was captured at her home in Dublin in November 1922. Humphreys was jailed until November 1923, undergoing a hunger strike and three months' solitary confinement. She was jailed again in 1927, 1928 and 1931.

WOMEN PRISONERS IN MOUNTJOY

FILL UP THIS FORM AND POST TO-DAY.

THE REPUBLICAN FILE

The Republican Press, Ltd.,
12 St. Andrew Street, Dublin.

Please forward me THE REPUBLICAN FILE every week for .... weeks, beginning with issue of ...., for which I enclose.........................

SUBSCRIPTION RATES (POST FREE)

Ireland and Gt. Britain.		U.S.A.
2s. 2d.	per Quarter	50 cents.
4s. 4d.	per 6 months	1 dollar.
8s. 8d.	per 12 months	2 dollars.

SATURDAY, 9th JANUARY, 1932.

AGAIN SUPPRESSED

On Thursday, December 31, detectives visited the Fodhla Printing Works and took away copies for scrutiny of the issue about to be printed. They returned in the evening and declared that the issue (for Jan. 2) was "seditious," instruct-ing the printers to remove formes from the machines. The issue consisted entirely of cuttings and quotations, as heretofore. No information was given as to what particular quotation was seditious. The present issue of THE REPUBLICAN FILE consists entirely of quota-tions or items drawn from the Press of the Irish Free State, bearing name of organ quoted from in each case. None of these papers has hitherto been declared seditious by the Tribunal.

A SLOGAN FOR ALL SEASONS.

The world-wide depression in trade is being felt in Ireland, and people who, hitherto, have been in-different to economic questions are beginning to see the folly of sending out of the country money which could easily be kept at home to the advantage of everybody. In England the knell of Free Trade has sounded, and the task of conserving the home market for the British manufacturers has already begun. The slogan, "Buy British," has been adopted by leaders of every section of the com-munity with beneficial results. We would commend the feasibility of a similar crusade in Ireland. "Buy Irish" (without any qualification) is a motto which should appeal to everybody. So far, it has only been half-heartedly adopted. The "National" Press is too busy defending the interests of "our best customer" to devote any attention to such a petty proposal.

—*An Camán.*

CORRESPONDENCE.
IN ARBOUR HILL.

To the Editor, *The Irish Press.*

A Chara,—I am informed by one of the released prisoners that my brother, George Mooney, who is undergoing a sentence of six months in Arbour Hill prison, is looking very ill. His health causes me great anxiety as he has not had time to recover from the effects of his recent confinement in Mountjoy. He has been in solitary confinement for some weeks past and is not getting any exercise. The cold is intense; there is no heating in the prison; food is bad and insufficient and medical treatment for sick persons neglected. The rules are rigid and the slightest departure from these is punished by bread and water. And all this is done in the name of Christianity.

BRENDA MOONEY.

SHEILA HUMPHREYS.

KATHLEEN MERRIGAN.

MAEVE PHELAN.

AWAITING TRIBUNAL TRIAL

Miss Sheila Humphreys, Mrs. Kathleen Merrigan and Miss Maeve Phelan, arrested on December 17, held in Bridewell for some days, transferred to Mountjoy Prison on Saturday, December 19. Await-ing trial before Military Tribunal.

WHO ARE THE LAW-BREAKERS?

To the Editor, *The Irish Press.*

A Chara,—Mr. J. Fitzgerald-Kenney, K.C., is very fond of preaching the sanctity of constitutional action. It would be interesting, therefore, to know what particular Saorstat statute permits him to violate all normal canons and conventions of civilised law in the following fashion.

At an early hour this morning (Dec. 17) a little squad of his plain-clothes men rushed into my mother's garden. With a total disregard of anti-burglarious law, two of them broke into the house through the back, and tore through the dwelling in order to open the front door for their companions. Re-united in force they then proceeded to make an unannounced assault on the household sleeping quarters.

R. HUMPHREYS, B.L.

ARRESTED IRISHWOMEN
New York Protest.

The following telegram from New York was received yesterday by "The Irish Press":—

"Associated Irish Societies (ninety-six bodies) emphatically protest against Sheila Humphreys, Kathleen Merrigan, Maeve Phelan, under Constitution Act. Huge demonstration planned New York about middle of January.—Michael O'Kiersey."

A strongly-worded telegram of protest against the recent Constitution Amendment (No. 17) Act has been sent to the Free State Government on behalf of seventeen hundred men and women of Irish birth, by the Boston Gaelic School Society.

DENIED ADMISSION

CARMELITE PROVINCIAL INTERVIEWED

The Very Rev. Father Devlin, Provincial of the Carmelites, Whitefriar Street, Dublin, interviewed by an "Irish Press" representative in connection with the refusal of Mountjoy Prison Authorities to allow him to administer to the spiritual needs of the three women prisoners who are detained there under the Constitution (Amendment) Act, said: "The report given of my visit to Mountjoy is somewhat misleading. One would think, on reading it, I presented myself at the prison gates as an intruder, without any formal authority. Whereas, the very contrary is the fact, as I had the fullest authority of the Prison Chaplain to make my visit."

"In all institutions, prisons, hospitals, etc., all over the world, the chaplain is recognised without question by the civil authorities, as supreme in the spiritual control. With his permission and assent any other priest visiting the prison is allowed free entrance. And yet, strangely enough, the official at Mountjoy intimated to me that the chaplain had no authority to allow me to enter the gaol, even in my purely spiritual capacity, and that I would have to get permission from the Minister for Justice.

"Just imagine it; that one would have to seek permission from the Minister for Justice to exercise his faculties as a priest. Why, I doubt if they have tried that on even in Russia."

"Well, I am quite content," Father Devlin added, "to forget the sorry and humiliating incident, and feel even consoled over it, if this publicity gains for the unfortunate interned a recognition, on the part of the State, of that freedom of conscience which Holy Church gives to all her subjects in the sacred matter of the Confessional."

—"Irish Press."

Report on the imprisonment of Sighle Humphreys, *Republican File*, 1932. The *Republican File* was a short-lived replacement for *An Phoblacht*, which was banned in 1931.

FOREIGN RESERVE

In theory, the IRA forbade its members from leaving Ireland without permission, but in reality hundreds were doing so in the post-Civil War period. As the IRA explained: 'Large numbers of volunteers from all along the west coast emigrated, and a considerable number also from other parts of the country. The reason for which most of these men emigrated was because there was no hope of their obtaining a livelihood in Ireland in the near future'. In 1925, the organisation set up a Foreign Reserve in the hope that the process could be controlled somewhat. IRA volunteers who intended emigrating were ordered to join the Reserve: evidence suggests only a minority did so.

Óglaigh na h-Éireann

(IRISH REPUBLICAN ARMY)

FORM No. F.R.1.

Application for Transfer to Foreign Reserve List

To:
THE ADJUTANT GENERAL

I am forced to leave Ireland through extreme economic distress in order to obtain a livelihood (or for reasons stated in attached sheet). I wish to be transferred to the Foreign Reserve List for a period of five years. I promise to return at the end of that time if I do not get an extension, and to abide by the conditions set out hereunder:

1. To be bound by the same disciplinary code as active Volunteers, i.e., all my actions to be sober and upright and a true soldier of the Republic.
2. To save up as soon as possible and keep intact the price of return journey to Ireland.
3. To return to Ireland immediately General Headquarters informs me that my presence in Ireland is necessary and orders me to return.
4. To keep the Adjutant General informed of my address through the prescribed channels
5. To endeavour to increase my efficiency as a soldier and as a citizen in order to be of greater use in defending and building up the country when I return.
6. To do my utmost to promote the interests of the Republic and to help all organisations working for that object in the country to which I go.
7. Not to organise or join any organisation into which it is proposed to admit only Foreign Reservists of the Irish Republican Army.

(Signed) John O'Dea

Unit and Appointment C. Coy 4th Batt. Clare Bago (Sec-Leader)

Date 5-4-26

Proposed Destination New York

I, the undersigned, hereby declare that the statements in above application are true, and I believe the applicant will, as he has promised, abide faithfully by above conditions.

(Signed) O.C. 4th Batt.

Unit and Appointment

Date 5-4-26

TWOMEY PAPERS, UCD ARCHIVES

CLAN NA GAEL

The IRA wanted its members to remain politically active while they were abroad and in America to join the Clan na Gael. Many failed to do so: some dropped out of politics entirely, while others disliked or distrusted their American comrades. Nevertheless, the Clan did play a social role for some republican emigrants in the post-Civil-War period. It was less successful in raising money: most of its members in the late 1920s had very little to send to Ireland and after the Wall Street crash of 1929, even less was available for the IRA. This leaflet from 1931 shows some of the social attractions of republican activism.

TWOMEY PAPERS, UCD ARCHIVES

A Message to all Lovers of Irish Freedom
from the
Brooklyn and Queens

I. R. A. RESERVES & LADIES AUXILIARIES I. R. A.
(Clan-na-Gael)

Latest reports from Ireland indicate that the Irish Republican Army, Fianna-na-Eireann and Cumann-na-mBann units, have reached a state of efficiency and enjoy the co-operation and support of the Irish public to an extent that has not been equalled at any stage during the long years of Ireland's fight for complete independence.

Recent public admissions made by Cabinet Ministers of His Majesty's Irish Free State Government made known the fact that the forces of the Irish Republic are something to be reckoned with in the near future. Con-sequently it is up to each and every one of us to do all in our power to aid the forces of the Irish Republic in bringing about a condition in Ireland that will bring Mother Eire nearer to its goal of Freedom. We may do this successfully by supporting I. R. A. functions which in this area are regularly conducted in Greater New York's most beautiful ballrooms, known as the PRIDE of ERIN Ballrooms, located at the corner of Atlantic and Bedford Avenues, Brooklyn, N. Y. To the unaffiliated I. R. A. men and Cumann-na-mBann ladies here, a special appeal is made at this time to get in touch with the organization and work from within.

In these halls, the American music is supplied by Jack Healy's Radio Orchestra, and of course Paddy Killoran needs hardly to be announced as being the conductor of the famous radio orchestra of Irish dance music.

Particulars of the BEAUTY CONTEST to be conducted in these ball-rooms may be had on application to the proprietors of the Hall, Messrs. Tom and John Gallagher, at the above address, or direct with Brooklyn I. R. A. Club Headquarters, 183 Vanderbilt Avenue, Brooklyn.

Support I. R. A. Functions and read An Poblacht the only official organ of Irish Republicanism, which may be had by communicating with C. McGinn-ity, at I. R. A. Halls, 147 Columbus Avenue, New York City.

Do not travel on British lines—United States and German Lines offer up-to-date and reasonable transport facilities.

FIANNA FÁIL

During November 1925, Frank Aiken had signalled his disatisfaction with the IRA's lack of political direction. As far as he was concerned, the prospect of overthrowing the state by force seemed unlikely. Within the organisation rumours were current that he was prepared to support Sinn Féin taking seats in Leinster House. At the IRA convention Aiken made clear that in certain circumstances he was prepared to endorse this. He was replaced as chief of staff by Andy Cooney, but remained on the IRA's executive. In a letter to his colleagues he explained why he felt that volunteers holding views such as his should not be debarred from the IRA. At the General Army

Aiken's letter to the IRA Army Council TWOMEY PAPERS, UCD ARCHIVES

November 18th. 1925.

my Council

of Army Council at their first meeting will have to
r things, what they are going to do with me, and
matters I should like to give them information and
, I request you, if you please, to read this letter

nt to say that I will insist on my right to advocate
outside Volunteer work, any honourable political
thening the nation to achieve independence. I insist
ause I think it is the duty of Volunteers to insist on
ime I am ready, as long as the Army Authorities abide
on, to serve as a Volunteer in any capacity in which
e useful, and to uphold in public and in private the
Irishmen to be trained and armed without the control
hostile or inimical to the Republic of Ireland.

ou my services thus explicitly for the sake more of my
d than anything else. I am greatly afraid that most
what I consider, far-seeing enought at the present time
anyone holding my views to positions which I believe
lled in the interests of the Nation by people holding
our attitude relieves me of a position which nothing in
sense of duty would tempt me to fill, and it is only
the difficulties from both friendly and enemy sources,
myself and you all that I am ready, if I am given the
the game through, that I now offer you my services in

probably take time and bitter experiences to teach some
it is the height of foolishness to debar in advance the
ng any honourable means to help them to secure our
Lord knows I think the fight before our country should
t enough to any sensible man without seeking to limit
thin narrower bounds than those open to honourable men who
nise the legitimacy of any Government hostile or inimical
of Ireland.

ven worse than foolishness, to put it mildly, to believe
n should have that much tactical elbow-room in theory and
now when she is in a life and death struggle in order to
ople who will not think the matter out until our enemies
ight. It is, I maintain, an honourable policy to use the
he Free State or Six County governments possess in order
independence of our country, provided we don't have to
egitimacy by any oath or declaration or by any other way
nd that we maintain openly that our object is to establish
rnment for the Republic; I haven't the slightest sympathy
with people who would decalre now that they will not agree
y and who would, when our present policy fails, either
declarations of allegiance themselves to these bodies or
rs who would; neither have I much sympathy with people who
ll the chances of national success in our generation on the
ote possibility of a successful coup d'etat - the former
the type of swash-buckler who threatened a lot about what
with the people who voted for the treaty and then discarded
en the civil war broke out; the latter of the honest but
nists who thought they could defeat the Free State in

nearly time for people who can influence the national
nd who have the proper national faith, to realise that faith
good for national salvation; that they must use forsight and
common-sense/

2

common-sense if they are to do the country good instead of harm. I hope to goodness the present Army Council will agree to the suggestion I am going to put forward and stand by it even though it may be misrepresented or disagreed with temporarily by some of our friends.

My suggestion is this: That the Army Council should pass the following resolution and issue it to all ranks and stand firmly to any temporary dissatisfaction no matter from whom it may arise:-

"Having carefully considered the question raised by the motion proposed at the Convention to the effect that any Volunteer who favoured Republican T.Ds. entering Free State Parliament, if the oath of allegiance were withdrawn, should not be eligible for the membership of the Army Executive , and the subsequent withdrawal of those motions and election on the Executive of the then Chief of Staff who advocated this policy, we have decided that the Constitution does not debar any man who holds such opinions from being a Volunteer or holding any appointment, provided of course that he does not in any way yield a voluntary support or allegiance to any Government or power within Ireland hostile or inimical to the Republic of Ireland".

The sooner you all realise that you must taken openly the stand that men who hold these views are by the very fact debarred, or are not debarred, from holding appointments in the Army, the better it will be for the Army and the Nation as a whole. The question is one that will call for an expression of opinion from the Army Council before long in order to give a guide to all ranks as to how they are to behave in the matter. The Convention, of course, left the question an open one for each Volunteer because the two resolutions which proposed to make the holding of such views a punishable offence were withdrawn, and I, who defended the policy, was elected, by 20 voted out of 39, on the Executive. This leave given tacitly by the Convention, must be given explicitly by the Army Council in order to prevent Volunteers or anyone else misunderstanding what took place at the Convention.

We Volunteers believe that without the Army Ireland cannot gain her freedom. With a lot of our men this belief is only an human military instinct; they have never thought the matter out, I have thought it out; for, being as I was Chief of Staff, on me devolved principally its defence when its abolition was sought be people who believed themselves to be its friends. It is because I have convinced myself with good, sound, clear reasons that without a good Volunteer Army, we cannot achieve freedom in our generation that I want to stabilise and strengthen ours and prevent, if I can, from splitting over every disagreement regarding policy that is bound to arise between this and our goal . The manner in which it meets the present situation is going to decide whether in our day it will be of any immediate benefit. To fulfil its purpose and be of the greatest possible use to the Nation the Army should not act as if it relied solely on force of arms to achieve victory and thereby give the support of the people as a gift to the anti-Republicans North and South; it should not try to withdraw into itself and become a society of select brethern who will admire one another instead of openly giving a helping hand in its spare time to civilian organisations that are fighting honourably for the same ends: it should not attempt to curtail the legitimate rights of citizens when they become Volunteers by refusing to allow them to get close to the people in order to give them a helping hand along the right road; it should not, in short, forget that it is an organisation for the enrolling and training of all Irishmen who are willing to fight for Ireland and give allegiance to her only, and that, as such an organisation it will have to provide , if it means to be successful, to make use of men who will differ on every question under the sun - religious, social, political - except on the one question; that Irishmen owe allegiance to Ireland and therefore must be prepared to uphold her sovereignty at all times and by all honourable means.

Frank Aiken.

Convention the majority of IRA officers voted that the organisation break all political ties and become completely independent. From November 1925, the IRA was not formally linked to any political party, but a wide variety of views were represented in its ranks.

Fianna Fáil was founded in May 1926, by Eamon de Valera, who led a split from Sinn Féin after that party rejected his proposal that it take seats in Leinster House, if the Oath of Allegiance were abolished. But many who supported de Valera still sat on the IRA executive or were in command of its local units. It was not until the general election of June 1927 that many IRA officers were forced to make the break with the organisation, having agreed to become election candidates for Fianna Fáil, thus disobeying the IRA's General Order No. 28 ('Volunteers as Parliamentary Candidates'). The most prominent of these was Frank Aiken, but Tom Derrig, Michael Corry and Tom MacEllistrim were also well known. Many of the men who were court-martialled as a result of their decision went on to have significant careers in Fianna Fáil: Aiken became Minister for Defence in 1932, while Tom Derrig became Minister for Education in the first Fianna Fáil government.

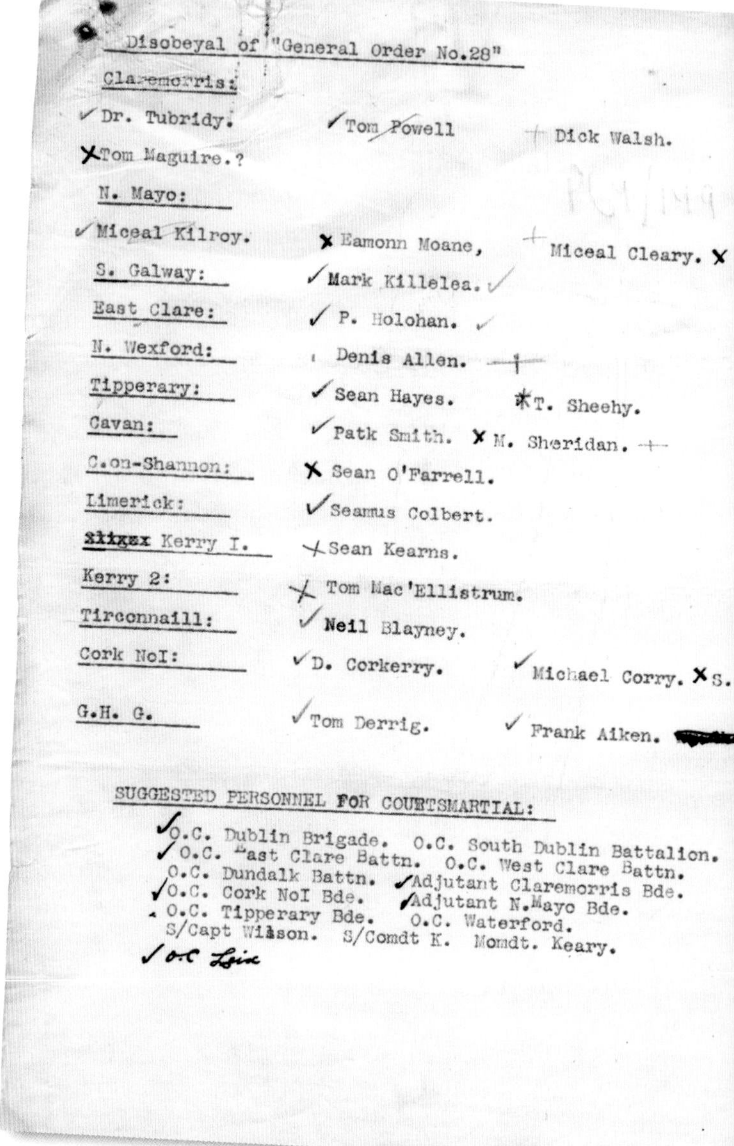

Disobeyal of "General Order No.28"

Claremorris:
Dr. Tubridy. Tom Powell Dick Walsh.
Tom Maguire.?

N. Mayo:
Miceal Kilroy. Eamonn Moane, Miceal Cleary.

S. Galway: Mark Killelea.
East Clare: P. Holohan.
N. Wexford: Denis Allen.
Tipperary: Sean Hayes. T. Sheehy.
Cavan: Patk Smith. M. Sheridan.
C.on-Shannon: Sean O'Farrell.
Limerick: Seamus Colbert.
Kerry I. Sean Kearns.
Kerry 2: Tom Mac'Ellistrum.
Tirconnaill: Neil Blayney.
Cork NoI: D. Corkerry. Michael Corry.
G.H. G. Tom Derrig. Frank Aiken.

SUGGESTED PERSONNEL FOR COURTSMARTIAL:
O.C. Dublin Brigade. O.C. South Dublin Battalion.
O.C. East Clare Battn. O.C. West Clare Battn.
O.C. Dundalk Battn. Adjutant Claremorris Bde.
O.C. Cork NoI Bde. Adjutant N.Mayo Bde.
O.C. Tipperary Bde. O.C. Waterford.
S/Capt Wilson. S/Comdt K. Komdt. Keary.

IRA officers who stood as Fianna Fáil candidates in 1927
TWOMEY PAPERS, UCD ARCHIVES

The list here also includes those who stood as independents or for Sinn Féin. These included Daniel Corkery, a Cork IRA officer who later joined Fianna Fáil and Tom Maguire of Sinn Féin, who withdrew from the election. A notable absentee from the list was Oscar Traynor, who stood as a Sinn Féin candidate and joined Fianna Fáil in 1928.

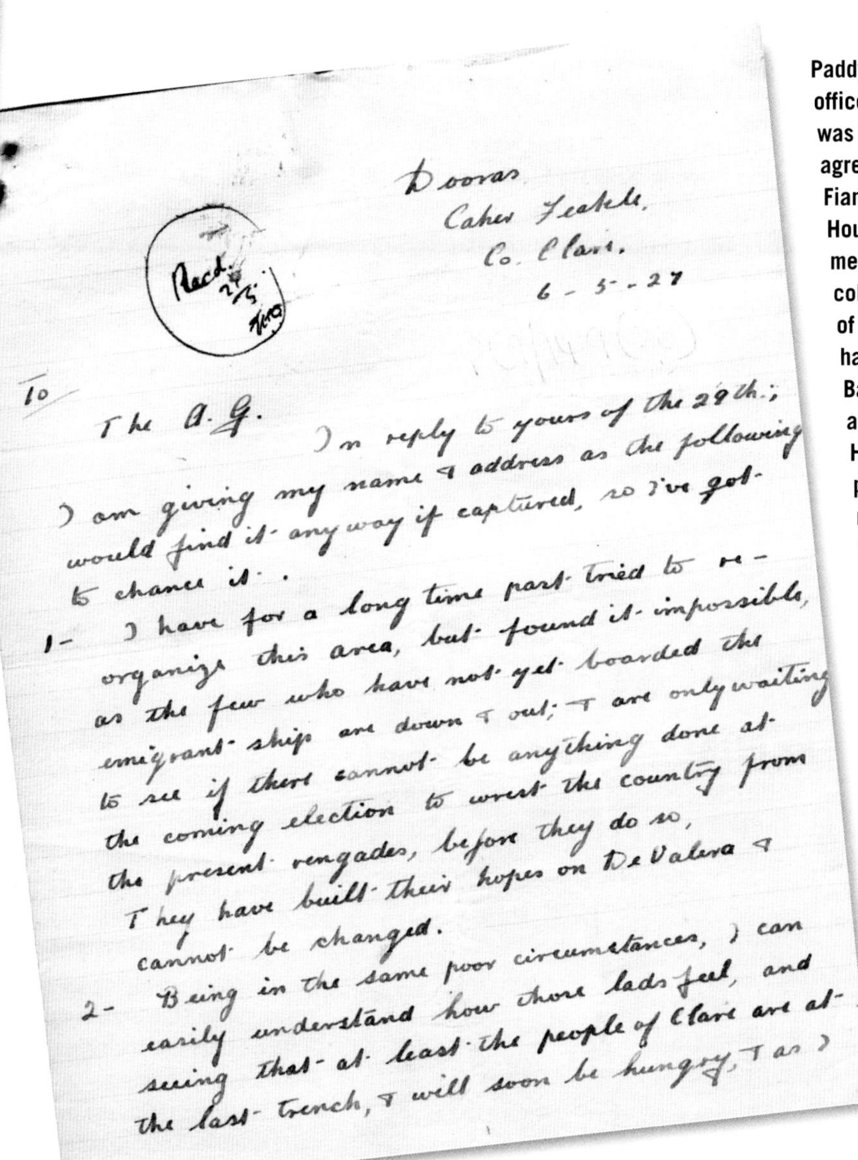

Dooras
Caher Feakle,
Co. Clare.
6-5-27

To
The A.G.

In reply to yours of the 29th.; I am giving my name & address as the following would find it anyway if captured, so I've got to chance it.

1- I have for a long time past tried to re-organize this area, but found it impossible, as the few who have not yet boarded the emigrant ship are down & out; & are only waiting to see if there cannot be anything done at the coming election to wrest the country from the present renegades, before they do so, They have built their hopes on De Valera & cannot be changed.

2- Being in the same poor circumstances, I can easily understand how those lads feel, and seeing that at least the people of Clare are at the last trench, & will soon be hungry, & as I

Paddy Houlihan, an IRA officer in east Clare, was one of those who agreed to stand as a Fianna Fáil candidate. Houlihan had been a member of a flying column during the War of Independence and had taken part in the Ballyturin House ambush in Galway. His letter shows the pressures which led many IRA members to place their hopes in Fianna Fáil. Houlihan was elected and remained a TD until 1932.

TWOMEY PAPERS, UCD ARCHIVES

Initially Fianna Fáil did not enter the Dáil. But on July 10 1927, Kevin O'Higgins, the Minister for Justice, and a hate figure for republicans since the Civil War, was shot dead by IRA members (who seem to have acted independently). The Free State feared a new insurrection and passed a series of stringent security measures that included forcing election candidates to pledge to take the Oath of Allegiance on nomination. Faced with the prospect of being permanently excluded from Leinster House de Valera and his supporters took their seats on 12 August 1927.

This was not the end of Fianna Fáil's links to the IRA, however, as locally many IRA officers remained close to de Valera's party.

THE EASTER LILY AND ANTI-IMPERIALISM

During March 1926, Sighle Humphreys and Fiona Plunkett of Cumann na mBan proposed a campaign to make the lily the symbol of the republican dead. They were conscious of the success of the British Legion in using the poppy and hoped the lily would rival it. (In the late 1920s the RUC described lilies as 'republican poppies'). It was a very successful innovation and it was claimed that half a million lilies were being sold by 1935. During the mid-1930s, Fianna Fáil launched its own 'Easter Torch' to rival the Lily: it was not a success. The lily is still used to commemorate the republican dead and is worn at Easter.

COURTESY OF THE NATIONAL LIBRARY OF IRELAND

42

1916 1932

Break the Connection with the British Dominions.

"We declare the right of the people of Ireland to the ownership of Ireland and to the unfettered control of Irish destinies to be sovereign and indefeasible . . . Standing on that fundamental right and again asserting it in arms in the face of the world, we hereby proclaim the **Irish Republic as a Sovereign Independent State** and we pledge our lives and the lives of our comrades-in-arms to the cause of its freedom, of its welfare and of its exaltation among the nations."

Asserting Ireland's right to freedom in this Proclamation the Men of Easter Week challenged the might of the then powerful British Empire. They suffered a military defeat, and paid the penalty of their glorious defiance.

But their sacrifice kindled a flame of fire which acts as a beacon light whenever compromise and weakness tend to turn men from the straight road to Freedom

Their clearness of their aims and the courage of their acts inspired the noblest minds in Ireland.

For their Standard of Liberty, for the Irish Republic hundreds of Ireland's noble young soldiers have given their lives during the last six-teen years.

At Easter time we commemorate the memory of all the Dead wh died for Ireland and pledge ourselves never to falter or to halt until th last link between Ireland and the British Empire is broken.

People of Ireland, *Unite then in one supreme effort break that connection and establish a free sovereign Ir Republic bounded only by the sky and the ocean.*

Wear an Easter Lily at Eastert

THE EMBLEM OF REPUBLICAN IRELAND

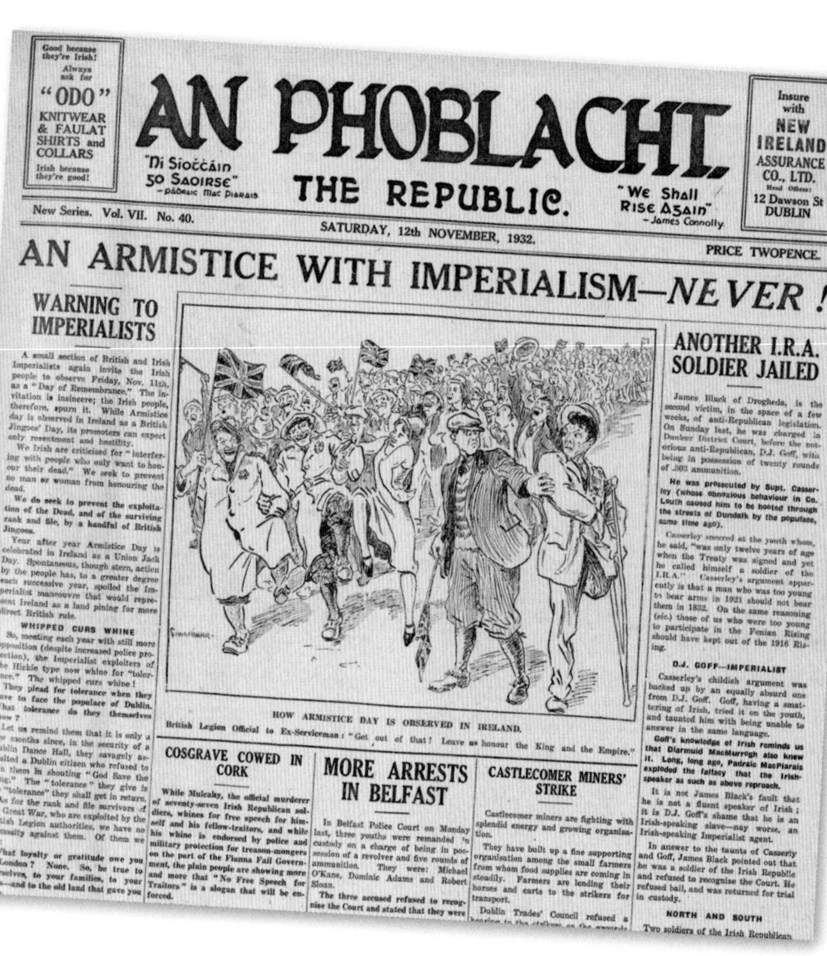

Good because they're Irish! Always ask for "ODO" KNITWEAR & FAULAT SHIRTS and COLLARS Irish because they're good!

AN PHOBLACHT

"Ní Siocáin go Saoirse" – Pádraic Mac Piarais

THE REPUBLIC.

"We Shall Rise Again" – James Connolly

Insure with NEW IRELAND ASSURANCE CO., LTD. Head Offices: 12 Dawson St DUBLIN

New Series. Vol. VII. No. 40. SATURDAY, 12th NOVEMBER, 1932. PRICE TWOPENCE.

AN ARMISTICE WITH IMPERIALISM—*NEVER !*

WARNING TO IMPERIALISTS

A small section of British and Irish Imperialists again invite the Irish people to observe Friday, Nov. 11th, as a "Day of Remembrance." The invitation is insincere; the Irish people, therefore, spurn it. While Armistice day is observed in Ireland as a British Jingoes' Day, its promoters can expect only resentment and hostility.

We Irish are criticised for "interfering with people who only want to honour their dead." We seek to prevent no man or woman from honouring the dead.

We do seek to prevent the exploitation of the Dead, and of the surviving rank and file, by a handful of British Jingoes.

Year after year Armistice Day is celebrated in Ireland as a Union Jack Day. Spontaneous, though stern, action by the people has, to a greater degree each successive year, spoiled the Imperialist manoeuvre that would represent Ireland as a land pining for more direct British rule.

WHIPPED CURS WHINE

So, meeting each year with still more opposition (despite increased police protection), the Imperialist exploiters of the Hickie type now whine for "tolerance." The whipped curs whine!

They plead for tolerance when they have to face the populace of Dublin. What tolerance do they themselves show ?

Let us remind them that it is only a few months since, in the security of a Dublin Dance Hall, they savagely assaulted a Dublin citizen who refused to join them in shouting "God Save the King." The "tolerance" they give is the "tolerance" they shall get in return.

As for the rank and file survivors of the Great War, who are exploited by the British Legion authorities, we have no animosity against them. Of them we ask:

What loyalty or gratitude owe you to London ? None. So, be true to yourselves, to your families, to your class—and to the old land that gave you birth.

HOW ARMISTICE DAY IS OBSERVED IN IRELAND.

British Legion Official to Ex-Serviceman: "Get out of that! Leave us honour the King and the Empire."

ANOTHER I.R.A. SOLDIER JAILED

James Black of Drogheda, is the second victim, in the space of a few weeks, of anti-Republican legislation. On Sunday last, he was charged in Dunleer District Court, before the notorious anti-Republican, D.J. Goff, with being in possession of twenty rounds of .303 ammunition.

He was prosecuted by Supt. Casserley (whose obnoxious behaviour in Co. Louth caused him to be hooted through the streets of Dundalk by the populace, some time ago).

Casserley sneered at the youth whom, he said, "was only twelve years of age when the Treaty was signed and yet he called himself a soldier of the I.R.A." Casserley's argument apparently is that a man who was too young to bear arms in 1921 should not bear them in 1932. On the same reasoning (sic.) those of us who were too young to participate in the Fenian Rising should have kept out of the 1916 Rising.

D.J. GOFF—IMPERIALIST

Casserley's childish argument was backed up by an equally absurd one from D.J. Goff. Goff, having a smattering of Irish, tried it on the youth, and taunted him with being unable to answer in the same language.

Goff's knowledge of Irish reminds us that Diarmuid MacMurrogh also knew it. Long, long ago, Padraic MacPiarais exploded the fallacy that the Irish-speaker as such as above reproach.

It is not James Black's fault that he is not a fluent speaker of Irish; it is D.J. Goff's shame that he is an Irish-speaking slave—nay worse, an Irish-speaking Imperialist agent.

In answer to the taunts of Casserly and Goff, James Black pointed out that he was a soldier of the Irish Republic and refused to recognise the Court. He refused bail, and was returned for trial in custody.

NORTH AND SOUTH

Two soldiers of the Irish Republican

COSGRAVE COWED IN CORK

While Mulcahy, the official murderer of seventy-seven Irish Republican soldiers, whines for free speech for himself and his fellow-traitors, and while his whine is endorsed by police and military protection for treason-mongers on the part of the Fianna Fail Government, the plain people are showing more and more that "No Free Speech for Traitors" is a slogan that will be enforced.

MORE ARRESTS IN BELFAST

In Belfast Police Court on Monday last, three youths were remanded in custody on a charge of being in possession of a revolver and five rounds of ammunition. They were: Michael O'Kane, Dominic Adams and Robert Sloan.

The three accused refused to recognise the Court and stated that they were

CASTLECOMER MINERS' STRIKE

Castlecomer miners are fighting with splendid energy and growing organisation.

They have built up a fine supporting organisation among the small farmers from whom food supplies are coming in steadily. Farmers are lending their horses and carts to the strikers for transport.

Dublin Trades' Council refused a

An Phoblacht 12 November 1932.

An Phoblacht was the IRA's weekly newspaper from 1925–36. DUBLIN CITY LIBRARY & ARCHIVE

Armistice Day was a major occasion in Dublin during the 1920s and 1930s, with thousands of British Army ex-servicemen parading on 11 November and the area around Grafton Street bedecked in red, white and blue bunting. However, from 1925, the event saw republican mobilisations, aimed at disruption. These often ended in rioting. The IRA's activities during this time extended to the bombing of statues of British royalty and British Legion halls. Usually, the organisation claimed that it bore no animus to ex-sevicemen themselves, who it argued were being used by imperial interests, hence this cartoon on *An Phoblacht's* front page.

COURTESY OF THE NATIONAL LIBRARY OF IRELAND

INDIA CALLING!

Thousands of miles across the oceans India calls for help.

For generations India has been kept in subjection by Britains usual barbarous methods.

But India has arisen, has proclaimed her right to freedom and to rule her country in her own interests.

FROM IRELAND India has learnt many things.

She has learnt how to organise her Republican Army.

She has learnt how to ambush the common enemy.

She is learning how to deal with her Sir Henry Wilsons.

She is learning, from our mistake how to treat "peace" and surrender proposals.

BUT WHAT OF IRELAND TO-DAY?

Ireland which fought the British Empire in the hey-day of its power, lies peaceful and inactive NOW when that Empire is crumbling—

Ireland has allowed its proudest province to be torn from her.

IRELAND'S MILLS lie idle while England floods the country with the shoddy goods refused by India.

IS IRELAND DEAD OR SLEEPING?

ENGLAND'S DIFFICULTY HAS ALWAYS BEEN IRELAND'S OPPORTUNITY. Never before has England been in such difficulties, with AUSTRALIA and Canada waging an economic war on the "mother" country, with India and Egypt claiming complete freedom, will IRELAND ALONE remain a willing slave of the British Empire?

GOD FORBID!

IRISHMEN AND WOMEN. Learn from India. In her fight for freedom India has united all her peoples, and they are many and varied.

Ireland has only ONE people, but England keeps us divided. Only a renewal of the demand for COMPLETE FREEDOM will unite our people. NOW is the time to renew that demand.

Two puppet governments the "Free State" and Northern governments stand between us and freedom. Were the men of Ireland united, those governments could not last a day. Once overthrown they will never again regain power.

What Say the men of Ireland?

India Calls! India Provides the opportunity!

Join the Irish Republican Army and help Ireland to avail of that opportunity.

Issued by Cumann na mBan, 27 Dawson Street,
September, 1930

'INDIA CALLING'

The main recipient of republican support internationally during the 1920s was the Indian nationalist movement. Speakers from India regularly visited Ireland and addressed republican rallies and *An Phoblacht* promoted the Indian cause. IRA leaders also met members of African and Asian revolutionary organisations often through the auspices of the Soviet Comintern, an international organisation of communist parties. Republicans attended Comintern-sponsored events in Belgium, Germany and Moscow and set up branches of the Friends of the Soviet Union in Ireland. Less publicly, the Soviets provided funding to the IRA and discussed the possibility of cooperation in espionage in the west. Some IRA leaders, such as Peadar O'Donnell, were committed to socialist politics, while others were happy to align themselves with the Soviets in the hope of gaining military aid.

AN T-ÓGLACH

OFFICIAL ORGAN OF THE IRISH REPUBLICAN ARMY.

New Series No. 16. JULY, 1931. PRICE 2d.

EDITORIAL

There has been an amazingly rapid resurgence in feeling throughout the country during the present year. The question we must ask is: Are we availing of it to collect young men into Oglaigh na h-Eireann? If we are not, then it means that Officers and N.C.Os. are negligent, or have not the right idea of what is required of them. Most encouraging progress is being made in many units. Several Companies and Battalions have doubled and trebled their strengths in the present year. The opportunities for recruitment are not confined to any particular county or district; they exist everywhere.

Lethargy or weariness is passing; National feeling is returning; lazy and tired Volunteer Officers have been wed out. The greatest progress has been made where the Officers are young. It is only natural, as it is young Officers who can more easily make contact with young minds. We must push these young enthusiasts ahead. They must be encouraged and helped in developing the qualities of leadership, and it is responsibility that will do so quickest. We must not be unduly influenced by those who say: "It is good to have the young men, but the older men must guide and advise them." Well and good, provided this does not mean retarding progress. We must not allow "wisdom" or "caution"—other names very often for tiredness and timidity—to hold back development. The future of the Revolutionary Movement depends on the young men now flocking in.

We must select as Officers and N.C.Os. young men of the highest and strongest character, courage, and personality, and not because they are popular, though popularity joined with essential qualities would be a further advantage. Leadership—character, confidence, initiative—can only be developed on the training-ground, therefore there must be intensive training. There must also be the highest development in organisation and administration. The Volunteer Movement must be laced and interwoven throughout the entire country. The devastating isolation of recent years must be smashed through and left behind.

Units must be brought into contact; we must have rallies, field-days and demonstrations. Each unit should know what neighbouring units are doing; Staffs of these units should meet; there must be no districts of "No man's lands." In every town and village,in every parish and townland we must organise Volunteers. After the General Convention this year G.H.Q. Staff aimed at, and believed it possible to achieve, a hundred per cent. increase in strengths in a year. This will be exceeded if present rate of increase is continued.

Hand-in-hand with technical military training must go National and Political education. Not only must we train men to fight, but we must also teach them why and for what they are to fight. Political consciousness, and a sense of political values, must be taught; not only that the Nation is unfree, but why it is not free, and the root causes and the means by which it is kept in subjection.

Let us profit from the recent past. The Republic was overthrown in 1922 largely because the Volunteers did not understand and were not taught the fundamental principles on which it was based, or the economic and social principles it enshrined. Volunteers were deluded by false phrases and slogans. For instance, they were misled into believing that the part of the National territory the British soldiers and police had evacuated was free. They did not realise that these foreign troops and police were really only defending the political and economic interests which were exploiting and robbing the people. These interests remain unaffected and undisturbed in their exploitation. Native traitors and their dupes were found to safeguard these interests for hire.

Freedom therefore must mean more than freeing the National soil of foreign troops, and the restoration of a Republican Government. It must mean: The smashing of exploiting institutions and agencies, which are robbing and despoiling our People; the abolition of landlordism in the soil and natural resources of the Nation, which was created by robbery and violence; creating of conditions which will end the exodus, under fierce pressure, of the Gael and which has resulted in decimating the Nation; an ending of poverty and hunger, of unemployment and the physical and moral decay of the workless. These great ends can be brought about, and existing evils ended, by utilising the resources and credit of the Nation, in the interests of the People, and not as at present for the advantage of a small privileged class.

Volunteers must never let the idea get hold of them that because they are Volunteers they are apart from the mass of the People. They must have the feelings of the People from whom they spring; feel the same wrongs, hurts and injustices which are oppressing them, and so often crushing them. They must have a burning hatred of these things, and a desire for the opportunity to end them. Only when they are ended can it be claimed that the People are free, and that Ireland is a free Nation.

TRAINING.

Realising that a high percentage of Volunteers are recruits, or men with short service, and therefore without training or experience, it is advisable to emphasise how vital training is. Without training, bodies of men, though termed Army units, would become mobs if faced by disciplined troops. Training is not alone the teaching of men how to skilfully handle and use military weapons, and carry out military movements and manoeuvres, but also the inculcating and developing in them of a strong sense of discipline and unity.

The first essential in a military force is discipline, and all that it connotes—loyalty to principles, comradeship, obedience, and a readiness to make sacrifices. Discipline can only be promoted on the training ground. It is here that Volunteers get to know one another, to know their Officers, and their Officers to know them; here it is that they become accustomed to act together at a single command, to obey, as it were, one will. A revolution or a war cannot be carried to success unless there is this discipline, this unity. It is only men who believe the same things, who fight and stand together for the same objective who can succeed.

Many object to continuous training and find parades irksome; repetition jars on them; they become impatient. But this constant training and parading, and repetition, is absolutely necessary. You cannot come along when a fight is on, take a man, hand him a rifle and ammunition and say "You are now a soldier." He won't be one, though you may persist in calling him one. He and you may believe that he is until he meets a soldier—that is a trained military man. It is not enough to be "a good shot." In the late wars here individual initiative and action counted for much, but individual action proved fruitless in the war 1922-1923.

The more parades, marches, field-exercises, shooting practices there are the better. There can be no question of being over-trained, all the dangers are in our being under-trained.

After a strong sense of discipline and unity is instilled on the parade-ground, through the obeying of orders and drill, the next stage will be Weapon Training. Weapons must be made available to the Companies for training. This is a crucial phase. Men may march in excellent spirits and formation to battle, but the issue will largely depend on their using their weapons with skill and effect. Not only being "a good shot," but also knowing when to shoot, and at what to shoot, matters. Musketry instruction: aiming, sighting, judging distances, regulating sights, fire control, are vital items of the infantry man's training.

At the present time our immediate task is to take in hand the training of the young men who are being rapidly recruited. A great responsibility rests particularly on Company Officers and Section Commanders. Battalion Officers must be active in directing and supervising Company training. The Battalion Commander must arrange for Battalion field-exercises. These give Officers opportunities of handling large bodies; promotes comradeship and confidence in the Battalion. Besides, they enable the employment of all Staff Officers in practical work.

It is absolutely essential to develop the qualities of leadership in Officers, and to do so Officers must get as much special training as possible. The first quality is confidence. Officers are shy and ineffective in handling a Company if they feel incapable. They need encouragement at the outset to bring forth this quality of confidence, and the exercise of their intelligence. With the will to learn, the officer of ordinary intelligence and determination will succeed.

In training and instruction it is necessary not only that Volunteers should be got to carry out evolutions, but that their meaning and purpose, in the light of war conditions, should be explained. As the training of Volunteers develops, exercises should be carried out as small tactical manoeuvres. It is in this manner that men can be got to visualise war conditions.

An outline, or Syllabus for the training of Infantry is being printed in this issue. Officers and Section Commanders will

RADICAL POLITICS, 1931

This issue of *An tÓglác* was published at a time when the IRA's embrace of radical politics and its increased activity seemed to be paying off. The IRA's confidence was vividly expressed when the government failed to prevent its annual commemoration of Wolfe Tone at Bodenstown, Co. Kildare in June, despite banning the gathering. Thirty thousand people took part in the commemoration, including a large number of Fianna Fáil TDs. At Bodenstown, Peadar O'Donnell warned that, 'All the powers in their hands we must take into ours, and in the final phase we must be prepared to meet force with force'.

Maurice 'Moss' Twomey, IRA Chief of Staff, felt that Bodenstown showed the authorities were 'losing their grip'. There was certainly alarm in official circles. One garda officer in Kerry warned that if '. . . the Soviet comrades are not dealt with more determinedly, the state will perish'. Other gardaí complained that in several districts there was no cooperation from locals. The IRA had also carried out three murders in early 1931, killing two if its own members (accusing them of informing) and, most dramatically, shooting dead a garda superintendent in Tipperary.

Moss Twomey, Bodenstown, 1933. Maurice 'Moss' Twomey was IRA Chief of Staff from 1926-1936. He played a major role in rebuilding the IRA in the late 1920s and in holding a movement of disparate factions together.
PHOTOGRAPH: MAURICE TWOMEY JR

Facing page: *An tÓglác*, July 1931 TWOMEY PAPERS, UCD ARCHIVES

While the government pondered harsh repressive measures in response (and solicited the aid of the Catholic heriarchy) the IRA leadership pushed ahead with a political project. There was general agreement that the new republican party would be radical. In May, Moss Twomey had been bold enough to write that, 'if it is Communism to undo the conquest . . . to end robbery and exploitation by a privileged minority; then Tone, Emmet, Mitchel, Lalor, Connolly, Pearse, and Mellows were Communists, and the Irish Republican Army is a Communist organisation'. Hence the political party Saor Éire, launched by the IRA during the autumn of 1931, was openly socialist.

February 19th, 1932.

Dear M.

The I.R.A. and Fianna Fail must be fused at once. They
have at bottom the same national and social outlook. There is
really less friction between them to-day than often exists unde[r]
within one organisation. Just now the way is open to complete
________. If it does not take place now, when neither has
power over the other, it will be a thousand times more difficul[t]
when Fianna Fail gets control of the affairs of the twenty-six
counties. A complete spontaneous fusing now would double the
sum of their separatesstrengths. The national morale would be
strengthened a thousand fold, and many things that are impossib[le]
of achievement with divided forces would not only be possible
but certain.

So long as the activites of the national forces were
not directed and controlled by men who stood openly and wholeheartedly by the fundamental national principles there were
many reasons why men who were prepared and willing to fight
for them should have desired and maintained an independent self
controlled organisation. One of the principal fears has been
that when the people elected a majority of representatives who
were prepared to act up to these principles that the Government
institutions would not be handed over to them. It was that rea[son]
that was uppermost in the minds of those who fought hardest
against a surrender of arms at the end of the Civil War. If a[nd]
when a Fianna Fail Government gets control of the Governmental
institutions of the twenty-six counties, and accepts and acts
upon the principles contained in the Peace Proposals agreed up[on]
by the Irish Republican Army published by the President,
Eamon de Valera, on the 27th of April, 1923, there can be no
occasion for such fears. The arms and services of the members
of the I.R.A. could then be placed at the disposal of that
Government, and in my opinion ought to be ~~done~~ immediately. Mo[...]
It is of the greatest national importance that the willingness
the I.R.A. to agree on their side to the Peace Proposals of 19[..]
should be proclaimed at once. The announcement by the present
Executive that they are prepared to act up to the proposals ag[reed]
upon unanimously by all who were members of the Army Executive
from June 1922 to April 1923 would, I feel sure, be approved b[y]
all present members of the I.R.A., just as they were accepted [by]
all members of the I.R.A. in 1923 who were free, and by the
prisoners in both Free State and Six County jails. The Fianna
Party would undoubtedly respond and announcetheir willingness
accept and act up to them. They have asked for and got a mand[ate]
for the removal of the oath.

Aiken's letter to Moss Twomey, 1932
AIKEN PAPERS, UCD ARCHIVES

The government's response to the IRA's growth was a drastic clampdown during October 1931, introducing a Constitutional Amendment Bill, which outlawed the IRA and several left-wing organisations, suppressed several newspapers including *An Phoblacht* and established a tribunal composed of army officers to try 'political' cases. The tribunal had the power to impose the death penalty. The clampdown was accompanied by a bishops' pastoral letter condemning the IRA and its links with communism. The letter stated that, 'You cannot be a Catholic and a Communist. One stands for Christ, the other for Anti-Christ'.

While the clampdown of 1931 failed in its twin aims of destroying the IRA and by implication, damning Fianna Fáil as Red, it did have a lasting effect on the IRA: many of its members broke from the organisation, fearing clerical censure. As a result the IRA leadership decided quietly to bury Saor Éire in 1932.

-2-

The announcement should be made within the next few days. Any delay would, under the present circumstances, be fatal. FIANNA FAIL has not received a majority. The doubt in the people's minds as to whether Fianna Fail could secure internal peace had the effect I told you it would have at the time of the passing of the Constitutional Amendment Act when I appealed to you to get the I.R.A. to declare their willingness to negociate on the basis I outlined in the Dail. We are now dependent upon Labour upon whom pressure will undoubtedly be brought to join Cumann na nGaedheal in the formation of a "National Coalition Government". Many of them will be inclined to accept in the event of our failure to prove our ability to secure internal peace. Remember Jinks. The British papers are beginning to thunder already. All the usual re-actionary forces will be whipped up to force Labour and ourselves to agree to this Coalition, and the levers of the Eucharistic Congress, trouble with England, world depression, etc. will be used for all they are worth. We will be on the defensive and may fail to secure the reins of Government unless you come to the national rescue by showing that you will accept our authority wholeheartedly when the oath is removed. The elections in Sligo-Leitrim have still to be fought, and may decide who is to be the Government.

We have now a chance to secure real national unity against the re-actionaries which only comes once in a generation. You can round off a splendid record by an act honourable to the I.R.A., and of everlasting value to the cause of freedom and social justice. Any hesitation or delay may result in letting an opportunity pass which may never present itself again, and both the I.R.A. and Fianna Fail will be condemned to utter failure to advance nationally or socially, and in the end both will peter out. If the way is not cleared for a fusion of forces we are doomed to a period of indecision and weakness in dealing with the urgent international, financial and economic and social problems which will lead to a defeat of the Fianna Fail Government, if it should get control, and the anti-national reactionary forces will again get control.

A fusion now of the national forces, that is of the labourers and the working farmers will ensure that the national march to freedom and social justice and cultural and economic development will commence with rapid movement and overwhelming strength.

I appeal to you for God's sake, and for the sake of the people of Ireland to clear the way by making the announcement <u>at once</u> that you are prepared to accept and act up to the principles which the men who fought the civil war agreed upon.

Le gac deagh guidhe

FIANNA FÁIL AND THE IRA, 1932-33

In early 1932, the IRA suspended its orders forbidding volunteers from working or voting in parliamentary elections and instead ordered them actively to work for the government's removal, i.e. the removal of Cumann na nGaedheal under W.T. Cosgrave. In practice this meant the IRA threw its weight behind Fianna Fáil's election effort. Privately the IRA admitted that due to the 'Coercion Act, Terrorism, and the ill-treatment of prisoners, the hatred against the Coercionist regime was so intense that Volunteers could not be restrained from voting against their candidates'.

The IRA's decision meant that several thousand men were available to help steward Fianna Fáil rallies, to put up posters, to paint walls, to canvass and, allegedly, to cast multiple votes. In the immediate aftermath of the election, in which Fianna Fáil won 72 seats, enough to form a minority government with the support of the Labour Party, Frank Aiken contacted Moss Twomey. In his letter, Aiken offered Twomey and the IRA the opportunity to reunite into one organisation with Fianna Fáil. He claimed that there was little difference in reality between them and that the backlash which was sure to come both from Britain and internally could best be confronted by a united republican movement. As a show of goodwill, on 9 March 1932, Aiken, now Minister for Defence in the new Fianna Fáil government, released all IRA prisoners held in the Free State. The IRA leadership were wary of this offer and despite several face-to-face meetings with Aiken during 1932, ultimately declined it.

August 25th. 1932

Dear Brother Mc'Garrity,

I was very pleased to get your letter dated June 24th. Do not considdr me discourteous for not replying to it earlier. It was because Con being here, and knowing he was reporting regularly, I did not do so, lest my attempt to expaain the situation to you may not b successful.

This is a situation which it was hard to foresee, especially some years ago. Then we all saw either the Republic or the Free State. Nobody visualised a Free State which Republicans were not supposed to attack! And that is just what we have today in the Twenty Six Counties.

The clear issue for us today is: will we stick by the republic, or compund with our principles and tacitly submit to the Free State, and trust to evolution for a republic!

Of course this perhaps may not be new. We had it in 1922. Some people then compunded, others of us would not do so.

We are all clear on many things in this situation:

1. Republican principles must be upheld regardless of the fortunes of parties or of individual consequences.

2. That the "Treaty" must not get recognition.

3. That the right to establish the Independence of Ireland by force, ifxp must be insisted on, and must not be abandoned.

4. But that if the Republic can be restored without violence so much the better.

Our difficult today is that most things we do to maintain and strengthen ourselves is branded as obstructing Fianna Fail! And it is amazing the people who think so.

We don't want the Cosgrave Imperial gang back, and we wish to avoid doing anything which may provide the pretext for their come back. We have expressed our readiness to work with Fianna Fail in the present situation. This offer was not accepted.

Letter from Moss Twomey to Joe McGarrity, 25 August 1932
TWOMEY PAPERS, UCD ARCHIVES

But with Fianna Fáil in power there *was* a new situation. Twomey explained some of the IRA's problems in a letter to Joe McGarrity, the central figure in the Clan na Gael in America. A native of Tyrone, McGarrity had become a businessman in Philadelphia, but dedicated his life to support for the IRA. Twomey explained to him the problem of having a 26-county government led by de Valera: 'Nobody visualised a Free State which Republicans were not supposed to attack!'

Crowds greet the release of IRA prisoners outside Arbour Hill prison in Dublin on 9 March 1932. The new Fianna Fáil Minister for Defence (and former IRA leader) Frank Aiken had visited the prisoners shortly beforehand. COURTESY OF THE NATIONAL LIBRARY OF IRELAND

Group of released IRA prisoners at reception in Dublin in March 1932. Back row, left-right: Seán McGuinness (Offaly), J. O'Shea, Claude O'Loughlin (Dublin), James Hannigan. Second row: George Gilmore, Charlie Gilmore, Frank Ryan, Thomas Breen, T.J. Ryan (Clare), George Mooney, Thomas O'Driscoll. Front row: Seán Mulgrew, Brian Corrigan (Achill), John M. O'Connor, Seán O'Farrell (Leitrim), M. Sherry.
COURTESY OF KYA RICHARDS

THE 'NEW IRA'

A communication from the IRA's intelligence department warns of a number of rumours being spread by Fianna Fáil supporters during 1932. At this stage Fianna Fáil and the IRA were not in conflict: Fianna Fáil TDs still attended IRA commemorations and IRA volunteers were also employed by Fianna Fáil. Yet it is clear that there was an effort to put distance between the organisations, hence the reported criticism of the IRA from Fianna Fáil's Oscar Traynor. The use of the term 'New IRA' would become common by 1934 and was used by Fianna Fáil spokesmen, especially Seán MacEntee, to assert that there was no connection between the army of 1916-23 and that of the 1930s. (U.R.A. refers to the United Republican Association, a short-lived organisation of IRA veterans.)

ÓGLAIGH NA h-ÉIREANN.
(IRISH REPUBLICAN ARMY)

Dept. Intelligence.
Ref. No. W.H/D. 31.

Árd-Oifig:
Brigáid Átha Cliath.
28th July 1932.

To/
D. 9. G. H. Q.

1. Further to mine W.H/D.30. I understand that you are in possession of all the material facts in connection with Dempsey's release.

2. Withx reference to a recent communication from the Chief-of-Staff to Brigade O/C concerning the presence of rumours and allegations against the Army I have the following Reports,

OSCAR TRAYNOR T. D. in the course of conversation with a girl (name not known)said last week that the Army are not giving Fianna Fail a chance that they had no right to make a public protest the night after Dempsey's arrest.

JOE REYNOLDS - a supposed Army Reservist at any rate a man who was attached to 3rd Batt. Dublin Brigade up to 4 or 5 years ago made a statement to my informant that there was deep antagonism between the "old I. R. A." and the "new I. R. A." that all Fianna Fail was behind the Government in the arrest of Dempsey that no man on the platform in College Green on the occasion of the Anti-Imperialist League Demonstration had a National Record, That the " so-called Army Council" were"a cowardly pack" on the occasion of the passing of the Coercion Act that they refused the challenge of the Cosgrave Administration "to come out and fight. These Vapourings may appear of no importance to you but this individual (although attached to a Fianna Fail Cumman) pulls a good deal of weight in Army and ex-Army circles . He is a member of the eexecutive Committee of the U. R. A.

3. As far as I can ascertain there seems to be similar ideas expressed by a number of these ex-army U. R. A. members. These individuals talk in an "old warrior" strain and are doing a great deal of harm to the Brigade where recruiting is concerned.

4. A reservist named P. Saunders who is Driver to Sean T. O'Kelly T.D. referred to in correspondence between the Brigade Adjt and G. H.Q over a month ago was recently asked by a Capt Gallagher O/C Transport F. S. Army McKee Barracks to sign some pay form which in Saunders opinion was equivalent to acceptance of F. S. Army Status. He refused as did 5 (five) otherx new drivers there is apparently some sort of deadlock at present. These six men have according to their own stories refused from the first to take orders from any one

AN PHOBLACHT.

"Ní Síoccáin go Saoirse" – Pádraic Mac Piarais

THE REPUBLIC.

"We Shall Rise Again" –James Connolly.

New Series. Vol. VII. No. 23. SATURDAY, 16th JULY, 1932. PRICE TWOPENCE.

MONSTER MEETING IN COLLEGE GREEN

ANTI-IMPERIALIST RALLY

Republicans Challenge Imperialism

Last Friday at College Green a large meeting (numbering, it is estimated, 10,000 persons) was held under the auspices of the Irish Anti-Imperialist League. Mr. Maurice Twomey presided, and revolutionary Republican groups were represented on the platform, which included living links with 1916 in the persons of Nora Connolly O'Brien (daughter of James Connolly) and S. Mallin, son of Commandant Michael Mallin. The speakers were Michael Price, Peadar O'Donnell, Madame McBride, Michael Fitzpatrick, George Gilmore, J. Mallin, James Larkin (junior), Nora Connolly O'Brien, H. Sheehy-Skeffington and Frank Ryan. Mr. V. Patel, the veteran Indian leader, was on the platform, receiving an enthusiastic ovation on his arrival. He was dressed in white in Indian costume and wore proudly the famous Gandhi cap, which all rebel Indians now wear, in spite of official attempts at banning.

RESOLUTIONS PASSED AT MEETING :—

1. "That whereas the connection with

workers of Great Britain and calls on them to resolutely oppose the aggressive action of the British Tory Government against the people of Ireland who are striving for Freedom from the stranglehold of Imperialism and Capitalism which has impoverished the mass of the people and partitioned our country.

"We call on the workers of Great Britain to demand that all British military and naval forces be withdrawn from the whole of Ireland.

"We call on our race in Britain and throughout the British Empire to protest against the shameless Imperialist attack on the Irish people; we appeal to them actively to associate themselves with all genuine Anti-Imperialist activities within their reach, so that the Imperial stranglehold on this nation may be broken and Irish life so organised that our exiled brethren may come home to a free united Irish Republic where Capitalist exploitation and its attendant evils and unemployment and slumdom shall have been for ever abolished."

Proposed by MICHAEL FITZPATRICK.
Seconded by JAMES LARKIN (junr.).

3. "That whereas millions of our race are citizens of the Republic of the United States of America, through the enforced exile to which Imperial rule has condemned the youth of our nation for generations, and whereas this same Imperial tyranny is once more threatening desperate warfare against the Irish people, demanding crushing burdens of tribute from us while at the same time manoeuvring for relief from her own debts.

"Now, we, therefore, the Citizens of Dublin, call on our kith and kin in

AN ADDRESS from the Army Council of the Irish Republican Army to the Men and Women of the Orange Order

Fellow-Countrymen and Women,

It is a long call from the ranks of the Irish Republican Army to the marching throngs that hold the 12th of July Celebrations in North East Ulster. Across the space we have sometimes exchanged shots, or, missiles or hard words, but never forgetting that on occasions our ancestors have stood shoulder to shoulder. Some day we will again exchange ideas and then the distance which now separates us will shorten. For we of the Irish Republican Army believe that inevitably the small farmers and wage-earners in the Six County area will make common cause with those of the rest of Ireland, for the common good of the mass of the people in a Free United Irish Republic. Such a conviction is forming itself in an ever-increasing number of minds in North-East Ulster.

The Irish Republican Army—within North-East Ulster as well as in the rest of Ireland—believe that the mass of the Working Farmers and wage-earners must organise behind revolutionary leadership if they are to rescue themselves from a system within which the few prosper and the many are impoverished.

GLENGORMLEY ARMS RAID SEQUEL

("IRISH NEWS" REPORT)

Prisoners Sentenced to Eighteen Months Hard Labour Each

"**I am an Irish Republican and do not recognise the jurisdiction of this British Court,**" said Arthur Thornbury, Clondara Street, Belfast, when arraigned at the Antrim Summer Assizes on Friday on a charge of armed robbery at the house of Mr. T. C. L. Newell, at Glengormley, near Belfast, on 17th March last, during which five rifles were stolen.

James Connolly, Falls Road, who was charged with Thornbury, when arraigned also replied: "**As an Irish Republican I refuse to recognise the jurisdiction of this Court to try me.**"

"Very well, this British Court will recognise you," said Lord Justice Best, directing that pleas of "Not guilty" be entered in each case.

The accused were not represented.

Mr. T. C. L. Newell, a civil servant, said he was at his home at Ballyclare Road, Glengormley, on the evening of the 17th March last, and was in the sitting-room with his family when a knock came to the door. His daughter-in-law went to the door, and he heard some people ask her if "the boss" was in.

His daughter asked them to come in. In the meantime his son had retired to the kitchen. He next saw his daughter-in-law being pushed into the room by the first man who came in.

His son then came from the kitchen to see what was wrong. His son asked the man what he wanted, and the man, who had on a waterproof and a cap, replied: "We are the Irish Republican Army and we have come for the arms."

There were, said the witness, five rifles, two shotguns, two Webley revolvers, and an automatic pistol in a bedroom in the house.

"**I would like to ask him if he has good eyesight.**"

When the witness replied in the affirmative to the question Thornbury remarked: "Read a few lines from the prayerbook; I am not prepared to take your word for it."

The witness then put on a pair of glasses and read a few lines from the prayerbook, whereupon Thornbury remarked: "**Do people with good eyesight usually wear glasses,**" and witness rejoined—"I only use them for reading."

Arms from India and Africa.

The Judge (to witness)—How did you come to have so many arms in your home?—**I had these in India and Africa,** and prior to coming home I wrote and asked for authority to bring the arms home. I left them in bond in London, and got a permit from the police here. **They are more for curios than anything else.**

Address to the Orange Order,
An Phoblacht 16 July 1932 DUBLIN CITY LIBRARY & ARCHIVE

During July 1932, in time for the Orange Order's annual parades, the IRA issued an appeal to northern Protestants to embrace republicanism. As well as being published in *An Phoblacht*, IRA units were ordered to distribute the Address across the North. Written by Peadar O'Donnell, the Address asked Protestant workers and small farmers to make common cause with their Catholic counterparts against exploitation.

The Address was partly motivated by the information that the IRA was receiving about widespread Protestant working-class anger in Belfast over the effects of unemployment. However, predictably, the appeal met with hostility. Unionist MP James Chichester-Clark denounced the IRA's appeal to the '. . . small farmer and to the wage earner whom they claim are being exploited by capitalism . . . forgetting that (capitalism) is merely a nickname for civilised life, forgetting that there is no alternative (to it) but barbarism and death'. The initiative was not well received inside the IRA either. In Armagh the local IRA burnt the Address rather than distribute it. The Derry IRA posted up copies of the Address but felt that 'it is a gesture that will not have the slightest effect'.

IRA CONVENTION, 1933

Unlike regular armies, the IRA had a formally democratic structure, with officers elected and major decisions taken at General Army conventions. The debates at the IRA's 1933 convention reflected continuing confusion over the movement's political direction. In this extract Moss Twomey expresses the frustration of republicans like himself, who wanted the organisation to participate in social activity but knew the backlash that being associated with 'communism' would cause. Cork's Tadgh Lynch, meanwhile, expresses the view that 'freedom' rather than any political policy should be the IRA's objective. Despite endorsing more social agitation, including intervention in strikes, the 1933 convention also formally barred communists from IRA membership.

15

We are not in conflict with any particular individual if the land he holds is used to the best advantage of the community. We took over farms during the Black and Tan war.

C/S. It is a very dangerous doctrine to preach that we are soldiers only. We are revolutionaries. The Army feels that by force of Arms is the only way at present by which we can achieve that freedom. We should be more than soldiers. We are told by the "Old I.R.A. men" that we are "Bolshevists". We have not a civil arm to-day. The Army Council should take over the responsibility of Government. In 1922 we took over the Banks showing that we realised that the peoples money was necessary for our freedom. The only mistake was that we did not take enough. We took farms - we should have taken over all the ranches and put the Free State Army in the position of protecting these large farmers. I think that the policy of Fianna Fail is far more dangerous than Cosgraves. Cosgrave did not attempt to start industries. The Fianna Fail Government are starting industries under capitalist lines - and capitalism may succeed and this situation if it extends for ten years , the country will be in a worse state than ever before. You will have economic chaos. Everybody accepts here that for some time there must be a revolutionary government. You must have a revolutionary government because England is going to increase the economic pressure - you are not going to have a Republic functioning quietly - England will not allow it. The setting up of a Republic is simple - but could we maintain it when set up. Here is the necessity for a programme beforehand and a force to carry it through. There are many who have property who, although the would lose financially would for the common good accept this proposed programme. You would also get a man sweeping the streets who would be opposed to it. The question is asked even by our own men "Is this communism" I do not know whether it is or not. I don't care - all that concerns me is that it should be able to stand up to critixxxx and be for the general good. I ask you to vote for or against this resolution one way or the other have it definitely. Be wholehearted about your decision. If you think that we should not go out to collect public opinion decide on making a perfect military machine and not waste time by dividing attention.

Mick Price. Proposes closure.

Chair. I think it is too early to close this.

J.J.Sheehy, Tralee. I see a split in the movement if this be pressed - every man should get an opportunity to speak.

Discussion remains open.

Tadgh Lynch, West Cork. The only position which we can accept is a free Republic for 32 counties. Because I do not agree with some other members on the social programme is not a reason why either of us should leave the A rmy. Should we decide on the killing in active service as to whether one man has a shilling more or less than another man. The justification of our killing should be that we resist the thing that stands between us and our objective. Is it wise for us to inflict our opinions on those who differ from us socially. We should not decide a social aim as the chief aim of the I.R.A. The possibility of our Republic may come in six months. - Is it wise to establish it if we have not our social programme ready. If the motion is passed do I take it that we accept everything that is in it. Are we out to free the Country for the capitalist or for the worker - no, we are out for the freedom of all. I can give instances of monied people who were as nationally minded as any other part of the community. What part of the community has a monoply patriotism. We should carry this as a body or reject it as a body.

IRA General Army Convention, 1933

TWOMEY PAPERS, UCD ARCHIVES

'ORANGE AND GREEN UNITED IN BELFAST'

During October 1932, Belfast was shaken by a protest movement involving Protestant and Catholic unemployed workers. Anger exploded over the miserly and humiliating system of 'Outdoor Relief': the sums paid to the unemployed after a means test. Barricades were erected in both the Falls and the Shankill Roads and there were numerous clashes with police. Two protesters (one Catholic and one Protestant) were killed by RUC gunfire. The IRA leadership saw the events as very significant, as *An Phoblacht's* headline illustrates. But on the ground in Belfast the local IRA's reaction had been haphazard and uncoordinated. Despite Unionist claims to the contrary, the organisation was not the driving force behind the protests: in fact the small Revolutionary Workers Groups (Communists) were more important. Nevertheless, the events signalled to the IRA that economic unrest might offer an opportunity to destabilise the northern state.

An Phoblacht, 22 October 1932 DUBLIN CITY LIBRARY & ARCHIVE

Reserve Oct. 29 for the I.R.A. CEILIDHE (see page 8)

AN PHOBLACHT.

"Ní Síoċċáin go Saoirse" – Pádraic Mac Piarais

THE REPUBLIC.

"We Shall Rise Again" – James Connolly

The Irish Republican Weekly with the LARGEST SALES

New Series. Vol. VII. No. 37. SATURDAY, 22nd OCTOBER, 1932. PRICE TWOPENCE.

ORANGE AND GREEN UNITED IN BELFAST

BRUTALITY AND DIPLOMACY FAIL TO SPLIT THEM

WORKERS' VICTORY

A city of revolution—barricaded streets, deep entrenchments, armoured cars around the city, armed police in groups, lorries full of armed police careering around the city, armed police in groups at every corner, curfew, police and police-spies everywhere. And in the working-class districts the people active, but sullen and bitter. This was the state of the capital of the Loyal Province last week. No wonder the Imperialists spoke and wrote bitterly of their "humiliation!"

(FROM OUR CORRESPONDENT)

Their work of years appeared undone overnight. Worst of all—by those on whom they had felt they could count indefinitely as their dupes.

The end came, and the leader of the militant workers of Belfast was able to proclaim that "a glorious victory" had been won by them. The exploiters of the workers had suffered a humiliating defeat. The victory in Belfast will be regarded as the first of many to be won by the workers throughout the whole of Ireland. The workers had triumphed over murder, terrorism, and brutality, and their just demands had to be conceded by their enemies.

BRUTAL MURDERS.

A demonstration by strikers was proclaimed by the Imperial authorities. They went ahead with their arrangements only to be met with armed force. They refused to submit and offered resistance. Numbers of them were shot down by the militarised police forces.

Samuel Baxter was brutally murdered by the police at point blank range; John Geegan died as a result of bullet wounds; others lie dangerously wounded.

The funerals of the victims were wonderful demonstrations of loyalty to the principles for which these workers were martyred.

POLICE BRUTALITY

Faced with armed force the workers resorted to street-fighting tactics; bar-

testant and Catholic stood and fought side by side. They went to and fro from district to district helping and encouraging one another. The "Belfast Telegraph" confessed this as follows: ". . . There was an exchange of mischief-makers all over the city so as to confuse the local police force," and again:

"It was significant that for once the religious question did not enter into the trouble. Youths from Protestant areas were to be found in Catholic districts and vice versa. . ."

For days the Imperialists could not believe that sectarian strife, their old and hitherto successful weapon in keeping the working-class at bitter enmity, was failing them. They tried to revive it. Under cover of curfew, police and their agents were busy painting the Shankill (Orange) district with the old political slogans to arouse sectarianism, such as: "Sinn Fein is in the Shankill"; "The I.R.A. are behind this strike." But the plan did not work this time. When the workers arose they proceeded immediately to efface these inscriptions. The Imperial game had failed. The Strikers' Committee warned the workers of the trap. But there was no need as the objective was too plain, indeed crude.

As part of the plan too, the police refrained from using their guns freely in what were Orange areas, relying on their batons instead.

AND CRAIGAVON FAILS!

Craigavon tried his hand. He made

I.R.A. MAN IN THE DOCK

Sneering Justice

"I'm a soldier of the Irish Republican Army, which I recognise as the one lawful army in this country. These arms and ammunition are the property of that army, and I demand that they be handed back, as no person has the right to steal them."

So said John O'Shea, of Crusheen, at Ennis District Couurt, when he was charged with being found in unlawful possession of two rifles and ammunition.

C.I.D. man, Looby, deposed to finding the rifles; Supt. Moore prosecuted.

When accused refused to recognise the court Justice Gleeson taunted him with not knowing the Irish language. He returned him for trial. Accused refused bail.

District Justice Gleeson thought he was scoring a point when he was taunting Volunteer O'Shea with not knowing the Irish language. The Volunteer has not had the facilities the pro-British D.J. had. We remind Gleeson that a mere knowledge of Irish does not make an Irishman. Dermot Mac Morrough knew Irish. He, like Gleeson accepted British rule and sentenced Irish patriots under British laws.

SAVAGE AND BARBAROUS

Judge on C.I.D.

"Savage and barbarous assault," said Judge McElligot, at Ennis, last week, when awarding thirty guineas damages against James Cronin for assault committed while he was in the C.I.D. force, in February, 1932.

Patrick Mooney, plaintiff, described how Cronin assaulted him, stripped him, beat him with a revolver, banged his head against a wall, sluiced him with water and stuffed his Fianna Fail literature down his throat with a revolver barrel. Medical evidence corroborated Mooney's statement.

There are scores of thugs like Cronin in the C.I.D. force Why are they not dealt with? And why have the victims

UNEMPLOYED ORGANISING THROUGHOUT IRELAND

'GIVE US BREAD'

As we go to press great demonstrations of unemployed are being organised throughout Ireland. In Dublin, on Wednesday, the workers are to march to Government Buildings to demand a hearing. Thus the South, as well as the North, is raising the cry "GIVE US BREAD." In Belfast, in Derry, in Sligo, Cork, Kilkenny, Limerick, Clonmel and Dublin, the unemployed are busy organising and formulating their demands, arranging hunger marches on local bodies and to both parliaments.

WORKLESS HAVE FIRST CLAIM

We approve of the action of the Belfast workers in their strike against their intolerable lot. Let us ask ourselves frankly whether our applause comes merely from the fact that we hate the government responsible for coercive methods against our comrades in Belfast, or whether it springs from an innate sense of the inherent justice of the claims put forward by the workless for work or maintenance. For, if their cause is just, then so are similar claims put forward by the unemployed in other parts of Ireland, whether in rural or industrial centres.

"WORK OR MAINTENANCE."

Until there are sufficient industries set up for urban workers, until in the country the ranches are divided up, the unemployed must be assured their daily bread. The cruel spectacle of hungry men, women and children—a daily one under our present system of soulless capitalism—is one that must be banished. Governments have a plain duty in this matter towards all their citizens: To see that none starve—that until there is bread and work for all, the State should provide for those deprived of work. Too long have the workless been fooled with doles and charity, with the dope of resignation and patience and misplaced tolerance. It is high time that they insisted on their just demands being granted. Swift action is called for.

"THOSE WHO HUNGER HAVE FIRST CLAIM

Ballymena—To alleviate the acute distress existing amongst the unemployed of the town, the staffs of several local firms have agreed to subscribe a percentage of their weekly wages to the relief fund.

Cork.—A deputation of Cork unemployed waited on South Cork Board of Assistance and said if they did not get an adequate increase on relief they would march into the union, and that would put more on the rates.

Kilkenny—Kilkenny Corporation have accepted the resignation of six Councillors—members of the Business Party—who stated that they felt compelled to take this step as a result of the Corporation meeting, when the Assembly Room was invaded by hundreds of workers. So did the French aristocrats try to escape, once upon a time! That trick won't work, Kilkenny Capitalists!

Limerick.—The City Board of Health decided to apply to the L.G.D. for sanction to a loan to enable the Board to purchase cheaply 400 to 500 tons of coal for distribution in kind to deserving poor.

Clonmel.—A meeting of unemployed decided to march to the Health Board meeting and demand an increase of home assistance; and to march to the Corporation Committee to protest against the opening of tenders for work by contract. Direct labour is demanded instead.

UNEMPLOYED LEADER THREATENED

William Conway, Secretary of the Irish Unemployed Workers' Movement,

RAIL STRIKE, 1933

In January 1933, a rail strike took place in Northern Ireland. When strike breakers were recruited to run the trains, under police protection, the IRA intervened. There were sniping and bomb attacks on trains and rail offices and in February 1933, IRA men engaged in a gun battle with police protecting a railway depot in Belfast. RUC constable John Ryan was killed, the first member of the force to be killed by the IRA (Ryan was a Catholic and a native of Tipperary). During the strike, Seán Russell, Quartermaster General of the IRA, was sent to Belfast to coordinate its intervention. This communication to Twomey illustrates how seriously the organisation took the dispute. It also contains a claim that striking Protestant railway workers, including members of the B-Specials, were cooperating in IRA attacks on the rail network. Russell claimed the bombs used in an attack on the GNR and Midland Railway depots in Belfast were 'supplied by the O/C Belfast and thrown by B-Specials'.

28. 2 '33.

1/32V

To: C/S.

Belfast

It would be difficult to measure the value of the situation existing in the North if we handle it with any degree of judgement. It is the most promising sign at all to find the "B" specials who are on strike in search of IRA assistance. It is quite clear, they realise that we are the only people capable of assistance: the only organisation that has seemingly their confidence and sympathies. What a change to find one group of "specials" searching the houses of our men, whilst another can be found collaborating with them! Should the strike continue long enough, and should our policy be based on sound judgement and be reasonably well carried out a colapse of the enemy

Belfast

morale

The

station

considera

the O/C

specials

a driver

unable t

ance the

a hole

concrete

further

by the O/C

The

complete

paraded

Officers an

an escam

units.

TWOMEY PAPERS, UCD ARCHIVES

'HITLERISM IN DUBLIN'

During March 1933, mobs, inspired in some cases by sermons preached during Lenten masses, attacked property associated with the left in Dublin. On 27 March a crowd of several thousand besieged and eventually sacked Connolly House, the headquarters of the communist Revolutionary Workers Group, on Great Strand Street. During the fighting Dublin IRA officer Charlie Gilmore helped defend the building, firing shots at the mob. *An Phoblacht* condemned the attacks but the IRA wished to avoid any association with communists and Gilmore was publicly disciplined for having taken part in the defence of Connolly House. This in turn provoked resentment and ill-feeling within the Dublin IRA.

An Phoblacht, 1 April 1933 DUBLIN CITY LIBRARY & ARCHIVE

II

e expected.
used upon the railway
fast a few days causing
amage were supplied by
and thrown by B
e just missed its mark —
d Hobson, who is now
k. He colapsed twice
own. The bomb made
feet in depth in the
station. I am sending
to Dundalk for collection
fast on Wednesday (tomorrow).
ny conventions will be
morrow. B company
on 25th inst. The
of Belfast are certainly
many of our Southern

An Phoblacht
The ORGAN of IRISH REPUBLICANISM

Offices : 'Phone 21458
12 ST. ANDREW ST., DUBLIN.
Subscription Rates :
(Post Free.)
One Year .... 13s.
Six Months .... 6s. 6d.
Three Months .... 3s. 3d.

SATURDAY, APRIL 1, 1933.

HITLERISM IN DUBLIN

Hitlerism is a disease, which until now appeared to be confined to the European Continent. But it now appears to be developing into a plague, and likely to sweep all over the world. It has manifested itself in Dublin in the last few days. Like witch-hunting of old it is to become a sport, unless rudely checked. The Jews have not yet been attacked in Dublin. The campaign has opened with an attack on a meeting of unemployed workers, and this in spite of the fact that this particular Body of unemployed workers are constantly reiterating their loyalty to Catholic social principles. The fury of the attack is apparently to be directed against the unemployed, and against the Workers' Revolutionary Groups, whose offices were attacked.

We are quite certain that many of those engaged on these wrecking, hooligan tactics, are loudest, when it suits their own political views, in shrieking against any violation of what they term "free speech." When, during the election campaign, traitors were prevented from preaching treason, these disciples of Hitler and of reaction in Dublin were probably dumb-founded with horror !

Who are behind these hooligan mobs, because it is evident there is a central direction for the campaign? Who are the directing faction behind these dupes, who are being led into they know not what?

AN PHOBLACT has often commented on the development of a situation in which it would be declared heresy and criminal even to protest against the existing economic and social order, or to declare that it should be altered. This new doctrine was enshrined in Cosgrave's infamous Coercion Bill of 1931-'32. For instance, it was then declared both sinful and criminal to state that Tribute should not be paid to England. Yet, during the last election campaign, the authors of the Coercion Bill made repudiation of Tribute the chief plank in their election platform !

This latest revival of the new doctrine is just sheer hypocrisy and dishonesty. Scoundrels who see collapsing the economic order within which they can maintain their privileged position, are inciting ignorant and fanatical dupes by an unscrupulous appeal to religious scruples.

But this campaign of heresy hunting will be defeated by the intelligence of the people, just as Cosgrave was overthrown. Nothing throw of the Cosgrave junta as their Coercion Bill.

The real instigators of this newest wrecking campaign must be exposed, and when they are exposed, they too will be repudiated.

This journal has no connection with the Workers' Revolutionary Groups, nor with the Unemployed Organisations, both of which are being attacked.

But we must insist that any organisation or group which has an economic or social programme has an absolute right to be allowed complete freedom to expound it.

It should be needless for us to re-state emphatically that we do not stand for any interference with religious freedom, and that we do not stand for any attempt to suppress religion or bring it into contempt. But we do not believe that these new-found followers of Hitlerism are inspired by any religious motives in their acts of hooliganism.

WE WONDER WHAT EXCUSE

Republicans have long ceased to be surprised at the acts of our 'Republican" Twenty-Six-County Treaty Government. Yet some of their acts still unconsciously make one wonder at the shortness of human memory.

The belated removal of O'Duffy and Neligan had led many Fianna Fail supporters to believe that their Government was at last going to change its policy of protecting the traitors in its employment at the expense of Republicans..

Now we hear that a Bill is to be brought to give Mr. O'Duffy an additional pension—for he already has one. We also hear that a job has been created for Mr. Neligan and that he is to be a Higher Executive Officer in charge of the R cords in the Land Commission. In charge of records at that—though in the same week we read that he was responsible for burning some of the most important records in the Free State Secret Service Department. If Mr. Neligan was given this job in the hope that he might use his destructive capability on the records of the Land Commission it might be well that the Fianna Fail Executive should so inform its irate organisation !

We wonder what excuse Mr. de Valera will give to the next Fianna Fail Ard Fheis—or will he merely threaten to resign if they don't agree with him.

For our part, we have long ago accepted the fact that the Fianna Fail Government has forgotten about the Republic and that the rest of its policy is based on that forgetfulness.

ANTI-WAR ACTION

To the Editor, AN PHOBLACHT.

Sir: There are one or two questions which I should like to ask you. The English papers are full of anti-war and anti-Imperialist demonstrations. Why is Ireland silent ?

Our position in the case of war would be extremely difficult. There does not seem to be any anti-war Society in the South of Ireland, and

AN PHOBLACHT

"Ní Síoċáin go Saoirse" — Pádraic Mac Piarais

THE REPUBLIC.

"We Shall Rise Again" — James Connolly.

New Series. Vol. VII. No. 36. SATURDAY, 15th OCTOBER, 1932. PRICE TWOPENCE.

BELFAST IN REVOLT

WORKERS SHOT DOWN BY POLICE

The strike of the Belfast Relief Workers, now more than a week in progress, took a new turn on Tuesday last when all the forces of the Six-County Government were mobilised to terrorise the strikers and bludgeon and shoot them into acquiescence.

Previously the sectarian instrument had been tried—unsuccessfully. Enraged at the unity of the exploited working-class, the government sent military, police and armoured cars to shoot them down.

As we go to press there is a fierce conflict in progress. Already there has been one striker killed and many wounded by gunfire. All the signs of revolution are there. Barricades, trenches. And—at last—organisation.

At a large meeting in College Green on Sunday last, resolutions of sympathy with the Belfast strikers were passed. Headed by the W.U.I. band, over 2,000 marched to College Green carrying banners with descriptive slogans, such as, "Bankers Flourish, Children Starve," "Work or Maintenance." Norman Taggart and Betty Sinclair (Belfast) addressed the meeting. Robert Stewart, of the Belfast Workers' Committee, dealt with the state of affairs that had brought about a crisis in Belfast, where the policy of its Board of Guardians was brutally callous in their treatment of the workless and their families. They were now united in a fight for a common cause and in that fight religious and political differences were being submerged.

James Larkin (junior) stated that they were going not only to appeal for Belfast strikers, but they were asking the people of Dublin and of the country generally to take action also.

Peadar O'Donnell said that he would like to associate with the body of the city workers in Belfast and Dublin those of the country now bottled up, who formerly were driven by economic necessity to America, but who now could no longer do so. While there were resources at hand it was meaningless that the unemployed should continue in patient passivity.

Mrs. Despard, Mr. Sean Murray, Councillor J. Dixon, Dun Laoghaire, and Mr. D. Layde, also spoke, appealing for help and support for the workers of Belfast in their present grim struggle.

APPEAL FOR FUNDS.

We ask your moral and financial assistance on behalf of 2,000 Relief workers in the city of Belfast at present on strike against inhuman starvation conditions. These workers have arrayed against them the wealthy interests who control the Board of Guardians, the City Council and also the imperialist Government of Lord Craigavon.

The working people of every creed and colour have rallied, as never before in the history of the North, to the cause of the striking workers. A demonstration of 50,000 people tok place last Monday in Belfast.

All working men and women, all friends and sympathisers with the cause of a united Ireland, are duty bound to show their practical support for the striking Belfast workers. All Labour and Nationalist organisations have now a splendid opportunity of striking a blow for Irish unity by rallying to the support of these workers.

We ask you to forward a donation to the Fund for the relief of the strikers. We ask you to get your friends to subscribe also. The undersigned are authorised to make collections on their behalf.

They who give quickly give twice.

Yours fraternally,

JAMES LARKIN (Junr.), T.C.
MARY DONNELLY.

All subscriptions to be sent c/o Mrs. Donnelly, at 10, Belgrave Road, Rathmines, Dublin.

YO-YO DUFFY'S ARMED POLICE

WHAT ONE OF HIS MEN THINKS

To the Editor, AN PHOBLACHT.

SIR,—McNeill has gone. Let us hope that his exit marks the beginning of the general exodus that is so urgently necessary if our country is to live. We are much too inclined to "forget and forgive," and too ready to appoint our enemies of yesterday, our "leaders" and our "masters" to-day. Many of those who were our sworn enemies of yesteryear occupy important positions in all political parties of to-day, and our blood brothers—who fought in the van, all through the thick of the fight, and in the rearguard—remain "hewers of wood and drawers of water." If old I.R.A. men had held the "key" positions since 1922, the shedding of much unnecessary blood of brothers would have been avoided, the spirit of Nationalism would have been fostered, and progress to Nationhood would have been made, because it must be remembered that the overwhelming majority of those of the I.R.A. who accepted the Treaty accepted only as a "stepping stone."

The politicians knew this, and, as they accepted the Treaty as a final settlement, they appointed their spineless henchmen, and West Britons who were pap-fed on British blood money, to all the "key" position to make it final. A clean sweep of all these double-crossing hirelings is necessary.

A country cannot stand still; it must either go forwards or backwards. Ours has gone backwards. We are more English to-day than we were in 1914. We still take our laws (by precedent) from England. We are, though parvenus in this respect, more snobbish in the observation of English social conventions than are Englishmen. And we ape their mannerisms, their accents, and their sartorial inventions to exaggeration.

JACKALS OF 1922.

This one and that one, on this side and that, has been blamed for the Civil War. It is my opinion that only one man is to blame. If the then Chief of Staff had held the "I.R.A. Convention"

KILMALLOCK FIGHT

NO FREE SPEECH FOR TRAITORS

The provocative attitude of the so-called White Army has led to trouble in various centres. In Kilmallock on Sunday last, members of this organisation, imported for the occasion, fired shots at a procession. The processionists retaliated by charging the gun-bullies. There was fierce fighting and military had to be summoned to extricate the "White Army."

In Mallow on Tuesday night, a meeting was held to form a branch of the "Pensioneers," as they are now popularly called. No one attended the meeting, but a crowd collected and stormed the hall in which the promoters were. Police and military were again summoned to save the "White Army" that was, in the words of its founders, "to save the country!"

THE GUN BULLIES.

When the Pensioners' organisation was first organised by Dr. Higgins, we called for prompt action against it. We pointed out that, at the very least, it would seek to create disordered conditions. "The conspiracy," we wrote, "could be defeated without bloodshed." We pointed out that about 3,000 pensioners, mostly ex-officers, receive between them, this year, £158,000 in pensions. They should be deprived of these pensions. They should be deprived of the arms they hold since 1922-23. "Above all," we said, "they can be defeated by a public opinion thoroughly roused."

MIGRATORY THUGS.

So far as the Fianna Fail Government was concerned, our call—the call of the people—was in vain. No action was taken by them. The Pensioners are, undoubtedly, insignificant in numbers. But they have the backing of most of the daily papers, and in addition, their financial resources are large. Their ringleaders gather squads of these gun-bullies from the few centres in which they are organised and transport them to venues of public meetings where they are transformed into the "audience."

THE KILMALLOCK BATTLE.

Kilmallock on Sunday last is a case

ist dailies are exploiting the Kilmallock Affair. "Free Speech" is their slogan now. For ten years they throttled free speech. They endorsed every coercion Act. They were slavish publicists for the British. Yet they have the audacity to talk about "free speech."

What kind of free speech do they want? Free speech for traitors. Now, we do not stand for that kind of free speech. And we say that the people of Kilmallock were quite within their rights in resenting free speech for traitors.

PROTECTING TREASON.

The Fianna Fail Government should not allow free speech to traitors. Any other government would not allow treachery to be publicly voiced. It would prevent it, and punish it. Yet, in Kilmallock, we had the strange spectacle of Government police and Government soldiers actually protecting traitors who were imported into a Republican area, to foment trouble by publicly voicing treason. And the government organ—the *Irish Press*—condemns the people of Kilmallock for doing what that Government should have done!

No wonder the treason-mongers and their hired gun-bullies openly flaunt their treason. They know that—despite all its threats—the Fianna Fail

An Phoblacht, 15 October 1932 DUBLIN CITY LIBRARY & ARCHIVE

THE BLUESHIRTS

During October 1932, clashes erupted between republicans and the Army Comrades Association in Kilmallock, Co. Limerick. The ACA had been formed by ex-Free State army officers during late 1931 and had stewarded Cumann na nGaedheal meetings during the 1932 elections: it was the forerunner of the Blueshirt organisation. In Kilmallock, former IRA Chief of Staff Richard Mulcahy was one of the ACA speakers. A large crowd of republicans had gathered and soon clashes broke out, during which ACA members fired shots. Armed soldiers were eventually needed to escort ACA members from the town. Similar violence escalated during the spring of 1933, especially after the general election in which Fianna Fáil won an overall majority.

Initially the IRA leadership sought to avoid clashes and ordered its volunteers to ignore the ACA: these orders were often disobeyed. In November 1932, Frank Ryan seemed to give the go-ahead to confrontation when he annonouced that there should be 'no free speech for traitors'.

After Eoin O'Duffy was sacked as Garda Commissioner by de Valera in 1933, he took over as leader of the ACA, who adopted the Blueshirt uniform. There were major riots in Tralee, Kilkenny and Drogheda during the winter of 1933-34 and several fatalities. Yet the IRA leadership continued to disavow these clashes. What became clear was that the leadership only exercised loose control over its volunteers in some areas. The policy of non-confrontation was also a bone of contention with the IRA's left.

REPUBLICAN CONGRESS, 1934

Editorial Offices: 113 Marlboro' Street, Dublin.

SUBSCRIPTION RATES: (Post Free)
Months 3/-
Months 6/-
Months 12/-
$4 per annum.

An Comdáil Poblactae
REPUBLICAN CONGRESS

Build for the REPUBLICAN CONGRESS
Organise a Group in your Area.
Write for advice to the Hon. Secs., ORGANISING BUREAU, Republican Congress, 112/113 Marlboro' St., Dublin.

"We cannot conceive of a Free Ireland with a Subject Working Class."—Connolly.

No. 8. SATURDAY, JUNE 23, 1934 Price: TWOPENCE

ISGRACEFUL SCENE AT TONE PILGRIMAGE

TTACK ON BELFAST REPUBLICANS

y Order of I.R.A. Leaders

UBLICAN Congress forces had to fight for their banners at he Wolfe Tone Commemoration on Sunday last.

The most astounding and shameful feature of the scenes was that Protestant workers from Shankhill Road and Ballymacarrett had ght for their banners too—on this, their first attendance at nstown.

"Irish Independent" and "Irish of Monday last have more or curately described the scenes. We o wish to give added publicity to sgraceful attack on the Congress Nor do we wish to boast our over the lads who were ordered ack us. Our attitude to them is ned in an editorial in this issue.

trouble in Assembly Field No. 2 llins arose over the warlord of the I.R.A. leaders, which re- to allow national and working-

"Republican Congress Groups."

"Wolfe Tone Commemoration, 1934. Shankill Road, Belfast, Branch. Break the Connection with Capitalism! Connolly's Message our Ideal. On the the Workers' Republic."

"James Connolly Club, Belfast. United Irishmen of 1934."

"County Dublin Congress Groups."

The task of seizing those banners was given to a Company of Tipperary No. 3 Battalion of the I.R.A., under the com-

Shankhill Road Contingent at Connolly's Grave.

FROM SHANKHILL ROAD TO CONNOLLY'S GRAVE

ALLEGED ASSAULT IN BRAY

Woman Knocked Unconscious

That the wife of an unemployed man was refused her supply of free milk; assaulted and knocked unconscious:

These allegations are made by a Bray correspondent in a report which we give hereunder.

(From a Bray Correspondent.)

Free milk for babies is supplied to the poor from a local dairy. For a few weeks, this—a branch of one of the biggest Dairy Companies—delivered the milk to the houses. Then a new regulation was made: The poor now have to call to the local dairy. The hours are from 9 a.m. to 11 a.m. The manageress isn't always ready at 9 a.m. The poor must wait often until 9.30 a.m.. And (of course) the poor aren't allowed in the front door.. They have to go around to a shed in the back. It's free milk—for the poor, you know.

On Tuesday, June 12th, Mrs. Vicars,

ARMED RAID ON SCABS

AT DE SELBY QUARRIES

The splendid solidarity shown by the men of the Workers' Union and of the Irish Transport and General Workers' Union in their demands for a wage increase

Republican Congress, 23 June 1934
DUBLIN CITY LIBRARY & ARCHIVE

At its March 1934 convention, the IRA split. Peadar O'Donnell, George Gilmore, Mick Price and Frank Ryan all left the organisation and issued a call for a 'Congress of Republican opinion'. The new organisation, Republican Congress, published a newspaper and made links with the Irish Citizen Army and various trade unions and local groups, such as the Republican Labour Party, in Tralee. For a short period Congress generated great enthusiasm and engaged in a wide variety of agitation; on housing in Dublin, land in Achill and anti-fascism. But Congress suffered its own debilitating split in September 1934 over whether to remain a broad front or become an openly socialist party, fighting for a worker's republic. Mick Price and his supporters left the organisation, eventually joining the Labour Party, where he would be a vocal presence on the left until his death in 1944.

The most iconic image of Congress remains that of its contingent at Bodenstown in June 1934, when, led by a group of Belfast Protestants, it became embroiled in clashes with the IRA. The cause of the clashes was the refusal by Congress to agree to the IRA's demand that they march without their banners. (The Communist Party, who acceded to this demand, were allowed to march unhindered.) When Congress refused to take down their flags, fighting with IRA stewards ensued. The IRA did not attack the group because they were Protestant: despite later assertions, this was never suggested in contemporary reports. As Congress veteran Paddy Byrne put it: 'If there was sectarianism, it was of the political variety.' By 1936, Congress was defunct, though many of its activists would be central to organising Irish support for the Spanish Republic.

FIANNA FAIL'S REVENGE.

THE FIANNA FAIL GOVERNMENT is revenging itself now for " AN PHOBLACHT'S " exposure, during the newspaper strike, of the disgraceful conditions of the workers in the " Irish Press " by suppressing " AN PHOBLACHT " every week.

No reason is ever given for the suppression of " AN PHOBLACHT,"

But when pressed for a reason last week Mr. de Valera's C.I.D. censors referred to two articles, one of which had been previously published in the " Mayo News " and the other in the " Irish Press "!

THE FIANNA FAIL GOVERNMENT uses the Free State Army Military Tribunal in its campaign to drive " AN PHOBLACHT " out of existence, just as CUMANN NA nGAEDHEAL GOVERNMENT used it three years ago for the same purpose.

THE FIANNA FAIL GOVERNMENT affords armed police and military protection to Imperialists and Fascists in their treasonable campaign against the nation. It professes to be opposed to a dictatorship and Fascism, and to stand for freedom of expression.

THE FIANNA FAIL GOVERNMENT claims to be a Republican Government, yet it orders its police to seize " AN PHOBLACHT," the organ of Republicanism, and refuses to give any reason to the proprietors. Yet that Government is scrupulous as to legal forms when dealing with Imperialists and Fascists.

Towards Republicans and Republicanism the Fianna Fáil Government adopts the methods of Dictatorship and of Fascism in suppressing Republican opinion.

DOWN WITH FIANNA FAIL FASCISM!

By mid 1934, *An Phoblacht* was subject to increased police scruitiny. Gardaí read proofs of the paper before it went to press and demanded that certain articles be cut. As a result, many editions appeared with blank spaces. In addition, IRA members were now being jailed by military courts and clashes with police were common. Especially prominent in these clashes were the so-called 'Broy Harriers', former republicans, including IRA veterans, who were recruited into the Free State detective branch during 1933. Hence the rhetoric in this leaflet accusing Fianna Fail of facilitating the Blueshirts while persecuting republicans. In fact, 349 Blueshirts were sentenced by Military Courts during 1934 and de Valera's government was winning support for its policy of clamping down on both sides. In 1935, *An Phoblacht* was suppressed altogether.

DUBLIN CITY LIBRARY & ARCHIVE

Facing page: Three IRA volunteers, including Claude O'Loughlin, training in the Wicklow Mountains c. 1933.

COURTESY OF KYA RICHARDS

Frank Ryan addresses an estimated 30,000 people in Dublin's College Green in March 1932.
NATIONAL LIBRARY OF IRELAND

FRANK RYAN AND SPAIN

Frank Ryan was one of the IRA's most popular officers and had a reputation for leading from the front in street protests. He left the IRA in 1934 and became editor of the Republican Congress newspaper.

In November 1936, Ryan became leader of the Irish volunteers fighting in support of the Spanish Republic. This was not a popular position in nationalist Ireland: there was mass public support for Franco's coup, mobilised by the Catholic Church and the *Irish Independent* newspaper during the summer of 1936. The IRA's official position was that volunteers were forbidden from going to fight for either side in Spain. However, some disobeyed, with several joining Ryan. Many of the Irish Republican volunteers were also ex-IRA volunteers, having joined the Republican Congress or the Communist Party. But a few IRA volunteers also joined Eoin O'Duffy's Irish Brigade and went to fight on the fascist side, showing the diverse political nature of the IRA in the mid-1930s. Ryan himself was captured in Spain, jailed under harsh conditions and narrowly escaped death. In 1940, he was taken to Nazi Germany, where, under the protection of German Intelligence, he was reunited with IRA leader Seán Russell. Both men were returning to Ireland by submarine when Russell suffered a burst ulcer and died. Ryan returned to Germany and died in Dresden during 1944, a strange end for one of the leaders of the republican left during the 1930s.

Chapter 4

THE TWILIGHT YEARS

In 1936, the IRA was banned by the Fianna Fáil government. The next decade saw the organisation shrink in size but engage in confrontation on both sides of the border. The years of World War II saw a bleak catalogue of internments, hunger strikes, shootings and executions. There was also confusion and demoralisation after the IRA began a bombing campaign in Britain in 1939 and established links with Nazi Germany. By 1945, the organisation was at a low ebb, with many believing that the IRA was finished as a real force.

CLAMPDOWN, 1936

On 26 April 1936, the IRA shot dead John Egan, a young Dungarvan man and former member of the organisation. They accused him of being an informer, but the killing caused widespread revulsion. Coming a month after the equally unpopular killing of retired Vice-Admiral Henry Boyle-Somerville in Cork, it gave further impetus to the Fianna Fáil government's moves against the IRA. During May, Moss Twomey was captured and sentenced to three years in jail, where over a hundred IRA members were already held. During a debate in the Dáil during June, Acting Minister for Justice Gerald Boland (brother of Harry Boland and a former IRA officer) stated that 'stern action must be taken against any organisation that claims to have the power of life and death over its members or ex-members', and, referring to conflicts with the Blueshirts claimed, 'We smashed them [and] we are going to smash the others', meaning the IRA.

On 18 June, the IRA was declared an unlawful organisation and the Bodenstown commemoration prohibited. A large force of gardaí and soldiers prevented republicans from assembling, and unlike in 1931, the event did not go ahead.

Michael Conway, Irish Republican Army, Sentenced to Death.

THE CRY FOR JUSTICE.

Michael Conway, the boy hero of Tipperary, condemned to death on July 21st by the Military Tribunal set up by Cosgrave in 1931 in his last desperate effort to destroy the soldiers of the Irish Republic, and which is to-day being used by De Valera for the same purpose.

The verdict of Conway's so-called trial was dictated by Cabinet Minister McEntee a month previous, June 21st, from a public platform in Lucan. Free State Officer Bennet responded worthily to the dictation of his renegade master when he read the death sentence on Michael Conway, July 21st.

Conscious of his innocence of any crime save that of loving his country and striving as Emmet and Pearse and Mellows had striven, to secure its freedom, Michael Conway defiantly faced the Norburys who sat in judgement on him, proudly proclaiming his allegiance to the Army of the Irish Republic.

Calmly, bravely, with the courage inspired by the justice of the Cause he served Michael Conway heard his death sentence, Unfalteringly he faced the hangman's rope—willingly offering his young life in vindication of his Republican faith.

But the Soul of Ireland Revolted Against the Martyrdom of the fearless young Hero.

De Valera and his co-ercionist colleagues realised that in sentencing Michael Conway to the gallows—they but hastened their own downfall as British Cabinet Ministers in Ireland.

***THEIR WAY OUT*—PENAL SERVITUDE FOR LIFE FOR THE HEROIC TIPPERARY LAD.**

People of Tipperary—People of Ireland—the cry FOR JUSTICE for Michael Conway calls to you from his convict cell.

JUSTICE FOR MICHAEL CONWAY

Justice demands freedom for the young soldier who so nobly, so generously, so fearlessly faced death for you and for Ireland.

DEMAND MICHAEL CONWAY'S RELEASE

Leaflet calling for the release of Michael Conway DUBLIN CITY LIBRARY & ARCHIVE

Michael Conway, from Clonmel, Co. Tipperary, was arrested, tried and found guilty of the Egan murder before the Military Tribunal during July and sentenced to death by hanging, to be carried out on 12 August 1936. This was the first death sentence passed under Fianna Faíl against an IRA activist. But the evidence against Conway was based on one fingerprint and he had refused to recognise the court. Furthermore, during June 1936, while being heckled by republicans during a public meeting, Fianna Fáil minister Seán MacEntee had stated that the gardaí had captured the murderer of John Egan and that they would 'hang him'. After appeals that this had prejudiced the case, the death sentence against Conway was commuted and he was sentenced to life in prison. As this leaflet shows, his imprisonment remained a focus for republican campaigning. In May 1938, he was one of a number of republicans released as a gesture on the inauguration of the new president of the Free State, Douglas Hyde. Conway returned to IRA activity and became a training officer during preparations for the bombing campaign in Britain. He was shot and wounded by gardai in 1940 and then interned until 1944. On release he was involved in the IRA leadership in the post-War period. Conway joined the Cistercian Order in 1950 and remained a monk until his death in 1997.

SEÁN RUSSELL

Seán Russell was one of the longest serving members of the inter-War IRA leadership. He joined the Irish Volunteers in 1913, fought in the Easter Rising and was on the staff of the IRA's General Headquarters by 1921. In 1927, he became Quartermaster General and as a result, knew every IRA unit and officer in Ireland. He had shown little interest in the various debates that had riven the IRA during the 1930s but was personally popular within its ranks. During 1936, Russell visited the United States. He had visited there once before, during 1932, and built up a rapport with Joe McGarrity. During this tour Russell was convinced by McGarrity of the necessity of a campaign targeting partition, to be waged in Britain itself. While in America, Russell sent a letter to the German ambassador in Washington, signalling his willingness to cooperate with the Germans at a future date. Russell seems to have thought that Britain's enemy could be Ireland's friend. McGarrity's Clan na Gael network in the US had contact with German agents from the mid-1930s.

Between 1936 and 1938, Russell had become commited to the idea of an IRA campaign in Britain, inspired somewhat by the American Fenian 'dynamite' campaign of the 1880s. McGarrity believed that de Valera might tolerate a campaign that avoided action in the Free State itself. However, Russell found the majority of the IRA leadership distrustful of his plans and suspicious of his relationship with McGarrity.

Russell was disciplined for allegedly witholding finance from the IRA and dismissed as Quartermaster General. In fact, Russell did advise McGarrity not to send money or arms to Ireland until a commitment to a new campaign had been secured.

After Moss Twomey's arrest, Seán MacBride became IRA Chief of Staff: his tenure was short-lived and in 1937, he was replaced by Tom Barry, one of the most famous commanders of the Civil War. Barry promised a campaign in the North, beginning with a raid in Armagh, but this was aborted, due, it was claimed, to information leaking to the public. Barry stood aside for Mick Fitzpatrick to become the IRA's leader but by 1938, Russell had accumulated enough support to take the top position himself. Russell's policy appealed to young IRA volunteers who felt that the organisation had spent too

Ms 17,485 1936–38

His Excellency, Dr. Hans Luther,
German Ambassador to the United States,
Washington, D. C.

Your Excellency:

The government of the Irish Republic desires me to call to your attention a news item reporting refusal by the Irish "Free State" government of landing rights in our country for your international air service. As special Envoy to the United States and Quartermaster General of the Irish Republican Army, I am asked to express to you on behalf of my government the sincere regret of our people that the German Nation, in return for past friendships to us, should be refused a right apparently conceded without question to England, the traditional enemy of the Irish race.

The "Free State" government depends for its very existence on the British parliament whose puppet it is, and the action taken must be viewed as the carrying out of the directions of the master rather than as the expression of the free will of the people from whom it pretends to derive its authority.

The Government of the Republic and the people of Ireland are, and will continue to be, mindful of the debt they owe to the German people and their government for assistance in a fight calculated to rid our country of the foreign rule that now uses the "Free State" as its domestic agent. That this is true may be attested by the fact that our Chief of Staff, many senior officers and our best men are in jail and that those who would prepare the Army and the people of the Republic for a successful termination to our centuries of struggle to be free have brought on themselves the undying enmity and the ceaseless persecution of that which, while it protests to have kept the faith with Pearse and Casement, is so belied with its actions that nobody is in doubt that the future will mirror the past.

It was not for such an end that we enlisted your aid in the past.

Ms 17, 4

-2-

It was because we sought then to end such rule that we might be free fr treason at home and tyranny from abroad. We ask that you believe this we would have you believe, too, that Ireland a nation is disposed to, shall be glad of the arrival of the time when she may, make returns to friends in Germany for their valued assistance in the early days of th present phase of our fight.

With esteem for you and your people, I beg to remain, on be of the government and people of the Irish Republicm

Sincerely and gratefully yours,

(Signed) SEAN RUSSELL

Special Envoy of Ireland to the
Quartermaster General of the I.R

Oct 25 —
1936

much time talking and he also enticed a number of veterans, such as Patrick McGrath and Jim O'Donovan, out of retirement.

The campaign, based on O'Donovan's so-called 'S-Plan' (developed originally in 1922), would involve a series of attacks along the Border, followed by a wave of bombings in England. On 28 November 1938, three IRA members (J.J. Reynolds, J.J. Kelly and Charles McCafferty) were killed in an explosion at Castlefin, Co. Donegal, whilst making preparations for the bombings. But operations went ahead as planned the following day: customs posts were destroyed by the IRA at six locations along the border.

1st December 1938

Dear Mr McGarrity

In your last letter to Moss you said I was a poor correspondent. You are right I know, but up to the present I had but promises only to give. Now it is different. On Tuesday night last we launched our campaign. We have as you see by enclosed newspaper clippings, started, as you and your council suggested, in the North. With the exception of a very sad accident, what we did was thoroughly done. The accident, for accidents and casualties we will have, in no way took from the operations, on the contrary it added considerably to it and to our advantage. It helps, firstly because three men lost their lives in attempting to destroy the huts, secondly and of no lesser importance, our men on the other points of the border carried on with their work and completed their jobs fifteen

Letter from Seán Russell to McGarrity, 1 December 1938
COURTESY OF THE NATIONAL LIBRARY OF IRELAND

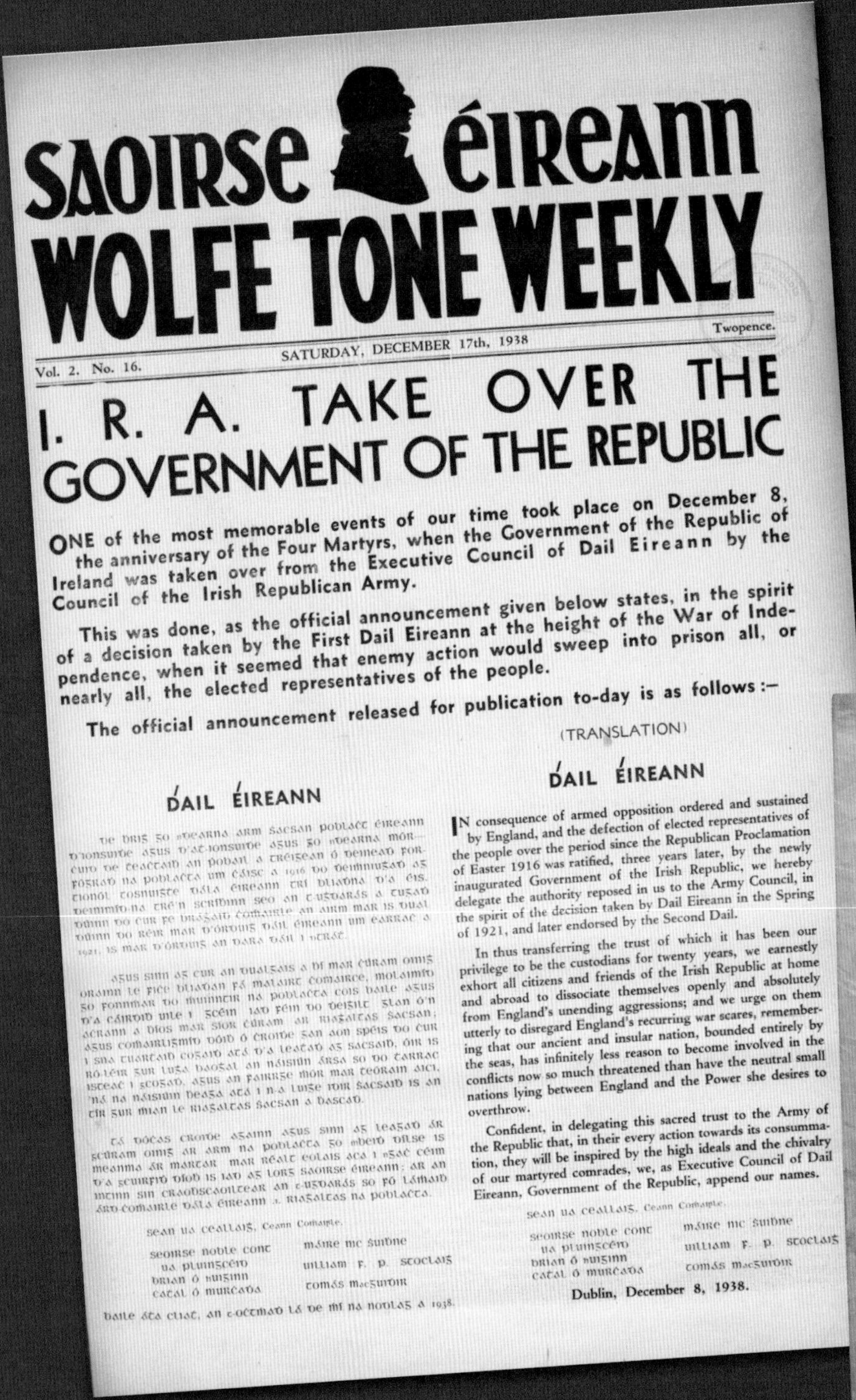

SAOIRSE ÉIREANN
WOLFE TONE WEEKLY

SATURDAY, DECEMBER 17th, 1938

Vol. 2. No. 16. Twopence.

I. R. A. TAKE OVER THE GOVERNMENT OF THE REPUBLIC

ONE of the most memorable events of our time took place on December 8, the anniversary of the Four Martyrs, when the Government of the Republic of Ireland was taken over from the Executive Council of Dail Eireann by the Council of the Irish Republican Army.

This was done, as the official announcement given below states, in the spirit of a decision taken by the First Dail Eireann at the height of the War of Independence, when it seemed that enemy action would sweep into prison all, or nearly all, the elected representatives of the people.

The official announcement released for publication to-day is as follows :—

DÁIL ÉIREANN

De bris go ndearna arm Sacsan Poblact Éireann d'ionsuide agus d'at-ionsuide agus go ndearna mór-cuid de teactaib an pobail a tréigean ó deireadh fógrad na Poblacta um Cáisc a 1916 do deimniugad ag tionól tosnuiste Dála Éireann trí bliadna d'a éis, deimnímíd-na tré'n scríbinn seo an t-ugdarás a tugad dúinn do cur fé brágaid Comairle an Airm mar is dual dúinn do réir mar d'órduig Dáil Éireann um earrac a 1921, is mar d'órduig an Dara Dáil i ntrát.

Agus sinn ag cur an dualgais a bí mar cúram oinig orainn le fice bliadan fá malairt comairce, molaimíd go fonnmar do muinntir na Poblacta cois baile agus d'a cáirdib uile i gcéin iad féin do deigilt glan ó'n achrann a bíos mar síor cúram ar Riagaltas Sacsan; agus comairligmíd dóib ó croide gan aon spéis do cur i sna tuartaib cogaid atá d'a leatad ag Sacsaib, óir is ró-léir gur luga baogal an náisiún ársa so do tarrac isteac i gcogad, agus an fairrge mór mar teórain aici, 'ná na náisiúin beaga atá i n-a luige idir Sacsaib is an tír gur mian le Riagaltas Sacsan a bascad.

Tá dócas croide againn agus sinn ag leagad ár gcúram oinig ar Arm na Poblacta go mbeid dílse is meanma ár martar mar réalt eolais aca i ngac céim d'a gcuirfid díob is iad ag lorg Saoirse Éireann; ar an intinn sin craobscaoiltear an t-ugdarás so fó lámaib Árd-Comairle Dála Éireann .i. Riagaltas na Poblacta.

Seán Ua Ceallaig, Ceann Comairle.

Seoirse Noble Cont Ua Pluinncéid — Máire Mic Suibne
Brian Ó hUiginn — William F. P. Stoclaig
Catal Ó Murcada — Tomás MacGuidir

Baile Átha Cliat, an t-octmad lá de mí na Nodlag a 1938.

(TRANSLATION)

DÁIL ÉIREANN

IN consequence of armed opposition ordered and sustained by England, and the defection of elected representatives of the people over the period since the Republican Proclamation of Easter 1916 was ratified, three years later, by the newly inaugurated Government of the Irish Republic, we hereby delegate the authority reposed in us to the Army Council, in the spirit of the decision taken by Dail Eireann in the Spring of 1921, and later endorsed by the Second Dail.

In thus transferring the trust of which it has been our privilege to be the custodians for twenty years, we earnestly exhort all citizens and friends of the Irish Republic at home and abroad to dissociate themselves openly and absolutely from England's unending aggressions; and we urge on them utterly to disregard England's recurring war scares, remembering that our ancient and insular nation, bounded entirely by the seas, has infinitely less reason to become involved in the conflicts now so much threatened than have the neutral small nations lying between England and the Power she desires to overthrow.

Confident, in delegating this sacred trust to the Army of the Republic that, in their every action towards its consummation, they will be inspired by the high ideals and the chivalry of our martyred comrades, we, as Executive Council of Dail Eireann, Government of the Republic, append our names.

Seán Ua Ceallaig, Ceann Comairle.

Seoirse Noble Cont Ua Pluinncéid — Máire Mic Suibne
Brian Ó hUiginn — William F. P. Stoclaig
Catal Ó Murcada — Tomás MacGuidir

Dublin, December 8, 1938.

Wolfe Tone Weekly,
17 December 1938

COURTESY OF THE NATIONAL LIBRARY OF IRELAND

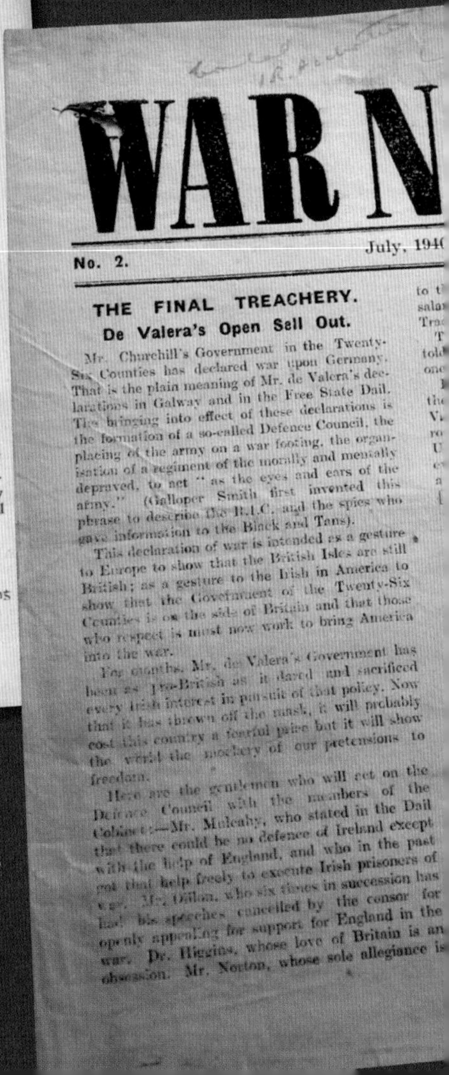

WAR N

No. 2. July, 194

THE FINAL TREACHERY.
De Valera's Open Sell Out.

Mr. Churchill's Government in the Twenty-Six Counties has declared war upon Germany. That is the plain meaning of Mr. de Valera's declarations in Galway and in the Free State Dail. The bringing into effect of these declarations is the formation of a so-called Defence Council, the placing of the army on a war footing, the organisation of a regiment of the morally and mentally depraved, to act "as the eyes and ears of the army." (Galloper Smith first invented this phrase to describe the R.I.C. and the spies who gave information to the Black and Tans).

This declaration of war is intended as a gesture to Europe to show that the British Isles are still British; as a gesture to the Irish in America to show that the Government of the Twenty-Six Counties is on the side of Britain and that those who respect is must now work to bring America into the war.

For months, Mr. de Valera's Government has been as pro-British as it dared and sacrificed every Irish interest in pursuit of that policy. Now that it has thrown off the mask, it will probably cost this country a fearful price but it will show the world the mockery of our pretensions to freedom.

Here are the gentlemen who will act on the Defence Council with the members of the Cabinet:—Mr. Mulcahy, who stated in the Dail that there could be no defence of Ireland except with the help of England, and who in the past got that help freely to execute Irish prisoners of war. Mr. Dillon, who six times in succession has had his speeches cancelled by the censor for openly appealing for support for England in the war. Dr. Higgins, whose love of Britain is an obsession. Mr. Norton, whose sole allegiance is

War News,
July 1940

NATIONAL ARCHIVES OF IRELAND

LEGITIMACY

On 8 December 1938, it was announced that seven TDs elected as part of the Second Dáil in 1921, who had refused to support either the Treaty or Fianna Fáil after 1926, had met and transferred their authority to the IRA Army Council. This was at Russell's request and as far as those involved were concerned, it conferred governmental authority on the IRA leadership. Of the seven signatories, only Tom Maguire had been active in the IRA, though Mary MacSwiney was well known as a republican agitator. The other five, however, were marginal figures and J.J. O'Kelly (Scelig), Chairman of the 'Dáil' and the author of this statement, was one of the most right-wing republicans and a virulent anti-Semite. The event was announced in the *Wolfe Tone Weekly*, edited by Brian O'Higgins, another one of the signatories to the statement. This 'handover' has acquired great significance for some republicans. Russell believed that it gave the IRA the authority to launch the British campaign which began on 16 January 1939. Targets as diverse as power stations, post offices and cinemas were bombed. By the summer over a hundred republicans were in jail in England while a similar number of Irish people had been deported.

WS

Price 1d.

WAR NEWS

The IRA began its publication of *War News* during July 1939, arguing that as a campaign was now being waged outside Ireland, it was more important than ever that the propaganda of the government be countered. Seán McNeela from Mayo was involved in its production and also in the operation of the IRA's Dublin radio transmitter (which broadcast on Sunday, Wednesday and Friday nights) until he was captured in late December 1939. For a while, the magazine was printed in Galway and there were separate editions at various stages in Belfast, edited by Tarlach Ó hUid, and in Cork. The production quality of the newspaper varied. It was distributed surreptitiously by hand or post: many copies were sent unsolicited to individuals. It was also left in bus stations and cinemas with instructions to 'pass it on'. Its reports on the 'expeditionary force' in Britain were often fantastical, claiming that IRA members had sunk submarines or had guided German warplanes to their targets. By 1943, it had effectively ceased publication, replaced in Belfast with *Republican News*, edited by John Graham, one of a number of Protestant recruits to the IRA in that city.

HUMPHREYS PAPERS, UCD ARCHIVES

BARNES AND McCORMICK, 1940

On 7 February 1940, 32-year-old Peter Barnes and 29-year-old James McCormick were hanged in Birmingham, having been convicted of involvement in the IRA bombing in Coventry that had killed five and injured over fifty people on 25 August 1939. The bomb is thought to have been meant for a power station but was left in a bicycle carrier-basket in Coventry city centre. The IRA's campaign had caused considerable disruption in England during the spring and summer of 1939: two people had been killed but, until Coventry, large-scale civilian casualties had been avoided.

McCormick, originally from Mullingar, was the IRA's commander in Coventry: he was tried under the pseudonym 'Richards'. Both he and Barnes proclaimed their innocence until the end (and the gardaí suspected Belfast IRA members of responsibility).

There were widespread protests in Ireland at the executions, with flags flown at half-mast and sporting fixtures cancelled: the Fianna Fáil-supporting *Irish Press* gave extensive coverage to the campaign for a reprieve. De Valera's government appealed for clemency on the basis that the executions would damage Anglo-Irish relations and fuel resentment in Irish America. Fianna Fáil TD Martin Corry expressed the hope that, 'Hitler would blow the British to hell' after the hangings. Ironically, there was to be a marked difference in the reaction of the Irish government and press to executions of IRA members carried out in the 26 Counties itself. (In July 1969, the bodies of Barnes and McCormick were returned to Ireland for burial and their funerals were the occasion of a major republican mobilisation.)

The Hunger-Strikers are Dying

Seàn MacEntee has stated on behalf of the "Free State Government" that they are not concerned with the fate of the prisoners. He accuses Mrs. Tom Clarke, Lord Mayor of Dublin of "sordid cynicism" because she leads the Irish people in their demand for political treatment for Republican prisoners.

FORCE DE VALERA TO SAVE THEIR LIVES !

Seàn MacEntee has repeatedly apologised for once serving the Republic. **Micky Traynor of Belfast is giving his life for the Republic.** Are you with MacEntee or Micky Traynor ?

FIFTY DAYS ON HUNGER-STRIKE.

The heroic six are in an extremely dangerous condition. Partially blinded, wasted and vomiting.
John Plunkett, Thomas M'Curtain, Jack M'Neela, Thomas Grogan, Tony D'Arcy and Micky Traynor, await the terrible death to which De Valera leaves them.

Voice Your Demand ! Save Them before it is Too Late !

Republican leaflet demanding action to save the hunger strikers MACENTEE PAPERS, UCD ARCHIVES

HUNGER STRIKE

During March 1940, IRA prisoners in Dublin's Mountjoy jail began a hunger strike, to demand that they be treated as prisoners of war. As their condition worsened, there were calls for the government to concede to at least some of the prisoners' demands. De Valera was strongly urged to resist the strike by Gerald Boland, Minister for Justice. Boland told the Dáil on 5 January that year, that a lot of his old comrades '. . . had unconsciously become criminals . . . if crimes were committed, the people who committed them could not be called anything but criminals . . . I don't care whether he has been a friend or comrade of mine in the past or not, it is all the same to me if he commits a crime, he should be made amenable for it'. While press censorship ensured that many of the protests relating to the strike went unreported, the cabinet decided to make no concessions to the strikers. On 17 April, Tony D'Arcy died, followed two days later by Seán McNeela. The strike ended in confusion.

A week later the IRA bombed Garda HQ at Dublin Castle and shortly afterwards two detectives were ambushed and badly wounded while guarding diplomatic mail. In a speech broadcast on Radio Éireann, de Valera warned that while the government had shown what he called 'excessive patience' towards the IRA, now, 'The policy of patience has failed and is over . . . Danger now threatens from within as well as from without . . . I warn those now planning new crimes against the nation that they will not be allowed to continue their policy of sabotage.' The scene was set for war.

"We have loved him in life, let us not forget him in death."—St. Ambrose.

Jesus, Mary and Joseph, may I breathe forth my soul in peace with you. 100 days.

Jesus, meek and humble of Heart, make my heart like unto Thine. 300 days.

OF YOUR CHARITY
Pray for the repose of the soul of
Sean McNeela,
Claggan House, Ballycroy, Co. Mayo,
Who died on the 19th April, 1940,
At St. Bricin's Hospital, Dublin, after 55 days' Hunger Strike.
Aged 25 Years.
R. I. P.

Thy Will be done, O Lord, Thy Will be done!
We bless Thy Name and welcome this our cross.
From rising unto setting of the sun
O, help us bear the anguish and the loss!
Thro' all the wakeful hours of every night
One thought give to our minds:—"The Lord knows best."
And then this blessing when our souls take flight—
To meet our martyr in Thy Home of Rest.

HUMPHREYS PAPERS, UCD ARCHIVES

'FOR THE REPUBLIC' 1940

During the War years, de Valera became as much a hate figure for the IRA as Cosgrave had been before him. The Fianna Fáil government interned over 500 IRA suspects and jailed a further 600 members of the IRA under the Offences Against the State Act. This poster lists the names of republicans who had died since 1936: Seán Glynn from Limerick was found hanging in Arbour Hill prison that year. Republicans blamed his death on ill-treatment by the authorities. Peter McCarthy was shot dead by gardaí in Dublin during 1937, the first IRA volunteer to be killed by state forces since de Valera came to power. McNeela and D'Arcy died on hunger strike during 1940, McGrath and Harte were executed the same year and John Joe Kavanagh was shot during an attempted escape from Cork prison.

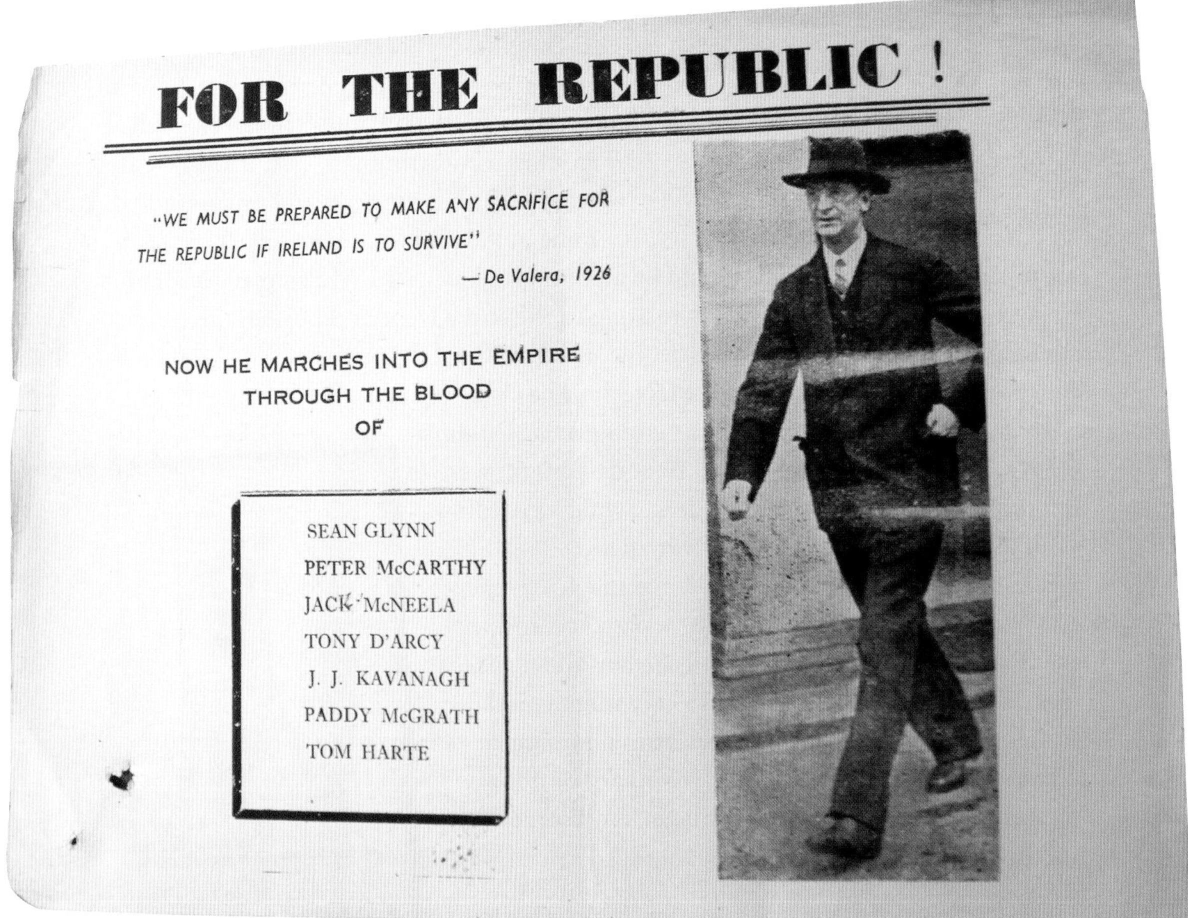

NATIONAL ARCHIVES OF IRELAND

'GERMANY AND IRELAND', 1940

During 1940, the dramatist George Bernard Shaw published an appeal to Irish nationalists, including the IRA, to put aside their past differences and support Britain against Germany. The IRA rejected his advice in *Ireland's Answer*, published in July 1940. Their reply argued that the Nazis had no designs on Ireland other than to help it free itself and that if the Germans landed in Ireland they would come as 'liberators'. Curragh IRA internee Sean Mulready remembered his shock when hundreds of his fellow inmates celebrated the collapse of France in June 1940: 'The whole camp just went berserk, berserk. The prisoners ran around in sheer delirious joy that the Germans had defeated and were about to occupy the cradle of modern, militant republicanism.'

GERMANY AND IRELAND.

" The Third Reich, as the guardian and energising force of European policy is inevitably interested in the continuity of these principles of national freedom enunciated in the past by Germany and the other Great European Powers and if, in the prosecution of the present war, German forces should land in Ireland, they will land, as they did in 1916, as friends and liberators of the Irish people.

" Germany desires in Ireland neither territory nor the fruit of economic penetration: her reward for any help that she may accord, directly or indirectly, is the freedom of civilised nations from the intolerable yoke of Britain and Britain's satellites and the reconstruction of a free and progressive Europe.

THE PERVERTS GOVERNMENT.

" Why is it in the face of the known and proven attitude of Germany that Mr. de Valera while sprinkling himself and his followers with the blood of the Irish Republican Cabinet of 1916, reverses their policy, denies their wisdom, attacks their patriotism and their honesty ? Every one of them according to Mr. de Valera (and Lord Craigavon) was a Dermot Mac Murrough, for not only did they invite German aid for Ireland, but boasted of it and as recently as 1922 Mr. de Valera was still asking for German support. German aid less valuable now than it was in 1916, because the Kaiser has been succeeded by Herr Hitler or because modern Germany has proven that she can and will smash Britain here. Just as she has already smashed her from Spain to the Balkans and from Iceland to Africa. For twenty-five years Mr. de Valera has claimed to be a Separatist and a Republican and has sworn solemnly that he kept the faith of Tone, Pearse and Casement. Why then is it that when the Republic could have been achieved almost without the firing of a shot, Mr. de Valera finds that a Republic is not desirable and that Tone and Casement were really traitors ? Why do Mr. de Valera, Lord Craigavon and Mr. Churchill, adopt exactly the same attitude to Irish Republicanism ? Why does Mr. de Valera appoint to his Government ignorant and wilful men whose allegiance is to Britain ? Why are the key positions in the Civil Service staffed with Britishers ? Why is the Defence Council composed solely of men who have publicly and repeatedly advised the Irish people to support Britain in this war ? Why is Mr. de Valera's own newspaper so pro-British that it published a series of articles on Germany written by an American—articles that were so vile that they were boycotted even in England ? Why are the key positions in the newspaper held by a succession of British hacks from Editors to sports writers? Why have we the British Censorship, the British A.R.P., the British Blackout, the secret deals with the British police and the British Government? Why, in short, i[illegible]e present Government of the Twenty-Six Counties, more meanly malevolently pro-British than Cosgrace when he was murdering Irish prisoners or the Redmond and Dillon party when they were cheering in the House of Commons for the murder of the 1916 leaders ? Why, in short, is the Government of the Twenty-Six Counties doing exactly the same things in the same way and with the help of the same people as the Government of 1914 ? The same class of mugs (sometimes the same mugs) are guarding the bridges as in 1914-1915. The same class of foxy English Army Officers and Shopkeepers with a little money to lose are advising people to join the British Forces. The special police of that date are the Local Security Force (Carey Column) of to-day.

THE ANSWER.

" The answer to all these questions is obvious—Mr. de Valera was never sincere in anything. When appealing to the people to elect his party to power he promised :—

To establish the Republic.
To eliminate unemployment.
To reduce Taxation.
To purify public administration.
To restore the Irish Language.
To build up a defence force and a mercantile fleet.

What he did was:—

He finally disestablished the Republic of 1916 (in so far as his Free State Parliament could do it).
He increased unemployment.
He increased taxation.
He appointed to the administration ruffians that even Cosgrave rejected.
He insisted that Irish was necessary for boiler cleaners but not for teachers and propagandists
He instituted an Army composed mainly of wastrels and ex-tommies armed with English guns.
His public life has been an unbroken series of broken promises, of hypocritical patriotism, of weakness masked by obstinacy and poisoned by fear.

SIGNED ON BEHALF OF THE GOVERNMENT OF THE REPUBLIC.

P. FLEMING, Runaidhe."

July 25, 1940.

Ireland's Answer, July 1940

NATIONAL ARCHIVES OF IRELAND

The general tone of the IRA's *War News* was often pro-German and, on occasion, anti-Semitic. In some ways this reflected popular prejudice: pro-German sentiment was far from confined to the IRA in the early years of the War, but there had also been a notably right-wing drift to the IRA's politics in the late 1930s. Both Peadar O'Flaherty and Jim O'Donovan, senior IRA members from the late 1930s, were right-wing in their political thinking. During 1940 two of the IRA's leading northern officers, Sean McCaughey and Charlie McGlade, approached the former Blueshirt leader (and Nazi sympathiser) Eoin O'Duffy and asked if he was willing to become an intelligence operative for the organisation.

By 1940, Sean Russell was involved in planning a role for the IRA in German invasion plans for Britain, which necessarily involved landings in Ireland. As a result, he went to Germany, reaching Berlin in the summer of that year. There, he was given diplomatic privileges and allowed access to German military camps. Among those with whom he had discussions was the Nazi Foreign Minister, Joachim von Ribbentrop.

4 WAR NEWS

The British Are Still Here

Are We The Only People To Accept Occupation?

THERE are many people in Ireland to-day, conscious of the country's tradition of freedom, recognising the worth of this tradition in the past, yet unable to see that at this moment the country's need is as great as ever and the opportunity greater. The flame of revolution against English rule and influence has burned since the first English-paid soldier trod here and in the hearts of right-thinking people it has warded off despair or led to martyrdom. It has been for all these centuries and generations the most constant thing in the national life—matched in constancy only by one thing—England's greed and enmity to us.

Never in all our centuries of acquaintance with it have this greed and enmity changed, never relaxed or grown old. It has seeped through the nation, marking the baser fabric with its dye generation after generation, until the point was reached where a definite proportion of the population was regarded by English politicians as loyal to the crown. By plantation, bribery, coercion, blackmail, teaching and all the weapons which England uses so dexterously this had been brought about. At last, unwilling to continue the losses of the war in Ireland, Britain's leaders decided to treat with the Irish, and, remembering their civil garrison here, they felt secure enough to remove the military one.

NEW WEAPONS.

The fight then went on a different footing; in the North it was won immediately and the border came into being. In the Free State it was more complex, but it was there too, as far as it could be won. The civil garrison saw to that. A nationless band of place-hunters, money-grabbers and hangers-on, they carried on the work of the R.I.C. and the British Secret Service without a halt, and still do. Their greatest ambition is complete union with England; their greatest fear, a German victory in the war. They are everywhere. For twenty years they have walked in and out of Leinster House, some with portfolios. Vote-seeking, they have played on the age-old desires of the people, rehashing for new occasions the words they used when (they say now) they were foolish and over-enthusiastic young men. Personal ambition has betrayed them and their country's betrayal is not too much for them to stoop to.

THE CHANGE.

When Mr. de Valera took office the English man-in-the-street feared that he might proclaim a Republic; the civil garrison of England here were frightened for a few weeks and the old hope of Ireland shone bright in the faces of the Republicans who remembered the better speeches of the man of Boland's Mill. Freemasons, Jews and ordinary traitors opposed him with their hands on their cash. They nearly won, but they might never have feared; it was not long before they began to see that he was not the Republican he seemed. Gradually he became a friend of theirs and their Press acclaimed him whenever it could. Not that **they** had changed—nothing so hopeful—but Fianna Fail's torch had dimmed in the smoke of London and Mr. de Valera had become a politican instead of a patriot.

The Cosgrave regime died, just as last year's leaves died, because new leaves were on the way to do the same work in their place. Gradually taking up the strings of Mr. Cosgrave's policy, improving where he was allowed by London, Mr. de Valera has outdone Cumann na nGaedheal in dealing with the civil garrison's problems, the greatest of which has always been the I.R.A.

THE BETRAYAL.

Mr. de Valera's hopes for Ireland become more and more cloudy at a time when the people cry out for a definite word; swaddled in phrases, the word "Freedom" comes into his speeches occasionally, shyly, not certain that it ought to be there at all. It is a long time back to Easter week and instead of a pike or a rifle we find a cheque-book in his hands—the national cheque-book. With the people's money he has bought off what opposition could be so meanly influenced and has hired an army to deal with the rest. Parliamentary opposition has become a rite performed to the music of clinking cash and Republicans are betrayed into the mercy of armed guards and quicklimed graves.

All this is merely some of the detail, the figures in a sum, the answer to which is that the people have judged and the truth of their old faith in the national destiny shows up the canting propaganda, the lies, the subterfuges, of this stale, canting administration. The heart of the nation strains back to the path of freedom; Republicanism is riper, more virile than ever, and **our day** is here.

De Valera accused of consorting with Freemasons and Jews, *War News*, February 1940

NATIONAL ARCHIVES OF IRELAND

There were a variety of views on the war within republican ranks and support for Russell did not equal being pro-fascist. Some of those involved in the bombing campaign in Britain had been active in the movement against Oswald Mosley's Blackshirts in the mid-1930s. Jim O'Regan, one of those jailed during the campaign, had actually fought with the International Brigades in Spain. During 1940, the leadership of Cumann na mBan wrote to the IRA to express their worry about the desire of many republicans to have German forces land in Ireland. In this letter they also express disapproval of the bombing campaign and complain of being ignored by the IRA.

Cumann na mBan letter to the IRA, June 1940
HUMPHREYS PAPERS, UCD ARCHIVES

concern to us that we are in ignorance of the policy or general plans or means which Oglaigh na hEireann intends to pursue.

Of late, our chief work has been concerned with those who may be called casualties of the struggle. We endeavoured to aid those on Hunger-strike in the two recent strikes: we called together and helped to work the McCormack & Barnes Committee, and we assist The Irish National Prisoners' Aid Society, which we founded.

But some of us have worked with lessened enthusiasm; provided we are re-assured on certain points we will all go to work wholeheartedly with renewed enthusiasm on increased activities.

<u>Points on which information is wanted.</u> 1. The chief reason we wish to see your C/S is to get information about the I.R.A. attitude in the present crisis. We do not, of course, want to be told any of your military plans or proposals. (But you must realise how impossible it is to do any publicity on your behalf when we have not got the slightest idea of your intentions. This is not the time for vague general appeals. People want specific instructions). According to the newspapers there would appear to be co-operation between the Germans and the I.R.A.. And many unthinking Republicans are most anxious to invite the Germans over here. But we do not think that a responsible body like the

3.

I.R.A. would be so foolish, from a military point of view, as to invite the Germans to our country. A t present the Germans are fighting Ireland's battle, and the battle of all oppressed nations within the Empire, in the best possible place. The collapse of the British Empire will result automatically in the freedom of Ireland, provided the Irish people are prepared and organised to maintain that freedom. The collapse of the Empire cannot be hastened one iota by turning Ireland into an international battle-ground and thereby saving England again from the necessity of fighting for her life on her own territory. Too long has Ireland suffered the agony and torture of a war in her own country in the effort to force England to release her clutches. Now we can thank God that we have lived to see the day that a foe ,(powerful enough to crush the British Empire) has undertaken and steadily advanced in the task. Our interference at this stage would probably serve the Empire's interest as it might prove an inducement to America to enter the war on the side of England (Irish Republicans should organise and prepare to defend the coming de facto Republic).

In view of the foregoing we would be glad to have you confirm that it is not your intention to make a cockpit of this country, when it is obvious that the desired result can be obtained without doing so

~~xxxxxxxxx~~ doing so

2. Another point - we were led t

4.

believe that the freedom of Ireland would be achieved by the campaign in England. This we very much doubted at the time. That campaign has now completely fizzled out, leaving as its only results two Irish soldiers in quicklime graves, three other soldiers blown to atoms in Donegal and hundreds serving what amounts to life sentences and enduring inhuman tortures in English jails: in addition, the many homes broken up, means of livelihood lost, and England and De Valera given warning so that they could deal drastically with the Republican movement before England had b ecome deeply involved in difficulties.

In view of the complete collapse of the policy of the army in the last two years we are very anxious to know what you expect from the Irish people and what the Irish people can expect from you.

3. If we are to do propaganda we need facts. These were always given in the days when Cumann na mBan carried on effective propaganda work. You state that propaganda and publicity is our work, but you surely must see that it is impossible for us to do publicity when we do not know what your attitude is to any aspect of Irish political life or what your present policy is.

For instance, it was impossible for us to counteract Fianna Fail propaganda concerning the Holles Street activity when

5.

EXECUTIONS, 1940–41

On 16 August 1940, two garda detectives, Patrick McKeown and Richard Hyland, were killed during a gun battle with the IRA in Rathgar. Among those captured at the scene were Patrick McGrath and Thomas Harte. McGrath was an IRA veteran, who had fought in 1916. He had been released from prison after a hunger strike during December 1939. Harte, from Lurgan, was just 20 years of age. Both men were tried rapidly by a court of army officers and sentenced to death. They were executed on 6 September, the first such sentences carried out under a Fianna Fáil government. Under emergency leglislation, IRA suspects could be tried by military courts, which were non-jury and had the power to impose the death penalty for a range of offences.

WAR NEWS

No. 7. SEPTEMBER 28 1940.

REPUBLIC MOURNS MURDERED SOLDIERS

| | Lieut.-General P. McGrath | |

PATRICK McGRATH joined the Irish Volunteers on their inception in 1913. He took part in the 1916 Rising under P. Clancy, who was in command at Ch- urch Street Bridge. After the Rising, Mc Grath was interned at Frongoch, being released at Christmas 1916. He took an active part in the re-organisation of the Volunteers and was on Headquart ers staff of the Army of the Irish Re- public.

During the Tan War, he took part in many important engagements, including the attack on Lord French and the rescue of Robert Barton. After a raid on the B. & I. Steam Packet Co. he received two wounds, one in the arm and the other above the heart. This bul- let lodged behind the main artery, and Patrick McGrath carried that English

(continued on page 4.)

| | Staff-Capt. T. Harte | |

THOMAS HARTE was born in Lurgan, Armagh, and when the ultimatum of the Irish Republic to England had ex- pired, he was one of the Expeditionary Force which proceeded to England to carry on the war against that country. He was eventually arrested by the ene- my and deported.

Back in Ireland, he was attached to Headquarters Staff under Patrick Mc Grath, and he carried on the work of the Republic until his arrest on August 16th, 1940. During the battle in Rathgar on that day, he was wound- ed. Though only twenty four years of age, he bore himself with the same indomitable courage as his veteran com rade, when he faced the Free State firing squad on September 6th, 1940

In Proud Memory of

Richard Goss

(Divisional O.C., I.R.A.)

DUNDALK, CO. LOUTH

who was shot to death at Portlaoighse Prison, August 9, 1941, for the crime of being a faithful soldier of the Republic of Ireland. He met his death with courage and Christian fortitude.

Imeasg Laoċra Éireann go raiḃ a anam i ḃFlaiṫeas Dé

Goss execution, 1941
HUMPHREYS PAPERS, UCD

War News, September 1940
NATIONAL ARCHIVES OF IRELAND

THE GOSS EXECUTION

On 9 August 1941, IRA man Richard Goss was executed at Portlaoise Prison for wounding a soldier. Goss had taken part in the robbery of banks in Oldcastle and Castlepollard, stealing £1,300 during June that year. He and his unit had hidden out at the family home of Barney Casey (killed in the Curragh the previous December). When gardaí, backed up by soldiers, raided the house, there was a shoot-out and a soldier was hit, though there was disagreement at Goss's trial (by military court) about whether he had, in fact, fired the shots which injured the soldier. However, the military court had the power to impose the death sentence for resisting arrest, and in this case, it did. From Dundalk, Goss had been a strong supporter of Seán Russell's leadership bid in 1938 and had been active in the bombing campaign in Britain.

Goss's execution took place against a background of increasing IRA raids on banks and post offices. By 1940, the IRA was in a poor position financially. There was little money from Clan na Gael coming in and a garda raid had captured $18,500 that had been brought into Ireland by the German spy, Hermann Goertz. Hence, the IRA revived a fundraising tactic not used since the Civil War (when, during May 1922 alone, over £50,000 was taken in raids by the anti-Treaty IRA). During 1940, there were several bank and post-office raids in Belfast. There were more bank raids in Dublin during 1941. In Belfast the Civil Defence Headquarters was raided and £5,000 taken and IRA member Bob McMillen shot and wounded: an incident believed to have inspired F.L. Green's *Odd Man Out*, and the film of the same name, directed by Carol Reed. The Player Wills factory in Dublin was also robbed of its wages in 1943. But the tactic was disastrous for the IRA's image, seeming to confirm the government's accusation that they were gangsters. The IRA did not carry out another robbery for finance until 1969.

THE NORTHERN 'CAMPAIGN'

The high hopes entertained by the 1930s' IRA leadership about cross-community unity in the North proved to be misplaced. By 1934, sectarianism was again very much on the rise and July 1935 saw the worst rioting since 1922 (and the worst before 1969) with ten killed in Belfast. The IRA's response to the violence was confused: again there was no clear instruction as to its exact role and most members of the Belfast IRA were outside the city when the trouble occured. But as the IRA in the Free State declined, the IRA in the North began to grow.

The War years were marked by a number of high-profile actions in the North. Even before the bombing campaign began, the authorities in Northern Ireland were also clamping down on the IRA. Internment was introduced on 22 December 1938 and 34 men, all, bar one from Belfast, arrested. Internees were held in Derry Jail, Belfast's Crumlin Road and for a period on the *Al Rawdah* in Strangford Lough.

But in February 1940, an IRA raid netted 30 rifles from the British Army's Ballykinlar Camp in Co. Down.

On Christmas Day of that year, 120 prisoners rioted in Derry Jail: in March 1943 a total of 21 men managed to tunnel out of the same prison (18 were recaptured in Donegal and interned in the Curragh). In 1942, an IRA Northern Command, under Hugh McAteer, was established to begin a campaign. McAteer was captured that year but in January 1943, along with Jimmy Steele, Paddy Donnelly and Edward Maguire, he escaped from Crumlin Road. At Easter 1943, the IRA took over the Broadway Cinema on the Falls Road and McAteer appeared and read out the organisation's Easter statement.

But it was an earlier IRA Easter operation that led to the most remembered incident of the War years. At Easter 1942, the IRA planned to defy the authorities and to hold a public commemoration on the Falls Road. To help divert police attention, they organised a number of attacks. After the IRA fired at an RUC patrol on Kashmir Road they were pursued to a house in Cawnpore Street. During the ensuing gun battle the unit's 19-year-old commander, Tom Williams, was wounded and an RUC constable, Patrick Murphy (a Catholic and father of nine) killed. Six IRA men were captured, charged with murder and sentenced to death, though Williams claimed that he had fired all the shots that killed Murphy.

There was an outcry and appeals for clemency from the Catholic Church and from

Last letter of
Lieutenant THOMAS WILLIAMS
to his Chief of Staff.

Hugh A Chara,

Just a note to let you know how my comrades and I are getting along.

I am proud to know that you are our leader. My comrades and I are sure that you will use your utmost powers to free our dear beloved country, and bring about the re-establish-ment of the Republic and its Constitution.

It is beyond the powers of my humble intellect to describe the pride of my comrades in knowing that they are going to follow in the footsteps of those who have given their lives to Ireland and the Republic, or to describe the courage and coolness shown when sentenced to death.

My God, can we tell you and our comrades who will carry on the fight of the gladness and joy that is in our hearts. To know that the Irish people are again united aye and well may England quake, Ireland's awake, Ireland's awake. After twenty years of slumber our Nation will once again strike, please God, at the despoilers who have infringed the Nation's liberty and freedom and murdered her sons and daughters ; who have given us a foreign tongue and shall, please God, strike and strike hard and make the tyrants go on their knees for mercy and forgiveness.

But shall we make the mistake of 1921 ? No, no, 'tis men like you and your staff will see to it that no farcical so-called treaty shall in any way be signed by a bunch of weak-kneed and weak-willed Irishmen. Better that the waves of the mighty ocean sweep over Eire than take and divide our Nation and murder her true sons again. Better would it be that the heavens should open and send fire to destroy Eire than to accept another treaty like it.

In writing this, dear Hugh, do not think that I am saying it to you merely, or to the gallant soldiers of Oglaigh na h-Eireann ; it is from my heart I say it to the weak-willed and credulous Irishmen who may put any trust in England. My only regret now is that I will not be with you in the fight, and the last stage of Ireland's battle for freedom. But, with the help of God and His Blessed Mother, we may be in heaven looking down upon our dear, beloved, tortured and crucified Eire, and looking with pride on the men and women who will carry on the fight until victory.

Well, dear Hugh, I will close with this message to Oglaigh na h-Eireann : carry on, no matter what odds are against you ; carry on no matter what the enemy call you ; carry on no matter what torments are inflicted on you—the road to freedom is paved with suffering, hardship and torture. Carry on my gallant comrades until that certain day.

Your comrade in Ireland's Cause,
LIEUTENANT TOM WILLIAMS,
Belfast Battalion,
Oglaigh na h-Eireann.

Pamphlet detailing final letter of Tom Williams
HUMPHREYS PAPERS, UCD

de Valera's government. On 29 August, the death sentences of five of the men were commuted. However, on 2 September 1942, Williams was hanged, the only execution of a republican in Northern Ireland (though Michael Pratley, hanged in May 1924 for killing a man during a robbery in Belfast had also been a member of the IRA).

Following Williams' execution, the IRA carried out several attacks in Armagh and Tyrone and in early September, killed two policemen.

The case highlighted the Irish government's differing attitude to IRA activities on either side of the Border: the press in the South was forbidden by the government censor from referring to Constable Murphy's death as 'murder'; but they were ordered to use the term 'murder' when reporting the deaths of gardaí in similar incidents. Williams' co-defendants (who included Joe Cahill) were released in 1949. In January 2000, after a long campaign, Williams' body was reinterred at Milltown Cemetery in Belfast.

STEPHEN HAYES' 'CONFESSION'

In September 1941, the IRA leadership published details of a 'confession' by their chief of staff Stephen Hayes, in which he claimed to have been acting as an agent on behalf of Fianna Fáil since 1935.

Hayes was from Enniscorthy and had been commandant of the IRA in Wexford during 1921. He took the anti-Treaty side and was interned in the Curragh until 1924. He was well known as a figure in the GAA, winning a Leinster senior Gaelic Football title in 1925 and becoming chairman of the Wexford County Board. He remained active in the IRA and was on its executive from 1935. He stood as a republican candidate in a by-election in August 1936, winning 1,031 votes.

Hayes was a strong supporter of Seán Russell and the bombing campaign in Britain. When Russell left Ireland for America in April 1939, he appointed the 37-year-old Hayes acting chief of staff. From September 1939, when he narrowly escaped capture in a garda raid, Hayes was on the run. Under Hayes the IRA carried out the dramatic raid on the Magazine Fort in the Phoenix Park on 23 December 1939, stealing over one million rounds of the Irish Army's ammunition. In turn, this led to more determination on the government's part to clamp down on the organisation. Many of the IRA's leading officers were jailed during 1940 and Hayes seems to have relied heavily on his brother-in-law, Larry de Lacy (who had been active in Clan na Gael) and an IRA contact in the garda Special Branch, Jim Crofton. At the same time, Hayes was trying to manage the IRA's relations with German intelligence, meeting the spy, Hermann Goertz. On the run and isolated, Hayes drank heavily.

OGLAIGH NA h-EIREANN

(Irish Republican Army).

Dept. :—Adjutant-General. **G. H. Q. Dublin.**

SPECIAL COMMUNIQUE

ISSUED BY THE ARMY COUNCIL.

On June 30th, 1941, STEPHEN HAYES, aged 39, of Enniscorthy, Co. Wexford, and at that time Chief of Staff of the Irish Republican Army, was arrested and charged with treachery and conspiracy to betray the Republic, and imprisoned. As a result of sbusequent investigations tne Army Council directed that Hayes be court-martialled on the following charges :—

1. **THAT YOU, STEPHEN HAYES, CONSPIRED WITH THE "IRISH FREE STATE GOVERNMENT" TO OBSTRUCT THE POLICY AND IMPEDE THE PROGRESS OF THE IRISH REPUBLICAN ARMY.**
2. **THAT YOU, STEPHEN HAYES, ARE GUILTY OF TREACHERY BY HAVING DELIBERATELY FORWARDED INFORMATION, OF A SECRET AND CONFIDENTIAL NATURE CONCERNING THE ACTIVITIES OF THE IRISH REPUBLICAN ARMY, TO A HOSTILE BODY, TO WIT, THE "IRISH FREE STATE GOVERNMENT."**

The Court-martial was held on Wednesday, 23rd July, 1941, and Accused was found guilty on both charges, and sentenced to death, the President of the Court stating that Accused was a party to the most heinous conspiracy of crime in Irish history.

After promulgation of the findings and sentence of the Court Accused expressed the desire to make a complete confession. Relevant excerpts from that confession are quoted in the body of this Communique, where reference is made to a number of major incidents for which, among upwards of one hundred others, the Accused accepted responsibility.

Explanatory notes have been inserted throughout the Confession, between brackets, tnus : [—], and it should be observed that in each instance where the word "Army" occurs the Irish Republican Army is meant.

Accused's Confession reads as follows :—

"I, STEPHEN HAYES, have made the following confession of facts concerning my complicity in the conspiracy with the Free State Government, through their Agents, Dr. James Ryan, T.D., Minister for Agriculture, Thomas Derrig, T.D., Minister for Education, Senator Chris. Byrne and Laurence De Lacy, to wreck the Irish Republican Army. It has been made with the hope that it will undo some of the harm and injury I did to Oglaigh na h-Eireann (Irish Republican Army) through my cooperation with them.

"I decided on making this Confession after I was made aware of the verdict of the Court-martial.

"I further affirm that this Confession of facts is the truth, the whole truth and nothing but the truth, and nothing but the truth, and has been made voluntarily by me."

Signed : STEPHEN HAYES.

Dated this 28th August, 1941.

HOW THE CONSPIRACY ORIGINATED :

I have always been on friendly terms with members of the Free State Government party in my own County both before and after their accession to power in 1932. I was a close companion of Michael Flusk, Frank Cullimore, Robert Moran and Liam Walsh who were the principal Fianna Fail henchmen in Wexford town. The Irish Republican Army and Fianna Fail in the County Wexford were on friendly terms and this continued to be so right along. In 1935 through Michael Flusk I met Chief Superintendant Martin Lynch at P. McCabes Public House, Westgate, Wexford. Lynch and I often met in McCabe's place from that on right up to the time I left in 1938..........

"He knew the position I held in the Army. He prevented any undue police activity from taking place in the County as I guaranteed him that there would be no unpleasant incidents, such as shootings, beatings, etc., and that parades would be held as secretly as possible. To show results to his superiors for his way of doing things he asked me for some arms. Two riflees, a Lewis gun and two .45 shot arms were given to him over a period of two months or so in 1935. The stuff was in pretty good condition. Lynch guaranteed me immunity from arrest on political charges also. My reason for this deal with Lynch was that from my discussions with him he gave me to understand that he wanted peace and quietness in his area, and I did not want any trouble either, hence the agreement.........

"I gave Lynch a verbal report of all Executive Council meetings I attended during that period from 1935 to 1938. I was anxious that Lynch remain in the County, in view of our verbal agreement and I did not take the Army **seriously.**

RUSSELL INITIATES ENGLISH CAMPAIGN.

"In January 1938, Sean Russell came down to see me in Enniscorthy, after his return from the United States, to discuss the possibilities and the best ways and means to make the English Campaign the Policy of the Army. We met in Bennet's Hotel........... I told him the possibility of getting support for his policy was good..... He told me the Clann [Clann na Gaedheal organisation America] would give the Campaign its full support with finance and materials. He also asked me did I know anyone in Dublin who would help in anyway. I gave him the address of Larry De Lacy [Brother-in-law of accused and a sub-editor in the "Irish Times" lives at 20 Clare Road, Dublin. Accused introduced De Lacy as his chief adviser and confidante and he came to be regarded by the G. H. Q. Staff as a completely genuine and trust worthy Republican of considerable ability. Actually he was a trusted Fianna Fail agent].......

"I was in Dublin about three weeks afterwards at a Leinster Convention G. A. A. I called up to see De Lacy after it. I told him of my interview with Russell and the plans and preparations being made for the adopting of the English Campaign policy. He asked me when I would be up again, and I said in about a fortnight's time. I went to see him to get his advice, as I knew he would be able to get the Government's attitude and reaction to such a line of policy. That interview was in his own house.

"I called to see him in the "Irish Times" Office, a fortnight afterwards early in March. He told me to go ahead with the preparations for the adoption of the Campaign policy by the Army. The Government he said would more or less welcome it as it would give wide publicity to the partition issue and would give them an argument for Britain that—'if you wont make a deal with us you will have to deal with the I. R. A.' I knew De Lacy knew of my relations with Lynch as he asked me on a few occasions how was my friend Martin Lynch. When he told me to keep him informed on the progress of events in the Army, he knew I would. He told me he was keeping the Government posted on events in the Army. He advised me to make myself prominent in pushing the Campaign policy and get into an executive position on the Council. He said he would see Russel if he called on him, but otherwise he would not bother about him.......... He seemed to think that Russell was more a dreamer than a man of action.

"He told me when all was over I would get an executive position in one of the Government Departments. I did not see him again till after the Army Convention in April, 1938. [Russell's plan for an English Campaign was ratified at this Convention, and he was returned to power] In the meantime I had carried out his advice and become Chairman of the Army Council, and Secretary to the Executive. I saw him the night after the Convention, and told him how the proceedings went. He was pleased with the results. He asked me how long would it take to launch the Campaign. I told him it would be at least six months. He asked me if any date had been mentioned. I said, 'No, not yet,' however, I would let him know in time. As I would be in Dublin pretty often now, I told him I would give him a call oftener and keep him posted up-to-date."

"From this time onwards Army activity was concentrated on speeding up organisation in Britain and training units in incendiary and sabotage work generally, and laying in of raw materials for explosive and incendiary work.......... De Lacy knew from me of the progress being made. In the meantime the Government sponsored an anti-partition drive in England, after the Munich conference. This was all part of the idea to gain from and use the publicity that would be created all over the world, on British injustice in Ireland, by the Campaign. It was also intended as a smoke-screen organisation to which Irish support in Britain could rally instead of going all out Republican. They foresaw that Irish opinion would be awakened in England, and unless they had some organisation there, that opinion would eventually be lost to the Government here. Further they considered that by making a big show about the partition question at the period, they could blame the Campaign afterwards for the non-results of the agitation, and if they gained any concession as a result of the Campaign they could claim the credit for it themselves.

SIX COUNTY REPUBLICAN INTERNED.

"As preparations for the Campaign progressed the Six County units were anxious to start operations in that area at the same time as the Campaign opened in England. De Lacy advised against it. He said such a Campaign would force the Government to take action.... ...... and if they openly opposed the Campaign there, which they would be forced to do, they would lose all support from the people at home. The Campaign was to start around Xmas 1938, and the Belfast men were fully prepared. De Lacy instructed me to get the date postponed for a further fortnight or three weeks, and in the meantime the Government here would arrange with the Six County Authorities to have a 'Round-up' of the Irish Republican Army Officers in Belfast and other areas.

"The date was postponed on the plea that Xmas was not an appropriate time to start a war. Instructions were sent to Belfast for all the men to return to their

Front page of Hayes' confession

HUMPHREYS PAPERS, UCD ARCHIVES

way back to Dundalk. It was held up and captured near Swords [On July 19th, 1940, a lorry containing over 5,000 rounds of .303 ammunition was held up by the police at Swords and captured]. The subsequent report brought out by Crofton [A Dublin Castle detective who was working for the Army. The Government knew this and concocted false and fictitious police reports for his benefit. He is now serving a sentence of 5 years in Maryborough Gaol] was to the effect that the night before the ammunition was captured a guard rang up Asst. Commissioner Carroll from Monaghan and told him of the job next day. The owners of the lorry, Quinns had informed the Guard. To add credence to the report the Quinns were released some hours after the capture and got back their lorry. This report was sent to Divisional O/C Dundalk area with orders to shoot Quinn. Dundalk Army men protested but the order to shoot Quinn was repeated by me and the shooting took place which resulted in Quinn being seriously wounded [John Quinn was wounded by shots outside Dundalk on November 20th, 1940]. In arranging for the concocted police report Dr. Ryan, of course, understood that I would act on it and take drastic action against the victim mentioned in such report.

"My next meeting with Dr. Ryan was early in September, 1940. I met him in the Shelbourne Hotel. He was accompanied by Senator Byrne. He was annoyed at this meeting at the effect of the recent executions of Paddy McGrath and T. Harte on the people. He said the Government would have preferred to avoid such awkward situations.......... Many of their own supporters were rather sore over executing Paddy McGrath on account of his record. They hoped to remove some of the resentment by reprieving T. Hunt whose address I had sent him, and who was being tried on the same charges as P. McGrath and T. Harte. He believed that with this gesture and with a close censorship the whole episode would be forgotten as far as the general public was concerned..

MURDER OF AN INNOCENT VICTIM.

"Dr. Ryan had told me at a previous meeting that he would get concocted police reports in order to throw suspicions on to some victim or other as there were bound to be awkward questions on account of the number of raids and arrests for which there was no explanation. .... During the raid on Lansdowne Park [22nd August, 1940. Arms were captured and two men and two women arrested] the police occupied the place for nearly a week. On the Saturday of that week, a Battalion Officer from Wexford named Michael Devereux arrived at Lansdowne Park. He was detained by the police until Monday when he was released and allowed to return home. On that Monday Crofton brought out a police report that Devereux had told the police about two dumps in Wexford and that Detective Sergeants Fergus and Gill were leaving or had left to go down and collect the stuff. It also stated that Devereux had been released and had got some money for the information........ One of the dumps was captured but the local unit cleared out the other before it was raided.

"Dr. Ryan explained to me at this meeting in September that when he heard of Devereux's arrest he looked upon it as a good opportunity to cover up the leakage. He said he knew from me of the existence of a dump of gelignite near Piercestown and of another containing arms in .... both of which it had not been possible to collect without bringing the local police in on it. This he could not afford to do as he had to keep his confidence within a very narrow circle. To have word sent from Dublin to the police in Wexford might make some of them suspicious of me being the only person up here who knew of their existence. He arranged with the police whom I believe were Superintendent Gantley and Asst. Commissioner Carroll to concoct the report brought out by Crofton, to release Devereux and to collect the two dumps. In spite of the fact that Devereux was innocent the result of all this was that the dump of gelignite was collected.... and the guilt for it fell on to Devereux's shoulders, while some also suspected him for Lansdowne Park.

"Dr. Ryan felt that it would be necessary to shoot Devereux as if he lived he would be likely to become suspicious and probably be able to place the blame on the right shoulders. The order for the shooting of Devereux was sent down by me to the Divisional O/C of Wexford area immediately, who carried out my orders... ...... It was at this meeting that Dr. Ryan informed me of Russell's death in Gibraltar as a result of an 'accident' and was buried at sea. This information was conveyed to Dr. Ryan through Mr. Dulanty in London. All information was sent through Dulanty, as Dr. Ryan referred to him on a few occasions, when discussing the English Campaign, by saying—'I can get the necessary information passed on through Dulanty'............

"Dr. Ryan asked me how we were financially. I told him we were poorly off......... He asked me had De Lacy not mentioned Bank raids to me. I said 'yes'...... He pointed out to me that raids on Banks would do the Army a lot of harm. Even if one or two small jobs were successful the amounts to be got would not compensate for the bad name the Army would get and the consequent loss of supporters............ He said I ought to urge on the Army the necessity for cash and suggest the Bank raids.

DR. RYAN PLANS DUBLIN CASTLE EXPLOSION.

"After this meeting orders were issued to Divisional O/C Dublin area to prepare plans for a couple of Bank jobs in the city. Plans were prepared by the Dublin unit. Those plans were caught on one of the Dublin Staff who was picked up in the street with the O/C Dublin and another member of the Staff after they had left the office where the O/C worked on Eden Quay. I had sent word to Dr. Ryan that those plans were being prepared. The 'tecs were watching the O/C. I knew the plans were completed and sent Dr. Ryan word. As a result the three men mentioned above were arrested. The Government made a lot of propaganda out of the captured plans and the Army suffered by the severe criticism of members of their families and supporters.........

"The Dublin Castle explosion, April, 1940, was the result of a suggestion by Dr. Ryan to De Lacy [A landmine exploded in the grounds of Dublin Castle on April 25th, 1940, and 6 people were injured]. I had sent word to Dr. Ryan after the Hunger-Strike that the Army was demanding reprisals. He sent back word with De Lacy that he would have access to the Castle made easy and the idea of it would be dropped to Crofton, as he knew he would bring it out to the Army Director of Intelligence. He suggested that we set off a landmine inside in the grounds. This would satisfy the Army as to reprisals and at the same time rouse people's opinion against them for unnecessary destruction of Irish property and endangering the lives of brother Irishmen. The Director of Intelligence got information from Crofton about an easy access to the Castle and brought me word. I then told him to place a mine in the place as a reprisal for the Hunger-Strike deaths. This was done. The people looked upon it as a senseless job, and Government propaganda worked up the destruction of Irish property and endangering the lives of brother Irishmen idea.........

It further strengthened the Government's hands and helped people to forget the Hunger-Strike deaths........

"At meeting in September, 1940, subsequent to the executions of P. McGrath and T. Harte, Dr. Ryan had told me of the resentment expressed by some of their own old supporters over the executions. The principal ones he told me and the most bitter over it were a group of old I.R.A. men led by Simon Donnelly and Sean Dowling. I told him I knew of this and since the executions they were beginning to fall in wholeheartedly behind the Army. He said something would have to be done about it. He suggested an attack on them in 'War News.' I told him that he had better mention it to De Lacy as he was looking after the publicity and knew more about it than I did. He said he would. A short time afterwards an article appeared in 'War News' which was a personal attack on some of the principal old I.R.A. men who were belonging to a group dissatisfied with the executions and the Government Policy generally. This article had the effect of estranging those men once again from the Army. Whilst it did not throw them into the arms of the Government it caused bitterness and resentment amongst them against the Army. Some of those men had been helping for a long time in providing houses and contacts. After the publication of the article they refused to do any more such work.

FOOLING THE FREE STATE ARMY.

"Dr. Ryan's explanation to me after the Meath Hotel raid in March, 1940, for having military on the job was to promote a feeling of antagonism in the Free State Army against the Irish Republican Army. He said there had been a lot of propaganda spread amongst the rank and file in previous months through the medium of 'War News' and similar sheets. It had begun to have a very serious effect and Officers were complaining of slogans of 'Up the Republic' and 'Up the I.R.A.,' being chalked around the lavatory and dead walls of the barracks. As well, many of the younger soldiers on pay-night when returning to barracks with drink taken were shouting similar slogans. It was hoped by bringing them out on raids from time to time to give them the feeling that the Irish Republican Army was their enemy, and that this would help in its own way to counteract some of the harm already done by propaganda. It was their fixed policy also to place military guards wherever Army men were serving sentences or were interned. This would help to sustain a feeling of bitterness between the two. They themselves were also taking measures to put more propaganda of their own into the Free State Army. They intended to make use of the Radio and Stage for this purpose apart from books or papers. They also intended to spread out the old-timers in the Free State Army amongst the units. All those men, he said, were anti-Army and would help to quieten some of the younger fry who were likely to be carried away by seditious propaganda.

GOVERNMENT ORDERS BANK RAIDS.

"At a meeting with Dr. Ryan and Senator Byrne at Dr. Ryan's place, end of January, 1941, Dr. Ryan asked me had we got any further financial aid since last year. I told him 'No.' He then suggested that the Army do a few Bank raids in the country. He felt that such raids would have a deeper impression on country people. When done in a city they blow over but when done in country areas they are talked about for months. As well, he said, it was easier to track down the men on such a job in the country areas once there was any indication as to who they were. Further, the amount of cash to be got in country banks would be only a few hundreds. I told him I would see what could be done. Subsequent to this meeting the then Adjutant-General sent instructions to Divisional O/C Meath-Louth areas etc. to be on the look out for a suitable Bank job in his area. This instruction was repeated by the acting Adjutant-General after the Adjutant-General's arrest and the Divisional O/C of the area made preparations for two jobs, one at Oldcastle and the other at Castlepollard [£704 were taken at the Northern Bank, Oldcastle, 5th May, 1941; and £636 were taken at Hibernian Bank, Castlepollard, 9th June, 1941]..

"I met Dr. Ryan again the last week of April, 1941, in Shelbourne Hotel, he was accompanied by Senator Byrne and Mr. T. Derrig, T.D............... I told Dr. Ryan that I expected word that preparations were made for a Bank raid in Meath or Louth and would let him know....

"I sent Dr. Ryan word of my granting permission for raid in Oldcastle. I learned who was in charge from the acting Adjutant-General and sent word to Dr. Ryan. Richard Goss was the man in charge. Later I sent Dr. Ryan word of the Castlepollard raid and that Goss was again in charge. I told him in the message that Goss spent a lot of his time in Longford area and stayed frequently at Casey's house in that area [Richard Goss was arrested by military and police at Casey's house in Drumlis, Co. Longford, on 18th July, 1941, and shot dead at Maryborough Gaol, on August 9th]. The above two raids were the outcome of Dr. Ryan's instructions at meeting of the end of January, 1941, to have Bank raids in a few country districts. His ideas were to blacken the name of the Army and to cause discontent and disunity amongst the supporters. By having the raids on the country Banks the amount of cash likely to be taken would be insignificant in comparison with the amount of harm they would do the Army. Furthermore the raids in the country would be talked about for months and it would be much easier to track down the men on the job once they had got a lead as to who they were...........

The Army Council has issued the following announcement :-

It has now been definitely established—

1. THAT THIS CONSPIRACY WAS FOSTERED AND INSPIRED BY THE FREE STATE GOVERNMENT AS A FINAL AND DESPARATE EFFORT TO DESTROY BY TREACHERY THAT WHICH THEY FAILED TO DO BY FORCE
2. THAT A TREACHEROUS LEADER CO-OPERATED WITH OTHER TRAITOROUS IRISHMEN WHO WERE UNASHAMEDLY TRYING TO PERPETUATE BRITISH RULE IN IRELAND BY USING SINISTER AS WELL AS OPPRESSIVE MEASURES WHICH EVEN THEIR MASTERS IN LONDON NEVER DARED USE DIRECTLY.

The people of Ireland inured as they are to hardship and oppression will readily understand that none can bear it better than Ireland's faithful youth, and it is because of this sterling fact—that Ireland's true National Army is composed of her faithful and courageous sons, undeterred by death no matter what form it takes—that we are inspired to face with determination and confidence the final phase of the long struggle for Irish Freedom..

In the name of the people of Ireland we thank God for having given us the wit to uncover a foulness which would, had it gone on unhindered, have endangered our most precious National Heritage.

Signed :—ADJUTANT-GENERAL.

For and on behalf of the Army Council.

Dated this 10th day of September, 1941.

Final page of Hayes' confession

HUMPHREYS PAPERS, UCD ARCHIVES

At this time, two of the IRA's northern leadership, Sean McCaughey and Charlie McGlade, (appointed Adjutant General and Quartermaster General respectively by Hayes in 1941), became convinced that their leader was a spy. In June 1941, they took Hayes prisoner and began questioning him. For the next two months, Hayes was interrogated and occasionally beaten, while being moved from safe house to safe house. Eventually he admitted his 'treachery' and composed a confession, detailing extensive conspiracies and plots behind every disaster to have befallen the IRA. Hayes knew that while he wrote, he had a chance of survival. While being held in a house in Rathmines in early September he spotted a chance to escape, managing, though chained, to jump through a window and make his way to a nearby garda station. Raids soon followed and in the ensuing days, the IRA decided to publish the 'confession', causing much confusion within their own ranks and among the prisoners in the Curragh and Belfast.

McCaughey was captured and Hayes testified against him in court: the northerner was sentenced to death but the sentence was commuted to life in jail. The confession led to the gardaí renewing their interest in the case of Micheal Deveraux, a Wexford IRA man who had disappeared during 1940. Deveraux had been suspected of informing and had been executed and his body hidden in Co. Tipperary. In late September, his body was discovered and IRA men George Plant and Joe O'Connor charged with his murder: Plant was executed in March 1942. This added even more bitterness to the case.

Garda documents released in 2009 claim that the force had informants, ranging in rank from ordinary volunteer to O/C, in almost every area where the IRA organised in the Free State during the mid-1930s. These men were paid for their assistance and while some were motiviated purely by financial reasons, others hoped that helping gardaí would mean their locality saw little trouble. It is possible that Hayes provided information on occasion; but it is equally possible that the entire confession was fiction. McCaughey and McGlade seemed unable to recognise how isolated the IRA was from popular support in the South and how many of its problems were self-inflicted. The IRA had embarked on a bombing campaign in Britain and had embarrassed the government with the Magazine Fort Raid. During 1940 they had killed three garda detectives and wounded several others, killed an alleged informer, bombed Dublin Castle and attempted forcibly to free prisoners from Cork gaol. By 1941, the organisation was robbing banks and post offices to fund itself. The government was aware of republican contact with the Germans and fearful of this being used as an excuse for British military intervention. A determined state campaign against the IRA was completely logical and just as importantly, the IRA had been steadily losing whatever credibility it had since the mid-1930s.

Hayes served five years in prison and on release lived and worked in his native Wexford until his death in December 1974. He always claimed that his 'confession' was fiction, composed under torture. In 1951, his account of what happened was published in the literary journal *The Bell*. While many republicans remain convinced of Hayes' guilt, it is surely significant that this man, dubbed 'the greatest traitor in Irish history' by some, lived out his life without interference. But the fact that Hayes gave evidence against McCaughey damned him in many eyes, especially as McCaughey died a martyr's death after an agonising 31-day hunger-and-thirst strike during May 1946.

THE CURRAGH

During 1940, hundreds of republicans were interned without trial in the Curragh detention camp in Kildare. Conditions were rudimentary: the food was of poor quality, the huts that the internees were held in were hard to heat; once a week prisoners had a lukewarm shower and lice and illnesses spread easily in the huts. But some newspapers and reading materials were allowed and the IRA's camp regime, under its O/C Billy Mulligan, was relatively relaxed. Secretly, the prisoners were also building a network of escape tunnels.

However, in December 1940, a number of IRA officers, including Peadar O'Flaherty and Larry Grogan, arrived from Arbour Hill prison. O'Flaherty and Grogan were disgusted at apparent collaboration by some with the Free State camp authorities and believed that discipline among the internees was lacking. Thus, when the butter ration for the internees was cut shortly after they arrived, they demanded a protest. O'Flaherty hectored the internees that they would have to show the authorities whether they were 'men or mice'. He pushed for a symbolic burning of the internees' huts. When challenged, he pulled rank, as both himself and Grogan were Army Council members, though in theory an IRA officer lost his position in prison.

On the night of 14 December, seven of the huts were burned: in the confusion, some of them still contained internees' possessions. The destruction of the huts exposed a number of escape tunnels underneath and further outraged Camp authorities. Soldiers forced some of the prisoners back into huts that had been damaged by fire, beating with batons and rifle butts those who resisted. For two days and nights in freezing weather the prisoners were held without heating or adequate clothing. Finally released, the disorientated internees headed for breakfast rations in a confused state. More scuffles broke out and the guards opened fire, killing Barney Casey and wounding several others.

In Proud Memory of

Bernard Casey

(Battalion O.C., I.R.A.)

OCHILL, DRUMLISH

CO. LONGFORD

who, while an uncharged and untried prisoner, suspected of being a faithful soldier of the Republic of Ireland, was wantonly shot to death at the Curragh Camp, December 16, 1940.

Imeasg Laoċra Éireann go raiḃ a anam i ḃḟlaiṫeas Dé

HUMPHREYS PAPERS, UCD ARCHIVES

At the inquest into Casey's death, soldiers claimed that they had fired in self-defence, prompting Seán MacBride, acting as lawyer on behalf of Casey's family, to ask why he had been shot in the back. After the burnings, a new, harsh, regime of surprise searches and withdrawal of privileges was instituted. Discipline and morale suffered. A few prisoners took the option of signing out and renouncing IRA activity.

In January 1941, the IRA's new commander, Liam Leddy, ordered the internees to respond to a cut in coal rations by boycotting camp coal entirely. Cork IRA officer Tadgh Lynch refused to obey him, thinking the order lunacy in the winter weather. Leddy ordered Lynch ostracised but Lynch's comrades supported him and found themselves forced out of the IRA's structures, with the other internees not allowed to speak to or to have any dealings with them at all. Over the next year, more internees drifted into the Lynch group where the atmosphere was more relaxed and where discussion was tolerated. The political divisions within the prisoners were manifold. As World War II went on, internees discussed the pros and cons of the Allies and the Axis: some were attracted to the fascist Ailtirí na hAiséirghe party, which was very active during the 1940s and which promised to end partition by force. But there was an anti-Nazi response, too: International Brigade veteran (and Cork IRA man) Michael O'Riordan was one of the camp's communist group, which published a journal entitled *An Splanc (The Spark)*. A larger group of internees under Pearse Kelly and Seán McCool, adopted a more 'neutral' perspective, hoping for a British defeat but not being pro-Nazi. The camp saw a 49-day hunger strike during 1943, which ended in failure, though there was no repeat of the violence of December 1940.

By 1944, the number of factions at the Curragh had increased, with three main groups, split into several sub sections. There were some positive experiences. Hundreds of men learned Irish for the first time while interned. Máirtín Ó Cadhain, their teacher, a Galway IRA officer, began work on his *Cré na Cille*, which became one of the most important Irish-language novels of the twentieth century. Internee Sean Ó Tuama was elected president of Conradh na Gaeilge; newspaper reports gave his address only as County Kildare. For a period the communist Neil Goold taught Russian classes, while those of the opposing political bent learned German. Youngsters like Cathal Goulding and Brendan Behan, neighbours and childhood friends from Dublin, arrived in the camp in 1944 joining Leddy's hard-line faction. Behan had rejoined the IRA after he returned from borstal in England and had been jailed in Mountjoy where he began work on his play 'The Quare Fellow' and wrote its best known song, '*The Auld Triangle*'.

Blessed be the Name of God !

In Proud and Loving Memory
of

Charles Kerins

Who gave his life for the Republic of Ireland, on the Scaffold in Mountjoy Gaol. December 1, 1944, aged 26 years.

✠

He loved his God, he loved his land,
He served the cause of Right,
In danger's gap he took his stand
To wage the olden fight.
Faithful and fearless to the end,
He sought a shining goal.
May Mary Mother be his friend!
May God receive his soul!

Queen of Martyrs, Pray for us !

Mother of Perpetual Succour, pray for our Dead, for us, and for Ireland!

Crucified Lord Jesus, have mercy on the souls in Purgatory!

HUMPHREYS PAPERS, UCD ARCHIVES

'THE BOY FROM TRALEE'

Charlie Kerins, chief of staff of the IRA, was 26 when he was executed by hanging on 1 December 1944, at Mountjoy jail. He had been found guilty of the murder of garda Detective Sergeant Denis O'Brien during September 1942. The hanging was carried out by the British state executioner, Albert Pierrepoint, as the Free State did not have its own professional hangman.

Kerins had joined the IRA in 1939. He was suspected by gardaí of involvement in several robberies and shootings prior to his arrest in June 1944, when he was captured with arms and documents. He had become deputy chief of staff during early 1943, a sign, in part, of how arrests were crippling the IRA, and after the organisation's leader, Hugh McAteer, was arrested in Belfast, became chief of staff. The gardai were determined to capture Kerins and Belfast man Harry White, who they suspected of carrying out the killing of O'Brien. Denis O'Brien himself had fought in 1916 and during the War of Independence and taken the anti-Treaty side during the Civil War. He was one of a number of former IRA members who were brought into the garda detective branch during August 1933, in anticipation of clashes with the Blueshirts. As a prominent 'Broy Harrier' O'Brien gained a reputation for zealous hunting of his former comrades. Unlike the other five detectives killed by the IRA during the war years, O'Brien was targeted at his home in Ballyboden and ambushed while leaving for work.

Kerin's body was later returned for burial in Tralee. The O'Rahillys GAA Club in Tralee's Strand Road, for whom he had played, was later renamed Kerins O'Rahillys in his memory. Fellow Kerryman Dan Spring, along with Labour TD Jim Larkin and the Farmers Party's Patrick Finucane, was ordered from the Dáil chamber for disruption while the execution was being debated.

Kerins was the last IRA man executed in the 26 Counties. But the death of Seán McCaughey on hunger strike in Portlaoise during May 1946, provided a grim conclusion to the war years. Few foresaw an IRA revival. Gerald Boland reputedly claimed that the IRA was dead and that he had killed it.

Chapter 5

TOWARDS OPERATION HARVEST

Despite the setbacks of the War years, by the late 1940s, the IRA was reorganising, aiming now at a campaign to end partition while avoiding conflict in the South. The movement eschewed any association with left-wing ideas, promoting a conservative ethos politically. Successful arms raids attracted new recruits and Sinn Féin was revitalised as the political wing of the movement, with a monthly paper, *The United Irishman*. The effort culminated in 'Operation Harvest', the 1956-62 Border campaign.

Tomás Mac Curtáin at Bodenstown
WORKERS' PARTY OF IRELAND

THE MAC CURTÁIN APPEAL

In 1949, the IRA in Cork issued an appeal for funds. The appeal is significant because it makes clear that the IRA had no desire for aggressive action in the South. It is issued in the name of Tomás Mac Curtáin, one of the key figures in the IRA's reorganisation of the late 1940s. The two other major figures in this era were Tony Magan and Padraig McLogan. Magan, a Meath farmer, became chief of staff in September 1948. McLogan, a member of the 1930s' army council (and former abstentionist MP for South Armagh) became Sinn Féin president in 1950. (During 1949, the IRA made a decision to reassert its link with Sinn Féin, broken since 1925 and effectively to take the party over).

The three men agreed that the central aim of the IRA should be to prepare for a new armed campaign against partition. To avoid the mistakes of the past, there should be no conflict in the South. This order, to avoid hostilities in the 26 Counties, was eventually formalised in 1954 as General Order No. 8.

Óglaigh na h-Éireann
(IRISH REPUBLICAN ARMY.)

Briogáid a h-Aon,
Corcaigh.

To:-

A Chara,

The Irish Republican Army has one primary object, A successful military campaign against the British Army of Occupation in the Six Counties.

In view of the fact that any disturbance in the 26 Counties area would hinder the achieving of this object the Army has definately ruled out any kind of aggressive military action in the 26 Counties.

We who are in the I.R.A. are willing to give our time, our liberty and if necessary our lives in order that the ideal of a free Ireland may be realised.

But if we are to succeed we must have funds.

Therefore we find it necessary to appeal for financial aid to those who have stood by us in the past.

A collector, bearing authorisation will call on you within the next few days.

A receipt will be given for all subscriptions.

Is Mise,
Tomás Mac Curtáin
....
Brigade Commander.

The decision was particuarly interesting given Mac Curtáin's history. Born in 1915, he was the son of Tomás Mac Curtáin, Lord Mayor of Cork, who was murdered by police in March 1920.

Mac Curtáin Junior was active in the IRA from an early age and by the mid-1930s, had been arrested on several occasions. While jailed during 1936, he went on hunger strike for 31 days. He became commander of the IRA in Cork city during the late 1930s and was involved in several violent confrontations with gardaí. In January 1940, they attempted to arrest him and in the ensuing struggle, Detective John Roche was shot dead. Mac Curtáin was sentenced to death in June 1940 for murder (he had already endured another hunger strike by this point). The death sentence was commuted to jail for life and Mac Curtáin was sent to Portlaoise Prison. There he refused to wear prison dress and spent long periods in solitary confinement. A number of other wartime IRA prisoners in Portlaoise, such as Eamon Smullen, Liam Rice, Seán McCaughey and Jim Crofton, (who had spied for the IRA inside the Special Branch), also refused to obey prison rules and endured perhaps the toughest prison time of the War years.

Above: MacCurtáin Appeal, 1949 AIKEN PAPERS, UCD ARCHIVES

IRA MANIFESTO, 1949

In January 1949, the IRA responded to the 26 Counties leaving the British Commonwealth and declaring itself a republic. The IRA made it clear that they did not accept this. While the island was divided, they would fight on. The republic had been declared by a new coalition government which ousted Fianna Fáil in 1948.

There had been signs that, once the War was over, resentment at de Valera's repression was affecting Fianna Fáil's support. A long school-teachers' strike had also damaged the party's relationship with its supporters. In the presidential election of 1945, Patrick McCartan, standing as an independent republican, won 19.6% of the vote. During 1946, the Republican Prisoners Release Association was formed, drawing support from many IRA veterans. As a lawyer, Seán MacBride had defended IRA members accused of murder during the War years and in 1946, during the inquest into the death of Seán McCaughey, embarrassed the authorities by forcing them to admit that the conditions in Portlaoise were inhumane. MacBride played a leading role in canvassing among republicans for a new party. In July 1946, Clann na Poblachta was formed.

FORḞÓGRA

Mar ḟreagra ar an saoṫar atá ar siuḃal ċun bríġ bréige do ċur le stáid na h-Éireann i láṫair na h-uaire toisc gur cuireaḋ an Reaċt um Ċúrsaiḃ Coigcríoċ ar feiḋm, is mian le Comairle Ceannais Óglaċ Éireann forḟógra do ċraoḃscaoileaḋ d'ḟonn fírinne an scéil do ṁíniuġaḋ go beaċt.

Do réir Reaċta d'ar cuireaḋ i ḃfeiḋm i ḃFeis Ṡacsan bliaḋain 1920 agus gan oireaḋ is duine le Ṫeaċtaiḃ Éireann i láṫair, agus de ḃríġ gur glacaḋ le sna h-Airteagalaiḃ a Ceapaḋ um Réiḋteaċt, cuireaḋ cosc le n-a raiḃ ar siuḃal ag an bPoblaċt a forḟógraḋ um Ċáisc a 1916 is a bunuigeaḋ le Teaċtaiḃ Éireann uile bliaḋain 1919, agus cuireaḋ i n-a h-ionad ḋá ḟo-Ḟeis deiġilte d'ḟonn Éire do ċoimeád fa ḃuan-smaċt.

Ar an gcuma san deineaḋ Éire do ḋeiġilt ó ċéile tré ḟoiréirgean Ṡacsan, agus deiġilte atá sí ó ṡoin.

Ní déanfar an ḟírinne sin do ṡáruġaḋ is cuma cad deintear ċun stáid nuaḋ do ṫaḃairt do sna Sé Contaete Ḟiċead ar uċt "Poblaċt na h-Éireann" do ḃaisteaḋ mar ainm orta.

Tá smaċt ag Riaġaltas Ṡacsan fós ar Sé Ċontaete de Ṫír na h-Éireann agus arm gaḃála aca san ḋúṫaiġ sin ċun an smaċt do ċoimeád i ḃfeiḋm.

An ḟaid is leantar de'n smaċt soin ní ṫiocfaiḋ le luċt cosanta na Poblaċta a aḋṁáil go ḃfuil deireaḋ leis an aċrann atá ar siuḃal eadrainn le sna ciantaiḃ.

Iad so gur dual dóiḃ ḃeiṫ dílis do'n Ṗoblaċt, ní féidir dóiḃ dílse do ṫaḃairt d'aon ċeann de'n dá ḟo-Ḟeis deiġilte d'ar ċeap Rioġaltas Ṡacsán gan cuireaḋ gan iarraḋ; ní féidir leo a aḋṁáil go ḃfuil aon ḃríġ le dí-feiḋmuiġaḋ an Reaċta um Ċúrsaiḃ Cóigcríoċ aċt mar ḃeaḋ le h-iarraċt polaitiḋeaċta ċun a ċur i n-a luiġe ar ṁuinntir na h-Éireann go ḃfuil saoirse a dtíre buaiḋte aca ċeana.

An ḟaid is tá aon fóḋ de Ṫalaṁ na h-Éireann fá ġaḃáltas airm le tír iasaċta, ní féidir a ráḋ le fírinne gur aṫbunuiġeaḋ Poblaċt Éireann. Dá réir sin, is eaḋ is dual don uile ḋuine de luċt na Poblaċta leanṁaint go dlúṫ dá ndíċeall croiḋe go scaoiltear Éire, glan, ó gaċ rian de'n riaġaltas iasaċta atá d'ár milleaḋ le fada.

Eanair 1949.

Comairle an Airm
Óglaiġ na hÉireann.

AIKEN PAPERS, UCD ARCHIVES

Though strongly anti-partition, Clann recognised the southern state and its members were prepared to take seats in Leinster House. During 1947, it won two seats, MacBride himself becoming a TD. Clann's leadership was largely made up of former IRA members: 22 of its first 27-person executive had been either IRA or

MANIFESTO

In view of the deliberate attempt to misrepresent the situation arising from the repeal of the External Relations Act, the Army Council of Oglaigh na h-Eireann considers it desirable to issue a statement defining clearly the actual position.

By an Act of the British Parliament passed at Westminister in 1920, in the deliberate absence of the entire Irish representation—and through the acceptance of the Articles of Agreement for a Treaty, the Irish Republic, proclaimed in arms Easter 1916—and ratified in 1919 by the elected representatives of the people of all Ireland—was prevented from functioning, and in its stead two Partition Parliaments were set up to govern Ireland.

Thus Ireland was forcibly partitioned by England and has remained partitioned since. Any attempt to give the Twenty-six County area a new status by representing it as "the Republic of Ireland" does not and cannot alter this fundamental fact.

England still retains direct control over six counties of Irish territory, and maintains within that area an army of occupation. While that position remains Republicans cannot concede the claim that Ireland's centuries-old struggle for freedom is ended.

In the circumstances those owing allegiance to the Republic cannot, without sacrifice of their principles, give allegiance to either of the Partition institutions created by Britain, or recognise that the Repeal of the External Relations Act is anything better than a political manoeuvre to mislead the Irish people into the belief that the freedom of Ireland has been achieved.

While any sod of Irish territory remains occupied by the army of a foreign country, it cannot be truthfully stated that the Republic of Ireland has been restored and so it remains the duty of all Republicans to continue their efforts to rid Ireland of the last vestiges of foreign rule.

Issued by the Army Council
Oglaigh na h-Eireann.

January 1949.

Cumann na mBan activists. At the 1948 general election, five former IRA leaders stood as candidates in different parties: Aiken for Fianna Fáil, Mulcahy for Fine Gael, and MacBride, Seán McCool and Mick Fitzpatrick for Clann. Fianna Fáil liberally accused Clann of being 'communist' and/or an IRA front using similar rhetoric to that of Cumann na nGaedheal in 1932. There were high hopes for Clann, which were somewhat dashed when it only won 10 seats (though polling over 173,000 votes).

In the aftermath of the election, MacBride agreed to help form a coalition combining Fine Gael, two rival Labour parties, a farmers' party and Clann, in which he would be Minister for External Affairs.

Clann's decision to go into government with Fine Gael, the party of the Treaty, was a shock to some. In the longer run, some younger members, such as Charlie Murphy and Seán South, would join the IRA. One former Clann TD, Peadar Cowan (an ex-Irish Army captain and expelled Labour Party member), signalled his disillusion with the lack of progress towards ending partition by announcing the formation of a new Volunteer force in 1950. When that body failed to have an impact some of its members again drifted towards the IRA, which was benefitting from the government's propaganda against partition but also its failure to do anything about it. In contrast, the IRA promised that it *would* take up arms against the British.

ARMS RAIDS

The first public sign of the IRA's determination to reorganise came on 3 June 1951, when the organisation's Derry unit successfully stole a quantity of weapons from Ebrington Territorial barracks in the city. The raid was carried out without the police or British army even being aware of it. It was a good propaganda coup and was evidence that the decision of the leadership during May 1951 to set up a miltary council to plan a campaign was a serious step.

Eireannaċ Aontuiġṫe

The United Irishman

THE ORGAN OF IRISH REPUBLICANISM

VOL. 3. No. 6. JUNE, 1951 PRICE 3d.

DARING RAID ON DERRY BARRACKS

ARMS CAPTURE BY I.R.A.

A fitting protest against the visit of English Royalty to Ireland was made by the Irish Republican Army when during the course of the visit, Ebrington Barracks, Derry, was successfully raided and a large quantity of arms and ammunition seized. The haul consisted of Bren and Vickers machine-guns, anti-tank guns, Sten guns and Lee Enfield rifles, and a quantity of miscellaneous ammunition numbering hundreds of thousands of rounds.

Great credit is due to the men who planned and carried out the operation for the foresight and efficiency displayed throughout. Every contingency was foreseen and guarded against and nothing was left to chance. This was especially noticeable when the actual entry was being effected. In planning out the mode of entry beforehand the various obstacles had been noted and provisions made to overcome them. When about to effect an entry an additional unforeseen obstacle was encountered, but all the necessary implements to deal with this were on hand.

Everything had been well rehearsed, each man knew his job and the part he had to play. In the silence of the night men moved like shadows to their various positions. Sentries were posted and the raiding party proceded to force an entry into the stores. To do this two large padlocks had to be smashed and a heavy door had to be sawn through. As this was being done each man held his breath wondering if the noise would be heard by the nearby sentries and arouse their suspicions.

Having succeeded in gaining access to the stores the volunteers set to work silently and efficiently, and in a surprisingly short space of time they were loading the precious cargo on to the waiting truck. Many hands make light work and soon the heavy lorry, loaded to capacity, was rumbling past the unsuspecting sentries, and within a couple of hours was back empty in its garage, its cargo having been delivered into the eager hands of the men waiting to receive it.

The officer in charge of the operation expressed regret that he had omitted to leave a note of thanks to their Most Gracious Majesties for their kind co-operation, by causing large numbers of the Crown Forces to be drafted from Derry to Belfast and thus facilitating him in making what he described as the only effective protest that can be made to England's claim to rule in Ireland, viz.: The placing of guns in the hands of men who are willing and anxious to use them to drive the British Army out of Ireland.

CONTENTS

REMEMBER
PILGRIMAGE TO BODENSTOWN
will take place on
SUNDAY JUNE 24th

SEAN RUSSELL MEMORIAL
will be Unveiled on
SUNDAY, 9th SEPT.

United Irishman, June 1951 UNITED IRISHMAN

The United Irishman

An t-Éireannaċ Aontuiġṫe

is í An Poblaċt ár gCuspóir

IML. VI. UIMHIR 7 | IUIL, 1954 | TRI PINGIN

DARING ARMAGH RAID

"ARMS WILL BE USED AGAINST BRITISH FORCES"

—I.R.A.

In a daring daylight swoop, a unit of the I.R.A. carried out a successful raid r arms on the British Military Barracks, Armagh, on Saturday, June 12th. The eration was carried off to such split-second timing and with such amazing olness that the routine life of Armagh City went on undisturbed.

n twenty lightning minutes the unit had taken control of the Barracks, ptied the armoury and made their getaway—not a single shot was fired. ere they came from and where they went nobody has found out—but the n are free and the arms safe.

Less than fifteen minutes afterwards, the greatest combined military and police activity ever witnessed in the country was taking place, but all in vain. While simultaneously the world's news lines were carrying it as a priority headline to every corner of the globe, thus focussing world attention on the British occupation of Ireland.

Later that same evening, I.R.A. Headquarters issued a bulletin, stating that one of their units had carried out a successful raid for arms in Armagh, but no further information was released. During the ensuing week, a second statement was issued from H.Q. refuting some newspaper insinuations regarding the proposed use of the captured weapons—they would be used, H.Q. said, against the British Occupation Forces in due course. The Armagh action was brilliantly planned and executed with unrivalled bravery by a 20-man-strong unit. It stunned the enemy and quickened the Spirit of Freedom at home and abroad.

The startling inside story of this raid is told by the men who made it, on page five of this issue.

TWENTY BRAVE MEN

nty brave men, and Ireland's name
ross the earth is blazed,
Empire tottering to her doom
one more blow is dazed.

nty brave men, and, lo! the light
at shines in old men's eyes
thought the Fenian flame was
ead—
now it licks the skies.

women pray within their hearts
at God would give them sons,
thful and as true as they
took the foeman's guns.

y brave men, and lo! the pride
t lifts the drooping head;
diness in every step—
ation's shame is dead!

again to Bodenstown
turn for strength to Tone,
Twenty deathless Irishmen
not stand yet alone].

brave men, and England's pride
mbled in Armagh;
dly thro' a wakening land
out a wild "Hurrah!"

ss those men, those rebel men;
guide the I.R.A.
el each heart a manly part
eedom's Cause to play.

M. O CINNEIDE

INSIDE STORY OF RAID ON PAGE 5

During 1953, while gathering intelligence in Armagh, Leo McCormack, a Dublin IRA member (and a former British soldier) had noticed that the sentry at Gough Barracks was armed with an unloaded Sten gun. He formulated a plan whereby the IRA would infiltrate the barracks' garrison and carry out a raid for arms. Seán Garland, a 20-year-old IRA recruit from Dublin, was ordered to join the Royal Irish Fusiliers, based at Gough and over several months provided the IRA with detailed plans of the barracks. On 12 June 1954, an IRA unit, led by Charlie Murphy, raided the barracks and without firing a shot, made off with 250 rifles, 37 Sten guns and 9 Bren guns. It was a major coup for the organisation and led to both positive publicity and new recruits.

United Irishman, July 1954

Following the success of the Armagh raid, the depot of the Royal Inniskilling Fusiliers at Omagh was chosen for a similar effort. Dubliner Paddy Webster enlisted, to gather information. The mission was more complicated than Armagh and the possibility of having to kill British soldiers was taken into account. In the early hours of 16 October 1954, the IRA raided the base but a gun battle ensued in which five British soldiers and two IRA men were wounded. Eight IRA men were captured and tried under a nineteenth-century 'Treason Felony' law. IRA man Eamonn Boyce was sentenced to twelve years; the other men to ten. Boyce made clear that he regarded the treason charge as, '. . . ridiculous . . . I am a Dublin man, and as far as I am concerned, you have no right to charge me with treason'. Despite the raid's failure there was a wave of sympathy with the prisoners and renewed interest in the IRA, which had, for the first time in years, engaged the British Army in a gun battle. In 1955, two of the prisoners, Philip Clarke and Tom Mitchell, were elected as Westminster MPs.

IRISH
RESISTANCE
TO BRITISH
AGGRESSION.

Issued by the Army Council,
Óglaiġ na hÉireann,
NOVEMBER, 1954.

'IRISH RESISTANCE TO BRITISH AGGRESSION'

This statement from the IRA during November 1954, formed the basis of a popular poster that featured at many republican rallies during this period. The statement was issued after the Armagh and Omagh raids and makes clear that the IRA had 'decisively ruled out' military action in the 26 Counties. It also warns that premature action could deflect the movement from its overriding aim. The other notable aspect of republican politics of the time is the appeal to the Unionist population (including the police and B-Specials) to 'stand aside' in the fight between the IRA and the British. While the IRA wanted to avoid sectarian conflict and considered northern Protestants to be Irish, there was little understanding that Unionists would actively oppose an IRA campaign.

HUMPHREYS PAPERS, UCD ARCHIVES

IRISH RESISTANCE TO BRITISH AGGRESSION.

" Northern Bridgehead " is too valuable to her in time of war to be allowed slip easily through her fingers and the occupation and exploitation is as much to the detriment of the unionist population as the nationalist.

It is but right that this should be pointed out clearly to the unionists of every class and creed and an appeal be made to them, be they plain civilians, members of the R.U.C. or of the B Specials, to stand aside and refuse to become embroiled in the conflict between the foreign forces of oppression and the volunteer soldiers of the Irish Republican Army. No Irishman of any creed, class or political persuasion has anything to fear from the I.R.A. as long as he gives his first allegiance to our common Fatherland:

" We are one at heart if you be Ireland's friend,
Though miles apart our policies may trend,
There are but two great parties in the end."

THE Irish Republican Army has a carefully planned and progressive policy of opposition to the British occupation forces in the Six Counties and any type of aggressive military action in the 26-County area has been decisively ruled out of the scheme. All attempts to provoke unwise or precipitate action will be recognised as such and steadfastly ignored by those who know only one enemy—England, and who will refuse to be provoked into bringing discredit on the cause which they serve. It is the responsibility of the people of Ireland to see to it that those " elected representatives " who claim to act in their name do not sabotage the efforts of the inheritors of the Fenian faith in what will, with God's help, be the last and victorious phase of a struggle that has lasted only too long.

RECENT military operations carried out by the Irish Republican Army have been condemned by certain politicians as " isolated acts of violence " etc. The point which has apparently been lost on those who condemn is that these operations were not carried out for propaganda purposes. The successful raid in Armagh and the unsuccessful, but by no means discreditable operation in Omagh were made solely for the purpose of capturing arms from the enemy for use in the hands of those who are pledged to fight the British.

If sufficient financial support were forthcoming it would not be necessary to resort to such hazardous means to arm the resurgent youth of Ireland. But until that support is available it will be necessary to risk the lives, limbs and liberty of our bravest sons to replace the deficiency.

In spite of the condemnations of the politicians, in spite of the doubts of the "elected representatives," there must be some spark deep down in the soul of every Irishman worthy of the name, which burst into flame at the proof that the age-old enemy had once more misjudged the temper of the men of Ireland and that there are rising up among them young men of the same calibre as those who stood in the Bearna Baoghaol in every generation.

THE people of Ireland have a decision to make. Let them think well on it, because they will stand at the bar of history to answer for it and let it not be said of this generation that they failed those who once again have hurled defiance at the crumbling ramparts of that imperial and blood-stained power which for so long kept our country under the iron heel of oppression.

England still holds part of our land by force and in the eight hundred years of occupation never once has she given the slightest measure of amelioration except under force or the threat of force.

The dispassionate logical conclusion to be drawn from the history of the two countries is that Ireland can only achieve unity and freedom when the whole people of Ireland tell the British Army to get out or be driven out.

With charity towards all, with malice towards none, the Irish Republican Army looks forward with quiet confidence to the struggle that lies ahead. The trained, armed, disciplined and resolute soldiers of freedom pledge themselves once more to the task and asking God's blessing on their arms appeal to the people of Ireland to stand by them and to achieve with them the ideal which has shone so brightly and so steadily in the dreams and hopes of our people.

" In the name of God and of the dead generations Ireland, through us summons her children to her flag and strikes for her freedom."

Marian Printing Co., Ltd., rere 33 North Summer Street, Dublin

GLÓR  ULADH

THE VOICE OF THE REPUBLICAN NORTH

Vol. 1. No. 8. NOLLAG, 1955. Luach 3bp.

The ARBOURFIELD RAID

We cull the following from the 'Daily Express' of the 5th November, which paper also carried a facsimile of the headlines of th article as it appared in the 'United Irishman', November issue.

Ten men carried out the I.R.A. raid on Arborfield Camp, Berkshire, and they trained for it for six weeks before—at a secret camp. The I.R.A. story of the raid on August 13, told "by one of the volunteers who took part in it," was published in Dublin yesterday.

The men trained by night. They were specially briefed and given maps, drawings, and photographs of Arborfield.

A plan of the camp's armoury is also printed in the monthly, the United Irishman.

The unnamed raider's story says the ten men were told how to travel to England and how to contact the officer in charge of the operation on arrival there.

In England the O.C. briefed them again. It was arranged for some members of the expedition to travel the route to and from the objective several times so they would be familiar with the roads.

A car and route map was provided for each man.

Practice Run

One I.R.A. man on a practice run gave a hitch-hiking soldier from Arborfield a lift outside London.

Near Arborfield he picked up other soldiers returning to the camp and claims they provided him "with some valuable up-to-date information"

Then comes the story of the raid. It began at 2.10 a.m. The guards patrolling the camp—two parties of two men each—had changed at 2 a.m. and the raiders had two hours in which to work before the guard changedagain.

The guard commander, a sergeant, was held up at revolver point. So was the sentry at the barrier.

Two I.R.A. men armed with Webley revolvers rounded up the 12 remaining members of the guard.

They were tied hand and foot—some without trousers—gagged with cotton wool and field dressings and made to kneel against the walls in the guard room.

A bogus sentry "complete to the last detail in shoulder flashes and cap badge" was posted at the camp entrance.

2.14. The first I.R.A. van drove into the barrack square and halted at the armoury. Two minutes later a second van arrived.

But the raiders could not find keys No. 45 and 46—the keys to the magazine and armoury. The guard commander's personal keys did not fit. The keys, the story says, had been taken away by the armourer the night before.

The raiders forced the magazine doors.

3.15. The first van left the camp, loaded with ammunition, 50,000 rounds of ammunition and "a number of selected weapons from the armoury."

Hoodwinked

&hree men remained as a covering party "to ensure that the alarm would not be raised till both vans had time to reach their destinations."

4.10. The cover party held up and took prisoner four sentries coming on duty.

4.50. The covering party withdrew.

Three of the raiders, Donal Murphy, of Dublin; Joseph Doyle, of Bray (Co. Wicklow); and James Murphy, of Castledermot (Co. Kildare), were arrested after one of the vans was stopped by a police patrol outside London.

Doyle and Donal Murphy, who were in the first van when it was stopped, by "practising delaying tactics by way of fairy tales and adventure stories succeeded in hoodwinking and delaying the police sufficiently long to give the second van time to get away."

Says the I.R.A. account: "To their bravery and resourcefulness the remainder of the party owe their liberty!"

The raider ends: "It is my hope that I may have the privilege of taking part in future operations."

AN CONNRADH I mBEAL FEIRSDE

"Bíonn barraíocht Gaeilgeoirí ag cainnt ar bhás na teangan agus ar bhás an náisiúin," dúirt Cathal Mac Criostáil Cathaoirleach, ag cainnt dó ag cruinniú chinn bliana Choiste Ceanntair Bhéal Feirste, de Chonnradh na Gaeilge, Dia Sathairn, 19adh Samhain. Cuireann an cinéal seo cainnte éadóchas, ar fhólaimeoirí agus ar bhearlóirí i gcoiteann. Caithfidh muid treoir a thabhart dóbhtha agus dóchas a chothú ionntú cionns gur orthú atá aith-bheochaint na Gaeilge ag brath."

Bhí teachtaí ó cheithre Craobhacha deag de'n Chonnradh i láthair, le tuarascála ar obair na bliana seo a chluinstin agus le obair na bliana seo chugainn a leagadh amach.

In a thuarascáil, dúirt an Rúnaí, Brian Ó Maoileoin, gurbh é an rud a ba tabhachtaí agus a ba phráinní dá rabh le deánamh, obair aith-bheochana na Gaeilge sa' ghalltacht a cheangal le slánú na Gaeltachta. Bhí treoir le fáil, a dúirt sé, ins na foclaí seo de chuid Néill Uí Dhomhnaill :— "Níor léiríodh go grinn an obair mhór atá le deánamh má's linn dáiríre an Ghaeilg a chur i réim."

"Na cuspóirí náisiúnta eile a bhí againn, míníodh go beacht iad ar feadh shé scór bliain go dtí go rabh siad uilig ion-tuigthe as aon fhocal amháin—POBLACHT."

"Cá h-uair a bhéas cuspóirí na Gaeilge, comh buailte isteach 'nár n-intinn a's go mbéidh siad uilig ion-tuigthe againn as an aon fhocal amháin —GAELTACHT ?"

Bhí súil aige go n-éireochadh leis an Ghluaiseacht Ghaelach, céim mhór a thabhairt ionns ar an bharr-shamhail sin sa bhliain atá romhainn.

Thug an Cisdeoir, Caoimhín Mag Uidhir cunntas ari chúrsaí airgid na bliana a thaisbean go rabh doigh mhaith ar an chisde agus ghabh an Coisde buíochas leis as a shaothar.

Taoghadh na daoine seo leanas mar oifigigh i gcóir na bliana 1955-56.

Cathaoirleach :— Cathal Mac Criostáil.
Leas Chathaoirleach :— Pádraig Mac Giolla Ruaidh.
Rúnaí :— Brian Ó Maoileoin.
Leas Rúnaí :— Seán Ó Cearnaigh.
Cisteoir :— Caoimhín Mag Uidhir.
Leas Chisteoir :— Seán Mac Ghoill.

Taoghadh Cathal Mac Criostáil, Pádraig Mac Giolla Ruaidh, Tomás Ó Monacháin agus Brian Ó Maoileoin le gníomhú mar theachtaí o'n Choiste Ceanntair ar Chomhaltas Uladh.

Ar na rúin a cuireadh i bhfeidhm bhí ceann amháin a mhol go mbunóchadh an Coiste Ceanntair Coiste Gaeltachta, le cuidiú le neartú Ghaeltacht Thír Chonaill. Socruigheadh fosda go mbunóchthaí fá-choiste bollscaireachta agus go gceapfaí oifigeach le timireacht a dheánamh eadar an Choiste Ceanntair agus Ghaeil uilig na Cathrach.

I dtaca leis an Choiste Gaeltachta de, dúirt Pádraig Mac Giolla Ruaidh, mar fhreagair ar an bharúil nach dtiocfadh le Gaeilgeoirí Bhéal Feirste, Gaeltacht Thír Chonaill a shlánú, go rabh Gaelú Chúige Uladh i dtuilleamuí ar neart na Gaeltachta sin agus mar gheall ar sin go rabh dualgas orthú chinntuí oomh fada agus thiocfadh leo chan amháin go slánochthaí í ach go méadóchadh sí go gasta.

Dúirt León Ó Mairtín, gur de thairbhe na Comhdhála Agóide, fó choiste eile de chuid an Choiste Ceanntair, a bunaíodh "Muinntir na Gaeltachta," agus gur chruthú sin go dtiocfadh le Gaeil Bhéal Feirste cuidiú a thabhairt do'n Ghaeltacht.

Ar na daoine eile a labhair bhí: Tomás Ó h-Éanáin, Seán Ó Labhra, Tomás Ó Monacháin, Seán Ó Cearnaigh, Seán Ó Ceallacháin, Séamus Ó Maolmóna, Liam Ó Dochartaigh agus Séamus Mac Díarmuda.

On 13 August 1955, the IRA attempted another arms raid in England. A team of IRA members, led by Rory Brady (later Ruairi Ó Brádaigh) entered a British army camp at Arbourfield, Berkshire, in the early hours of the morning. They subdued and secured almost 20 soldiers without raising the alarm and made off with two vans containing over 50,000 rounds of ammunition, 55 Sten guns and 10 Bren guns. However, the overloaded vans were spotted by police and ultimately the material recaptured. Three IRA men, Donal Murphy, Seamus Murphy and Joe Doyle, were given life sentences for their part in the raid: a vindictive response, given that nobody had been hurt in the operation.

Glór Uladh, Nollaig 1955

RESISTANCE

During 1955, Seán Cronin, a former Irish Army officer and journalist, who had spent several years in the United States, joined the IRA. Cronin became the chief strategist behind 'Operation Harvest', the IRA's plan for a campaign in Northern Ireland. Cronin argued that the lessons of the War of Independence and the recent experience of guerilla war in Palestine, Vietnam and Cyprus offered a template for the IRA. He suggested a campaign which would be waged by IRA columns based in the South against British installations and communications networks, creating 'liberated areas' and inspiring a nationalist uprising in the North. IRA volunteers would wear uniform and seek to adhere to the rules of the Geneva Convention.

Resistance was published during 1957 and outlined the progress of the IRA's campaign to that date. The cover design incorporates the tricolour flash worn on their uniforms by IRA volunteers from 1956-62. The booklet was written by Cronin, who became IRA chief of staff in 1959, was jailed on several occasions and emigrated to the U.S. after 1962. He was the *Irish Times* Washington correspondent for many years. This pamphlet, and IRA statements in this era, were signed by, 'J.J. McGarrity', in memory of the Clan na Gael leader who died in 1940.

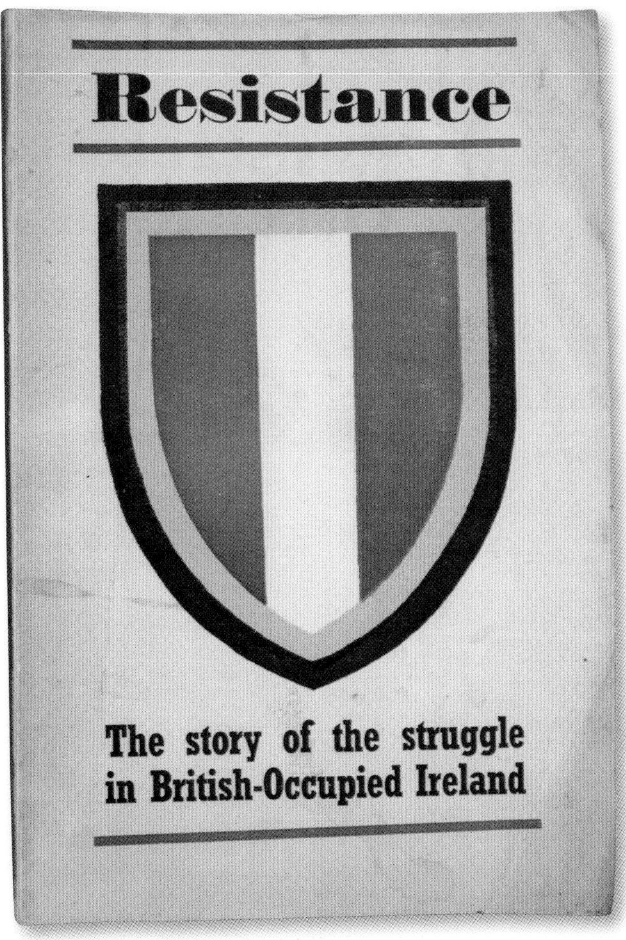

COURTESY OF THE NATIONAL LIBRARY OF IRELAND

THE CAMPAIGN BEGINS

During December 1956, IRA volunteers from across the South were brought to a farm at Athboy, Co. Meath, before being divided into columns and moved up to the border. The long-awaited campaign finally began with attacks on 12 December.

UNITED IRISHMAN

BULLETIN

NODLAIG 15, 1956 — 3 P.

National Resistance to British Occupation

ORGANISED RESISTANCE TO BRITISH RULE IN IRELAND BEGAN DURING THE EARLY HOURS OF DEC. 12, WHEN KEY BRITISH OCCUPATION POINTS IN THE SIX COUNTIES WERE ATTACKED BY ARMED UNITS OF THE REPUBLICAN MOVEMENT.

Striking forces penetrated the enemy's defences system despite the oft-repeated boasts and assurances by British and Stormont spokesmen that they were safe from attack.

Among the points hit were :

★ **The new British Territorial Army Barracks at Enniskillen which was almost completely demolished.**

★ **The B.B.C. booster transmission centre near Derry City which was totally dsetroyed.**

★ **Gough Barracks, Armagh, one of the main depots of the British Occupation forces in in the Six Counties.**

★ **Magherafelt, Co. Derry, where the Court-house was destroyed.**

★ **Torr Head in Co. Antrim, where a unit about to hit the Royal Air Force Radar Station, ran into an R.U.C. patrol and a clash occurred.**

★ **The Lady Brooke bridge at Lisnakea and the Garry Bridge near Enniskillen, Co. Fermanagh.**

As well, communications were cut in many areas and roads were blocked.

In these attacks the Republican forces suffered no casualties although many clashes with British military, armed B-Specials and police took place. Three Irish Republicans were seized at the Torr Head, Co. Antrim clash and two in Armagh City. They have been brought before Special Courts and charged with attempted murder.

THE CALL

An official statement to the Irish people explained the new phase the Irish struggle for freedom has now entered.

It was pointed out that resistance to British rule in occupied Ireland had now entered a decisive stage, that our people in the Six Counties were carrying the fight to the enemy. "They are the direct victims of British Imperialism and they are also the backbone of the national revolutionary resurgence."

United Irishman, Nollaig 1956 UNITED IRISHMAN

Special editions of the *United Irishman* reported that 'in these attacks the Republican forces suffered no casualties although many clashes with British military, armed B-Specials and police took place'.

UNITED IRISHMAN

BULLETIN

NODLAIG 22, 1956

3 P.

Second Week of Campaign Against British Rule

DURING THE SECOND WEEK OF THE CAMPAIGN OF RESISTANCE IN OCCUPIED IRELAND, THE ENEMY WAS HIT IN MANY AREAS, A REPORT FROM THE REPUBLICAN PUBLICITY BUREAU STATES:

On Dec. 17, at Nutfield—Munville Cross, half way between Lisnaskea and Brookeborough, Co. Fermanagh, an RUC patrol was ambushed by Irish freedom fighter guerrillas at 7.45 in the evening. A constable was shot twice in the leg and the patrol swiftly pulled out of the area and headed for Lisnaskea.

Later, RUC, B-Specials and British troops, scoured the Fermanagh area in a search for guerrillas. The freedom fighters returned to their Six-County bases.

A half hour later residents reported explosions in the Newtownbutler area.

THEIR SEARCH GOES ON

Police, Specials and military have now turned the Fermanagh area into a war-zone. Journalists touring the area have been halted many times, their identities double-checked, their cars searched and they themselves made to stand one side on the roadway while police went through their belongings.

The people report that police and Specials in the Fermanagh area are thoroughly scared. The presence of British troops hasn't made them any happier for they must now act as guides.

The Specials travel in groups 20-50 strong. They are employed to conduct raids on unoccupied dwellings or to terrorise peaceful citizens. The hazardous work of guerrilla warfare is not to their liking.

BROOKEBOROUGH

Lord Brookeborough, the Six County puppet Premier, went on a British television show to explain, as Stormont put it, his side of the case to 10 million listeners.

He wasn't very happy. In the middle of his speech he received an urgent message that a police patrol had been ambushed near his "country seat."

United Irishman, Nollaig 1956 UNITED IRISHMAN

Ulaidh ag Aiséirghe

TONE 1798 — MITCHEL 1846 — Ní Síothcháin gan Saoirse — CONNOLLY 1916 — McCAUGHEY 1946

RESURGENT ULSTER

Vol. 2, No. 22. SEPTEMBER, 1954. Price—THREEPENCE

THE LESSON OF POMEROY

On Thursday, 19th August, 1954 the inhabitants of Pomeroy and surrounding districts had gathered together to welcome home Mr. Liam Kelly Stormont M.P. and Senator in the 26-County Senate who had been released from prison early in the day. Headed by a Tricolour which they had been forbidden to carry, they were met by a strong force of R.U.C. and "B" Specials with drawn batons who attempted to seize the flag which was strongly defended by the standard bearers and guard of honour.

Ruthlessly, savagely and ferociously the people were batoned and bludgeoned—young and old of both sexes—by the guardians of Stormont's law and order. Bludgeoned back into their homes but not without their flag which they managed to retain. Some who had taken temporary shelter during the melee had again to face the hungry baton-warriors on their way to their own homes and many were met and beaten on the roads patrolled only by the armed Specials of Stormont. A reign of police terror prevailed that night in Pomeroy at the foot of those mountains where the song says "they kept the cause of freedom safe up on the mountains high."

In writing the story of the heroic men and women of Pomeroy who manned the Bearna Baoghail and courageously defended the Flag of the Republic on that August night in this year 1954 let it not be thought by Republican Ireland that we are accepting or condoning the politics of Liam Kelly or his political organisation Fianna Uladh; or that we are aligning ourselves in any way with him or his organisation.

Three main reasons can be given for our attitude in this respect.

1 Fianna Uladh is purely a partitionist organisation, confining their members to the Six Counties. 2 They recognise and accept the Constitution of the 26-County Govt—a Constitution which in itself recognises the **Legal Existence of the Six Counties.** Yet this is the Constitution Fianna Uladh wants extended to cover the Six Counties And lest we forget it is the Constitution under which 16 Republicans were martyred—10 being executed in the prisons or shot down mercilessly in the streets; 3 were allowed to die on hunger-strike, 2 died in prison and 1 was hanged by England's hangman who was imported for the occasion—included in the list was Sean MacCaughey who was born in Tyrone and Tom Harte from Lurgan. 3 Liam Kelly has already signed a written declaration that if elected to Stormont's Parliament, he will take his seat and abide by the regulations of Stormont. A man's word is his bond! . . .

Down through the years we have seen other men with great National records enter Leinster House with the same intentions—the same promises as Liam Kelly. To name but a few, Dan Breen, Frank Aiken, DeValera himself who once stated in Leinster House that "the rightful or legitimate authority in this country remains outside this House" meaning the 2nd Dail Eireann who refused to accept the Treaty of 1921, and yet let us scan the records of these men and the Government which they represented and we will find a reign of persecution, imprisonment and murder directed against the Republican Movement and its adherents.

We believe that the followers of Liam Kelly and Fianna Uladh are sincere in their Republicanism but let them take warning ere it is too late. Let them learn the lesson of those who put the same trust in DeValera and Co. and found that they had chosen a worse evil. Let them realise that Liam Kelly's Senatorship has been sponsored by Clann na Poblachta whose members joined the Coalition Govt. with the murderers of Rory O'Connor, Liam Mellowes, Dick Barrett and Joe McKelvey.

Let them realise that all these parties are opposed to the use of force as a solution to the achievement of our unity and independence and that neither they nor the executive of Fianna Uladh have publicly uttered one word of protest against the imprisonment of Republican soldiers at present both in England and Belfast.

Let them realise that they will be helping to split the Republican vote in the next General Election for Westminster which Sinn Fein announced before the setting up of Fianna Uladh that they would contest. Republican unity in the North must not be sundered at the whim of a few. It certainly will not be achieved at the 26 County Senate any more than by attendance at Stormont or Westminster.

Let them not make the mistake of those who seceded from Sinn Fein and the militant organisation in 1922 and again in 1926 when Fianna Fail were founded and on down the years with the idea that they had a better way of achieving freedom It has taken over 30 years to prove them failures, but at such a cost of Republican lives and suffering.

Armagh has shown us the strength of Republican leadership—Pomeroy has exemplified the courage and enthusiasm of the Republican rank and file. Let us weld both together in that organisation which has carried on the continuity of the struggle since 1916—Sinn Fein and kindred organisations—whose members have proved their sincerity of aims and objects down through the years—sincerity and loyalty which can be found on the little white crosses—on marble memorials which mark the last resting place of those who preferred Death to Disunity, Desertion or Dishonour.

There must be no more uneven struggles like Pomeroy—that is the lesson of Pomeroy.

They must not be forgotten in their lonely prison cells

Wakefield Prison, England—
Cathal Goulding, Dublin. 8 years.

Wormwood Scrubbs, England—
Manus Canning, Derry. 8 years.
Sean Stephenson, England. 8 years.

Liverpool Prison, England—
J. P. MacCallum, Belfast. 6 years.

Belfast Prison—
Joe Campbell, Newry. 5 years.
Leo MacCormick, Dublin. 4 years.
Kevin MacConnell, Dublin. 3 months.

Remanded in Belfast Prison—
Kevin O'Rourke, Banbridge.
James Rowntree, Newry.
James E. Kearns, Newry.
Matthew Loy, Newry.
Thomas Murtagh, Armagh.
Patrick Grimes, Pomeroy.

Join Sinn Fein

Are you helping in any way in the struggle for your country's Unity and Freedom? **Don't** you realise that your country is being denied **her** God-given right to Freedom by her oppressor, England? that for over 700 years your ancestors have carried on the struggle to release her from the chains of the invader? That thousands have suffered and died in that struggle—that they died for you? What way are you showing your gratitude? What way can you show it? You reply—By joining in that struggle—by serving as they served; by joining the Republican movement. Inquiries (personal) can be made to any of the following :—

J. Cahill, 60 Divis St., Belfast.
J. MacGurk, 37 Institution Place, Belfast.
P. Doyle, 45 Whiterock Crescent, Belfast.
F. MacGlade, 126 Ardilea St., Belfast.
J. Steele, c/o 5 Ballymurphy Rd., Belfast.

SAOR ULADH

In the post-1948 period the IRA had faced competition from a number of rival organisations, mainly made up of ex-members frustrated at the lack of military action. In Dublin alone during the early 1950s, there were An Rosc Catha, Arm na Saoirse and a group calling itself the Irish Republican Brotherhood (which carried out a bomb attack on the British Embassy in May 1951). The IRA eventually managed either to subsume such organisations or to intimidate them out of existence.

A more serious threat was Saor Uladh, a paramilitary organisation set up by IRA commander Liam Kelly in Co. Tyrone.

From Dungannon, Kelly had been jailed from 1941-45 and on release helped reorganise the IRA in his area. Kelly left the IRA during 1951 and maintained a strong base of support in east Tyrone. Politically, he was influenced by Clann na Poblachta, believing that the constitutional status of the 26 Counties was no longer an issue and that republicans should take seats in Leinster House. Kelly was elected to Stormont as an abstentionist anti-partition MP during 1953. However, he was jailed on charges of sedition in November 1953. While he was imprisoned, Fianna Uladh was launched as a political party. In July 1954, Kelly was elected to the Seanad on the nomination of Seán MacBride, who was back in government as part of a Fine Gael-led administration.

In his first appearance in the Seanad in November 1954, Kelly made it clear that in his view armed force was the only way to end partition. This article in *Resurgent Ulster* refers to the events that occurred when Kelly was released from prison in Belfast and welcomed back to Pomeroy in August 1954. Several thousand people gathered to greet him, displaying tricolours and republican flags. When the RUC attempted to seize these, major rioting broke out. The article illustrates the frustration felt by the republican movement about Kelly. The IRA considered his recognition of Leinster House to be treacherous, yet he was clearly a very popular figure in Tyrone. They were also aware that he was building up his own paramilitary network, Saor Uladh, recruiting new members from Co. Derry and Belfast. On 26 November 1955, his organisation attacked Roslea RUC barracks, Co. Fermanagh, and in the ensuing gun battle Connie Green, a veteran of World War II and a Saor Uladh training officer, was killed.

During 1956, there were more splits. A group of Dublin IRA members, unhappy with the aftermath of recent raids and frustrated by the lack of a formal campaign, broke away. The group was led by Joe Christle, a part-time UCD student and charismatic public speaker who had taken part in the Armagh and Omagh operations. Christle was warned by the IRA to cease activity but ignored them.

Facing page: *Resurgent Ulster* praises nationalist resistance to the police in Pomeroy, but warns that Liam Kelly accepts the southern state. September, 1954.

His group linked up with Saor Uladh and on 11 November 1956, they destroyed customs huts along the border.

Even when the IRA's own campaign began, Saor Uladh continued its operations, causing huge damage by blowing up the locks on the Newry Canal in May 1957, putting the port out of operation for two months (an action condemned by the IRA). Saor Uladh member Aloysius Hand was killed in action in Co. Fermanagh during July 1958.

In the Republic Saor Uladh carried out arms raids (exchanging shots with gardaí on one occasion). Unlike the IRA, if charged, its members recognised the courts. Saor Uladh members who were interned in the Curragh were ostracised by their IRA co-prisoners. Christle's group also carried out the destruction of British war memorials in the South (actions which again were renounced by the IRA).

In 1960, Liam Kelly emigrated to the United States. Over time a few Saor Uladh members returned to the IRA. Kelly himself was active in republican politics in New York after August 1969 and supported the Official IRA from 1970, becoming a leading member of its American network. Saor Uladh remained in existence and carried out operations in Tyrone during the early 1970s, until eventually most of its members joined the Provisional IRA.

'THEY GAVE THEIR LIVES': SOUTH AND O'HANLON

The first fatalities of the Border campaign occurred over the New Year's holiday 1956-57. An IRA column, led by Ruairi Ó Brádaigh, killed a policeman during an attack on Derrylin Barracks, Co. Fermanagh. At Brookeborough, Co. Fermanagh, a column led by Seán Garland attempted a similar attack. However, in the ensuing gun battle Seán South from Limerick and Fergal O'Hanlon from Monaghan were killed. The first deaths of southern IRA members in conflict with Crown forces for decades, their deaths unleashed a wave of emotional sympathy. Thousands attended the funerals and a pamphlet, *They Kept Faith*, sold over 10,000 copies in the space of a month. In November 1957, the worst republican losses of the campaign occurred at Edentubber, Co. Louth, when five men (four IRA volunteers and one supporter) were killed in a premature explosion. There was less of a public reaction to these deaths, however, reflecting declining interest in the campaign.

Facing page: *United Irishman*, January 1957

THE
an t-Éireannach Aontuighthe
UNITED IRISHMAN
is í an Poblacht ár gcuspóir
AMERICAN EDITION

IML. IX. UIMHIR 11. EANAIR, 1957 10 CENTS

REVOLT IN THE NORTH

RESISTANCE OF PEOPLE GROWS

In all Six Counties guerrillas struck back as Britain rushed troops to protect her colonial possession and strategic bridgehead in Ireland.

A proclamation called on the Irish people at home and abroad to support the fight for national liberation. Our people were asked to sink their differences and back their oppressed brothers and sisters in the north.

In the weeks since, despite mass arrests and wholesale terror tactics, the Resistance has gained ground everywhere and martial law in all but name exists in many areas. Stormont invoked the Special Powers Act and British troops blew bridges, cratered roads and engaged in widespread searches of mountainous areas with R.U.C. and B-Special Constabulary.

During the opening phase of the campaign the R.U.C. and Specials were not attacked. Instead, the Resistance called on them to either stand apart or take their place with their fellow Irishmen in the fight for freedom.

When this warning went unheeded, the R.U.C. and Specials became legitimate targets of the guerrillas for without these forces British rule could hardly maintain itself behind the cloak of "legitimacy" in occupied Ireland.

The 26-County authorities arrested many freedom fighters resting along border areas. Stormont attempted to exploit the myth that the campaign consisted of "cross-border-forays" but the camouflage grew thin as attacks occurred in points far removed from the border.

Stormont had even less luck ferreting out—aided by British troops—guerrilla bases. The people of occupied Ireland were solid to the core.

Two freedom fighters died following an engagement at Brookeborough. Four others were wounded. One of them died after being taken by enemy forces.

A weekly Bulletin giving full details of the struggle is published and distributed by this newspaper.

British occupation forces go into action in the Six Counties. Despite thousands of troops—reinforced by R.U.C. and Specials—Irish freedom fighters continued to hit British installations in occupied Ireland. Mainstay of the Resistance is the Nationalist population.

NEW DAY DAWNING

A new chapter is being written in the story of Ireland—but the Irish people for the most part are not aware of this.

Stormont has thrown a curtain of secrecy around events in the north. The only statements allowed are from Stormont sources and these are notoriously inaccurate and one-sided.

Our people in the south—and our exiles everywhere — have little opportunity of assessing for themselves what is really happening. The weekly Bulletin of the **"United Irishman"** has a limited circulation.

Our people in the south are not aware of the wave of enthusiasm passing through the north. And our people in the north are apt to blame their kindred in the south for not backing more strongly the fight for freedom.

For let there be no mistake about it: This is a fight for freedom.

This fight will be won when the united strength of our people is thrown in the scales against British imperialism. This tyranny has dominated us for too long. The time has now come when the hated invader must be driven from our land forever.

The enemy's bridgehead is weakening. We hope that in the months to come it will crumble completely.

Now is the time for all Irish men and women to stand shoulder to shoulder against the enemy of our people — British Imperialism.

THEY GAVE THEIR LIVES

Thousands of Irish men and women paid their respects to the two freedom fighters who were killed while engaging the enemy at Brookeborough, Co. Fermanagh, on Jan. 1, 1957.

They were: Sean Sabhait, a 29-year-old native of Limerick City and Fergal O'Hanlon, a 20-year-old Monaghan youth.

Irish men and women everywhere paid tribute to the memory of the two men who died fighting for freedom.

Sean Sabhait followed closely the Pearse ideal of an "Ireland not free merely but Gaelic as well, not Gaelic merely but free as well." These twin axioms were the motivating factors in his life.

He used the native national tongue on all occasions—even during the stresses and strains of a campaign. He taught by example and men who never spoke the language in their lives used their Irish — however limited— in conversation with him.

The more outgoing Fergal formed his philosophy around the belief that only by sacrifice could freedom be won. And he gave his young life in pursuit of this belief.

Sean Sabhait and Fergal O'Hanlon are names that will live on in the annals of the Irish people.

PUBLIC BODIES PROTEST

County Tipperary County Council has unanimously resolved that the British Government withdraw its forces from Ireland; that the 26-County Government desist from all operations along the border and release the prisoners now in custody as a result of their activities in the Six Counties. Other public bodies have passed similar resolutions.

Mr. D. Kennedy said that today in Ireland they had only a few who were keeping the spark of Republicanism alive.

The Chairman (Mr. Des Hanafin) said that he would like to be associated with the resolution and added that he would like to quote from Pearse's oration over the grave of O'Donovan Rossa:

"Ireland unfree shall never be at peace."

THIS ISSUE

We regret the late publication date of this issue. An attempt to wreck the machinery of our printer's plant was responsible for the hold-up.

CIRCULATE "THE UNITED IRISHMAN"

SUPPORT THE STRUGGLE!

Now is the time for Irish men and women at home and abroad to sink their differences and gather around the young men in their fight to-day for Irish freedom.

The young men of the 1956 Resistance to British occupation need your help urgently.

Without the support of the Nationalist people in the Six Counties there could be no fight for freedom.

THEY are giving their support. But the task lies heavily on them. They too need the backing of all our people.

Give it to them now.

their struggle within ... Counties only — that is within the area occupied and directly controlled by Britain. Their object is to drive Britain's occupation army from our country and hand back to our people the whole of this island to be administered as a united, independent, democratic Republic.

No part of this aim conflicts with the basic desires of the Irish people—or any section of the Irish people. These freedom fighters certainly have no quarrel with the young men in the armed forces of the 26-Counties They want none. And they seek none.

IRELAND FIRST

That is their aim and it should hardly need emphasising at this stage. The Irish Republican movement has declared this policy openly time out of

it will appear ... they are clashing with the 26-County authorities.

We do not have the resources or the propaganda media to refute these accusations. The newspapers have been warned not to report public meetings backing the Resistance in the North.

Young soldiers were sent to border areas just before Christmas to round up what were termed "irresponsible elements," and this was expected to get their backs up as they would blame their troubles on Irish Republicans.

THE POSITION

The freedom fighters in the North appreciate the awkward position the armed forces of the 26 Counties have been placed in.

They know that the feeling of freedom—of wanting to see this country released from

people stand when it comes to the test of England versus Ireland.

They know that the majority of the Irish people are behind them in this struggle. We may differ on other matters but in this one essential we are as one.

But the test is never allowed to be seen that clearly. The people with a vested interest in the maintenance of the present division will see to that.

Their job is to confuse the issue. Their job is to cast stones at the freedom fighters and call the Resistance all kinds of damning names. But this is one time when they will not succeed.

What is at stake is too basic to all of us. Our history and tradition is proof against their libels. The time is now. The opportunity is great. The Irish people will grasp both with firm hands.

One ... "Resistance Movement" against British occupation of our Six Counties is that outside nations are already taking a live interest in the p r o b l e m. The "Actionists" have timed their "protests" well, sparing life as far as possible but making their mark in a significant way for all the world to know.

Mr. Costello, whilst condemning the use of force in his radio pronouncement on Jan. 6 did not mention the fundamental cause of all the political unrest — The occupation of Ireland's national territory by England. Ireland unfree can never be at peace.

—Irish Echo, N.Y.

lism. True democracy, on the other hand is Christian, the commandments of God and the Sermon on the Mount put into practice.

I think that the philosophy of the continental Christian democratic parties is deserving of our attention. We have something to learn from the writings of Jacques Maritain. This great man has had the vision to see the past in its proper perspective, and from the past to know the answer to the problems of the future.

If to some the French Revolution is a manifestation of the Antichrist, it is to others a diluted or secularised Christianity needing only a living Christian ideology to make of it something truly magnificent. That is what I believe.

—FEAR FEASA.

FREEDOM FIGHTER

Resistance fighter from the occupied area gives exclusive interview to Dom Gordon for the C.B.C. Radio and Television network.

How long have you been a member of the Republican movement?

Over four years.

Why did you join the Freedom Fighters?

A simple answer is not possible. Environment and education were certainly major factors. By education I don't mean book-learning only: but what I learned as a boy and young man of Ireland's history from the people with whom I worked and played. The prosperity, piety and learning of our people before occupation was once an inspiration to Western Europe: the degradation and persecution throughout the centuries—right up to this present moment—of any Irishman who dare oppose by word or deed the might of English law and power impels us who are their children to vindicate them.

Acts of confiscation, proscription and treason felony—devilish devices to make murder, treachery and corruption legal, were used by England's parliament and Royal House to intimidate us. Jails, pitch-caps, gallows and firing-squads—the poison-cup, slander and lies were the instruments used to batter us into subjection.

There is a spirit in the Irish nation that will not surrender its right to freedom. I am a member of the nation and I have many comrades. We have a memory of an ancient glory that we would revive. Even if we die in its achievement and defence the generations yet to come will be able to live in peace and harmony with themselves and other nations. When we are free, England, now our only enemy, may well become our greatest friend.

Have you taken part in any raids?

Yes. I was at Lisnaskea, Derrylin and Brookeborough. At Lisnaskea we heard the inhabitants shout between machine-gun fire "Give it to t h e m, lads," sufficient evidence to us on the column that we had the support of the ordinary people.

What was the purpose of these raids?

What is the purpose would be a better question. It is threefold. (1) To spotlight the part that Ireland is still forcibly occupied by British troops. (2) that occupation is bitterly resented by 80% of the whole Irish people and by almost 40% of the people of the six occupied countries. (3) We aim to rally our people in their resistance to the occupation forces and to make the occupation difficult, costly and impossible.

Ireland can only become free when the nation is united to achieve its independence. In the past the Irish people have been cowed into sullen acceptance of conquest by a combination of England's military might and the timorous pleas of a small section of the Irish people who have prospered by becoming tools of English policy in Ireland. These people are known throughout Ireland's history as "The Queen's men and "Castle Cawtholics."

I notice, Mr. Brown, that you are in uniform. What is the significance of this?

Britain has always treated our resistance fighters as criminals and has tortured them and executed them on capture. Recent Geneva Conventions recognised Resistance Fighters as legitimate combatants entitled to full prisoner-of-war status if captured. Our men, wearing uniform with tricolour shoulder flash are Resistance Fighters, and if Britain executes any of them when captured she will be going contrary to the Geneva Conventions and will be guilty of official murder.

What plans do you and the other members of the Republican movement have for the future?

Our plans are to fight on till the British troops have been withdrawn from our country and a Parliament for the 32 Counties of Ireland has been established by the free vote of the whole Irish people.

United Irishman, January 1957

'FREEDOM FIGHTER'

This article appeared in the *United Irishman* of February 1957, based on the transcript of an interview of an IRA man by the C.B.C. network. It offers an illustration of the motivations of activists during the Border campaign.

JAMES CROSSAN

On 24 August 1958, James Crossan, a Sinn Féin organiser living in Co. Cavan, was shot dead by the RUC near the Mullan customs post on the Fermanagh border. Republicans claimed he had been ambushed by members of the Special Constabulary. In September 1958, the IRA warned that the B-Specials were now 'legitimate resistance targets'. The killing of Crossan was raised in Dáil Éireann by Clann na Poblachta, but the Flanna Fáil government ruled out an enquiry.

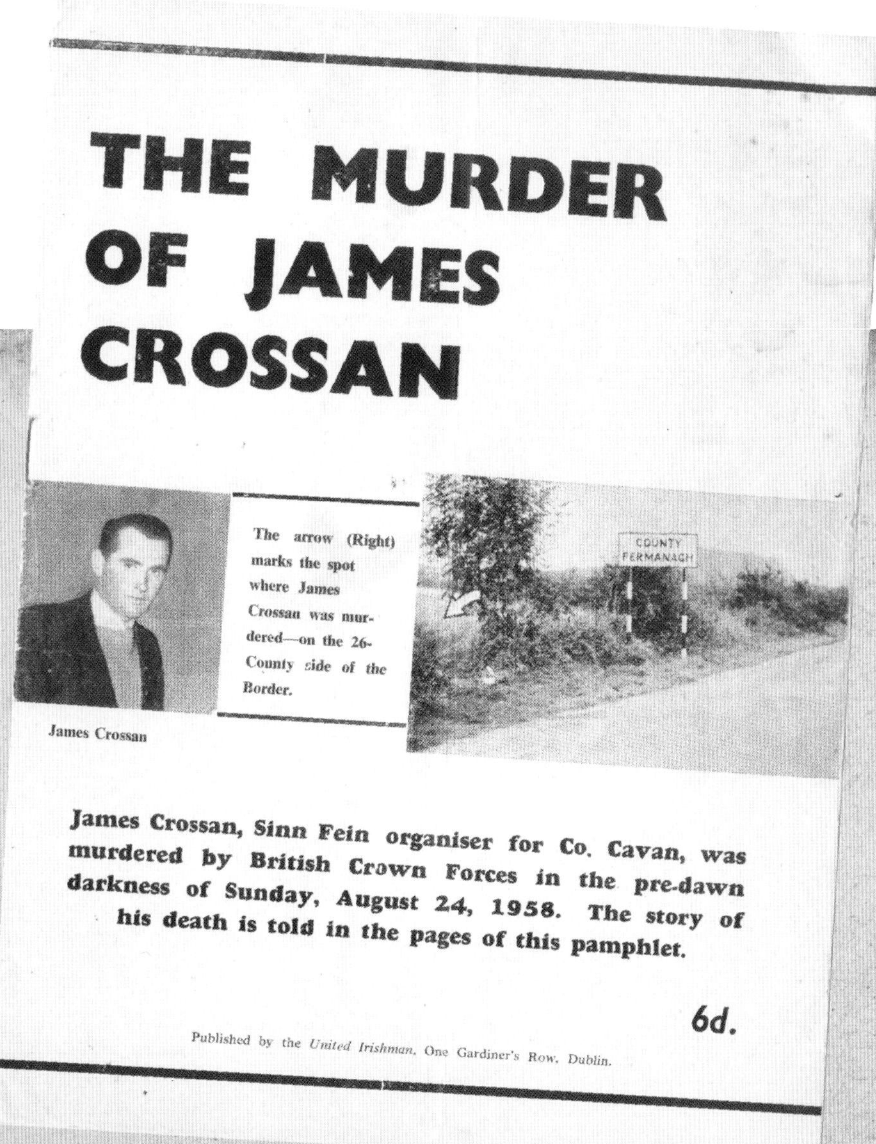

THE MURDER OF JAMES CROSSAN

The arrow (Right) marks the spot where James Crossan was murdered—on the 26-County side of the Border.

James Crossan

James Crossan, Sinn Fein organiser for Co. Cavan, was murdered by British Crown Forces in the pre-dawn darkness of Sunday, August 24, 1958. The story of his death is told in the pages of this pamphlet.

6d.

Published by the *United Irishman*, One Gardiner's Row, Dublin.

James Crossan, pamphlet cover, *United Irishman*, 1958

an t-éireannaċ aontuiġte

The UNITED IRISHMAN

IML. XIII. UIMHIR 2. FEABHRA (FEB.), 1961. 4d. (10 CENTS)

Kilkenny Raids and Arrests
Page 3

OPEN COLLABORATION WITH BRITISH FORCES

Important Sinn Fein Statement

THE pattern of collaboration is fully revealed in the tactics employed by rulers, North and South, and by the forces over which they exercise control, says a statement issued by the Publicity Committee of Sinn Féin on January 23.

The full text of the statement is as follows:

The proclamation of the Irish Republic in 1916 and its establishment in 1919, was a clear and definite expression of the will of the vast majority of the Irish people for an ending of British interference in the affairs of the Irish nation. In 1922, Dail Eireann, the established Government of the Irish Republic, was overthrown and partition of the national territory was imposed on the Irish people by Britain. Thus Britain remained in occupation of part of the Irish Nation.

The Six County and 26-County institutions of Government created to enforce and maintain partition have since been sustained with the aid of the military and police forces at their disposal. In order to make partition government effective and to obstruct and retard all efforts to end British occupation, military and police forces—North and South of the border—have worked in close collaboration.

HIDDEN FOR YEARS

For years this collaboration was maintained in a subtle and undercover manner, camouflaged and screened from the knowledge of the general body of the Irish people. Its existence was known only to those participating in it and to members of the Republican Movement who were its victims — because destruction of that Movement was its main target.

In latter years the Governments of Stormont and Leinster House have gradually abandoned their efforts to camouflage the collaboration between their forces in maintaining British rule in Ireland. At the present time little, if any, effort is made to conceal from the Irish people, or to screen from the eyes of the world, the collaboration that has existed all along and which is now blatantly exercised for all to see.

The pattern of the collaboration is fully revealed in the tactics employed by rulers, North and South, and by the forces over which they exercise control.

In the Six Counties Sinn Fein is banned. Membership of it, and even support of it, are punishable with imprisonment, with or without trial. Its members and supporters are victimised in every conceivable way. Their homes are touted and raided at will by British military and police forces. Their places of employment are visited and an effort made to intimidate their employers into sacking them.

TORTURE AND BRIBERY

In a number of instances prisoners have been beaten up and otherwise tortured, in an attempt to compel them to become common informers. In a further effort to extract information, men and women, boys and girls, are questioned and often offered jobs and bribes of money to reveal what they may know about members of the Republican Movement. As was to be expected under continued British occupation the coercion of Irish Separatists continued unabated in the Six County area.

The Irish people never expected that similar coercion would exist in the 26-County State. They were told that this area was independent and that its Government's primary aim was the Unity and Freedom of the National territory. However, a brief sketch of the picture in the Free State reveals almost an exact facsimile of the methods employed by Britain and her Irish collaborators in the Northern Statelet to smash the Republican Movement.

In so far as members and supporters of the Movement are concerned the natural and moral rights of the individual may be described in simple and plain terms as non-existent. Sinn Fein has not been officially banned but it is treated as a banned organisation. Members of Sinn Fein are subject to imprisonment, with or without trial. The venues at which their meetings, public and private, are held are continually touted by members of the 26-County police force.

Their homes, in many instances, receive similar attention and in pursuit of their daily avocations and amusements they are "trailed" by policemen. Their movements are questioned and they are asked to disclose any knowledge they may have about the movements of others. For refusal to inform on themselves and to turn informer on others they are imprisoned.

EMPLOYERS INTIMIDATED

In an effort to deprive members of Sinn Fein of their means of livelihood and thus reduce them and their dependants to the starvation level that compels emigration, places of employment are visited and employers intimidated. At the Ard-Fheisanna of 1958 and 1959 documents belonging to the Organisation were seized from delegates in the open street while police headquarters subsequently denied any knowledge of such seizure. After the Ard-Fheis of 1960 homes of delegates were visited by members of the police force masquerading as members of the Republican Movement, with the request that the agenda and other papers be handed over. Offers of cash and jobs are made in return for information sought. Members of Sinn Fein are approached by policemen posing as members of the Organisation "on the run"

(Continued on page 12)

Letter From Frank Aiken

To the Editor,

Sir,

The Free State Minister for Defence, in an interview yesterday, stated that the Six County Authorities have deliberately given sanctuary to prominent Republican Volunteers. That statement is untrue.

As far as Republicans are concerned, the Six County and the Free State Forces are one Army. Both forces, on the authority of the British King, and freely supplied with arms and munitions by England, have done their utmost to suppress the Irish Republican Army.

Both forces have been working in conjunction in their attempt to do so; and the success of either means partition of our country and establishment of British Authority in the area under their control.

We know definitely that Intelligence Officers of the Free State and Six County Forces meet regularly to exchange information regarding the movements and activities of Republican Volunteers.

Specials, having information from official Free State Army sources, often raid the homes of Volunteers on the night of their release from Free State Internment Camps, and the Home Affairs Departments of the Free State and the Six Counties exchange lists and descriptions of wanted Republican men and women.

On several occasions the Specials and Free State Forces, as if they were one army, made concerted swoops along the "border" in order to round up Irish Republican Army Columns.

Both forces have succeeded in killing and capturing a number of Republican Volunteers; but neither have been or will be successful in repressing the spirit of the Irish Republican Army in any of the Thirty-Two Counties of the Republic of Ireland.

Signed:
FRANK AIKEN, General.
Chief of Staff.

Feb. 1, 1924.

(Reprinted from 'SINN FEIN', Saturday, February 9, 1924.)

Member of Crown Forces Killed

WE have received the following statement from the Irish Republican Publicity Bureau, dated January 27, 1961:

The member of the British Crown Forces killed early today by Irish Resistance Fighters operating in the Roslea area of Co. Fermanagh, had been engaged on espionage missions into the Twenty-Six Counties under cover of social activities.

The information being sought by him would have a direct bearing on the lives and liberties of Irish people living in districts of the Twenty-Six Counties adjacent to British Occupied Ireland. During last summer he motored openly through the Knockatallon area of Co. Monaghan.

It has been the deliberate policy of the British Occupation Forces to send members into the Twenty-Six Counties in civilian dress to tout and spy and mark down for future attention Republican sympathisers residing locally.

Such people have been arrested, interrogated, ill-treated, jailed without trial, and, as has happened in the case of James Crossan, shot down on the roadside, at the first opportunity available to the British Crown Forces.

Four residents in Counties Louth, Monaghan, and Cavan, whose homes are close to the Border, have been imprisoned without charge or trial in Belfast for some years past as a direct result of spying expeditions into the Twenty-Six Counties.

Other members of the British Crown Forces who take part in "intelligence missions" of the type described include an R.U.C. man named Bell who is active in the Swanlinbar area of Co. Cavan, and R.U.C. Special Branch men Carson and Bennett who operate regularly in Dundalk and north Co. Louth. The fact, now revealed, that some of them wear full uniform under a civilian overcoat indicates how commonplace these activities have become.

Mr. Lemass' statement this morning rings very hollowly against the complete silence observed by him and his predecessor in office when James Crossan, a resident of the Twenty-Six Counties, was murdered in cold blood — shot in the back — in August of 1958 by the same British Crown Forces who crossed the Border into Co. Cavan.

And when a "rigged" inquest was held in Enniskillen, Mr. Lemass was not the first to rush into print in condemnation of this murder of an Irishman by British Crown Forces. He did not call for "co-operation in bringing the perpetrators to justice" nor had he any word of sympathy to offer to the relatives—for James Crossan had relatives too.

In fact, the known perpetrators of this foul deed come into Swanlinbar, Co. Cavan regularly and are never even questioned by the 26-Co. police about their activities in Co. Cavan on the night of August 23-24, 1958.

On balance, it appears that the only lives Mr. Lemass cares about are the lives of the armed British Garrison forces in Ireland.

(signed)
J. McGarrity, Secty.
Irish Republican Publicity Bureau.

RELEASE ALL PRISONERS

—MONAGHAN COUNTY COUNCIL

AT its meeting on January 9 Monaghan Co. Council unanimously called for the release of all political prisoners. The Council decided to send the resolution to the British, Belfast, and Dublin Governments.

Mr. P. Lonergan (Fine Gael), Vice-Chairman, who presided, said it had been the policy of the Chairman, Mr. E. Kelly (Indpt.), not to allow political discussions. He thought, however, that in as much as the present resolution was one of sympathy and charity he would not rule it out of order.

Mr. James McElwaine (Sinn Féin), said they should begin the new year well and he would propose they do so by passing a resolution calling for the release of all political prisoners held in British and Irish prisons. The so-called crime of these men was that they took part actively against the British Forces occupying their historic nation.

Mr. Denis McGuigan (Sinn Féin), seconding, said that the Stormont regime had been releasing men in twos and threes. Among those still held were 33 untried men. All prisoners should be released.

Mr. J. Deery (Indpt.), said he wished to be associated with the resolution because of the fact

(Contd. on page 12)

'MEMBER OF CROWN FORCES KILLED'

Almost all of the 18 fatalities in the Border campaign occurred in combat or were accidental. But in January 1961, the IRA killed an unarmed off-duty policeman near Roslea in Co. Fermanagh. Constable Norman Anderson had just dropped off his fiancée at her home on the southern side of the border when he was dragged from his car and shot dead. There was widespread condemnation of the killing and IRA prisoners in Belfast initally refused to believe that their organisation could have carried it out. The IRA claimed that Anderson was engaged in spying. While an unusual event in the context of the 1956-62 campaign, the killing was a precursor to many similar attacks after 1970.

CLAMPDOWN IN THE SOUTH

The Fine Gael-led inter-party government fell during March 1957, split on how to deal with the IRA's campaign. There was some evidence of support for the IRA during that year's general election: four Sinn Féin TDs were elected and the party secured 5% of the vote. But Fianna Fáil were returned to power and de Valera made clear that 'private armies cannot be tolerated'. Nevertheless, the government waited until the IRA killed a policeman in Armagh on 4 July before it moved. A total of 63 republican activists were arrested by gardaí, including Mac Curtáin and McLogan. The government then introduced internment without trial. By March 1958, a total of 131 republicans were held in the Curragh.

Mac Curtáin was the internees' commander. He had experienced harsh conditions in Portlaoise during the War and in the Curragh he, along with Magan, counselled caution and the avoidance of confrontation. This was resented by some of the younger prisoners. They demanded escapes and in May 1958, three prisoners absconded from the camp hospital, though they were soon recaptured. In September 1958, Mac Curtáin acceded to a request from the IRA leadership to allow the escape of Ruairí Ó Brádaigh and David O'Connell, who successfully got away and renewed IRA activity. However, in December, a large group of internees expressly disobeyed orders and attempted a mass breakout, using improvised smokebombs and wire cutters. Soldiers opened fire, wounding two, and eventually used tear gas to subdue the crowd. Nevertheless, fourteen men got away and presented themselves to the IRA. Despite their act of insubordination they were accepted back into the ranks, to the disgust of Mac Curtáin and Magan. The split widened further and simmered until the camp was closed in March 1959.

Facing page: 'Member of Crown Forces Killed' UNITED IRISHMAN

Bodenstown, 1959 WORKERS' PARTY OF IRELAND

In the midst of the Border campaign, republicans gathered at Bodenstown: chief marshal in 1959 was Cathal Goulding, recently released from jail in England, the chair was Tomás Mac Giolla, freed from the Curragh earlier that year and the main speaker was Ruairí Ó Brádaigh. All three men would play important roles in the IRA over the next decade. However, in June 1959, they were facing the reality that the campaign had lost whatever momentum it had possessed in its early stages.

THE END OF THE CAMPAIGN

On 5 February 1962, IRA units were ordered to withdraw from the Border. Their chief of staff, Ruairí Ó Brádaigh, then drafted a statement announcing a formal end to the campaign. The southern authorities were in no doubt that the stringent security measures introduced by the young Minister for Justice, Charles Haughey, forced the IRA to call a halt. (He had promised to 'use every means . . . including the army if necessary' to bring the IRA's 'futile, evil campaign of violence to an end'.) The introduction of the Special Criminal Court, presided over by army officers doling out long sentences, was certainly a factor in the IRA's decision.

Facing page: *United Irishman,* April 1962 UNITED IRISHMAN

Letters to the Editor

Coercion In Donegal

A Chara,

Reading the reports of the raiding of homes here in Donegal and elsewhere in the January and February issues of the U.I. I must say as an Irishman that I feel disgusted and ashamed of these 26-County police — the Gardai.

Is it any wonder that the politicians are trying to give an artificial look to the unemployment figures? The unemployed here who are in receipt of the "dole", many of whom have returned from Britain around the Christmas, have the Social Welfare Officer in their homes pretty often these days.

A ruthless investigation of the unemployed man's means is carried out; the few old hens are counted and, believe it or not, that wonderful little animal the donkey gets its name in the Social Welfare files these days.

Then we can hear Lemass and company tell the world, at some "Dinner" no doubt, that the unemployment figures have reached rock bottom. But, Mr. Lemass, you will not be honest with the people—you and the so-called national newspapers hide the truth.

The people here in Donegal in common with others throughout the country (and they are many) would welcome work. You have now stooped so low as to deprive them of the few miserable shillings of dole they were receiving. Will you investigate the means of the £1,000 a year clique in Leinster House? Oh, no.

All who are not in receipt of the dole here you and your shadow-boxers, Fine Gael, have driven into exile. Of course the unemployed have to forfeit their shillings to keep patrol cars and Gardai running about breaking into homes in the early hours of the morning and going as far as pushing around women and girls. It is about time you introduced a course on faith and morals in the Depot in the Phoenix Park.

On Sunday evening, December 17, 1961, a near neighbour of mine—God rest his soul—was fatally injured while walking home by a hit and run driver. When an effort was made to report the accident at the local barracks here, it was found that no Garda was on duty.

Yet reading the U.I. I see that they could muster 12 members of the force exactly one week earlier to raid and ransack the home of Sinn Fein Councillor Seamus Rodgers. Scores of other homes throughout Co. Donegal received the same treatment.

Then we had a young lady teacher being dragged from her classroom in Glenties by the police. (I.N.T.O. please note. Have you protested yet? You were very vocal some time ago).

It is a shame and a scandal to find these employees of Mr. Haughey forcing their way into ladies' bedrooms in a number of places in the county. If it happened in the Congo, Aiken would shout his head off at U.N.O.

Why is there nobody in high places to condemn these atrocities? If I were a member of the 26-County police I would be a man and refuse to be a party to such work, letting John Bull's orders—via Haughey and Lemass —go to blazes.

A Letterkenny woman's death was hastened by these activities, and I learn that a policeman attempted to seize a photo of that great patriot from near my own doorstep, "Plunkett" O'Boyle. We here in Burtonport and the Rosses will remember "Plunkett" with pride long after the peeler is gone.

Did we hear or read of Fianna Fail T.D. Cormac Breslin or Fine Gael Deputy "Pa" O'Donnell raising the question of these raids and arrests in Leinster House? Ah, no—after all those arrested were only Irish Republicans. Many things have happened around these parts more serious than membership of Sinn Fein, yet no great noise was made about them.

We're still being made the dupes of John Bull and the modern "Bodach" rules supreme. I will soon have to face the emigration ship and become another of the figures of emigrant statistics. Of course I am not alone in that respect, driven from my home by the modern Cromwells who deny me a living in the land of my birth.

However, I will be back again, please God, and I appeal to you ordinary people to stand by Sinn Fein; yes, to men and women, boys and girls who put their country before big names and fat salaries.

Don't forget that some gain at the expense of your children who are being exported daily. Perhaps that child you cared for so well you may never see again when you bid him or her goodbye at the bus stop.

I wish you and your paper all success. At least you are not afraid to publish the truth and you do not need to use the slogan "The Truth in the News" to do it either. Thank God for your paper—I am always looking forward to it—and God bless the brave young lads in the prison cells.

Their cause will yet triumph.

SINN FÉINER.

Burtonport,
Co. Donegal.
27/2/'62.

British Commandos

A Chara,

Just a note to inform you that on the 30th day of January, 1962, in Clogher, Co. Tyrone, a large number of British Commandos stationed in Ballygawley were charged with criminal assault on a 13-year-old girl.

The girl concerned was an orphan. She kept a diary which led to the arrest of these Commandos, some of them married men.

The court was held in camera. No one was allowed in or out—only those concerned. It was kept a very close secret.

I can assure you this is the truth and I sincerely hope you give it publicity. It has not been published in any paper in the North.

Seventeen men were charged in all.

Yours sincerely,

J. S.

Tydavnet,
Co. Monaghan.
14/2/'62.

ENDING OF CAMPAIGN

We have received several letters concerning the recent termination of the Resistance Campaign in Occupied Ireland which seem to indicate that the writers had not read in full the I.R.P.B. statement of February 26. We would direct the attention of readers who did not receive our March issue to the full text of this most important press release which we re-publish here.

THE leadership of the Resistance Movement has ordered the termination of the Campaign of Resistance to British Occupation launched on December 12, 1956. Instructions issued to Volunteers of the Active Service Units and of local Units in the occupied area have now been carried out. All arms and other material have been dumped and all full-time active service Volunteers have been withdrawn.

The decision to end the Resistance Campaign has been taken in view of the general situation. Foremost among the factors motivating this course of action has been the attitude of the general public whose minds have been deliberately distracted from the supreme issue facing the Irish people—the unity and freedom of Ireland. Other and lesser issues have been urged successfully upon them, and the sacrifices which could win freedom in the political, cultural, social and economic spheres are now stated to be necessary to bolster up the partition system of government forced on the Irish people by Britain forty years ago.

SECONDARY ISSUES

This calculated emphasis on secondary issues by those whose political future is bound up in the status quo and who control all the mass media of propaganda is now leading towards possible commitment of the people of the 26 Counties in future wars. The Resistance Movement stands firmly against any such course of action while Ireland is unfree and will use all its resources towards restoring in full to the Irish people their sense of national values.

For over five years Irish freedom-fighters have fought against foreign occupation, native collaboration and the overwhelming weight of hostile propaganda. Supported loyally by the Republican people of the Six Occupied Counties they have faced fantastic odds. 5,000 British regular troops, 5,000 territorials, 12,500 B-Specials, 3,000 R.U.C., 1,500 specially trained Commandos and sundry security guard forces totalling close on 30,000 armed men bar the road to freedom. Their considerable resources have included armoured vehicles liberally supplied by the British Government, heavily fortified strong-points and the most modern war equipment.

TORTURE AND TERROR

Terroristic tactics against the civilian population, draconian laws, imprisonment without charge or trial, torture-mills to force "confessions" from prisoners, long and savage penal servitude sentences, the shooting down of unarmed people at road-blocks and threats of even sterner measures including flogging and hanging have all been employed to maintain British rule in the Six Counties.

The collaborationist role of successive 26-County Governments—acting under British pressure—from December 1956 has contributed material aid and comfort to the enemy. Border patrols by 26-County military and police working in collaboration with the British Occupation Forces were instituted 48 hours after the opening of the Campaign. The press was muzzled and the radio controlled in the interests of British rule.

The methods and eventually the aims and objectives of the Resistance Movement were misrepresented to the Irish people and to the world by the professional politicians of the 26-County state. Top-level conferences with the Crown Forces and the continuous supplying of information to the enemy — secretly at first, but later quite openly—were other and lesser known features of collaboration.

26-COUNTY COLLABORATION

Unarmed freedom-fighters found within the 26 Counties were arrested and jailed while armed patrols of the British Forces could cross the Border at will. Jailing of Resistance supporters and even moral sympathisers throughout the 26 Counties followed while quisling Irishmen from the same area were permitted to join the enemy forces. Homes were raided and people followed about by the Special political police. The Curragh Concentration Camp was opened and maintained for close on two years with 200 uncharged and untried prisoners. When public opinion forced its closing down, the Prisoners' Dependants Fund was attacked and hundreds of collectors jailed.

When this tactic too was defeated proceedings against Resistance fighters and their supporters at 26-County District Courts were suspended by the introduction of a Military Tribunal in November last. The savage sentences since imposed for technical offences culminated in the imprisonment of a young freedom-fighter from Co. Derry for eight years. In the teeth of such provocative action by those whose aim appears to be civil strife in the 26 Counties the discipline of Irish Resistance fighters in adhering to their instructions over the entire five-year period has been magnificent.

When repeated warnings by the Resistance to cease bearing arms against their own people were disregarded, the R.U.C. and B-Special Constabulary were listed as legitimate military targets. The international provisions governing belligerent status including the wearing of means of identification, the carrying of arms openly and being under the the control of responsible officers have been observed by the Resistance Movement but in no case has the enemy recognised the status of the men fighting for their country other than as criminal.

OVER 600 OPERATIONS

During the five-year Campaign over 600 operations against enemy patrols, strong-points, communications, transport and civil administration have been carried out at enormous cost to the enemy. Casualties inflicted total six killed and 28 wounded. (This includes British soldiers, B-Specials, R.U.C. and Commandos.) In addition four members of the Crown Forces—apart from British military, naval and air force personnel for whom figures are not readily available—were killed other than by Resistance action.

In the same period the Resistance suffered two killed in action and seven killed accidentally. Also a Sinn Fein organiser was murdered by British Crown Forces near Swanlinbar, Co. Cavan. A small number of Resistance fighters were wounded. Forty-three prisoners of war are serving sentences of from four to 15 years in Crumlin Road, Belfast, and three are jailed in England, while Mountjoy Prison, Dublin, holds 42 Irish Republicans.

TRIBUTE TO SUPPORTERS

No aid from any foreign source has been received by the Resistance Movement. Irish exiles from many countries have been more than generous in their support of the Campaign while some returned to participate actively in the fight. The leadership of the Resistance Movement wishes to pay a long overdue public tribute to all the loyal Irish people of every class and creed who gave support—whether in the form of billets, transport, intelligence, funds, munitions or even encouragement—and to all who had the moral courage to speak out in private or in public in defence of the men fighting for Ireland. In future an even greater volume of support will be needed so that the Cause dear to the hearts and minds of all who have actively contributed to the Resistance Campaign of 1956-62 will ultimately triumph.

The Resistance Movement remains intact and is in a position to continue its Campaign in the occupied area indefinitely. It realises, however, that the situation obtaining in the earlier stages of the Campaign has altered radically and is convinced that the time has come to conserve its resources, to augment them, and to prepare a more favourable situation. The policy of not taking aggressive military action within the 26-County area remains unaltered and the Resistance takes its stand against any attempt to foment sectarian strife which is alien to the spirit of Irish Republicanism.

ETERNAL HOSTILITY

The Irish Resistance Movement renews its pledge of eternal hostility to the British Forces of Occupation in Ireland. It calls on the Irish people for increased support and looks forward with confidence — in co-operation with the other branches of the Republican Movement—to a period of consolidation, expansion and preparation for the final and victorious phase of the struggle for the full freedom of Ireland.

Signed :

J. McGARRITY,
Secretary.

Irish Republican Publicity Bureau,
February 26, 1962.

STOP! LOOK! READ!

A REMINDER . . .

. . . that there are still 75 Republican Prisoners held in British and Irish Jails.

In Belfast Jail there are 43 men sentenced to long terms of penal servitude, most of whom are already four or five years in prison (some almost eight years).

In Mountjoy Jail there are 29 men serving sentences ranging from four months to eight years.

In England two men are serving life imprisonment, while an Irish mother is serving 21 months.

The majority of these prisoners have dependents who are supported mainly by An Cumann Cabhrach.

Will YOU please help this charitable work by sending your donation to-day to:

AN CUMANN CABHRACH, P.O. BOX 187, DUBLIN 1.

You can also help by supporting the various functions —ceilithe, concerts, raffles, etc.—which are held from time to time.

PLEASE HELP US TO HELP THE PRISONERS

Support An Cumann Cabhrach

But the IRA leadership also considered whether the campaign was going anywhere. Despite all the effort, partition was as solid in 1962 as it had been in 1956. Had the campaign failed because the IRA was not ruthless enough? Indeed, by the standards of later IRA campaigns, it had been remarkably 'clean', with no civilians killed. Were the Irish people 'distracted' from the problem of partition by 'secondary issues', as the IRA statement claimed? Or had the IRA become isolated from the day-to-day concerns of ordinary people? In the general election of 1961, Sinn Féin lost the four seats it had won in 1957. Republicans had said little about the chronic economic state of the country during the 1950s and had avoided involvement in issues not directly linked to the 'national question'. In the Border campaign's aftermath, former leaders such as Magan and MacCurtáin left the IRA altogether.

Many of those who had risen to leadership positions during the campaign itself, such as Mick Ryan, Ruairí Ó Brádaigh and Cathal Goulding, were still committed to organising a new military effort to end partition. But there was also a recognition that there would have to be political rethinking as well.

Chapter 6

A NEW REVOLUTION

During the 1960s, the IRA grappled with the realities of a rapidly changing Ireland. Many of its leadership argued that to remain relevant, it needed to embrace social and economic agitation and to encourage a more prominent role for Sinn Féin. Indeed, by 1969, Cathal Goulding and others were endorsing the idea of taking seats in the parliaments of Leinster House and Stormont and forming an alliance with communist organisations. Political differences about this direction were intensifed by the upsurge in violence in Northern Ireland after 1968 and would produce the most important split in the IRA since 1922 by the decade's end.

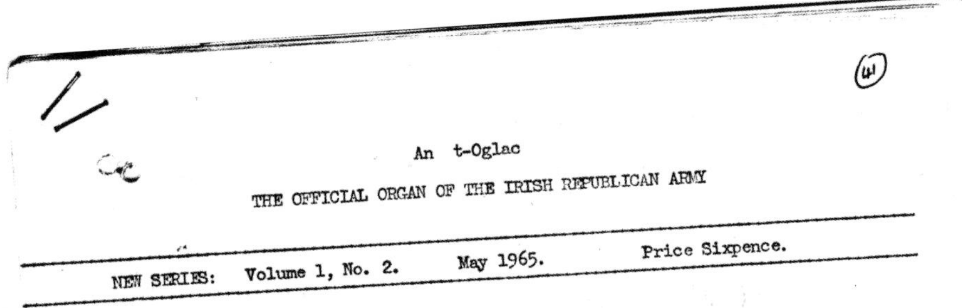

An t-Oglac

THE OFFICIAL ORGAN OF THE IRISH REPUBLICAN ARMY

NEW SERIES: Volume 1, No. 2. May 1965. Price Sixpence.

Statement from the CHIEF of STAFF

to all Volunteers

This, I believe, is the first time in many years that a Chief of Staff has addressed a personal message through An t-Oglach to all Army personnel. I decided on utilising the pages of this paper for a number of good reasons. Firstly, I wish to tell you of the interests and activities of the Army in a number of new fields. Secondly, I wish to inform each of you about some proposed changes which will shortly be presented to you for approval or rejection.

As you are aware, from the Convention Report which was read to you, the Army in Convention authorised the setting up of a Conference, or Commission, to consider the internal organisation of our Movement and the tactics which we have used in the past. The Conference has now prepared for our examination ten recommendations, all of which recommend changes. The document will shortly be circulated to your Unit and I urge you personally to study it with the utmost care, without emotion or prejudice. Bear in mind that to-day we grapple with problems which are no longer clear-cut. To the youth, which must be attracted to our standards if we are to win, many of our attitudes are doctrinaire, to them we are bound in a tradition sanctified by time rather than reason, by habit rather than effectiveness. In your hands lies the acceptance or rejection of each of these ten points.

To the Volunteers of long service to the Army and Republic I would address a special word. Think well on these recommendations. Let your final voice on them be based on our present and future needs, not on the past as such, but on what is practical and, therefore, necessary. Of all Volunteers I ask that each recommendation be treated as a separate document, that each point be accepted or rejected individually.

Recommendation number nine (9) raises the burning question of entering Leinster House. This is not the first time that this question has come before us, but it is the first time that such a course of action is recommended us by a Conference of Republicans. To very many of us it is not a question that can be dealt with briefly, some of our finest being in favour, some of our finest being opposed. All I ask of you is that/

'TO ALL VOLUNTEERS', 1965

During 1965, IRA Chief of Staff Cathal Goulding sent a special message to his organisation's volunteers, urging them to consider the organisation's future direction. Goulding had become the IRA's leader in September 1962, replacing Ó Brádaigh. Born in 1922 in Dublin, his family had been involved in republican politics since the 1870s. Goulding's grandfather had been a Fenian and his father had fought in 1916. He himself joined the IRA in the late 1930s and was jailed during the War years. He was one of the younger officers entrusted with reorganising the IRA locally after the War but was jailed again in 1953 when captured after an arms raid in Felstead, in Essex. After six years in prison in England he was released in 1959 and returned to IRA activity.

Facing page and below: *An tÓglác*, May 1965, Cathal Goulding's special message to his organisation.

- 2 -

An t-Oglach

May, 1965.

you give it your maturest thought, that you ponder the question scrupulously and give a reasoned and fair reply. With this recommendation in particular, an unemotional attitude is essential; should it happen that you are against the recommendation - you must not regard those who favour it as traitors; should it happen that you favour the recommendation you must not regard your opponents in the matter as either stupid or traditionalist. You will debate this question, as all others, with comrades and friends, not with enemies.

With our new and vital orientation in the fields of co-operation and land we are laying the basis for our future effort in the North. Without a solid and real base in and among the people our efforts will again come to nothing. We must equip ourselves for this work now.

To those who doubt the value of this social work I can only urge the reading of any history of a modern revolutionary movement. Read of Cuba, of Algeria, of Cyprus. We depend on an armed people for success. But first we must arm the people to combat the foreign take-over, the foreign landlord.

I intend that the next military campaign will be the final one. I work for that now. Work with me and ensure that the future will yield us the Republic for which so many generations have suffered and fought. I am confident that we now chart a course which will lead to victory, yet we must be mindful that our future is not a haphazard thing but something that we must create and which we will create.

C. McNeill,
C.S.

The IRA held an extraordinary convention in June 1965 to discuss ten proposals from their leadership about the organisation's future. This was part of a reasessment driven by Goulding, which aimed at avoiding the mistakes of the 1956-62 campaign and becoming more relevant to everyday politics. In part, Goulding was attempting to return to some of the ideas of the republican radicals of the 1930s. He was interested in, and influenced by the ideas of the Marxist, Dr Roy Johnston, who he invited into the republican movement during 1965.

The most controversal of the proposals was that the movement abandon its policy of refusing to allow republicans to take seats in the 'partition parliaments' of Leinster House and Stormont. Goulding attempted to reassure volunteers that the embracing of new strategies did not mean an end to the army's primary role: 'We depend on an armed people for success. But first we must arm the people to combat the foreign take-over, the foreign landlord', he said in his special message. But at the convention, the proposal to drop the absentionist policy was defeated and disagreement simmered, contributing to a growing distrust of Goulding among traditional republicans. Some attributed his political direction to having been 'converted' to communism by the East German spy Klaus Fuchs, while in prison in England. Among those who opposed Goulding at the 1965 convention was Seán Mac Stíofáin, who had been jailed with him in 1953, but who felt that the IRA's primary purpose was military and who strongly supported abstentionism.

LIAM MCMILLEN'S ELECTION CAMPAIGN, 1964

In 1964, the republican movement contested the Westminster elections, putting forward twelve candidates on an abstentionist platform. In the West Belfast constituency the candidate was Liam McMillen, the 36-year old Commander of the IRA in the city. McMillen, from Ton Street, had been an IRA member since the early 1950s (though he was affiliated to Saor Uladh for a period) and had been jailed during the Border campaign.

In the election he polled 3,256 votes, but his campaign was more notable for the violence that occurred. Ian Paisley, a fundamentalist preacher, had threatened to lead a march to the Falls Road if a tricolour flag was not removed from McMillen's offices in Divis Street. The RUC stormed the office and seized the flag. When the tricolour was displayed again the next day, the police returned in riot gear but were met by stones and petrol bombs. Several days of trouble followed. At a protest rally McMillen and a fellow republican candidate, Bobby McKnight, hung out another tricolour and led crowds in singing 'Amhrán na BhFiann'. Later that week

Top: Liam McMillen (at microphone) at the Official IRA Easter commemoration. Belfast, April 1975. A few weeks later he was shot dead by members of what became the INLA.
MARY McMILLEN

Right: Liam McMillen: election pamphlet 1964, in which his name is misspelled.

The Issue Restated

The Primary issue in this election is that of freedom for all Ireland. Political freedom is merely a means for the achievement of social and economic freedom. It will not be handed to us. We must prove we are determined to have it. Freedom and independence from England will mean the ending of all the social evils of our time, viz., emigration, unemployment, discrimination and the many other ill effects of British rule in Ireland.

The British connection has been the root cause of the discontent and hardship endured for so long by the Irish people. The elimination of the British connection, therefore, remains the first task in the establishment of a united, free and prosperous nation. It is essential that the Irish people use every means in their power to achieve this objective.

Use this election to show your determination to own your own country. It is the duty of every voter to cast his vote in the interest of the nation. This can only be done by voting Republican.

Voting for the Republican candidate means :

(*a*) *Demonstrating the determination of the Irish people to govern their own Country in their own way.*
(*b*) *Rejecting Britain's claim to rule any part of Ireland.*
(*c*) *Securing the election of candidates pledged to convene a parliament legislating for the whole nation.*

Participation in the British parliament means acceptance of British rule. Our task is to break the connection with Britain, not to bolster it. Elected Republican candidates will invite all parliamentary representatives in Ireland to establish a parliament which will actively legislate for the whole nation.

YOU want such a Parliament
NOW you can vote for it

We have a positive policy and plan for the ending of British rule in Ireland. With your support we can put it into action.

Do you want to remain a forgotten remnant of the British Colonial Empire or will you be the most vital part of a strong and progressive Irish nation ?

VOTE
FOR FREEDOM AND PROGRESS

VOTE REPUBLICAN

Published by William O'Neill, 160 Norfolk Street, Belfast. *Printed by* Ticards, Durham Street, Belfast.

FOR FREEDOM AND PROGRESS

Vote
Liam McMillan
REPUBLICAN CANDIDATE
for West Belfast

5,000 people marched behind the tricolour on the Falls Road, escorted by Fianna members carrying hurleys. The controversy gave the IRA some publicity and led to recruitment into the organisation: it also showed the potential for conflict that existed under the surface of society in Northern Ireland. In 1967, McMillen was a founding member of the Northern Ireland Civil Rights Association and sat in its first executive.

A NEW DIRECTION

During 1966, the republican movement had made a major effort to promote its new direction on the 50th anniversary of the Easter Rising. The IRA contrasted the ideals of the 1916 leaders with the reality of 1960s' Ireland. They argued that only the republican movement could reunite the country and provide social justice for all its citizens. At Easter 1966, republicans organised their own events in competition with the commemorations held by the Irish government. In Dublin, there were serious clashes with gardaí when detectives tried to sieze an IRA Dublin Brigade flag at one such event. In Belfast, a much larger commemoration passed off peacefully. In late 1966, IRA leaders were involved in discussions about a new campaign of civil disobedience in Northern Ireland: republicans would be central to the launch of the Northern Ireland Civil Rights Association in early 1967. By 1968, IRA volunteers were helping steward the early civil rights marches. In the South, republican protest on housing helped produce the Dublin Housing Action Campaign, while there was land agitation in the countryside.

But the IRA's discussions about its new role in social agitation provoked much dissent. There was no shortage of critics from both right and left. Some felt that the IRA should have no purpose other than gearing up for another campaign against partition. While military training continued and the IRA bombed British Army recruiting offices in Northern Ireland during 1967 and again in 1968, critics maintained that the army was being run down. Others thought the variety of leftist politics being embraced by the IRA was 'reformist', 'Stalinist' or simply, 'communist'.

Former Saor Uladh members were involved in a number of political groups during the 1960s: one member, Gerry Lawless, emigrated to London and was influential in the development of Irish Trotskyism, while others, such as Joe Christle, remained independent republicans. Members of both Saor Uladh and Christle's group were involved in blowing up Nelson's Pillar in Dublin's O'Connell Street in 1966.

A group of former IRA members in Cork formed the Irish Revolutionary Forces and published a journal called *An Phoblacht*, which was highly critical of the republican leadership. In 1967, another group of ex-IRA members robbed a bank in Drumcondra in Dublin and followed this up with several more robberies. By 1969,

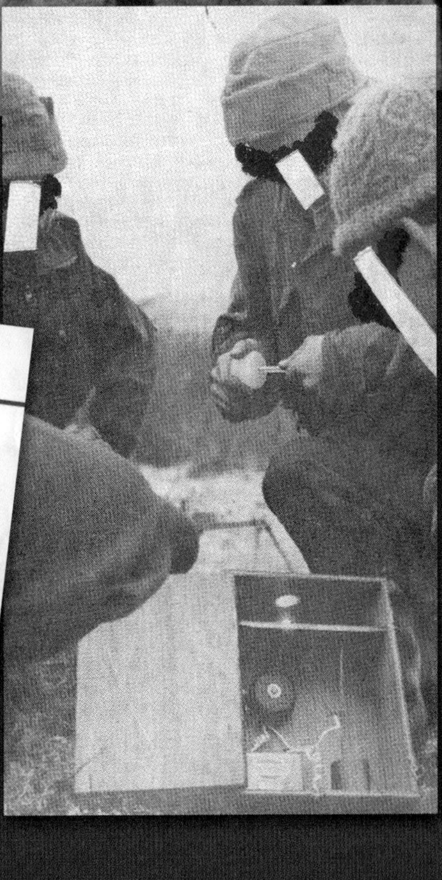

Top: Republicans clash with Gardaí in Dublin, Easter 1966
IRISH TIMES

Right: IRA bomb making class, 1966, from *The Separatist*

this group adopted the title Saor Eire Action Group. But during this time, most critics of the IRA leadership simply dropped out, many who had been jailed during the Border campaign returning to family life or to their careers, while remaining in touch with friends still in the movement. There remained those like Seán Mac Stíofáin, by 1967 the IRA's director of intelligence, who felt that the presence of ex-communists, such as Roy Johnston, among the leadership of the organisation, and the debates such as whether the Rosary should be said at republican events, marked a dangerous trend for the IRA. Others were worried about the evident enthusiasm of IRA leaders like Seamus Costello for contesting elections on a non-abstentionist basis.

In late August 1967, the IRA's senior officers met on a farm in Co. Tipperary to discuss the state of the organisation. There they heard that, despite attempts to reorient the movement over the previous two years, many volunteers were not

Below and facing page: Minutes of IRA Meeting, August 1967

IV.

In the temporary absence of the Adjutant General a prepared statement was read out on his behalf. In this statement the A.G. gave a breakdown on the strength of the Army throughout the country, the number of vols. in each area, the existence of splinter groups and hos estimate of the potential of the army. There were 6I4 vols. on the rolls of whom, in his opinion, 274 were effective. Of the total strength 2I2 were active members of Sinn Fein.

The report was generally critical of the local leadership at Command level and bore out the remarks of the C/S on that score.

The Director of Intelligence gave a report on the state of his dept. and of the I5 areas he discussed only two merited good, in his opinion, one was noted as fair and the remainder were poor, bad or non-existent.

The Director of Finance in his report painted a bad picture. In March of I966 the Army had a balance of £770 which was added to by a £IOO in subs. and by £395 in Sweep money. The concert tour was a failure to the tume of £500. The present situation was that the Army owed it's staff members £273 and £334 to individuals.

In the absence of the Q.M.G. a statement was read out giving the stock of equipment in G.H.Q. dumps. It appears that the Army has enough ammo. for one good job, a very limited amount of arms and explosives.

....Contd.

Moving on to a discussion of the C/S's speech to the meeting, it was agreed that it be broken up into points and that each point be discussed separately it being agreed that each man present could make a general statement on the following day on the Army position as a whole.

The first point for discussion was the reason for the failure of the campaign. Opening the discussion, LIAM MAC MILLAN stated that the reason for the failure was the lack of heavy equipment as well as the failure of the political wing of the movement.

MICK RYAN. put the failure of the organisation down to a miscalculation on the part of the leadership vis a vis the Free State. He said that we must get down to the grass roots if we are to be successful, that we must make clear that out ultimate aim is the creation of a socialist Republic. While he agreed that political organisation is essential he was satisfied that politics would not do it alone, that no social revolution was possible without the use of arms. The movement would make a real beginning, he said only when the movement believes in what it is trying to do. We must educate our members, we must get to the people. Once our own men are e ucated in what we are doing then the presentation of our ideas to the people will be easier. Money, he continued, was one of our great problems. On the solution of this problem depended the fielding of full time workers. Part time men are not enough.

TOMAS MAC GIOLLA. in anwwer to Liam Mac Millan, stated that heavey weapons were not the answer. In his view this statement on political failure by the C/S was the most important part of the statement. "How", he asked, "can we possibly sicceed without the support of the people?". Too many people, he continued, think only in terms of fighting in the north. We must think in terms of the 32 counties. The entire people must become involved in the actions of the movement.

SEAMUS COSTELLO. stated that the failure of the campaign and of Sinn Fein were related. There was a lack of real political activity before the campaign. Sinn Fein was created to cash in on the sentiment generated by the campaign and was never a serious political organisation. All present could remember the 90,000 unemployed in 1957 and Sinn Fein indifference to that situation. Sinn Fein, he said, stood for a 32 county republic and nothing else. It was not enough, the movement did not give the people credit for possessing any common sense. On this point of sense, Costello introduced the question of abstention which he described as not being a credible alternative, and something which could not be presented as such. He did not agree with Mac Millan on their being a shortage of arms. There were sufficient available but there was a lack of conviction on the part of the people using them.

involved in political activity. The movement was also low on funds and weaponry. Cathal Goulding, as chief of staff, stated that there, 'must be an end to indecision to doubts, to questioning. There must be a return to a conscious discipline on the part of everyone. We are not playing around for amusement's sake. We are not immortal and what is to be done must be done now . . . I want to hear each man here make an open and honest stand on the issues I have raised, I want to hear what is in each man's mind. If we do not have a mutual confidence expressed here in the face of the future, then we waste our time'. In the aftermath of the meeting, the IRA's intervention in social agitiation was stepped up and volunteers were ordered to become involved in Sinn Féin. The meeting also heard discussions about the need to raise finance through robbery and by forging new international links.

IRA Army Council member and Bray Sinn Féin councillor Seamus Costello (right) brings housing protesters into the council chamber during 1968. Costello was one of the republican leadership most keen to cast off what he saw as the shackles of abstentionism. PHOTOGRAPH: P. YEATES

AN TOGLACH

One of the demands made by those who attended the August 1967 meeting was that the IRA relaunch *An tOglach*. This they did later that year, the journal being edited by Mick Ryan and Sean Garland. This December 1967 editorial expresses pride at the IRA's 1956-62 campaign but also a determination to be successful in the future. It assured volunteers that 'armed struggle' was very much still on the agenda.

An tOglach

OFFICAL ORGAN OF THE IRISH REPUBLICAN ARMY. DEC. NO. 3.

EDITORIAL

In every generation the Irish People have asserted their right to National Freedom and Sovereignty in arms.

Eleven years ago this month saw the culmination of many years work and sacrifice in the launching of a campaign against the British Forces of Occupation by another generation in an attempt to win that freedom. That it failed, as the attempts of other generations failed, is no reflection on the many brave and great men who organised, planned and fought in the last campaign.

We can with experience and hindsight, look back and say to each other, with a certain smugness, "They did this wrong and they did that wrong", and perhaps, we would be right in our judgements.

But we can, and should, take pride in that they organised and fought,, a campaign against the British Forces of Occupation in this country, that was the greatest sustained effort for freedom since 1920.

We remember them with pride, and vow that this generation will, by learning from their, and past generations, example and experiences complete the tas for which the I.R.A. was formed.

There are many lessons to be learned from the last campaign, the most notable being that it is not enough to have men with guns in their hands. They must be men who know what they want, men who know what this struggle is about, that it is not for rocks and fields but for people we fight. We must have men who are capable of teaching the people what is wrong in this country of ours.

We must have men who are capable of working with and for the people. We must have men who are capable of leading the people in an armed struggle. For of this last let there be no doubt, there will be an armed struggle against the forces who are at present in control of this country.

This is a time of preparation. This generation must work harder, longer, and be even more dedicated and more ruthless than past generations.

We have had too many attempts and failures. For us the timeworn phrase "Better to have tried and failed than not to have tried at all" is out of date.

For this generation, nothing less than success will do.

****

Future issues contained articles on trade union interventions and practical advice on weapons and explosives. The Easter 1968 edition contained this diagram of the Molotov cocktail, described as an 'incendiary bomb used for assault purposes'.

An t-Oglach, Easter 1968

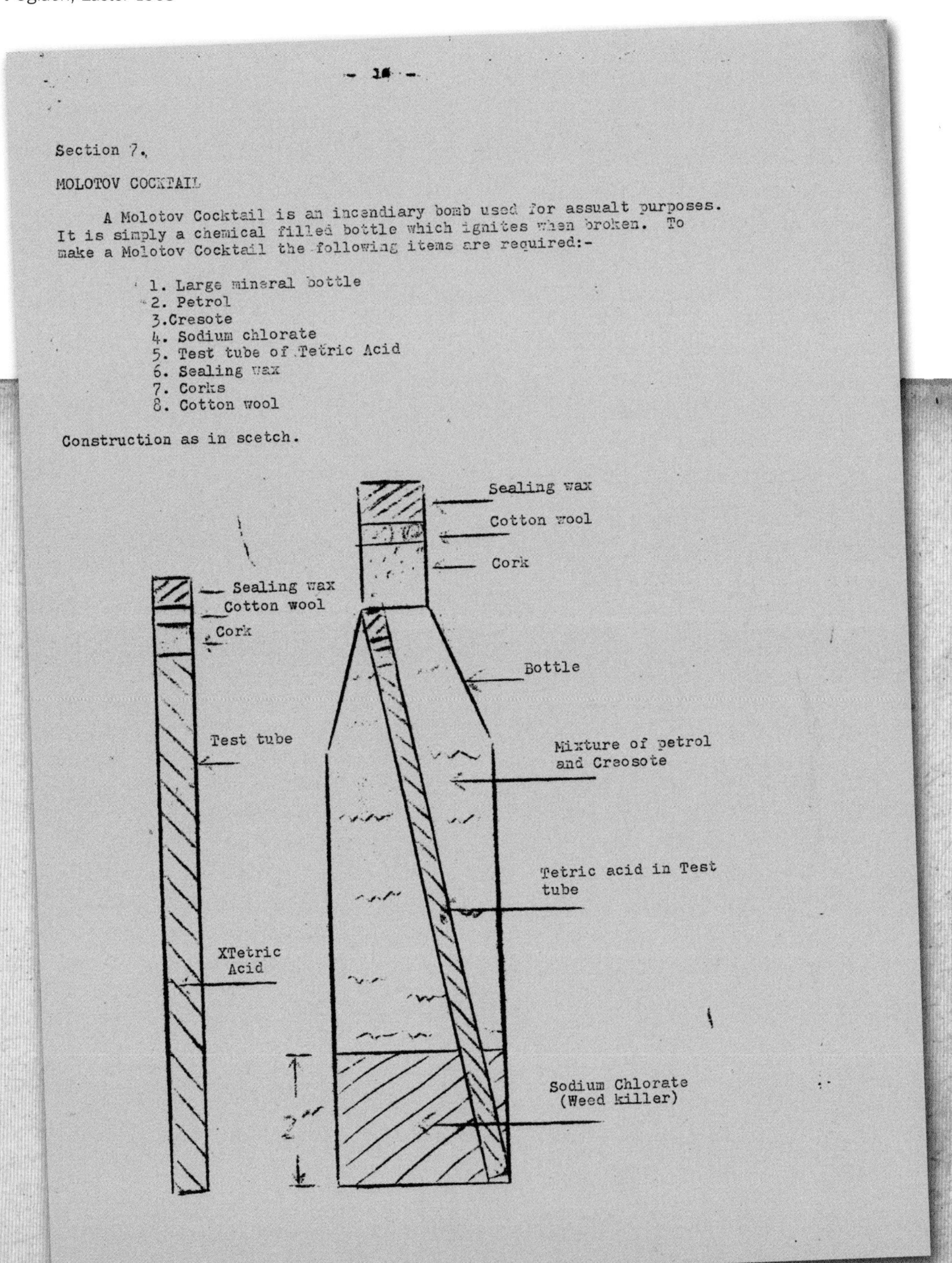

\- 14 -

Section 7.

MOLOTOV COCKTAIL

A Molotov Cocktail is an incendiary bomb used for assualt purposes. It is simply a chemical filled bottle which ignites when broken. To make a Molotov Cocktail the following items are required:-

1. Large mineral bottle
2. Petrol
3. Cresote
4. Sodium chlorate
5. Test tube of Tetric Acid
6. Sealing wax
7. Corks
8. Cotton wool

Construction as in scetch.

A group of Belfast Fianna Éireann members in Drumshanbo, Co. Leitrim, during the summer of 1968. On the right, standing, is Gerry Adams, then 19 years of age. From a strongly republican family, Adams took part in Liam McMillen's 1964 election campaign in Belfast. He worked as a barman, while becoming active in the IRA and its various political initiatives, such as the West Belfast Housing Action Campaign. On Adams' left is Seán Curry, who, along with some of the other youngsters in this photograph, would be active in the fighting in the Falls area during August 1969 (Curry, unlike Adams, took the Official side in the split of 1969/70). The youngster marked with an 'x' is Peter McGuigan, who has been misidentified in the photograph's caption as Gerald McAuley, the 15-year-old Fianna member killed in Bombay Street in August 1969 and regarded as the first republican fatality of the northern conflict.

The other adult in the photograph is Brendan Kielty from Antrim, who as a teenager had been an active republican and was jailed in 1932. In 1936 he joined Eoin O'Duffy's Irish Brigade and served with the pro-Franco side in Spain. Returning to Ireland he rejoined the IRA and was jailed during World War II.

Photograph: *An Phoblacht*, August 1970 AP/RN

IRA firing party at the reburial of Barnes and McCormick, Co. Westmeath, July 1969. The occasion saw a public attack on the Goulding leadership's polices by Belfast republican Jimmy Steele. Goulding is to the left of the firing party. IRISH PRESS ARCHIVES

The IRA's role in social agitation began to attract the attention of the authorities in the Republic. Since May 1968, when the IRA had burned buses being used to transport strike-breakers to a factory in Shannon, armed activities had increased. Shortly after this incident Seán Garland told republicans at Bodenstown that the 'fight for freedom' was a 'class struggle' and that the IRA was becoming an 'Army of the People'. In August 1968, an American-owned trawler was blown up in Connemara and the IRA also carried out attacks on foreign-owned farms during early 1969. In July that year, the gardaí estimated that the organisation had perhaps 1,200 members. A Department of Justice report alleged that several academics and journalists, in the press and television, were giving the IRA 'active assistance' and that 'a number of the IRA have been trained by an RTÉ technician in the use of shortwave radio transmitters'.

In May 1969, the IRA carried out an armed robbery of a security van at Dublin Airport, stealing over £24,000, the first time the organisation had done this since the 1940s. The Department of Justice recommended that as, 'in different parts of the country units of the IRA [and Sinn Féin] are uneasy about the new left-wing policy of their leadership and about the violent methods that are being adopted in the destruction of private property. Their uneasiness needs to be brought to the surface in some way with a consequent fragmentation of the organisation. It is suggested by the Department of Justice that the Government should promote an active political campaign in that regard'.

1969—THE SPLIT

The most important split in the IRA since 1922 took place in late December 1969, at Knockvicar House in Boyle, Co. Roscommon. A number of major issues came to a head at the IRA convention. The majority of the leadership, including Goulding, Tomás MacGiolla, Seán Garland, Mick Ryan and Seamus Costello, supported two motions that committed the IRA to becoming part of a 'National Liberation Front' with other radical organisations (including the Communist Party) and allowed republicans elected to either the Dublin, Belfast or London parliaments to take their seats. They were strongly opposed by their colleagues Ruairí Ó Brádaigh and Seán Mac Stíofáin. The motion supporting the NLF proposal was passed. This was followed by a debate on getting rid of the abstentionist policy. This, too, was passed by 28 votes to 12. But these victories disguised the fact that the IRA was badly split. Tension had been growing about the organisation's embrace of the left and particularly about its desire to take parliamentary seats.

But all of this was overshadowed by the upsurge in violence in Northern Ireland after October 1968. Republicans had been active in support of the civil rights movement throughout 1969. In August that year, fighting erupted in Derry during a march by the loyalist Apprentice Boys and nationalists succeeded in keeping a large force of police out of the Bogside area. In order to 'keep the pressure off the Bogside' the IRA in Belfast carried out a number of diversionary attacks to draw police forces away from Derry. Demonstrations were organised and RUC stations firebombed. Rioting soon engulfed much of west and north Belfast and (poorly armed) IRA members were active in defending nationalist areas. Over the night of August 14, the IRA exchanged fire with police and loyalists, while thousands rioted.

After two days, when British troops were sent onto the streets, seven people (five Catholic and two Protestant) were dead and hundreds of people, mostly Catholics, had been forced from their homes. There was a wave of sympathy for northern

RESISTANCE

IRISHMEN & IRISHWOMEN

THE UNITED IRISHMAN

BLAME BRITAIN

HOW BELFAST FOUGHT

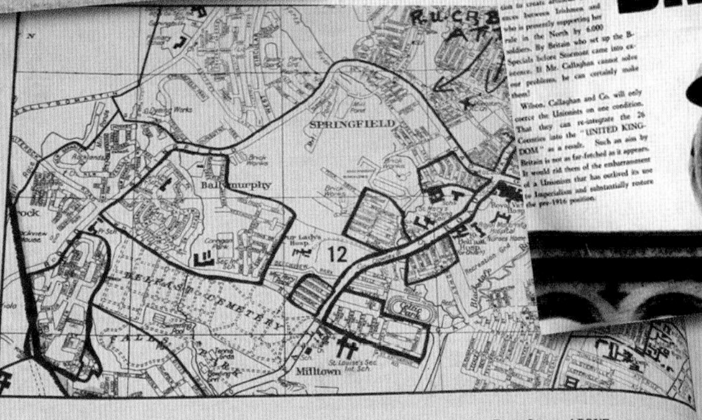

The pogrom in Belfast started about 10.30 p.m. on the night of Thursday, August 14 and the fighting, looting and burning died out after the arrival of the British troops at 7.30 p.m. on the evening of the next day, Friday, August 15.

In the fighting seven people had died, 427 were treated in hospital, 108 with gunshot wounds, and at least 400 houses lay in smoking ruins.

The fighting started just about 10.30 when people from Shankill Road, the Protestant area, led by men wearing white armbands, moved north onto the Crumlin Road at Ardoyne and south onto the Falls Road. Closely behind followed squads of R.U.C. and B-Specials.

As the Paisleyites moved down the approach roads to the Falls Road they stopped at the first Catholic houses on their line of march and began systematically to fire them as the inhabitants fled.

Citizens Defence Associations that had formed during the fortnight previous as the tide of intimidation and tension had risen reacted very effectively to the situation. Groups of them advanced from the Falls down the approach roads from the Shankill Road where the Paisleyite mobs had already commenced the burning of houses. Dover St., Percy St., Northumberland St., Boundary St., North Howard St., Cupar St., and Conway St. were the scene of fierce fighting as Defence Associations fought a holding action with the Orange mobs in order to give people time to evacuate.

In the meantime a Belfast Corporation bus depot was held up at gun point and more than forty buses commandeered to help build barricades on the Falls Road. Furniture, cars, lorries and beds were all pressed into service as the battle raged in the approach roads and streams of refugees flowed across the Falls into the protection of the growing barricades.

When it was obvious that the Orange mob had been checked by the defenders they were told to withdraw and leave the way for the hundreds of R.U.C. and B-Specials advancing on the Falls. Supported by armoured cars and firing indiscriminately with automatic rifles and machine guns, the combined forces of R.U.C. and Specials forced the Catholics back behind the newly erected barricades on the Falls. Behind them the Paisleyites burned and looted and the whole area blazed until there was nothing left to burn.

As the R.U.C. and Specials launched attacks on the barricades guarding the Falls area gunfire was returned for the first time from within the Catholic area.

I.R.A. firing continued until all ammunition was spent, according to reports. Weak though it was in comparison to that of the combined U.V.F., R.U.C. and B-Special forces, the I.R.A. firepower slowed up the advance of the rampaging mobs and helped to hold vital barricades and refugee centres. The full story of the I.R.A. part in the defence has yet to be told, however.

B-Specials anxious to loot handed over their weapons to Paisleyites and started smashing windows in Townsend St.

The chairman of the Northern Ireland Civil Rights Association, Mr. Frank Gogarty, appealed at 2 a.m.: "For Christ's sake tell someone to intervene. Tell someone in Dublin. There will be another four hours of murder here."

He said that the B-Specials were on the Shankill road handing out rifles and revolvers to civilians.

"There must be immediate intervention if more people are not to be killed by B-Specials and the Paisleyites they are leading through the Falls," Mr. Gogarty said.

"They are driving through the streets in tenders, shootin indiscriminately, firing into homes and shooting at anyone they see."

By 5 a.m. five people had died. The miracle was that hundreds had not died as people faced machine guns with bricks and petrol bombs in order to prevent a massacre.

Throughout the day sporadic shooting continued and refugees flowed in increasing numbers from the atmosphere of terror that gripped the Falls during the day. British troops, waiting outside the city, were held back until the last possible moment in order to ensure a welcome from the terrified populace.

The troops' entry to the riot-torn areas came simultaneously at 7.30 p.m. About 400 troops, drawn from the Second Battalion, Queen's Regiment, in Holywood, Co. Down, and from the First Battalion, Royal Regiment of Wales, Ballykinlar, advanced with rifles ready up the Falls and Shankill roads.

Buildings blazed about them as they marched. Gunfire, however, which had echoed throughout Falls Road, Springfield Road, Divis Towers and Percy Street all day, gradually reduced.

The dead included Mr. Herbert Roy, a prominent member of the U.V.F., in Belfast, Mr. David Linton, 48, whose funeral was later attended by the Rev. Ian Paisley; a soldier (Catholic), home on leave from the British Army, who was caught in a burst of machine-gun fire on the top of Divis St. Towers; and two Catholic youths, nine year old Patrick Rooney, killed by a bullet which pierced three walls of his home in Divis St. Towers and fifteen year old Gerald McCauley, a member of Na Fianna Eireann.

ABOVE: The map above shows the barricaded areas surrounded in black. The arrows marking the main line of attack between the Shankill and Falls Road and the approach roads that were completely burned out by the mobs.

BELOW: A grim-faced Paisley later attended the funeral of Mr. David Linton who was killed during the riots.

Never forget that behind the Orangemen, the Paisleyites, the B-Specials and R.U.C., it is Britain holds the real power. She has the troops and the responsibility under the Government of Ireland Act 1920.

After 50 years' injustice the "settlement" Lloyd George imposed on Ireland is crumbling. The Unionists can no longer rule in the old way. Neither can Britain. The Catholic people of the North have got up off their knees and are fighting. The Stomont junta ar shivering in their shoes while they ca into being their bristling armoury terror. "Ulster must not be coerced they say. By this they mean they m be allowed to do all the coercing. Protestant Ascendancy must last for and Nationalists continue to rer second-class citizens in their own h land.

LEGISLATE NOW!

We say: ULSTER MUS COERCED . . . if that is the on to get civil rights and basic de for the Catholic and non-Unioni lation.

Britain set-up the Six Cour in 1920 and has turned a blind years of bigoted backwardness aim of us all must now be to to revise that settlement in interest.

Section 75 of the Gove

notes and comments

nationalists across Ireland but there were recriminations within the IRA. A number of Belfast republicans, many of whom had dropped out of the movement after the Border campaign, argued that the IRA had let nationalists down because of its lack of preparation for the events of August. This, they claimed, was 'the logical outcome of an obsession in recent years with parliamentary politics, and the subsequent undermining of the Irish Republican Army'. The Dublin IRA leadership *had* been taken by surprise by events and though units were sent to the Border with orders to carry out attacks, there was confusion about their purpose. Cathal Goulding issued a public statement explaining the IRA's position, arguing that the organisation was committed to fighting for a united Ireland. This, in turn, drew criticism from those who felt that Goulding was to blame for not foreseeing the likelihood of conflict in the North.

After August, the IRA in Belfast gained new recruits, but it was torn between those, such as its commander Liam McMillen, who continued to support the Goulding leadership, and those, soon a majority, who agreed with the critics, who included Billy McKee, Joe Cahill and John Kelly.

At the same time, the Irish government was split over what policy to adopt towards Northern Ireland and elements within Fianna Fáil were making promises of money and weapons to nationalists, provided they did not interfere in southern politics. All this contributed to accelerating and driving a split within the IRA. Because of the situation in Belfast neither group from the city was represented at the Boyle convention. Having lost the vote about abstention and the NLF, Ó Brádaigh and Mac Stíofáin held their own meeting, set up their own Army Council and established a new organisation, the Provisional IRA. Among the first members of the new leadership were Ó Bradáigh, Mac Stíofáin, Daithí Ó Conaill, Paddy Mulcahy, Seán Treacy and Joe Cahill. The Provisionals' existence became public knowledge on 28 December. Tom Maguire, by then the only survivor of the group of seven TDs who had 'handed over' authority to Seán Russell's Army Council in 1938, also gave his blessing to the formation of the Provisional Army Council.

There were now two IRAs, and after January 1970, two Sinn Féins, Official and Provisional. Friendships were sundered, old comrades fell out and in Belfast, from an early stage, both organisations were fighting each other. By Easter 1970, the Officials had acquired a nickname, 'Stickies', because of their adhesive lilies, while the Provisionals were the 'Provos' or the 'Provies'.

Facing page:
Top left: 'Join the IRA' The aftermath on the Falls Road BELFAST NEWSLETTER
Top right: 'Resistance' *United Irishman*, September 1969
Centre right: 'Blame Britain' *United Irishman*, September 1969
Bottom: 'How Belfast Fought', *United Irishman*, September 1969

THE LAND OF IRELAND FOR THE PEOPLE OF IRELAND

The recent action at the Mannin estate was carried out by a unit of the Irish Republican Army in support of the demand by local farmers that this estate be acquired by the Land Commission and divided among the thirteen neighbouring smallholders, in order to improve the living conditions of those with no means of support other than their uneconomic holdings, and to prevent the estate falling into the hands of foreign or native speculators.

It is now up to the small farmers of Connacht to take the initiative and establish land leagues throughout the West wherever there are large estates – whether owned by native or foreign landlords – and demand that they be acquired by the Land Commission and divided among neighbouring smallholders, or re-organised as co-operatives, jointly owned and controlled by the people who work them.

To those who have fallen victim to the propaganda of the ruling class, or who unknowingly repeat the landlords' defence of the 'rights of private property', our answer is Fintan Lalor's answer:

'To any plain understanding, the right of private property is very simple. It is the right of man to possess, enjoy and transfer the substance and use of whatever he has himself created. This title is good against the world; and it is the sole and only title which can give a valid right of absolute private property a place to vest.

'But no man can plead any such right of property in the substance of the soil. The earth, together with all it spontaneously produces, is the free and common property of all mankind, of natural right, and by grant of God; and, all men being equal, no man therefore has a right to appropriate exclusively to himself any part or portion thereof, except with the common consent and agreement of all men.

'The sole right of property which I acknowledge to be morally valid is the right of common consent and agreement. Every other I hold to be fabricated and fictitious, null, void, and of no effect.'

The Republican Movement has committed itself to being in the vanguard of the people's fight for the re-conquest of Ireland, and the return of the land, fisheries, industry and general wealth of the nation to their rightful owners, the Irish people.

Issued by Galway Command, Irish Republican Army

Throughout 1969, the IRA had been active in social agitation in the South. This was now used by some critics to claim that the organisation had neglected the North. In these leaflets the IRA explains intervention in land disputes and promises to defend activists from repression.

It is clear that the police allowed themselves to be used as a partisan force by Fianna Fáil.

On behalf of the Irish Republican Army we now issue this statement:

Whenever and wherever Irish men and women wish to make a protest against any of the injustices so prevalent in Ireland, we, the Irish Republican Army, assure them of our full support. Further, we will not hesitate to take direct action against any individual or group of individuals, official or otherwise, who would attack these Irish men and women or deny them their rights.

Issued by General Headquarters, Irish Republican Army.

Desmond Fitzgerald

Adjutant General

IRA Statement: full text

The Army Council of the Irish Republican Army, acting in its capacity as the Provisional Government of the Irish Republic proclaimed in arms in 1916, and ratified by the universal suffrage of the Irish people in 1918, hereby calls on all Irishmen and Irishwomen, both at home and in exile, to forget all divisions and differences of the past and to stand in unity against the forces of British imperialism.

Already Northern units of the Irish Republican Army have been in action in defence of the lives and homes of the people which have been attacked by deliberately fomented sectarian forces, backed up by the B-Specials, with the aim of destroying the natural solidarity and unity of working class people. These units have played their part in defensive operations in Bogside, Derry, where they have put their discipline and experience at the disposal of the Citizens' Defence Association. In Belfast in the recent period the I.R.A. and other Republican Organisations have co-operated with the Citizens' Defence Groups and used their all-too-limited resources in the attempt to hold off the terrorist forces of reaction which have been unleashed upon peaceful men, women and children. The people of the Falls Road area have gratefully acknowledged this assistance in the past few days and have contrasted it bitterly with the failure of the Dublin Government to act in their defence.

UNITS OF THE IRA...

Violence

For a number of years past the Republican Movement has been committed to support of the moderate demands of the Civil Rights Movement in the genuine hope that reforms obtained by constitutional agitation would provide a framework within which a peaceful settlement might be arrived at to the outstanding problems of our people. Unfortunately, however, because of the intransigent stand of right-wing Unionism, and their meeting of moderate demands with terrorism and violence, we have been reluctantly compelled into military action to defend the lives and homes of the people in the Six County area.

In response to urgent calls for help from an almost defenceless people and because of the failure to date of the Dublin Government to use the forces at its disposal for the defence of the nation and its people, the Army Council has placed all volunteers on full alert [illegible] local Defence Committees, Citizens' Action Groups and other popular organisations which are at present the only recourse of the people of the North in the face of terrorist attacks from sectarian Unionist gangs.

These forces of the I.R.A. are being used in a defensive capacity wherever the people are being terrorised by Unionist mobs, backed up by armed B-Specials. Control will rest with local leadership and the instructions given to Volunteers are that they must co-operate fully with all local popular organisations, living with and merging themselves with the people they are called upon to defend.

At this vital juncture number of fully equipped units to the aid of their comrades in the Six Counties and to assist the in Irish history we repudiate the British Government's political confidence trick of trying to represent her military forces as saviours of the people and arbiters between Irishmen. The sectarian B-Specials rampaging through the streets of the North of Ireland are as much the responsibility of the British Government which permitted their establishment in the first place as they are of the bigoted Unionists in Stormont.

Warning

In this connection we issue a warning to the young British soldiers who now find themselves patrolling Irish streets and towns because of the Unionist Government's refusal to grant the just demands of the Civil Rights Movement and the criminal misgovernment and incompetence of the British Parliament at Westminster which has persisted in turning a blind eye to the situation in the Six Counties for so long.

As a result of your Government's continued interference in Irish affairs and its refusal over the years to insist that the North of Ireland be ruled with fairness and democracy, you now find yourselves caught between the terrorised Catholic minority on the one hand and the Orange mobs, supported by thousands of armed and uniformed "Specials," on the other. Irishmen have no quarrel with you as individuals, but we warn you that until the Westminster Government disarms and disbands the B-Specials, legislates for all the Civil Rights demands, and indeed removes you from the country altogether, you are in a very perilous situation. For this is not your country. It is our [illegible] Government and Parliament have divided in order to serve the interests of the imperialist monopolies, financiers and aristocrats who are a curse to the people of England, Scotland and Wales, as they have been a curse to Ireland.

We warn you that if you allow yourselves to be used to suppress the legitimate attempts of the people to defend themselves against the B-Specials and the sectarian Orange murder gangs, then you will have to take the consequences.

To the Dublin Government we say this: You must immediately use the Irish Army to defend the persecuted people of the Six Counties. You must then call an urgent meeting of the United Nations Security Council, followed by a meeting of the General Assembly, in order to expose the British claim that what is happening in the Irish cities of Belfast, Derry, Newry and elsewhere is Britain's own "internal" affair, for the insolent and ludicrous lie that it is. Britain must be exposed to the searchlight of world opinion for the mess she has made of the Six Counties, which she has tried to hide from the world for so long. The Irish delegation at the United Nations must talk about Ireland for a change, after years of talk about Tibet and Peru.

We recognise that a political solution to the present crisis in the North will have to be found in time. The only solution acceptable to Republicans and to the Irish people as a whole is one in which Britain gets out of our country altogether, withdraws her troops, and control over the whole of Ireland passes to a 32-County Irish Parliament, elected from among all the people of Ireland, North and South, on the proportional representation representation system of election, the only fair system which will be just to both Catholics and Protestants, under United Nations supervision. For a united, independent, democratic Republic is the only possible constitution within which Protestants and Catholics can live together in friendship under the common name of Irishmen, in which civil rights will be guaranteed to all, the Irish working class be reunited in one political community, and the way opened up for progressive advance in all fields of our national life, leading to the establishment of a socialist workers' and farmers' Republic for the whole country.

Pressure

Irish people in the 26-Counties . . . Put every pressure you can on the Dublin Government to support the victimised people of the North. Make Dublin justify its claim to sovereignty over the whole of the national territory. Contribute generously to the relief funds being set up to relieve Catholics and Protestants turned out of the homes. Organise rallies, meetings, demonstrations of support within the coming period. Trade Unionists, farmers, students, people of all political views . . . let us stand together in this hour of crisis.

The soldiers of the Republic are in the field to serve the people. Let all Irishmen support them so that we may build in our time a united Ireland and lay the basis for democracy and socialism in our country.

(Signed) Cathal Goulding,
Chief of Staff,
Irish Republican Army.

● When the gagging stops, the gassing b[...]

DEVLIN BREA[...]

By far the most energetic member of the Six Counties Labour Party is Paddy Devlin. Chairman of the party and M.P. for Falls, Paddy was interned at the age of 17 and is now the 43-year-old father of five. Dubliners will remember him from the impassioned speech he made from the G.P.O. platform and from his appearance on R.T.E. "We want guns", was Paddy Devlin's unashamed cry to the people of the 26-Counties; "Don't abandon us", his anguished appeal.

Dublin trip

It is not hard to explain the deadly earnestness and the utter desperation which Paddy Devlin showed during his Dublin visit when one remembers that, in his own constituency, during the recent flare-up of violence there, six people died, 127 had been injured and 5,000 people bombed or forced to flee from their homes.

To Dublin, at any rate, looking for help—any help—came the chairman of the party which has in its constitution the words: "The Labour Party firmly supports the basic constitutional relationship between Ulster and the rest of the United Kingdom." Naturally enough, the party keenly resented their chairman's trip south and rumours are rife about an imminent split between Paddy Devlin and the all but defunct Six Counties Labour Party.

Declining poll

If Mr. Devlin does decide to resign from the party he will have the support of all progressive people. It will be remembered that Mr. Devlin unseated the veteran Republican Labour man, Harry Diamond (an M.P. for over 25 years), in the last Stormont election in the Falls constituency. In this predominantly Republican area it is obvious that Paddy's vote was a personal, not a party one, and that few Falls constituents will mourn if Paddy Devlin removes his allegiance from the Northern Ireland Labour Party.

best be shown by the steady [...] total poll in [...] Stormont e[...] 76,842; 196[...] 45,113.

This an[...] perialist par[...] refused to [...] the pernici[...] Act and is [...] the Six C[...] main the [...] that it is. [...] things to [...]

[...] REA[...] IN [...] SO[...]

IRA statement in response to the fighting in August 1969, *United Irishman*

FIANNA FÁIL AND THE IRA

During August 1969, thousands of people in the Republic had demonstrated in support of northern nationalists. Among many in the South there was support for the idea of armed intervention in Northern Ireland. This pamphlet, *Fianna Fail and the IRA*, published by the Official IRA, and banned by the government, claimed that the 1969-70 republican split had been fomented by agents of Fianna Fáil in order to neuter an IRA that was becoming a threat to their power. In fact, both factions within the IRA had received money from Dublin government sources in 1969 and republicans were given military training in the South.

Taoiseach Jack Lynch shakes the hand of Unionist leader, Terence O'Neill.

DEFENDERS?

A great deal of the bitterness of the split revolved around the accusation that the Goulding leadership refused to defend Catholics in Belfast from Loyalist attacks. But it should not be taken for granted that this was ever seen as the IRA's primary role. During the last major sectarian confrontations in the city, in 1935, and from 1920-22, the IRA had also responded in a confused and inconsistent manner. What is true is that after 1969, many nationalists assumed that the IRA *should* be defenders.

Chapter 7

FROM WAR TO PEACE

The conflict that emerged after 1970 transformed the IRA and the popular perception of the organisation for good. The early years of the 'Troubles' saw violence on a scale unknown in Ireland since 1919-23. Thousands of young men and women, primarily northern nationalists from working-class backgrounds, were drawn into the IRA for the first time. Areas in which the IRA had a minimal presence until the 1970s would be now labelled 'republican strongholds'. Thousands would be jailed and hundreds killed or injured. But republicans would also feud with each other and involve themselves in activities that bitterly divided nationalist Ireland. Early predictions of a 'Year of Victory' changed to a strategy of 'Long War' and eventually into support for a 'Peace Process'. By then over 3,500 people had died as a result of the conflict.

'THE ROCK OF THE REPUBLIC', 1970

The Provisionals published two newspapers: *An Phoblacht*, published in Dublin and edited by Seán Ó Brádaigh, Colman Moynihan and then Eamonn MacThomáis, and *Republican News*, published in Belfast, edited by Jimmy Steele and then Proinsias MacAirt. (The Officials retained control of the *United Irishman*.) The first edition of *An Phoblacht* dwelt heavily on the Provisional IRA's claim to be the legitimate inheritors of the republican tradition, remaining steadfast despite the latest 'betrayal'. Hence the references to previous sellouts by the the Treatyites, Fianna Fáil and Clann na Poblachta. The paper describes the decision of the 1969 IRA convention to endorse the taking of parliamentary seats as an attempt to set up 'Free State Party No. 4'. Some of these assertions might have remained relatively esoteric had the relationship between northern Catholics and the British Army not deteriorated badly during 1970. After an intial period of uneasy peace, many began to resent the role of troops in policing nationalist areas. Major rioting broke out during Orange parades on 27 June and the Provisional IRA opened fire on loyalist crowds, killing three men. Later that evening, loyalist mobs attacked the Short Strand and the Provos killed three more Protestants during gun battles in the vicinity of St Matthew's Catholic church. One Catholic vigilante, Henry McIlhone, was killed by fire from his own side while leading Provo Billy McKee was wounded.

The defence of the Short Strand became a powerful recruiting tool for the Provisional IRA. A week later British troops raided a house in the Lower Falls, having received a tip-off that weapons were being stored there. Rioting broke out and as British troops were moved into the area, they clashed with the Official IRA. The British Army imposed a curfew on the Lower Falls, threatening to shoot anyone who remained on the streets. There followed rioting and several gun battles with

An Phoblacht

THE REPUBLIC
Official Organ of the Republican Movement

IML. 1. UIMH. 1. SRAITH NUA

FEABHRA (FEB.), 1970

9d. (U.S. and Canada 25 c.)

ON THIS WE STAND

A Worthy Memorial to Wolfe Tone

A worthy memorial to Theobald Wolfe Tone is now being prepared and will be unveiled at his grave in Bodenstown, Co. Kildare, this summer.

It will replace the memorial (pictured above) which was blown up in October last. The grave has been in the care of the National Graves Association for many years. Their Secretary, Seán Fitzpatrick, told our reporter that there had been a magnificent response to their appeal for funds.

The Association assumed the responsibility for reconstruction immediately after the damage was done and there was a prompt response to their appeal.

They were particularly pleased with the many letters of encouragement, such as one from a schoolgirl in Derry, one from an old-age pensioner (a Presbyterian) in Belfast, and one from Tone's great great grand-daughter in America.

Mr. Fitzpatrick had a special word of praise for the G.A.A., Trade Unions and National Graves Branch Committee in Kildare who have helped in a big way. Nár laga Dia a lámha.

ROSCOMMON STATEMENT

The following statement was released to the press subsequent to meetings of the Irish Republican Army of Roscommon and Galway: The Roscommon and Galway Units of the Irish Republican Army reject the policy to recognise the Westminster, Stormont and Leinster House Parliaments and pledge allegiance to the Provisional Army Council as the lawful leadership of the I.R.A.

The Rock of the Republic

In the very first issue of this paper we wish to say bluntly and openly that we are standing on "The Rock of the Republic," and from that position we refuse to budge. Let us explain.

On December 6, 1921, the Irish delegates from the Government of the Republic signed in London a document known as "Articles of Agreement for a Treaty between Great Britain and Ireland." That document was ratified by a small majority of Deputies in Dáil Eireann, and had the effect of setting up two States in Ireland, one known as the Irish Free State, and the other as Northern Ireland. These States had two Parliaments, one to govern the 26 Counties, the other to govern the Six, and the British Army was left in occupation of our six north-eastern counties.

THE FREE STATE

The two States in question were, and still are, England's alternative to the Irish Republic proclaimed in arms on Easter Monday, 1916, ratified by the votes of the Irish people in the All-Ireland General Election of 1918 and established by law on January 21, 1919, when the First Dáil Eireann met and solemnly proclaimed to the world that Ireland was, and would remain, a 32-County Independent Irish Republic completely free of any political link with the British Empire.

Those who supported the Articles of Agreement or, as we prefer to call it, the "Treaty of Surrender," attacked their former comrades with British-supplied guns. The newly-established Free State Army did England's dirty work in the so-called Civil War of 1922. Hundreds of men died to preserve the Republic, but from a military point of view the war was lost.

Then came 1926, when another group of Republicans, getting tired of the struggle to maintain the Republic, left the I.R.A. and Sinn Féin and formed Free State Party No. 2, now known as Fianna Fáil. That party came to power in the 26-County State on March 10, 1932. It wore a Republican mantle, but by 1939 the mask was off.

SEAN RUSSELL

When the I.R.A. under Seán Russell resumed the war against England, by sending an Expeditionary Force on to English soil, the Fianna Fáil Government in Dublin attacked the Republican Movement. Hundreds of men were arrested and I.R.A. men had again to face the firing squad and the hangman's rope because they would not accept England's alternative to the Republic. Paddy McGrath, Tommy Harte, Richie Goss, Charlie Kerins, Maurice O'Neill and George Plant went bravely to their deaths rather than accept that alternative, and Tony D'Arcy with his comrade Seán McNeela died on hunger strike rather than surrender. Seán McCaughey died on hunger strike in Portlaoise Prison in 1946 for the same reason, but 10 years later on December 12, 1956, I.R.A. units were again attacking the British Army of Occupation in North-East Ulster. Fianna Fáil's terror had failed to break the I.R.A. even though Free State Party No. 3 had been born and was now a part of the 26-County set up. We refer, of course, to Clann na Poblachta under the leadership of Seán MacBride, who once held the proud position of Chief of Staff of the I.R.A., as Frank Aiken did before.

And now, in 1970, we are asked to follow Free State Party No. 4. We are told that we should enter and take part in the deliberations of the Leinster House, Stormont and Westminster Parliaments. We are even told that this is the Revolutionary Road. That this is the way to the Republic.

But we will have none of it. We here and now repudiate again the "Treaty of Surrender" and every institution set up under that document, i.e., the Parliaments of the 26-County and Six-County States, the courts established under those Parliaments, and every instrument of terror which they possess to enforce the law of conquest on the Irish nation.

And we say to all Republicans that it is their duty to support us in maintaining the Republic. We repudiate also all forms of Free State-ism and all other isms which are not in line with traditional Republican and Separatist policy.

TONE'S GOSPEL

We accept the gospel according to Tone and with Pearse we say "Tone has spoken for all generations." The Rock of the Republic is solid and has very many defenders to-day. The authentic voice of Tone preaching the gospel of Republicanism is as clear now as it was in Easter Week. We cannot put it more simply than in Tone's own words: "To unite the whole people of Ireland, to abolish the memory of past dissensions, and to substitute the common name of Irishman for the denominations of Protestant, Catholic and Dissenter." These were his means. "To break the connection with England, the never failing source of all our political ills," that was his aim.

WE ARE PREPARED

There is no ambiguity about that. Tone was clear and on Tone's policy we stand. We say in the words of Mitchel: "Come Red War or Revolution we are prepared." Yes, we are prepared to play our part as every generation before us played its part. We know of only one way to do that. It is Tone's way, it is Mitchel's way, it was the way of the Fenians, the men of Easter Week, the men

To Page 8.

This paper has been launched at short notice and without any finance. The costs of production are very heavy, including not only printing but carriage and postage, blocks, wrapping, essential office equipment, etc. To keep it in existence and to put it on a sound financial footing we need money urgently. Consequently, we are launching a

PUBLICITY FUND

with a target of £500. We confidently appeal to all our readers and supporters, including our many exiles, for subscriptions to this fund. Initially, we need £250 before February 10. IT IS AS URGENT AS THAT.

Please Subscribe Generously

Please do it to-day

Send to: An Phoblacht, Irish Book Bureau, 33 O'Donovan Rd., S.C. Rd., Dublin 8. All subscriptions will be acknowledged.

TUS MAITH LEATH NA hOIBRE

ARD-FHEIS APPOINTS CARETAKER EXECUTIVE

At the conclusion of the adjourned Sinn Féin Ard-Fheis at 44 Parnell Square, Dublin, on January 11, the following statement was issued to the press:

"The delegates present here tonight consider themselves to be the adjourned Ard-Fheis of Sinn Féin. We left the Intercontinental Hotel because we were asked to give allegiance to an I.R.A. leadership which recognises the Westminster, Stormont and Leinster House Parliaments.

"We adhere to the Sinn Féin Constitution as upheld by the Ard-Fheis, but those who remained in the Intercontinental Hotel stated that they did not accept the Constitution and rules of Sinn Féin in so far as these preclude recognition of the three parliaments.

A caretaker executive was appointed from members of the new Ard Comhairle and Sinn Féin public representatives in attendance. A full Ard-Fheis will be held in due course."

The meeting reaffirmed its allegiance to the Irish Republic as

To Page 8.

The first *An Phoblacht*, 1970 AP/RN

the Officials. The British admitted firing 1,454 live rounds, killing three local civilians and a freelance photographer as they flooded the area with CS gas. 18 soldiers were wounded, 15 by gunfire. As the army entered the area, soldiers began extensive house searches, during which homes were wrecked and people beaten. Two Unionist MPs were then brought on a tour of the subdued area in the back of an army Land Rover. The Falls curfew was a key moment in the alienation of nationalists from the British Army. While the Officials claimed that it was the biggest confrontation between the British Army and the IRA since 1916, in many ways the Provisionals benefitted more. The Official IRA remained committed to defence but the Provisionals had other plans. Brendan Hughes, a leading member of the Belfast Provos, later recounted that throughout 1970, the Provisional IRA had been moving onto a war footing and waiting for the opportunity to go onto the offensive. With the Falls Curfew, it had gotten its chance. By the winter of 1970, bomb attacks and shootings were on the increase, as was recruitment and arms importation.

'TOTAL WAR'

Throughout 1971, there was a steady escalation in conflict between nationalists and the British Army. In Belfast and Derry in particular, rioting and confrontation became routine. In February 1971, three people (a British soldier, a Provisional IRA man and a civilian) were killed in fighting in Belfast. The soldier, Gunner Robert Curtis, was the first to be killed in Ireland since 1924. By the end of the year, 181 people had been killed, including 94 civilians and 44 British soldiers.

While the violence had been worsening during the spring and early summer, with both the Provisional and Official IRA targeting soldiers and carrying out widespread bomb attacks, there had still been certain constraints. When the Provisional IRA killed three off-duty Scottish soldiers during March they disclaimed responsibility, as the nature of the killing (the soldiers were drunk and in the company of their killers, who they believed were taking them to a party) was widely unpopular. As one Provisional explained: 'I know it's not a job Pádraig Pearse would have done'. Similarly most bomb attacks went unclaimed. But the British Army's killing of civilians and the general contempt they displayed for working-class nationalists radicalised many.

Then, in early August, the Unionist government introduced internment without trial, arresting over 300 men (all nationalists) in raids across the North. It soon became apparent that many of the internees were being ill-treated. The rage that followed internment engulfed nationalists of all descriptions. There was a surge in support for the IRA and the scale of the fighting that followed had not been seen in Ireland since the 1920s. In the Republic, there was also a wave of sympathy for nationalists and much support for the IRA. As far as the Provisionals were concerned, the opportunity to drive the British from Ireland, once and for all, had arrived.

Facing page: *An Phoblacht*, October 1971 AP/BN

An Phoblacht

THE REPUBLIC
Official Organ of the Republican Movement

IML. 2 UIMHIR 10 (Sraith Nua) DEIREADH FOMHAIR (October) 1971. 5p (U.S. and Canada 30c)

SUPPORT FOR THE I.R.A.

AFTER being fined on September 6 at Enniskillen Court for alleged disorderly conduct, Father Sean McManus C.S.S.R. made the following statement expressing his complete support for the I.R.A. and denying the right of an illegally constituted court to charge him.

Fr McManus said:

"I refused to recognise the court because it has no legitimate authority. But that is only the 'tip of the iceberg'. I do not, I never have and I never will recognise the colonial State of British Occupied Ireland. This State exists because of a (morally and politically) criminal action. It was illegally imposed by force, and it is illegally sustained by force, against the will of the Irish people. Therefore, its institutions, its laws, and its legal and political expressions are invalid.

"The creation and maintenance of this State blatantly violates God's law and the natural law, because its fundamental principle is: "ownership by right of conquest", i.e. ownership through violence and the gun. This State was conceived and born in violence, was imposed by violence and the gun, and by violence and the gun it is maintained. And those who created it, and those who sustain it, are the real men of violence – they are the gunmen; they alone – are the terrorists.

"This terrorist State I reject in its entirety. I reject in particular its judiciary: in principle it is illegitimate; in practice it has a despicable record of injustice, corruption and sectarianism.

"Refusing to recognise the court is the policy of the Irish Republican Army. I will immediately be suspected of being in sympathy with the I.R.A. Well, lets clear up this "suspicion": I want to state publicly and unequivocally that I am in sympathy with the I.R.A., indeed sympathy is too weak a word.

"Many people may wonder why I should want to publicly proclaim my convictions. The answer is simple: My conscience forbids me to be silent; and if I did not now speak out I could never live with myself, because for the rest of my life I would know that I had been a coward – no matter how hard I tried to justify my silence as prudence. I would know that I had been deceitful and treacherous to the patriots who are sacrificing their lives for the freedom of Ireland. I cannot join them in the fight for freedom of my country, but the very least I can do is speak up for them when they are being slandered and vilified by unscrupulously vicious propaganda.

"The oppressors of Irish freedom call the I.R.A. terrorists and murderers, but I call them by their proper titles; I call them freedom fighters, I call them heroes, and I venerate their dead as martyrs for Ireland. And I know that any true Irishman – or indeed any (informed) honest and fair-minded man – thinks and feels the same way.

"I could not live with myself if by my silence I traitorously stabbed these patriots in the back. I abhor the deceit and hypocrisy that condemns these men and women who are sacrificing their lives for the freedom of Ireland. I could not bear to be even remotely associated and by silence would associate myself, with such deceit and hypocrisy. It is only to be expected that the violent men who are oppressing Irish freedom should condemn the I.R.A. freedom fighters; but it is unforgivable when they are also condemned by many so-called Nationalist spokesmen.

"Yet in the light of history – condemnation from the latter is not surprising, for every struggle for Irish freedom has – traitorously – been condemned by these kind of people. (And yet our patriots, despite "this unkindest cut of all" still fought on because they were, and are, men of courage, integrity and dedication). And of this I am certain; that when our patriots free Ireland and free it they surely will, these very people will be the very first to jump on the band-wagon and salute the men they now condemn. They did it before and they will do it again.

"To praise Tone, Pearse, Connolly, Sean Treacy, Cathal Brugha and all the others, on the one hand, while on the other condemning those (and here I make no distinctions between the Provisionals and the Officials) is treachery and deceit of the lowest kind. How I detest such chicanry – it revolts and disgusts me, and I will have no part of it.

"I finalised my decision to speak out as I stood by a lonely grave. It was the grave of a man who was the personification of nobility, courage, and integrity: a typical member of the I.R.A. He is a man whose memory I honour and of whom I am deeply proud: my brother Patrick who died for Ireland in 1958."

JOE MCCANN

The cover of the *United Irishman* of September 1971 featured Joe McCann, an Official IRA member, during gun battles in the Markets area of Belfast after internment was introduced. McCann had joined the IRA during 1964 and was one of the best-known members of the Officials in Belfast. He was shot dead by British troops in April 1972.

AN t-EIREANNACH AONTAITHE
Mean Fomhair (September) 1971, Iml. XXV. Uimhir 9. Luach 5p. (1/-), (U.S., Canada and Australia 25c.)

THE UNITED IRISHMAN

Army of the People

An Phoblacht

THE REPUBLIC Voice of Irish Republicanism

DERRY'S BLOODY SUNDAY 30th. JAN. 1972.

COMMEMORATION SUPPLEMENT

British Troops Murder 13

MANY OF THE VICTIMS WERE SHOT IN THE BACK

BARNEY McGUIGÁN

GERARD DONAGHY

JOHN YOUNG

MICHAEL KELLY

PATSY DOHERTY

MICHAEL McDAID

WILLIAM NASH

JACK DUDDY

HUGH GILMORE

JIM WRAY

KEVIN McELHINNEY

WILLIAM McKINNEY

GERRY McKINNEY

We stand and salute the 13 who were murdered by British Guns in Derry City – We salute also all who died by British Guns before January 30, 1972 and since that date let us insure that all these sacrifices have not been in vain.

Demand the withdrawal of British Troops from Ireland.

An Phoblacht, commemorative edition, January 1973 AP/RN

Following Bloody Sunday, when British paratroopers killed 13 civilians in Derry, popular support for the IRA in nationalist Ireland reached a level unseen since the 1920s.

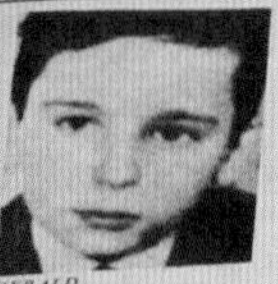
GERALD DONAGHY

Murdered by Paratroopers.

Derry Bloody Sunday.

PATRICK DOHERTY

Murdered by Paratroopers.

Derry Bloody Sunday.

JAMES WRAY

Murdered by Paratroopers.

Derry Bloody Sunday.

WILLIAM NASH

Murdered by Paratroopers.

Derry Bloody Sunday.

MICHAEL KELLY

Murdered by Paratroopers.

Derry Bloody Sunday.

BERNARD McGUIGAN

Murdered by Paratroopers.

Derry Bloody Sunday

PARA HQ. BLASTED AT ALDERSHOT

The headquarters of the notorious Paratroop regiment was blasted in an explosion at Aldershot during the month. The explosion occurred a few minutes before one o'clock when the officers' mess was crowded with those who planned and organised the dreadful murders in Derry on Bloody Sunday. Between thirty and forty officers were present when the bomb went off, and initial reports confirmed that several of the high ranking officers had been killed. British propaganda units then moved into action, and miraculously the dead officers disappeared.

The operation was marred by tragedy, in that civilians were killed.

It has been established, however, that all those killed were on the Ministry of Defence lists. The announcement that ordinary civilians had been killed was taken, however as a general signal by reactionary and hypocritical politicians to attack the Republican Movement and condemn the action.

But despite the efforts of these politicians and place seekers, the suggested civilian casualities did not hide the fact that the target chosen was a military one. This fact was conveniently overlooked in all the embittered comment on the incident.

What actually happened was simple. An active service unit of the IRA left their base in the North of Ireland, where the people are continually subjected to military terror, and crossed over to England. Extensive surveillance of the most likely targets was undertaken. Aldershot was chosen, according to IRA sources, precisely because the danger to civilians was at a minimum there. Most interesting in the light of later developments was the fact that although the bomb went off at three minutes to one, according to on the spot witnesses, British propaganda altered the time to 12.40 when there would be few officers there. But even their own reports admitted the injuries of seventeen officers. If the bomb had gone off at that time, as the British and their collaborators maintained, there would have been no officers present at all.

What is even more interesting is that similar disappearances of Paratroop officers occurred in South Yemen when various Aden groups were fighting for their national liberation. Even where the NLF and FLOSY claimed certain casualities the British were able to deny them, to the obvious propaganda advantage of the British. The Paratroopers are a regiment in which this is particularly easy, since a high proportion of the officers in that regiment have no family ties of any kind. Their deaths would be missed by no one. What the British had got away with in Aden they also hoped to get away with in the Aldershot case. This view is backed by the views of people in Aldershot, who maintain that there were at least thirty officers in the building when the explosion occurred. Since 280 lbs. of gelignite were used it is obvious that few people in the building would escape unscathed. Yet the only military casualities admitted were seventeen officers injured. What happened to the other thirteen? But publication of this information wouldn't help Britain's propaganda case.

Full praise must go to the brave volunteers who carried out the operation in the very heart of Britain's military headquarters. Taking that quantity of gelignite along roads on military premises, where security is daily announced to be tightened up even further is no easy job. But the IRA has shown that no amount of security can prevent determined and courageous men.

The Paratroopers, of course, came into particular prominence after the dreadful murders they committed in Derry. The military policy of the IRA has been repeated on many occassions to be one of defence and retaliation. If ever retaliation was justified it was against the Paratroop regiment. But who should suffer? The ordinary workers who swell the ranks of the Paras and are treated with total contempt by their upper class officers, or the officers who planned and directed the whole dreadful massacre? The IRA's answer was clear that the ruling elite are the ones who should be hit. That is why the Officers' Mess in Aldershot was chosen for an operation.

Retaliation has been taken on many occasions against British soldiers and installations in the North. The Aldershot operation was a specific exercise against the Paratroop Regiment for its actions in Derry. There is no question of a full scale military campaign in Britain, for the IRA is aware that terror is not the way to victory. But Aldershot showed that the IRA, like any genuine revolutionary movement, is prepared to and is capable of striking back against the imperialists in the heart of their homeland.

A full statement from the IRA was issued the following day as Union Jack Lynch began a campaign of intimidation against peaceful and democratic members of Sinn Fein. Every effort was made to link Sinn Fein, an open constitutional political party, with the military organisation of the IRA. The IRA's statement itself, which set out the full background to the Aldershot explosion was given minimal coverage by the mass media. This statement made the point that the target was a valid military target and that the volunteers were Northern based men who have to suffer British military terror daily. The statement denied any intention to carry out a campaign of bombing in England since that would be totally contrary to the political basis of the Republican Socialist ideology. The statement also pointed out the real and genuine regrets of the IRA for civilian casualities, but pointed out that all those working at Aldershot were specially screened by the Army and that if any were civilians the responsibility for their security rested with the British government.

Here below is the full text of the IRA's statement, signed by J. J. McGarrity:

"In the light of the mass of ill-informed and hypocritical comment on the Aldershot explosion the IRA would like to make the following points clear:

(1) The target chosen was a military target, being the Officers' mess of the Paratroop Regiment which perpetrated the Derry outrage. An Active Service Unit of the Official IRA left the North, crossed to England where it carried out the operation. The Unit has since safely returned to Ireland. 208 lbs. of gelignite was used which completely destroyed the building in which there were between 30 and 40 officers. Our intelligence reports indicate that at least 12 officers were killed.

(2) British propaganda has attempted to distort what happened, but this propaganda can be discounted when we remember earlier reports which indicated that between three and ten officers had been killed. This figure miraculously disappeared as the Army Information Bureau swung into operation. Our information asserts that all the dead were on the Ministry of Defence lists.

(3) The IRA certainly regrets any civilian casualities, and with far more sincerity than that of the hypocritical canting politicians. We would re-emphasise, however, that the target was a military one and that the responsibility for civilians lies totally with the British Authorities. It was they who declared a state of war on the Irish people which led to the Derry messacre. If they want to use civilians as stool pigeons on military premises they should ensure their security.

(4) We wish to deny any suggestion that the IRA is about to engage on a military campaign in Britain. We eschew all such ideas but restate our policy of defence and retaliation. Regiments guilty of atrocities and leading officers in those regiments are valid targets, wherever they be.

(5) This operation has shown that the IRA can strike at the British Army even in the heart of England. Serving officers should realise that their crimes can be avenged. It has also shown where Jack Lynch's loyalty lies — with Britain. This is the logic of his attempt to take Ireland into the EEC. (6) Finally we would point out that THE NEED FOR REPRISALS WOULD NOT ARISE IF THE British Army were withdrawn. This could open the way for genuine political initiatives: the institution of democracy; the ending of sectarianism and the guaranteeing constitutionally of civil and religious liberties for all. Those who call for peace should also call for justice.

WILLIAM McKINNEY

Murdered by Paratroopers.

GERALD McKINNEY

Derry Bloody Sunday.

HUGH GILMORE

Murdered by Paratroopers.

JACK DUDDY

Derry Bloody Sunday.

KEVIN McELLHINEY

Murdered by Paratroopers.

JOHN YOUNG

Derry Bloody Sunday.

MICHAEL McDAID

Murdered by Paratroopers.

ALDERSHOT, 1972

On 30 January 1972, British paratroopers shot dead 13 people in at a civil rights march in Derry in what became known as Bloody Sunday. Nationalist Ireland was gripped with rage and a week of marches, strikes and rallies followed, with the British Embassy in Dublin burnt down. The Official IRA Army Council gave the go-ahead for an attack on the headquarters of the Parachute Regiment at Aldershot in Hampshire. On Tuesday 22 February a car containing explosives was parked outside the officers' mess. At 12.45 p.m. it exploded, killing five women cleaners, a gardener and an army padre. The Official IRA initially claimed that they had killed at least twelve British officers. As the truth emerged, they expressed regret for the civilian dead but argued that responsibility for the deaths lay 'totally with the British authorities'.

Facing page: *United Irishman*, March 1972

STATEMENT
FROM THE
IRISH REPUBLICAN ARMY

"Statement from the Irish Republican Publicity Bureau.

"Announcement by Irish Republican leadership.

"We have been asked to release the following statement:

"The Irish Republican Army will suspend offensive operations as and from midnight, Monday, June 26th, 1972, provided that a public reciprocal response is forthcoming from the armed forces of the British Crown.

"The leadership of the Republican movement believes that a bilateral suspension of operations would lead to meaningful talks between the major parties to the conflict. The movement has formulated a peace plan designed to secure a just and lasting solution and holds itself in readiness to present it at the appropriate time.

Signed by the leadership of the Republican movement,

"P. O Neill, runai,
I.R.P.B."

AN PHOBLACHT
Iml. 3 Uimh. 7 6p Iúil 1972

VICTORY FOR THE HUNGER STRIKERS!

FROM THE CEASEFIRE TO THE FINAL SOLUTION

INSIDE

An Phoblacht, July 1972 AP/RN

'YEAR OF VICTORY?'

On June 26 1972, the Provisional IRA declared a ceasefire, during which talks took place between the leadership and the British government; the first such meetings since 1921. In January, the Belfast Provisional newspaper *Republican News* had declared 1972 would be 'The Year of Victory'. In May, the same paper illustrated 'how the War is being won' by explaining how the use of car bombs had shifted the balance in favour of the Provisional IRA:

'The IRA's new car bomb, which first appeared in early March. Prior to the introduction of this bomb four or five armed men placed low powered bombs which

SEÁN MAC STIOFÁIN

Mac Stiofáin, the Provisional IRA's first chief of staff, lost his position after being jailed in Dublin during November 1972. He began a hunger-and-thirst strike, during which the IRA attempted to rescue him from the Mater Hospital, but was eventually ordered off the strike in confusing circumstances. Released in 1973 he did not hold a senior post in the IRA again.

COURTESY OF SEAMUS MURPHY

only destroyed a single shop or building. Quite obviously the chances of being caught by the enemy were great. It is quite true to say that with this old type bomb the IRA destroyed the centre of Belfast. Nevertheless this bomb was rarely used in small towns for the obvious reason that men on foot doing this type of job would have no chance of escape. Consequently apart from Belfast, Derry and Newry there was little or no IRA bombing in any other town. Since March however nearly all major towns in Northern Ireland have been badly hit by the new car bomb. It is not clear whether Lisburn or Shipquay Street, Derry, was the first target of this bomb early in March. The Lisburn bomb destroyed eighty shops and the Derry bomb destroyed an entire street . . . then it was the turn of Banbridge, Bangor, Carrickfergus, Enniskillen and of course the centre of Belfast.'

In March, the British government had suspended Stormont and introduced direct rule from London: the Provos saw this as proof they were winning. Their chief of staff Seán Mac Stiofáin was joined at the talks in London by Belfast's Seamus Twomey, by Ivor Bell and by Gerry Adams (who was released from internment to take part) and by Derry's Martin McGuinness. Apart from Mac Stiofáin, Daithi Ó Conaill was the only southerner taking part.

The talks were inconclusive and the truce broke down after clashes in Belfast's Lenadoon district. The ceasefire had lasted just 13 days.

July 1972 saw nearly 100 people killed: by the year's end 496 were dead. Republicans had killed 108 British soldiers while 74 members of both IRAs had lost their lives. Many IRA members died in explosions, as in Newry during August when three IRA men and six civilians were blown up at a customs office. Nearly 260 civilians died, many in bombings that brought carnage to town centres across the North, most notably on 'Bloody Friday' when 20 car bombs were exploded in Belfast city centre killing nine and injuring 130. By the winter, random sectarian killings were also commonplace, especially in Belfast. It was not the 'Year of Victory', but at the time few foresaw another two decades of violence.

'SUPPORT THE PROVISIONALS'

A Provisional IRA volunteer in the Bogside, Derry, 1972. He is equipped with an Armalite rifle, quantities of which had begun to arrive in Ireland that year. Prior to this, a variety of weaponry including Lee Enfield, Springfield and Garand rifles, M1 carbines and Thompson and Sten sub-machine guns were being utilised. Often confused with the M-16, the Armalite became the weapon most associated with the Provisional IRA during the 1970s. The gun was idealised in song, 'My Little Armalite', and in rhetoric: at the 1981 Sinn Féin Ard Fheis, its Director of Publicity Danny Morrison asked, 'Will anyone here object if, with a ballot paper in this hand, and an Armalite in this hand, we take power in Ireland?'

PHOTO: EAMON MELAUGH

THE UNITED IRISHMAN

AN t-EIREANNACH AONTAITHE
Meitheamh (June) 1972. Iml. XXVI. Uimhir 6. Luach 5p (U.S., Canada and Australia 25c.)

I.R.A. DEMANDS

- *release internees*
- *withdrawal of troops*
- *establishment of political freedom*
- *amnesty for all offences*
- *abolition of special powers act*
- *progress towards full democracy*

The IRA has decided to suspend armed military actions.

News of the IRA's decision has caused a tremendous impact on the political situation and is regarded by observers as being the possible move that may yet prevent a full outbreak of a sectarian civil war.

The IRA's decision was taken in view of the growing dangers of that type of internal violence as a result of a request by the Executive of Republican Clubs in the 6 Counties. It opens up once again the possibilities of redeveloping political action.

The only exception to the general suspension of armed actions is the reservation of the right of self-defence and the right to defend any area under aggressive attack by the British military or by sectarian forces **from either side.** The oppressed minority in the North who have been able to rely with confidence on the IRA as a defender of the people may still have that confidence.

The reason for taking this crucial decision lay in a growing awareness by the leadership of the Republican Movement that we had been drawn into a war that was not of our choosing, and that we were being forced to fight on enemy ground. The IRA has decided to reaffirm its political programme in an effort to avoid sectarian war, to bring about a political confrontation between the Irish people and British imperialism.

It is to be expected that the Provisionals may try and sabotage this development. But the onus rests in the main on the British aggressor forces. Obviously, if there were any repeat of the Bloody Sunday episode in Derry the IRA would have to reconsider its position. But for the moment the prospects look good for political progress: already both the extreme Unionists and the Provisionals are finding themselves increasingly isolated, as people rally behind the Republican movement's banner. The Armagh march is the beginning of a new phase of civil struggle.

The statement from the IRA confirmed the original announcement made by the Northern Republicans (see page 3). The statement reads:— "The Army Council of the Irish Republican Army confirms the statement issued by the Executive of Northern Republican Clubs. All units have now been informed of this decision and have been instructed to suspend all military actions, excepting only that we reserve the right of self defence and the right to defend any who are under direct attack from the British Army or from any sectarian force. We have agreed to this proposal of the Republican Clubs because of our growing concern over the dangers of a sectarian civil war which could only set the cause of socialist revolution back many years. We feel that progress in the situation is dependent on a resumption of political activity, and would call on all Irish men and women to support the five points put forward by the Republican Clubs in their statement."

The immediate demands are listed in the five points.

(1) the release of all internees.

(2) a general amnesty for all political prisoners in British or Irish jails, for men on the run and for all those against whom charges are pending as a result of their involvement in the civil disobedience campaign or because of resistance to British troops; and a write-off of all debts incurred as a result of the civil disobedience campaign.

(3) the withdrawal of troops to barracks pending their ultimate withdrawal from the country, and an immediate end to military repression.

(4) the abolition of the Special Powers Act in its entirety.

(5) Freedom of political expression must be immediately established; the Republican Clubs in particular demand their full democratic rights of political existence.

On May 29 1972, the Official IRA announced a conditional ceasefire. There had been increasing worry at leadership level about the prospect of sectarian civil war in the North and the fact that the Officials' operations were seen as indistingushible from those of the Provisionals. The OIRA had already publicly stated that a military victory was impossible and that its aim from this point onwards was for the return of a mass movement on the streets.

OFFICIAL IRA CEASEFIRE

The meeting to decide on the ceasefire, at Mornington, Co. Louth, saw little outright opposition. The ceasefire was presented internally as conditional and as a tactical move to gain breathing space and not at all as the end of the road for the Official IRA's military role. The ceasefire allowed for so-called 'defence and retaliation'

the United Irishman

An t-Éireannach Aontaithe

RETALIATION

The following statement has been received from the Irish Republican Publicity Bureau.

The British Army has intensified its attacks on the working people of the Six Counties and has deliberately murdered three members of the Irish Republican Movement in recent weeks. The civilian population of some ghetto areas has been the object of murderous onslaught and routine brutality by thugs belonging to the British forces, in and out of uniform. Homes have been destroyed, people innocent of any involvement have been harrassed, assaulted, murdered with callous indifference, but careful intent.

Two members of the Irish Republican Army, Volunteer McGerrigan and Staff Officer Hughes were coldly murdered in Armagh. In Belfast, a plain-clothes murder gang was used to shoot down a Protestant member of the Republican Clubs, Robert Millan, while he was engaged, unarmed, in the protection of his neighbours with a group of Republican vigilantes. The Parachute Regiment shot dead two men in Ardoyne and Edmund O'Rawe was slaughtered in the Falls Road while standing, unarmed, against a wall.

The Irish Republican Army has prepared a list of over 20 incidents in which British forces assaulted men, women and children, either while invading their homes or on the streets of their cities and towns.

The Army Council of the I.R.A., consistent with its policy of defensive and retaliatory action, directed its units to intensify their roles in defence and retaliation for these callous and deliberate assaults. Units were ordered to exact retribution from both British soldiers and installations. Successful retaliatory actions have been carried out in Belfast, Armagh, Tyrone, Derry and Newry in which seven British soldiers have been killed and 20 injured. At least five British soldiers were seriously wounded when Gough Barracks, Armagh, was penetrated by an I.R.A. action unit.

The Irish Republican Army has frequently warned the masters of the British Army that aggression against the people of the Six Counties would not go unpunished. The I.R.A. will continue to defend working people and to retaliate for murderous attacks. These are the orders of the Army Council.

The assaults by the British Army on innocent civilians and on unarmed members of the Irish Republican Movement are neither haphazard nor accidental. They are part of the British Army's tactics, as the military agents of political masters, to lure the I.R.A. into direct confrontation at a time when the attention is being directed to political activity. The stratagem is clear.

The British Government wishes to install its middle class allies in the Six Counties in power. It wishes to destroy the possibility of any radical political alternative to the new Unionists. It recognises the Republican Clubs pose such an alternative. It aims to defeat and destroy the political challenge which the Republican Clubs represent.

No brutality, no murder by the British Army is or ever has been without a purpose. The purpose of recent murders and intensifying brutality is to push Republicans into a position from which it would be difficult if not impossible to fight the local government elections. The I.R.A. is determined that the Republican Movement will not be manoeuvered, by murder or persuasion, into any position other than that which the movement, in response to the demands of the people, chooses.

(Continued on page 4).

United Irishman, May 1973

actions if needed. This leeway in terms of 'defence and retaliation' meant that in May 1973 (a year after the ceasefire) the Official IRA would claim to have killed seven British soldiers in a series of attacks, including a car bomb at Gough Barracks, Armagh. However, by 1974, the leadership had succeeded in greatly reducing OIRA activity against the British forces.

Official IRA colour party at Bodenstown, June 1973. By the late 1970s the Official IRA disappeared from public view, while remaining in existence and operating within Sinn Féin the Workers' Party (later the Workers' Party) using the title 'Group B'.
EAMON MELAUGH

OFFICIAL IRA CONVENTION 1972

The Official IRA met in convention on October 22 1972, facing serious problems. The ceasefire declared in May remained in place but was under pressure, with several OIRA members killed in the previous few months. Cathal Goulding explained the thinking behind the Aldershot bombing and an assassination attempt on Unionist MP John Taylor as 'prestige type operations', while Seamus Costello outlined how the Officials had taken £70,000 in robberies over the previous two years. A total of £22,378 had been spent on arms but in some areas supplies had been depleted by British Army raids or by losses to the Provisionals. The convention was told of the development of a new weapon: this was a mortar which would be used in a series of attacks in early December 1972. There was also a major debate on the movement's future political direction taking place with chief of staff Goulding and Sinn Féin president Tomás MacGiolla taking a position opposed to Seán Garland and Seamus Costello. Goulding and Mac Giolla stressed the need to reach out to northern Protestants and concentrate on civil rights, while Garland and Costello argued that the national question remained central. At a further convention held in Kilkenny in December 1972, Garland and Costello's document would be accepted by a majority of delegates, though the alliance between both men would end in 1973 and further internal division develop. The names in the document are *noms de plumes*: 'Clancy' is Costello, 'Thompson', MacMillen.

Facing page and following spread: Minutes of the Official IRA Convention, 1972

Minutes of the General Army Convention held on the "2oth October I972
The convention which was attended by delegates and I5 visitors
commenced at 1o-45 Pm with the election of a chairman and secretary ;
Those elected were ; Chairman Cox
Secretary M Prior .

After the adoption of Standing Orders the convetnion at II pm adjourned
until 9-3o am on the 2Ist .

****

The convehtion resumed at 9-3o am on the 2Ist and appointed a steering
committee of 3 of the visitors .
The chairm n then went on to clarify the position re the distribution
of personal dozuments in particular the document circulated to delegates
by Ro the former ed of the dd .paper .
The Cs then read the AC statement during the course of which the Directors
of the following departments gave their reports . QMG : Training ; Operations
Intellignece ; Publicity : Organisation :Education : Finance ;
The report was adopted at II am and was then discussed . the following
are the main points which emerged .
£ 22378 , was spent on Weapons andthe the QMs department since the previous convention '7o.
Quite a large number of weapons were lost to the Provos and the BA ;
some areas in the North -in particular rural areas - were very short on
weapons ; QM reported on progress in the manufacture of the new weapon.
(Quigley protested the disclosure by the QM of details of the new Weapon)
Questions re the reasons for the decisions to carry out certain operations
such as Aldershot, Taylor , were answered by the CS who said that the II
AC acted on the basis of the need for prestige type operations for the
movement was goingto survive and maintain support and the loyalty of its
members and the credibility in the eyes of the public . In reply to a
question re Bernadette Devlins condemnation of the shooting of Barnhill,
the CS stated that prior to her public denouncement she had contacted him
and explained her reasons for the stand she was taking on the matter .
The CS further stated that the UI would be disclaiming the attack on B
Devlin contained in the article Capitalism Imperialism .
The Operations director stated that out of a total income of £ 92ooo for
the two years see page 2.

2

£ 70,000 came as the direct result of operations and £22,000 from USA etc. He suggested that we should not continue to depend solely on ops for income for reasons of theeffort in time and manpower andthe risk element; he suggested instead the imposition of a levy of £1000 per month from the combined foreign support organisations in the US ,England etc. Returning again to the question of weaponry it was agreed that some effort should be made to equip those southern units which were expanding and which had been stripped of stuff to equip northern units .

At 12 noon the Army Council statment was adopted unanimously .

Noon. Three tellers were apponted at this time andthe convention went on to discuss the Clar.

The first resolution to be discussed was No 1 on page 20 under Standing Orders which called for the convention to deal with all resolutions and in the event of IN sufficient time to deali with them that the convention be reconvened . The resolution was defeated but it was suggested that the convention could at any time consider such a move if it was thought necessary .

A motion to have standingordersuspendedfor resolutions dealing with policy taken first on the clar was passed - 40 / 16 .

A motion calling for the suspension of standing ord rs for the duration of the discussion of the Policy resolutions was defeated .

I pm The convention adjourned for lunch

2-45 pm Convention resumed with the proposing of Res No. 56 page 15 for th purposes of discussing policy . Then followed Clancys amendment , knonw as Document A which was seconded by Cummins ; this was in turn followed by Hogans amendment , known as Document B , and which was seconded by MacDonald, the former editor.

Briefly , the proposers of Document A felt that the movement had over recent times appeared to be abandoning basic Republican concepts and principles and whereas they agreed with the ERA policy and most other tactical aspects of the movements policy , they felt that the aims and objectives stated in Document A were the best means by which the movemnet could again identify with the Republican tradition and win the support ofthe public and the loyalty of and confidnece of its members .

Those who favoured Document B did so because they felt that the present policies of the movement were the only way by which the movement could a. help to deescalate the sectarian conflict ; b, to go some way towards winning the Protestant to a better understanding of Republicanism and the policies of the movement ; they repeated that national fre dom could not be won without the help and support ofthe Protestant population and that any abandonment of our present policies now andthe adoption of Document A would lead possibly to the movement moving gradually into the same position as the Provos .

The discussion on the documents was thorough with;23 people spoke and it went on until 5 pm when it was proposed by Thompson seconded by Oh that a. both dokument s be submitted to general meetings of each Command Area to assess their opinion and each Command to then instruct its delegates to on the attitude to adopt at a re convened convention which should be held on the Sunday nearest the 26th November .

B. [illegible] be submitted to the [illegible]ance [illegible] .

and C. that the documents only be submitted to the commands and that no arguments for or against by made by HQ or those who will chair each meeting .(the delegates to remain the same as originally selected).

5 pm . Security ; Cummins proposed that in the interests of security t delegate anyone who leaves a clar or other document out of their possession be denied a vote , and that visitors who do likewise be deprived of their documents for the rest of the convention.

6 pm convention adjourned until 7-3o.

7-3o resumed. with discussions on res 28 page 6 and an amendment to it, res 36 page I4 ; the amendment was defeated . The resolution with alterations was carried . some more resolutions discussed until Io pm when an adjournmdnt was called until 7 am on the 22nd.

FREEDOM STRUGGLE

The Provisional IRA's pamphlet, *Freedom Struggle*, was published in June 1973 and promptly banned. Nevertheless, it soon claimed a sale of 20,000 and was reprinted many times. IRA spokespeople were also banned from RTÉ television and radio from the early 1970s onwards, a ban extended to Provisional Sinn Féin.

But there were embarrassing reminders that support for the IRA was often more widespread than the authorities wished to admit. On 31 October 1973 the Provisionals engineered a dramatic escape of three of their leading members, Seamus Twomey, J.B. O'Hagan and Kevin Mallon from Mountjoy Prison. A helicopter was hired by an American 'film producer', hijacked, and its pilot forced to fly to Mountjoy and land in the prison yard. Within weeks the Wolfe Tones' 'Helicopter Song' was No. 1 in the Irish charts. By the mid 1970s the playing of overtly republican songs on radio had also been officially discouraged. The way in which censorship affected southern perceptions of the IRA and downplayed violence against northern nationalists was a constant source of republican complaint throughout the 1970s and 1980s.

'VICTORY TO THE IRA'

In January 1974, the Provisional IRA leadership promised an escalation of the armed struggle. They were still confident that a British withdrawal could be secured. 1974 was another bloody year, with 303 people killed, with the 51 British Army dead well outnumbered by over 200 civilian fatalities. In Belfast, in particular, loyalist gunmen were carrying out daily attacks on nationalists. An attempt by the British and Irish

Facing page: AP/RN

An Phoblacht

Iml. 5. Uimh.2. 5p. Eanáir 11, 1974

This is a copy of a colour poster at present to be seen in many parts of the Six Counties, particularly Belfast. The colours are white, rose and black.

All–out onslaught on British terrorism

TOP priority of the Republican Movement this year will be the defeat of the British terror campaign, according to a new year statement issued by the leadership of the Republican Movement through the Irish Republican Publicity Bureau.

Here is the statement in full:

"On entering the fifth year of the struggle for freedom, the leadership of the Republican Movement renews its pledge of loyalty and service to the people of Ireland. We look forward with confidence to 1974 as the year during which British rule in Ireland shall be destroyed and the curse of alien power banished from our land for all time. The full resources of our Movement will be directed towards that end and, with the experience of the past and the support we presently enjoy, we have no doubt as to the successful outcome of the struggle.

The defeat of the British Army terror campaign will remain the top priority of the Movement for the coming year. The terror campaign is being waged against our people irrespective of religious affiliations with the express purpose of beating them into acceptance of Britain's new conquest of Ireland.

The actions of the Irish Republican Army will be directed more vigorously against those who wage war on the Irish people. The enemy will be hit where and whenever we deem it necessary until England recognises she cannot win a colonial war in this day and age.

Without the military campaign of terror, England has no hope of imposing her political designs on Ireland. She relies greatly on a Free State–Unionist Axis to help her cement the division of our country and prevent the emergence of an independent, sovereign Ireland. The politicians of Dublin and Belfast are now united under London control to deny the people of Ireland their right to self-determination and to place the entire country under complete British domination.

SDLP betrayal

We call upon the whole people of Ireland to disown the politicians who are determined to sell our country. The S.D.L.P. have betrayed those who placed their trust in them. Their alliance with the architects of repression and their feeble attempts to act as tax gatherers for the British Government warrants outright condemnation. The Republican Movement will intensify the Civil Disobedience Campaign, extend the Rents and Rates Strike and prove to the new Unionists of the North that they do not represent the aspirations of our people.

We can expect further coercion in the South in the coming year. Free-Stateism at its ugliest continues to grow every day. Police brutality is on the increase; censorship of the news media is common; and the stifling of effective political opposition is a major aspect of government policy.

We would remind the politicians of Dublin that, in a war of national liberations, there are only two sides: the enemy's and the peoples. The politicians have made their decision through their policies of collaboration and we must take cognisance of such.

North's heavy price

The price to secure freedom has borne heavily on the Northern people. Hundreds of families have lost parents, sons and daughters, through either death or imprisonment. We take this opportunity to express our deepest gratitude to these people for the heroic way in which they have shouldered their cross and the fortitude they have shown in the face of unbelievable suffering. The loyalty shown by the families of the men and women in jail has been a source of inspiration for all who carry on the struggle.

We sincerely wish to see an end to the conflict as soon as possible. We have outlined the basic conditions which will lead to an end of hostilities. The right of the Irish people to self-determination must be acknowledged by the British Government. The Sunningdale agreement denied this right and, as such, contributed nothing towards a lasting solution.

A commitment by the British government to a planned and orderly withdrawal from Ireland is the second requirement for peace. Our third demand is a general amnesty for all political prisoners.

It is futile to believe that new, political institutions can operate while 1,500 people languish in prison cells. Peace, based on justice, is our goal and the energy of the Republican Movement will be directed towards that end in 1974", the statement, signed P.Ó.Néill, rúnaí, concludes.

DON'T LET THEM DIE

Everyone to the home of the BRITISH AMBASSADOR next Sunday afternoon

Cill Gobain (Stepaside), Co. Dublin

governments to secure a power-sharing deal ('Sunningdale') was scuppered by a loyalist general strike during May, in the midst of which car bombs killed 33 people in Dublin and Monaghan. The Ulster Volunteer Force later claimed these bombs, though from an early stage, the involvement of British intelligence was suspected.

Members of the Provisional IRA leadership had secretly met UVF leaders for discussions: both opposed the Sunningdale power-sharing agreement and welcomed its collapse. Provisional IRA units in Britain had stepped up bombings during the year, culminating in carnage in Birmingham in November when 21 people were killed.

Despite the predictions of IRA victory, the mainly southern-based Provisional IRA leadership seemed well aware of the war-weariness of many in the North and during late 1974, were engaged in talks, firstly with Protestant clergy and then British officials, that produced a ceasefire in early 1975. The Provisionals did recognise that the Unionist position would have to be considered in a united Ireland and Ruairí Ó Brádaigh in particular put great stock in the Éire Nua policy, which proposed a federal four-province Ireland after a British withdrawal. This, he felt, would give a large measure of autonomy to Ulster Loyalists. However, the UDA and UVF escalated their sectarian killings during 1975 and the Provisionals responded, carrying out sectarian attacks themselves, contributing to making the year a bloody one. In October 1975, a feud between the Official IRA and Provisional IRA would claim a further 11 lives. The Ceasfire ended soon after.

THE IRISH NATIONAL LIBERATION ARMY

During the Official IRA ceasefire, discontent had grown over the lack of application of its 'defence and retaliation' policy. Many volunteers wanted more action against the British Army and, especially in Belfast, permission to respond to Loyalist attacks. This frustration coalesced around Seamus Costello, Director of Operations of the OIRA. During 1974, Costello was court-martialled and dismissed from the OIRA (and Official Sinn Féin). He gathered support from some of the disaffected and also from those who argued that the Officials were becoming 'reformist'. In December 1974, Costello formed the Irish Republican Socialist Party (IRSP). At the same time he was putting together a new army, as yet unnamed. Costello was its Chief of Staff, with Derry activist Johnnie White, Adjutant General. OIRA members from Belfast, Derry and Armagh, Wicklow and north Munster formed the nucleus of the new group.

The organisation did not announce itself as the Irish National Liberation Army until December 1975. By then, however, as well as a number of attacks on the British Army and on loyalists, it had been embroiled in a savage feud with the Official IRA.

The IRSP's *Starry Plough* Newspaper, May 1975

In Belfast, the OIRA had moved to strangle the IRSP at birth, sparking off a round of blood-letting that saw former comrades shoot each other. Five people were killed, including Liam McMillen, the OIRA's commander in the city. In October 1977, Costello himself was assassinated by the Official IRA in Dublin.

Attempting to compete with the Provisionals' military campaign, while also building a more radical socialist alternative to them, would prove no easy task for the INLA. The IRSP was subject to intense state harassment from an early stage, while the INLA was troubled by internal disputes and lack of equipment. However, in March 1979, the organisation carried out the assassination of leading British Conservative politician Airey Neave, with a car bomb at the House of Commons. Several leading INLA members, including Ronnie Bunting, were shot dead by unidentified gunmen during 1980, which many alleged was British state revenge for Neave's killing.

IRSP members played a major role in the H-Block campaign and three INLA members (Patsy O'Hara, Kevin Lynch and Michael Devine) died during the 1981 hunger strike. The party also had councillors elected during 1981. During 1982, for the first and only time, it killed more people than the IRA, 17 of them (11 soldiers

republican NEWS

Vol. 7 No: 7 SATURDAY, 19th February, 1977 England/Scotland/Wales 10p (USA 45 cents) PRICE 7p

THE VOICE OF REPUBLICAN ULSTER

PANIC HITS LOCAL CAPITALISTS AS ——

IRA ATTACKS GRASS ROOTS IMPERIALISM

Veteran IRA leader Seamus Twomey in a rare interview on French television last Monday night declared: "All British industrialists are targets. They are exploiting the Irish working-class... everyone directly connected with British imperialism are definite targets."

Already the business community are reeling under IRA attacks-first initiated under the Belfast Brigade last summer-and although the ruling-class cannot be overthrown by individual attacks, the revolutionary strategy of the IRA has changed the nature of the challenge to the capitalist bourgeoisie.

Historically the ruling-class has been faced with strikes and trade-union agitation in opposition to their capitalist exploitation at home; and in their 'adventures' and imperialist quests in the colonies they created and supplemented a local bourgeoisie which ruled behind the scenes whilst up front the armed forces and State police suppressed all opposition.

away in the ghettoes your

"The men, two Amer-

own membership to the

ulation, which airs its opinions and attitudes

Republican News, 19 February 1977 AP/RN

'PANIC HITS LOCAL CAPITALISTS AS IRA ATTACKS GRASSROOTS IMPERIALISM'

In early 1977, the Provisional IRA shot dead Jeffrey Agate, the managing director of the Du Pont plant in Derry. His killing was one of a number of attacks on businessmen that year. *Republican News* claimed that, 'The business community are reeling under IRA attacks...and although the ruling-class cannot be overthrown by individual attacks, the revolutionary strategy of the IRA has changed the nature of the challenge to the capitalist bourgeoisie.' The article ended by declaring, 'Victory to the IRA! Victory to the Irish Working Class!'

The language reflected a sharp turn to the left by the Provisional IRA's Belfast leadership. This was part of a wider shift, partly inspired by disillusion at the 1975 ceasefire and the unsuccessful talks in which the mainly southern-based leadership of the IRA had engaged. In Long Kesh, opposition to the ceasefire, and to the rationale behind it, had grown up around Brendan Hughes, Ivor Bell and Gerry Adams, who argued that the IRA should reorganise to meet the challenge of a long war. In this particular instance, the tactic of attacks on businessmen was soon abandoned. To many republican supporters the rhetoric was bizarre and there was little evidence of popular support for such killings.

and six civilians) in a bomb attack on the Dropping Well bar in Ballykelly, Co. Derry. But the organisation was also notable by then for its willingness to undertake openly sectarian killings, such as the shooting dead of 20-year-old Sunday-School teacher Karen McKeown in October 1982.

Internal divisions and rivalries resulted in a series of brutal feuds, making the organisation's name synonymous with splits and hindering any real chance it had of expansion. Several people died in 1987 during the worst of these feuds, including leading member Thomas 'Ta' Power. In the mid-1990s, several more activists were killed, including sometime chief of staff, Gino Gallagher. The 1987 split saw the formation of a new Irish People's Liberation Organisation (IPLO) which, before it was forced to disband by the IRA in 1992, had developed a more extreme reputation for sectarianism and criminality than any other republican group.

(The INLA rejected the Provisional IRA's 1994 ceasefire and killed several people in this period, including the notorious Loyalist leader Billy Wright in Long Kesh in December 1997. It declared a ceasefire in the aftermath of the Omagh bomb in 1998 but remained active. In February 2010, the organisation formally decommissioned its weapons.)

GUNS AND POLITICS

This 1979 IRA publicity poster features activists armed with an M60 machine-gun and an RPG-7 rocket launcher. Quoting James Connolly, it asserts that the movement is fighting for a socialist republic. The combination of military imagery and socialist rhetoric was the norm in contemporary republican propaganda. In the late 1970s, the M60 featured in many IRA propaganda shots and in several attacks. Seven M60s had been stolen from an arms depot in Massachusetts in the mid-1970s and were secured for the IRA by their main arms supplier in the U.S., George Harrison. Harrison, a native of Mayo, had lived in New York since the late 1930s. He had smuggled some weapons during the Border campaign but after 1970, he was responsible for sending thousands of guns to Ireland.

REPUBLICAN NEWS

THE VOICE OF REPUBLICAN ULSTER

VOLUME 8 NUMBER 10 Saturday 11th March 1978 PRICE 10p. England, Scotland & Wales 12p.

SOLIDARITY WITH THE ARABS

Revolution is definitely only the business of us ignorant, immoral, uncultured working class and unemployed masses. We Republicans in a supporting capacity to the armed struggle, and in a very active militant capacity when it comes to street protest, salute the young lad behind a battery and 200 yards of bell-wire lying out in the fields, and are proud of our urban guerillas of the revolutionary Irish Republican Army on the streets of Derry and Belfast.

So opposed to any vestige of Irish nationalism is the British Army that the flying of the Irish tricolour is "illegal". Last Saturday a soldier was killed when he tried to remove a tricolour from a booby-trapped telegraph pole. Suddenly the English press showed respect for the tricolour and spoke of it being "besmirched" by the rebels. Because we know they were only joking and only being themselves, they didn't hurt our feelings.

At 17.20 hours (Cairo Time) last Friday afternoon in Donegall Street, in Belfast's city centre, Volunteers with admirable courage and dressed as Arabs (it was Student's Rag Day) killed a British solider and a female member of the loyalist para-military "civilian searcher" unit.

Last Tuesday afternoon hundreds of students in reactionary fashion protested at the ingenuity of the IRA Volunteers and marched to THAT PLACE where we tried to march to last August 10th. REPUBLICAN NEWS sends greetings to those 20-odd people who are in jail, having tried to march to the City Hall seven months ago.

INTERNATIONAL REVOLUTION OK WITH STUDENTS.

If two members of the Palestine Liberation Organisation had killed two Israeli paramilitaries on the occupied West Bank dressed as students it would have been cause for joy in the student circles of "INTERNATIONAL REVOLUTION AND SOLIDARITY WITH OUR REPRESSED COMRADES IN OCCUPIED PALESTINE, ZIMBABWE, NAMIBIA, AZANIA, CHILE AND ARGENTINA ETC...ANYWHERE BUT IRELAND'.

Nobody has any objections to the students galloping about the town like happy idiots once a year, especially when they are collecting for charity. And if they want to ignore the repression of armed British imperialism in nationalist ghettos that's OK as well.

Playing ostrich is sound; but for them to raise their heads with British morality in the middle of a war of national liberation is both reactionary and hypocritical. There are almost 300 young people bricked-up, and we mean BRICKED-UP, in H-Block, in the worst prison conditions known about in the world.

There was no further education for them, no Rag Days. They are supervised and beaten by British animals posing and dressed-up as human beings.

At night when the Bears that supervise our prisoners go off duty these lads shout through 1/8" cracks in the steel doors to comrades whom they can't see. They are held in naked, solitary confinement. They don't know what clothes feel like to wear. When they describe their lot, as they do in smuggled pieces o paper which we repro duce, it makes 'good reading to an outside But to us, their familie comrades or supporters, makes us passionate angry, and it is bloody human disgr that these principled you people should be subje to this inhumanity.

NOW LET US H THE STUDENTS ON T HUMAN RIGHTS' IS OR ARE THEY RE WHAT WE SUSP PRO-BRITS DRE UP AS STUDENTS?

PRISONERS' SUNDAY

Last Sunday protests organised by the RAC took place in different parts of Belfast to mark the second anniversary of the Brits' attempts to 'criminalise' the prisoners.

(See "Prisoners' Sunday" Page 11 and "London protests" Page 10).

Irish Independence party - a key to option two?

See centre pages

Republician News, 11 March 1978
AP/RN

'SOLIDARITY WITH THE ARABS'

On 3 March 1978, the IRA shot dead a British soldier and a female civilian searcher at a security checkpoint near Belfast city centre. As it was the Queen's University 'Rag Day', large numbers of students in fancy dress were in downtown Belfast. Four gunmen, wearing 'Arab' costumes, were able to approach the checkpoint and open fire at close range. This *Republican News* headline is a satirical response to the criticism from student groups about the killings and a reaffirmation of the movement's revolutionary stance: 'We...salute the young lad behind a battery and 200 yards of bell wire lying out in the fields, and we are proud of our urban guerillas of the revolutionary Irish Republican Army.'

'H-BLOCK COMMANDANT EXECUTED'

In November 1978, Albert Miles, Deputy Governor of the The Maze prison, was shot dead at his home. His killing was part of a campaign against prison staff being waged by the IRA. The campaign was partly to raise awareness of the ongoing crisis within the H-Blocks and partly to 'punish prison staff for their brutality towards prisoners'.

In 1975, the British government had withdrawn special-category status for paramilitary prisoners which meant that from then on, members of the IRA and other organisations would have to wear prison uniform, do prison work and serve their sentences as 'criminals'. Most male prisoners would be held in a new state-of-the-art 'H-Block' prison at Long Kesh, (The Maze).

During 1976, IRA prisoner Kieran Nugent refused to wear a uniform. His example sparked off the 'blanket' protest, whereby prisoners refusing the uniforms were clad only in blankets from their cells. Participation in the protest meant confinement to cells, loss of reading material and regular clashes during searches prior to and after visits. The campaign, involving over 300 IRA and INLA prisoners (and also women in Armagh) escalated to a no-wash 'dirty protest' in 1978. The protesters complained of beatings and petty brutality from warders, while the authorities claimed that the prisoners' problems were self-inflicted. Actions such as the killing of Albert Miles were popular with those on the blanket: they felt they were hitting back. Inevitably, however, they brought reprisals on the prisoners themselves and were counter-productive in winning public support. A protest campaign for political status and waging an armed struggle did not always complement each other. Another key aspect of British policy at this time was 'Ulsterisation', which meant that locally-recruited troops and police were placed in the front line. Killings of locals, invaribly Protestant, intensified the sectarian image of the war, as did disasters such as the La Mon bombing of February 1978 that killed 12 people.

Republican News, December 1978 AP/RN

H-BLOCK COMMANDANT EXECUTED

IN A precisely executed military operation last Sunday evening the Irish Republican Army shot dead in his North Belfast house, the Deputy Governor of Long Kesh prison camp. From when the POW's struggle to defend political status began over two years ago, this man, Albert Miles, had been in charge of running the barbaric H-Blocks. In a supplied statement the IRA pointed out that: *"This man was fully aware of the beatings and torture of the men 'on the blanket' and was in fact instrumental in sentencing political prisoners to solitary confinement and dietary punishments".*

FLEXIBLE TACTICS

With this operation being followed within twenty-four hours by the successful ambush of a UDR man, also in Belfast, the IRA has once again demonstrated its flexible tactics and decisive striking power. The war goes on with a vengeance!

Last Sunday's execution of the H-block commandant has provided a tremendous morale boost for the beleagoured people of the nationalist ghettoes, especially for the heroic blanket men and their relatives.

Predictably following Mason's guidelines, the media and all the 'Democratic Unionists' to the equally falsely named 'Republican Clubs' condemned the IRA's action in hysterical terms.

Yet only two days earlier, this time in Derry City, another unarmed fifty-year-old man had been shot dead and this particular political assassination produced barely a whimper from all the selfstyled 'concerned humanitarians'.

Perhaps it was because Derry man Patrick Duffy was an auxiliary volunteer of the Irish Republican Army, shot dead by the British army in a classical SAS-type 'stake-out', and neither Paisley nor the Sticks nor all the other political opportunists could see any political capital to be made out of this particular death.

Investigative journalism by the news hounds of the media and politicians' carefully contrived postures of horror and grief somehow always stop dead when it is a British finger on the trigger. Even the supposedly nationalist Belfast **'Irish News'** feels it to be its duty to slavishly run a front-page eight-column banner headline " **Chorus of Condemnation follows shooting of Deputy Maze Governor"** whilst consigning the Brit assassination of an unarmed middle-aged Republican to the small print.

SELF-INFLICTED

The total lack of credibility in Brit claims that their 'stake-out' victims **ALWAYS** go to shoot them against impossible odds remains unexposed by the media.

Judging by his Sunday evening statement, an increasingly hysterical Mason, never very bright at the best of times, appears to have had what few brains he had, blown away by the recent IRA bombing offensive. Quite how shooting dead the H-block commandant can be Republican **"hypocrisy"** is mystifying, given that screws, large and small, have long ago been declared **"legitimate targets"** by the IRA. Unlike the blanket men the screws can leave the H-blocks if they so wish. Their 'plight' as IRA targets and their filthy working conditions are clearly self-inflicted.

Apart from their sectarian delight in brutalising Republican POW's it is £150 per week which provides the continued attraction to a job which may well prove fatal to them as their mercenary English boss discovered to his cost. Their motives stand in sharp contrast to the Republican idealism of such men as Patrick Duffy.

MASON'S

'WAR NEWS'

The IRA's weekly activities were detailed in the 'War News' column of *Republican News* (*An Phoblacht-Republican News* from 1979). These illustrate the sheer volume of operations carried out by the IRA which, whilst they never made more than temporary news and did not always cause death or even injury, ensured that Northern Ireland could not be seen as 'normal'. Other IRA activities included punishment shootings and beatings, of which thousands took place in nationalist areas from 1970 onwards. Given the relatively small population of Northern Ireland (1.5 million) a very high proportion of its people were affected by this violence. Not all IRA actions were covered in War News.

Waging an armed struggle was financially costly and at various stages there were over a thousand IRA members in prison, whose dependents needed support. The IRA (and the INLA) helped fund itself through armed robberies. From being rare in the late 1960s, a decade later bank and post-office robberies were daily occurances. Smuggling and kidnapping were also utilised as ways of raising money.

Page 2 – REPUBLICAN NEWS, Saturday, August 19, 1978.

WAR N

IN SUPPLIED STATEMENTS THE IRISH REP
SIBILITY FOR THE FOLLOWING OPERATION

AUGUST 8–9

BELFAST:
Six gun attacks against British forces through

FRIDAY AUGUST 11

DERRY:
A mobile active service unit of the Derry
clothes soldier of the Special Air Services (
ordination with several other undercover Brits
After the attack they were withdrawn fr
was challenged as to the status of the soldier
However, had the soldier assassinated a Re
as a member of the "crack SAS regiment".)

BELFAST:
Belfast Brigade IRA launched two sep
at Henry Taggart Hall.
Just after lunchtime a hand grenade was
fire at the sentry. Later in the evening a
the base. It exploded shortly afterwards, s
Infantry.

IRA di

IN a supplied statement the Belfast Bri
responsibility for the recent bombing of
kill Road.

On the eve of internment Tuesday A
to several small business premises in t
IRA disclaimed any responsibility for d

REPUBLIC

THE LONG WAR

In 1978, the IRA explicitly referred to the policy of being 'committed to, and more importantly geared to, a long term war', *Republican News* explained. 'The Republican Movement considers that for both political and economic reasons the British remain extremely determined to hang on to the six occupied counties. Therefore owing entirely to this British intransigence the war to liberate and unify this country will be a bitter and long-drawn-out struggle. There is no quick solution to our British problem . . . there are no short cuts to our 32-county Socialist Republic.'

This marked a major departure from the IRA's slogans of the early 1970s and from the hopes engendered by the 1975 ceasefire. An indication of new thinking had come at Bodenstown in 1977, when Jimmy Drumm had delivered a speech written by Gerry Adams and his supporters which warned that, 'the British government is NOT withdrawing from the Six Counties . . . indeed, the British government is committed to stabilising the Six Counties and is pouring in vast sums of money to improve the area and assure loyalists, and secure from loyalists, support for a long haul against the Irish Republican Army.' Ó Brádaigh's Éire Nua policy was also increasingly criticised as a sop to loyalism.

Adams and his allies made it clear that there could be no compromise with what they saw as a supremacist ideology. The Bodenstown speech argued that the struggle would be a long one, and that while the IRA would provide the cutting edge, republicans had to win support for their political policies as well, North and South.

Dundalk Protest

'British are resp
for H-Blocks'

RAL GUERRILLAS

Vol. 8 No. 48 SATURDAY, DECEMBER 9, 1978.

(ENGLAND, SCOTLAND and WALES 12p) PRICE 10p

IRA GEARED TO A LONG WAR

A MASSIVE wave of co-ordinated bomb attacks launched by the Irish Republican Army, has rocked the British occupied six counties yet again. Last Thursday evening 30th November within just over an hour active service units attacked commercial targets in 16 towns.

This second wave of widespread bomb attacks including the use of car-bomb hundred-pounders came only a fortnight after co-ordinated IRA bombing raids had devastated several commercial centres. In a supplied statement the IRA said these latest attacks should completely dispel any speculation that previous attacks were a flash in the pan or a dying kick.

This second bomb wave came only days after the Republican execution of the Long Kesh H-Block Commandant.

SERIOUS WARNING

While causing hysterical shudders of anger in the corridors of Stormont and Whitehall this explosive display of disciplined IRA military might have provided a tremendous morale boost for the nationalist people.

But the IRA has issued a serious warning to the nationalist people. The Republican Movement considers that for both political and economic reasons the British remain extremely determined to hang on to the six occupied counties. Therefore owing entirely to this British intransigence the war to liberate and unify this country will be a bitter and long drawn-out struggle. There is no quick solution to our British problem. Certainly the recently much floated "solution" of six county "independence" will lead us nowhere but to disaster; there are no short cuts to our 32-county Socialist Republic.

As the IRA stated last week: *"We are committed to, and more importantly geared to, a long term war".* The Brit media is promoting the recent attacks as being the opening blasts in a "Winter Offensive". Yet these attacks have in fact just been part of the IRA's on-going war effort. Certainly these attacks will not cease once the winter is over!

FLEXIBILITY IN TACTICS

Flexibility in military tactics (from commercial bombing to prestige bombing and from car bombs to incendiaries) and the ability to surprise the Brits, remain decisive weapons in the IRA's arsenal.

Yet the rigid imperialist mentality of the Brits makes them incapable of understanding this, and the extent of the popular base upon which the IRA's war effort necessarily rests. A base which is superficially passive to an ignorant observer, but which in fact provides fertile pastures for Republican growth and renewal. Mason has been forced to eat his arrogant words of victory, his foolish claims of having defeated the IRA. Addressing diplomats' wives at a dinner in London last week he claimed that he always said the IRA retained its ability as an effective strike force!

GUTTER-PRESS

Almost a year ago to the day in an interview published in the Brit gutter-rag the *'Daily Express'* (dated December 5th 1977) he claimed: "We are squeezing the terrorists like rolling up a toothpaste tube. We are squeezing them out of their safe havens. We are squeezing them away from their supplies of money and explosives".

Particularly in the past three weeks Mason has been forced to eat his words. The Republican "toothpaste" remains securely embedded in the "tube" which is the nationalist population of the six counties.

IRA BOMBING ON!

The "morning after" in Armagh City's Scotch Street which was one of the many commercial targets blasted by the I.R.A. in their second recent widespread wave of co-ordinated attacks.

Republican News, 9 December 1978
AP/RN

Drumm stated that republicans would 'never accept the legitimacy of the "Free State" a fascist state, designed to cater for the privileged, capitalist sycophants'. Thus, republicans would need to overthrow both states to achieve a socialist republic.

The IRA's ongoing activities were also important in countering the statements from Northern Ireland secretary Roy Mason that the organisation was weakening. In December 1977, Mason had claimed that, 'We are squeezing the terrorists like rolling up a toothpaste tube. We are squeezing them out of their safe havens. We are squeezing them away from their supplies of money and explosives'. During 1979, the IRA would deliver serious blows to that analysis.

AP/RN

'IRA MAKE BRITAIN PAY'

On 27 August 1979, the IRA carried out its most devastating attacks ever on the British Army. At Narrow Water, near Warrenpoint, Co. Down, the IRA killed 18 soldiers with two bombs. The first bomb killed six soldiers and IRA members also fired on the remainder of the convoy from across Carlingford Lough. The surviving soldiers took up positions behind nearby gates and a wall, where the IRA had left another 800 lb bomb: this exploded half an hour later as reinforcements arrived and the wounded were being airlifted to hospital. Twelve more soldiers were killed, including Lieutenant-Colonel David Blair, the most senior British officer to die in the North. An English civilian, Michael Hudson, was shot dead by troops while watching the carnage from across Carlingford Lough. Sixteen of the 18 dead were members of the Parachute Regiment and the incident was described as its worst loss since Arnhem during World War II. The Paras were widely despised by nationalists and because of Bloody Sunday, seen as a prestige target.

The shock of Warrenpoint was magnified by the killing on the same day of Lord Louis Mountbatten, a cousin of the Queen and former senior naval officer. The 79-year-old Mountbatten, 82-year-old Lady Patricia Brabourne, 14-year-old Nicholas Knatchbull and 15-year-old Paul Maxwell were blown up while boating at Mullaghmore, Co. Sligo.

The Provisional IRA were jubilant at the attacks, as can be seen from the front page of *An Phoblacht/ Republican News.* The IRA had made world news headlines, had carried out a technically brilliant operation at Warrenpoint and had struck at the British establishment. They were also unrepentant, warning that if the British public would not grasp the reality of Britain's role in Ireland, then the IRA would, 'rip out its sentimental, imperialist heart'. The attacks were popular with republican supporters and gave confidence to those, like the prisoners in H-Block, who felt their sacrifices should be avenged. But in southern Ireland in particular, the killing of the elderly Lord Mountbatten, Lady Brabourne and two teenagers was not seen as legitimate warfare. Increasingly evident was the wide divergence in attitudes of those in the South, summed up by the comments of an 18-year-old woman from Limerick in the course of a discussion on attitudes to the IRA: 'They used to be a great organisation at one time, didn't they? But then they started all this killing.'

Women were recruited directly into the IRA for the first time during the late 1960s. However, the Cumann na mBan organisation remained in existence and sided with the Provisionals in the 1969/70 split. By 1979, Cumann na mBan was largely southern based, with most female Provisionals in the North simply joining the IRA. This 1979 poster declares the organisation committed to both armed struggle and socialism.

AP/RN

'NOT A MARXIST ORGANISATION'

During the late 1970s', there was increasing commentary on the leftist rethoric being used in *An Phoblacht-Republican News* and in IRA statements of the time. More importantly, there were signs of internal unease at the tone of some of the commentary. In October 1979, Gerry Adams, now Vice-President of Sinn Féin, was interviewed in *Hibernia* magazine and claimed that 'nobody' in Sinn Féin was influenced by Marxism. This was untrue: almost all republicans claimed to be followers of James Connolly, who was a Marxist, while Adams and his supporters had digested a range of literature by Marxist writers while in prison. Nevertheless, it pointed to the pressures on the republican leadership to play this down. There were often marked differences in rural Tyrone or Armagh compared to urban Belfast and Derry, or indeed between Dublin and Kerry. The IRA issued its own statement clarifying matters which claimed that, 'the Irish Republican Army is not a Marxist organisation', but also that, 'it is no secret, and we make no apology for it, that our aim is the establishment of a democratic socialist republic based on the 1916 proclamation'. Less controversal was general republican solidarity with organisations like the Basque ETA, the Palestine Liberation Organisation and the African National Congress. When this statement was published in the paper of NORAID, the IRA's support organisation in the U.S., references to 'socialism' were deleted.

I.R.A.'s Republican socialism is a radical native brand

THE FULL text of the IRA statement issued on 'Marxism' last week is:

"Down the years Irish freedom fighters have been slandered by political enemies and the media in an attempt to discredit the cause of Irish liberation. All previous smear attacks having failed our enemies have now resorted to the 'red scare' to which they believe our supporters at home and in America will be particularly susceptible.

"We place on record that the Irish Republican Army is not a marxist organisation.

"Copies of the constitution of Oglaigh na hEireann have been seized often enough by the Free State and British authorities. It states quite categorically, it is no secret, and we make no apology for it, that our aim is the establishment of a democratic socialist republic based on the 1916 proclamation.

"Our republican socialism is a radical native brand taken from Tone, Lalor, Connolly and Mellows. It is our determination and our success which is frightening the Free State collaborators and the British government, and their latest propaganda attacks should be seen in this light."

3 November 1979

AP/RN

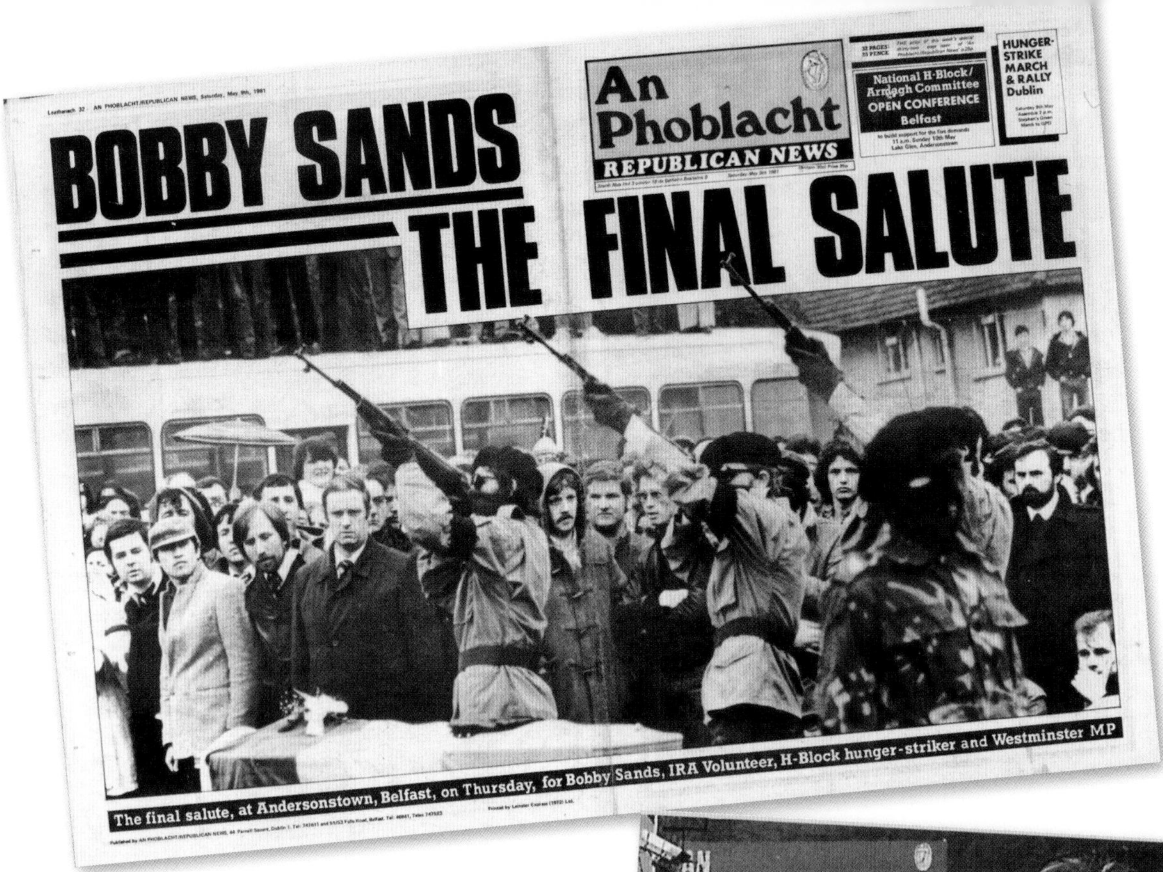
AN PHOBLACHT/REPUBLICAN NEWS, Saturday, May 9th, 1981

An Phoblacht

REPUBLICAN NEWS

32 PAGES 25 PENCE

National H-Block/ Armagh Committee OPEN CONFERENCE Belfast

to build support for the five demands 11 a.m. Sunday 10th May Lake Glen, Andersonstown

HUNGER-STRIKE MARCH & RALLY Dublin

BOBBY SANDS THE FINAL SALUTE

The final salute, at Andersonstown, Belfast, on Thursday, for Bobby Sands, IRA Volunteer, H-Block hunger-striker and Westminster MP

Above: *An Phoblacht*, 9 May 1981 AP/RN

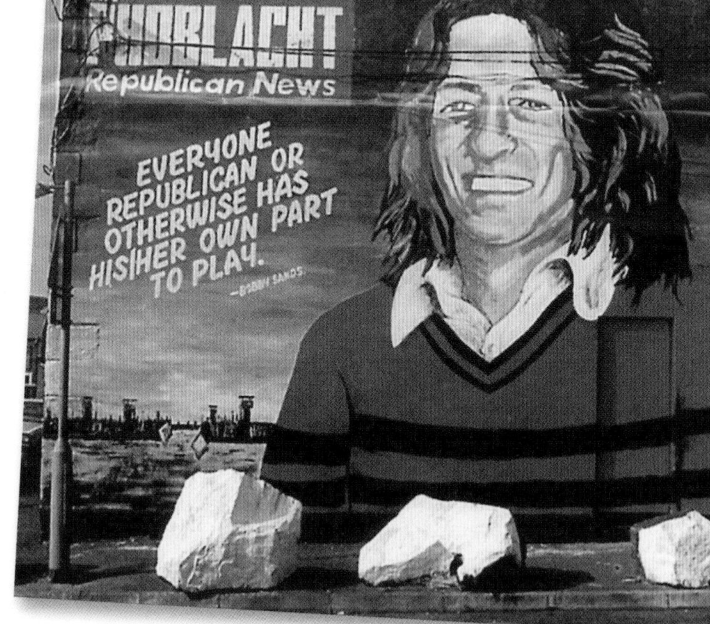

Right: Bobby Sands mural, Belfast AP/RN

HUNGER STRIKE

IRA prisoners took part in hunger strikes on several occasions during the early 1970s. Two IRA men, Michael Gaughan and Frank Stagg, died after long strikes in Britain in 1974 and 1976 respectively. But the longest lasting and most significant strikes occurred in 1980-81 in Long Kesh. The prison protests came to a head during 1980. While there was increased awareness of the issue of political prisoners outside the prisons, there seemed little chance of movement on the demand for 'political status' within Long Kesh itself. As a result, seven H-Block prisoners began a hunger strike in October (they were soon joined by three women in Armagh) which lasted until mid December, when, with one prisoner, Seán McKenna, in critical condition, their leader, Brendan Hughes, ended the fast. At the time it was suggested that a deal had been on the cards, but was reneged on by the British.

In March 1981, a new hunger strike began, led by 27-year-old Bobby Sands, from Twinbrook. Active in the IRA since the early 1970s, Sands had been jailed from 1973-76. On his release, he returned to active service and in 1977, was sentenced to 14 years. While 'on the blanket' Sands wrote poems and articles for *Republican News* under the pen name 'Marcella'. He became O/C of the IRA prisoners in 1980.

As the strike attracted increased attention, a decision was made to run Sands as a candidate in the Fermanagh-South Tyrone by-election in April. Sands won 30,493 votes, beating the Unionist candidate, and was elected MP to Westminster. However, the British government, led by Margaret Thatcher, refused to grant concessions and on 5 May 1981, Sands died after 66 days on hunger strike. His death provoked the worst street violence since the early 1970s, while his funeral at Milltown Cemetery attracted over 100,000 mourners. His election and the evident support for the hunger strike punctured the claim that republicans were an isolated, criminal conspiracy. Sands' seat was held in the subsequent by-election by republican Owen Carron. Another three hunger strikers died during May and by August ten men (seven from the IRA and three from the INLA) were dead. After pressure from the relatives of those still on hunger strike, the republican prison leadership called the fast off in October. Though political status was not granted, many of the prisoners' demands were conceded within the H-Blocks. During the strike, two prisoners had also been elected as TDs in the Republic and the popular support expressed during 1981 was seen by some in the republican leadership as evidence that an electoral base could be won for Sinn Féin.

In 1982, having decided to contest Northern Assembly elections, on an abstentionist basis, Sinn Féin won five seats and 64,191 votes (10.1% of the vote). It was a concrete sign of the potential that existed for political growth. Many trace the evolution of Sinn Féin as a political force to the hunger strikes, though many other republicans drew the lesson that the armed struggle would have to be intensified in their aftermath. Brendan Hughes later claimed that he called off the 1980 strike because he did not want fellow hunger strikers to die. In 2005, Richard O'Rawe, a former prisoner, alleged in his book, *Blanketmen*, that a deal that could have saved at least six of the strikers was turned down by the IRA leadership outside the prison, in order to maximise the political advantage for Sinn Féin. This claim was rejected by the IRA. Bobby Sands remains the best-known IRA martyr of the modern era and his image an iconic one.

IRA colour party at Bodenstown, June 1983 DEREK SPIERS/REPORT

The post-hunger-strike growth of Sinn Féin was most dramatically illustrated by the election of Gerry Adams as MP for West Belfast in June 1983. Overall, Sinn Féin won 102,701 votes or 13.4% of the total. (Danny Morrison also came within 100 votes of a seat in Mid-Ulster.) Adams was acutely aware that this was the first time a republican had ever won this seat (in 1918, when Sinn Féin had swept nationalist Ireland, the Home Rule party's Joe Devlin had held west Belfast against de Valera). In the aftermath of the election Adams was interviewed by Dublin-based *Magill* magazine. He was asked whether Sinn Féin's successes provided a mandate for the IRA's campaign. Adams replied: 'The IRA does not need an electoral mandate for armed struggle. It derives its mandate from the presence of the British in the Six Counties.' He was then asked that, since it was the case that 'revolutionary movements which use force usually argue that it is made necessary because political action is closed to them', did the fact that 'Sinn Féin has been able to take political action very successfully' not affect their justification for the use of force? Adams answered: 'It doesn't. I believe the use of force in the Six Counties is justified by the British presence. They don't give people much choice. At the end of the day they won't be argued or talked out; a movement that wants them out will either have to use force or the threat of force.'

BRIGHTON, 1984

AN PHOBLACHT
IRELAND'S BIGGEST SELLING POLITICAL WEEKLY
Republican News

IRA BLITZ BRITS

EXCLUSIVE
INTERVIEW WITH GHQ SPOKESPERSON

An Phoblacht, 18 October 1984 AP/RN

In the early hours of 12 October 1984, an IRA bomb killed five people at the Grand Hotel in Brighton, which was hosting the Conservative Party conference. More than 30 others were injured, including senior Tory politicians. The IRA narrowly missed killing British Prime Minister Margaret Thatcher and several of her cabinet.

In an interview with *An Phoblacht* explaining their reasoning, members of the IRA argued that if the bomb had been a success, they foresaw a massive clampdown on the organisation, including internment without trial being reintroduced. But they were willing to take this risk. They rejected condemnations from politicans who claimed their actions were anti-democratic: 'Nobody in Ireland elected Thatcher's cabinet. It is the Irish people who are denied democracy, who are denied self-determination, who are denied by the British government, which is the staunchest supporter of the Union and the loyalist veto, the right to elect a national government for this island.' They also claimed that, 'British politicians are hypocrites when it comes to the oppressed fighting back. To bring Germany to its knees, Britain waited until the towns of Hamburg, Dresden and Cologne were packed with refugees before fire-bombing hundreds of thousands of civilians. America justified the dropping of the atom bombs on Japanese civilians on the basis that the Second World War could be brought to a speedy conclusion. We detonated a bomb against the key people responsible for the violence and war in our country in order to bring this war to a speedy conclusion'. They described how they were, 'determined never to lay down our arms until the Irish people as a nation are allowed determine their own future. Britain clearly, after 15 years, cannot defeat us, so her occupation of Ireland is going to keep on costing her dearly until she quits'. Finally, they warned that, 'we were unlucky. But we only have to be lucky once; they will have to be lucky always. We feel we are going to be very lucky'.

Despite condemnations of the attack from political figures, this IRA action was popular with many people, even those who usually disagreed with them. Margaret Thatcher was despised by many nationalists in Ireland for her role during the hunger strike in 1981 (as well as for many of her other policies) and there were those who felt that targeting her, rather than low-level or part-time members of the security forces, made sense. It also demonstrated a high level of planning and ambition: few revolutionary organisations come close to killing the head of the state they are fighting.

'HISTORIC IRA CONVENTION', 1986

The Provisional IRA's first general army convention since 1970 took place in 1986. The organisation decided to end the ban on IRA volunteers discussing the taking of seats in Leinster House and to support republican candidates who were prepared to do so (in effect allowing IRA volunteers to sit in Dáil Éireann). The background to the convention was the continuing desire of the republican leadership to progress politically, North and South. In the 1984 European elections, Sinn Féin's Danny Morrison won 91,476 votes, or 13.3% of the total, in Northern Ireland (though he failed to take a seat). In the 1985 northern council elections, Sinn Fein won 75,686 votes (11.8%), gaining 59 seats.

Republicans now looked South, where their old rivals in the Officials (now the Workers' Party) were making gains in urban areas blighted by unemployment and neglect. However, to make a breakthrough in the Republic, the nettle of abstentionism would have to be grasped. Younger recruits in the South, many who had joined after the hunger-strikes, had few hang-ups about this. But to many of those who had founded the Provisionals, refusing to have anything to do with Leinster House was a bedrock principle. To them, accepting the legitimacy of the 26 Counties meant, in the long run, accepting British rule. The IRA's response was to argue that the suggestion, 'that the IRA is not legitimate because of the decision it has taken on abstentionism is ridiculous. The IRA predates the Second Dáil and the First Dáil, its constitution is a military constitution, and our legitimacy stems from organised popular resisistance to British rule in Ireland, a tradition which was reinforced in 1916, by the Fenians, by the Young Irelanders, by the United Irishmen. Its legitimacy stems from a tradition of resistance which has been a fact of history since Britain first encroached Irish sovereignty 800 years ago'.

This debate went on inside and outside the IRA. Since 1983, there had been those who felt that electoral activity was curtailing the armed struggle. (Long-time Belfast IRA leader Ivor Bell had been expelled from the organisation for complaining about this prior to 1986.) Those who were worried about the running down of military activity or that the end of abstentionism signalled the road to a 'sell out', were reassured that huge quantities of new weapons were on their way, which would enable the IRA to put British withdrawal back on the agenda. Not only would military activity not suffer, but it would be escalated to a level not seen since the 1970s.

The IRA leadership, dominated by northerners and led by Adams and McGuinness, won the argument. Ó Bradaigh and Ó Conaill left the movement, taking many of the original southern Provisionals with them, but having much less

Facing page: *An Phoblacht*, 16 October 1986 AP/RN

AN PHOBLACHT Republican News
IRELAND'S BIGGEST SELLING POLITICAL WEEKLY
Sraith Nua Iml 8 Uimhir 41 Deardaoin 16 Deireadh Fomhair Thurs 16th Oct 1986 (Britain 30p) Price 25p

Framework for repression

SEE CENTRE PAGES

Historic IRA Convention

ON TUESDAY, OCTOBER 14th, the following statement was issued by the Irish Republican Army:

'Recently, and after much careful planning, IRA delegates from all over Ireland secretly met in a General Army Convention for the first time in 16 years. At this meeting were members of the outgoing Army Council and representatives of the Army Executive, GHQ Staff and Departments, Northern and Southern Command Staffs, Brigades and Battalions and Units, all of whom were elected by their own conventions to attend.

The Convention opened with a unanimous pledge of rededication to the armed struggle and confidence in the armed struggle as being the means of breaking the British connection and bringing about Irish independence.

Several sections of the Constitution of Oglaigh na hEireann were amended and, by more than the required two-thirds majority, the delegates passed two particular resolutions. The first removed the ban on Volunteers discussing or advocating the taking of parliamentary seats. The second removed the ban on supporting successful republican candidates who take their seats in Leinster House.

Also reaffirmed was General Army Order No 8 which prohibits offensive action against the administration in the twenty-six counties or its forces.

The Constitution was modernised so that it reads in non-sexist language.

The objective of restoring the Irish language as the everyday language of the Irish people was reaffirmed.

The present strategy of the Irish Republican Army was discussed and endorsed, although the volume of resolutions made it impossible to deal with every issue.

By secret ballot, the delegates then elected a 12-person Army Executive, which in turn elected a new Army Council. The Army Council, the Chief of Staff it has appointed, and the Army Executive will study the outstanding resolutions which relate to how best to prosecute the struggle for freedom.'

P. O'Neill,
Irish Republican Publicity Bureau,
Dublin.

Above: Gerry Adams and Martin McGuinness at Dublin's GPO, Easter 1986 EAMONN FARRELL/PHOTOCALL

support in the North. They launched Republican Sinn Féin and won the backing of General Tom Maguire, the last survivor of the Second Dáil. A new military organisation, led by a 'Continuity Army Council' was also established, but what became the Continuity IRA did not have a public profile until the 1990s. There was also a less well-known rupture inside Long Kesh where around 30 prisoners formed the League of Communist Republicans. They argued that the vote on abstentionism showed that the movement was taking a reformist route but also that the armed struggle was not productive and should be brought to an end. In February 1987, Sinn Féin fought its first general election in the South with a non-abstentionist policy: no seats were won and the party polled just 1.8% of the vote. Nevertheless, the IRA's plans to escalate its campaign were in motion.

LOUGHGALL

IRA volunteers in Cappagh, Co. Tyrone, fire a volley of shots in honour of their comrades killed at Loughgall, May 1987 AP/RN

On May 8 1987, eight members of the IRA were killed in an ambush carried out by the British Special Air Service at Loughgall, Co. Armagh. It was the IRA's biggest single loss since Clonmult in Cork in 1921. An uninvolved civilian, Anthony Hughes, was also shot dead. The IRA men, all members of the East Tyrone Brigade, included the area commander Patrick Kelly, Patrick McKearney (who had escaped from Long Kesh in 1983) and Monaghan Sinn Féin councillor Jim Lynagh. The men were considered key operators in one of the IRA's most formidable units. The SAS, who had prior intelligence and had lain in wait to ambush the men, admitted to firing over 600 shots.

Loughgall was one of a number of occasions between 1987 and 1992 when IRA members were ambushed by the SAS. In March 1988, three IRA members, Mairead Farrell, Seán Savage and Danny McCann, were shot dead while unarmed but on an IRA mission in Gibraltar. Later that year, the commander of the IRA in mid-Tyrone, Gerard Harte, along with his brother Martin and Brian Mullin, were shot dead at Drumnakilly. During the early 1990s, several more IRA members were killed by the SAS in Tyrone and Armagh.

A number of IRA members were killed by loyalists, while loyalists also targeted Sinn Féin members and their families. The new ferocity of the loyalist campaign gave rise to fresh allegations of security-force collusion, with republicans convinced that the UVF and UDA were being directed by British Intelligence. There is no doubt that the use of the SAS and the loyalist campaign impacted on the ability of IRA to escalate the armed struggle. The IRA had received huge quantities of weapons from Libya in the mid-1980s. These included AK-47 rifles, General Purpose machine guns,

DShK heavy machine guns, and tonnes of Semtex explosive. In military terms the IRA was as well equipped as at any time in its history. Yet while many attacks were carried out, some of them causing major casualties, such as a bomb at Deal in Kent that killed 10 soldiers in 1989, the promised offensive did not materialise. Recurring allegations about the failure of the IRA to intensify its campaign have concerned the extent to which agents and informers had compromised the organisation, allegations which gained more traction when Denis Donaldson, a long-serving Belfast republican, admitted to being an informer for over 20 years in 2004.

AN PHOBLACHT
TWENTY-FOUR PAGES
Republican News

Déardaoin 14 Bealtaine Thursday 14th May 1987 (Britain 35p) Price 30p

Fuair siad bás ar son saoirse mhuintir na hÉireann

• Vol EUGENE KELLY • Vol TONY GORMLEY • Vol PADDY KELLY • Vol DECLAN ARTHURS

• Vol SEAMUS DONNELLY • Vol JIM LYNAGH • Vol PADRAIG McKEARNEY • Vol GERARD O'CALLAGHAN

LOUGHGALL MARTYRS

An Phoblacht, 14 May 1987 AP/RN

ENNISKILLEN

On Sunday 8 November 1987, an IRA bomb killed 11 people, most of them old-age pensioners, all of them Protestant, at a war memorial at Enniskillen, Co. Fermanagh. The IRA acknowledged the 'catastrophic consequences' of the bomb in this statement, but claimed that the bomb was triggered by a British-Army scanning device. In the early 1990s, the IRA admitted that the bomb had actually been a timed device and was detonated deliberately.

Enniskillen had a major impact on a republican movement that was trying to expand politically while maintaining an armed struggle. In the South, in particular, the bomb was seen as evidence of the IRA's sectarian nature. After Enniskillen, Gerry Adams commented that the bomb had dealt a 'body blow' to Sinn Féin's prospects for growth in the South. Indeed, in the 1989 general election, Sinn Féin's share of the vote dropped to just 1.2%. Nevertheless, many republicans felt that however terrible, events like Enniskillen were inevitable in war, and that the movement would recover from them.

IRELAND'S BIGGEST SELLING POLITICAL WEEKLY

AN PHOBLACHT Republican News

Sraith Nua Iml 9 Uimhir 44 — 12 Samhain — Thursday 12th November 1987 — (Britain 35p) Price 30p

Republicans will never forget it and in the ongoing struggle to end injustice and bring about a free, peaceful Ireland will carry it in their hearts and minds forever.

SEE OPINION – PAGE 2

ENNISKILLEN TRAGEDY

WHAT THE I.R.A. SAID

THE following statement was issued by the IRA on Monday, November 9th, the day after the bomb explosion in Enniskillen, in which 11 people were killed:

'The Irish Republican Army admits responsibility for planting the bomb in Enniskillen yesterday which exploded with such catastrophic consequences. We deeply regret what occurred.

GHQ has now established that one of our units placed a remote-controlled bomb in St Michael's aimed at catching crown forces personnel on patrol in connection with the Remembrance Day service but not during it. The bomb blew up without being triggered by our radio signal.

There has been an ongoing battle for supremacy between the IRA and British army electronic engineers over the use of remote-control bombs. In the past, some of our landmines have been triggered by the British army scanning high frequencies and other devices have been jammed and neutralised. On each occasion we overcame the problem and recently believed that we were in advance of British counter-measures.

In the present climate nothing we can say in explanation can be given the attention which the truth deserves, nor will it compensate the feelings of the injured or bereaved.

Signed: P. O'Neill,
Irish Republican Publicity Bureau, Dublin.'

Republicans do not attempt to justify or explain away what happened in Enniskillen last Sunday. There is no way that what the IRA has called the "catastrophic consequences" can be reversed or minimised. It was an appalling tragedy that should never have happened. But what is clear is that the IRA had no intention of injuring civilians, and did not themselves detonate the remote-control bomb. They did not anticipate the tragic results of the premature detonation of the bomb. That was a monumental error for which republicans have paid, and will continue to pay, dearly.

In the aftermath of Enniskillen, everything that republicans have said has been distorted where it has not been censored. This is to be expected but what cannot be denied is that the IRA has been consistent in claiming responsibility for an action so damaging to the Republican Movement and so useful to the enemy. Nor can it be denied that the war in the Six Counties which has claimed so many lives is not now and never has been the fault of the Irish people – nationalist, loyalist or republican – but that ultimately Britain is to blame.

An Phoblacht, Thursday 12 November 1987

AP/RN

The IRA killed over 50 civilians in the years between 1987 and 1989 alone: some accidentally, such as Eamon Gilroy and Elizabeth Hamill, in a bomb explosion on the Falls Road during July 1988. Others died because they were in the company of targets, such as Heidi Hazell, the wife of a British soldier, shot dead in Germany during 1989 and 21 year-old Gillian Johnston, killed in an attack in Fermanagh during 1988.

Civilian fatalities also included people accused of being informers, suspected loyalist paramilitaries and those who worked for the security forces. One of the most notorious of these attacks came during November 1990, when the IRA forced Patsy Gillespie from Derry, who worked at a British base, to drive a bomb into a British-Army checkpoint, killing himself and five soldiers.

The IRA's explanations for its 'mistakes' were never popularly accepted outside the ranks of its supporters. Even successful operations, such as the killing of six soldiers in Lisburn during June 1988 and eight soldiers in Co. Tyrone two months later, did not win it many new adherants.

While no political progress had been made in the South, Sinn Féin's electoral surge in the North had also faltered since the heady days of the mid-1980s. In the European elections of 1989, Sinn Féin received 48,914 votes (9.1%), to their main nationalist rival, the SDLP's 136,335 (25.5%). In the council elections the party won a substantial 69,032 votes (11.2%) but lost 16 seats (down to 43) and were still well behind the SDLP's 129,557 votes (21%). Even if it was not said publicly, it was apparent that the Armalite and the ballot box were not complementing each other.

The frustration felt by republicans at what they saw as the southern public's lack of comprehension of their cause was expressed vividly by Danny Morrison in *Hot Press* in August 1988: 'People in the twenty-six Counties who don't want the Six Counties, let us know. If they're telling us to fuck off, telling us that they're happy with the state they've got and fuck 1916, then tell us. Because if they don't want us, then I would have to look at the situation . . . if they think they've got an Irish nation inside the twenty-six Counties, they should build a wall and lock us out.' Morrison then countered questions about the IRA's lack of support in the South: 'The IRA doesn't claim to be representing the people in the twenty-six Counties. Nor does Sinn Féin. The IRA claims to represent the IRA and the oppressed nationalists who support it. The IRA don't plant bombs in the name of the people of the twenty-six Counties — the IRA plant bombs to bring about a political resolution to the problems of the North.' On this key point Morrison was wrong, however: the IRA *did* claim to represent all the people of Ireland, not just northern nationalists, and it was this claim that informed much southern criticism of them.

'THE GOOD OLD IRA'

The Provisional IRA's campaign was routinely condemned by Fianna Fáil and Fine Gael for disgracing the name of the 'old' IRA. One response was the polemic *The Good Old IRA*, written by Danny Morrison and published in November 1985. Morrison explained that, 'this pamphlet is not a definitive list of IRA operations in the 1919-21 period. Indeed, the majority of attacks on RIC, Black and Tans and regular soldiers are not included. Nor is the death of every civilian recorded. This list is morbid enough and is intended to illustrate a number of important points to confront those hypocritical revisionists who winsomely refer to the "Old IRA", whilst deriding their more effective and, arguably, less bloody successors'. He hoped that, 'Even if these operations are shocking revelations to those who have a romantic notion of the past then the risk of their disillusionment is worth the price of finally exposing the hypocrisy of those in the establishment who rest self-righteously on the rewards of those who in yesteryear's freedom struggle made the supreme sacrifice'.

The pamphlet also dismissed the argument that the IRA of 1919-21 had a democratic mandate, suggesting that, 'Nobody was asked to vote for war' in December 1918. For those who claimed the mantle of Liam Lynch and Michael Collins, it made uncomfortable reading.

Top: Publicity photo of IRA members with mortar AP/RN
Right: Cover of the pamphlet, *The Good Old IRA*

DOWNING STREET

On 7 February 1991, the IRA launched a mortar attack on the British cabinet while it met in Downing Street. Four people suffered minor injuries. Even critics of the IRA could not ignore the irony that it had bombed the British cabinet at a time when ministers were discussing the first war in Iraq, in which the Royal Air Force was carrying out hundreds of bombing missions.

Despite the audacious nature of the attack and the fact that bombings in Britain were taking place regularly during the early 1990s, some of them causing millions of pounds worth of damage, there had been secret contacts between the IRA leadership and the British since the late 1980s. These eventually led to an IRA ceasefire in August 1994. The ceasefire broke down in February 1995 but was renewed in July 1997.

IRELAND'S BIGGEST SELLING POLITICAL WEEKLY

AN PHOBLACHT

Republican News

Straith Nua Iml 13 Uimhir 7 | 14 Feabhra | Thursday, 14th February, 1991 | (Britain 40p) Price 35p

IRA bombs War Cabinet

"While the nationalist people in the Six Counties are forced to live under British rule, then the British cabinet will be forced to meet in bunkers. The British government has the solution to the conflict... It should initiate the process which will lead to British withdrawal from our country and create the conditions for a true democracy throughout Ireland."
— Irish Republican Army, Thursday, February 7th 1991.

IRA interview

SEE CENTRE PAGES

An Phoblacht, 14 February 1991
AP/RN

IRA members in Belfast's Short Strand, 1997. One of the major arguments against the decomissioning of IRA arms was that it would leave nationalist areas such as the Short Strand undefended. The imagery of the modern IRA and its emphasis on 'defence' reflects its roots in nationalist Ulster. Similarly, slogans such as 'Tiocfaidh ár lá (our day will come) and terms like 'the 'Ra' date from the 1970s and not the IRA's early-20th-century origins.

AP/RN

TÍRGHRÁ

The Provisional IRA carried out its first act of decommissioning in October 2001. Though wrangling over the issue continued, there was a sense that an endgame was taking place. In 2002, the families of IRA members who died as a result of the conflict were invited to a special commemorative gathering, for which *Tírghrá* was produced. The book listed 364 republicans (not all IRA members) who were killed or died between 1969 and 1999. A number of those included had not been claimed as IRA volunteers at the time of their deaths. These included Fergal Caraher of Crossmaglen, shot dead (while unarmed) by British soldiers in December 1990 and three IRA members killed by the UVF in Cappagh, Co. Tyrone in March 1991. The list also included Short Strand defender Henry McIlhone, killed in June 1970, two members of the Official IRA who were killed in Tyrone in 1972 and a member of Saor Uladh, killed in 1973.

The 30 or so IRA members killed by their own organisation as informers were obviously not listed.

A year after the book was published, 24-year old IRA member Keith Rodgers was shot dead in south Armagh, killed, republicans alleged, by criminals. Rodgers was 17 at the time of the IRA's 1997 ceasefire and his membership was evidence that the organisation had continued to recruit into the 21st century.

PROVISIONAL IRA DECLARES WAR OVER

In July 2005, the Provisional IRA (having been on ceasefire since 1997) declared an end to its armed campaign and cooperated in the decommisioning of its arsenal. For most of the previous decade, during the long peace process, the demand for decommissioning had been seen as an attempt to humiliate republicans, to make the IRA 'surrender'. IRA supporters were assured that it would never happen: 'Not a Bullet, Not an Ounce' read the graffiti.

By 2005, however, the republican leadership argued that increasing political strength had opened up new opportunites for republicans. Since 1998, when the party had endorsed the Good Friday Agreement, Sinn Féin had become the majority party among nationalists in the North and had real, if limited, success in the Republic. Its leaders, having been reviled as terrorists and banned from TV airwaves until the early 1990s, were now internationally known figures, invited to the White House and Downing Street. By 2008, Martin McGuinness would be deputy first minister in a new Northern Ireland administration, in coalition with the Democratic Unionist Party. Republicans argued that the armed struggle had made all this possible and that in the long run the logic of the process would lead to a united Ireland. They could also point out that the majority of nationalists obviously endorsed this strategy.

The fact remained, however, that the war had been waged on the basis that the British would be forced to leave Ireland, not that republicans would become part of a government within the Six Counties. Under the terms of the Good Friday Agreement, republicans accepted that Northern Ireland would remain

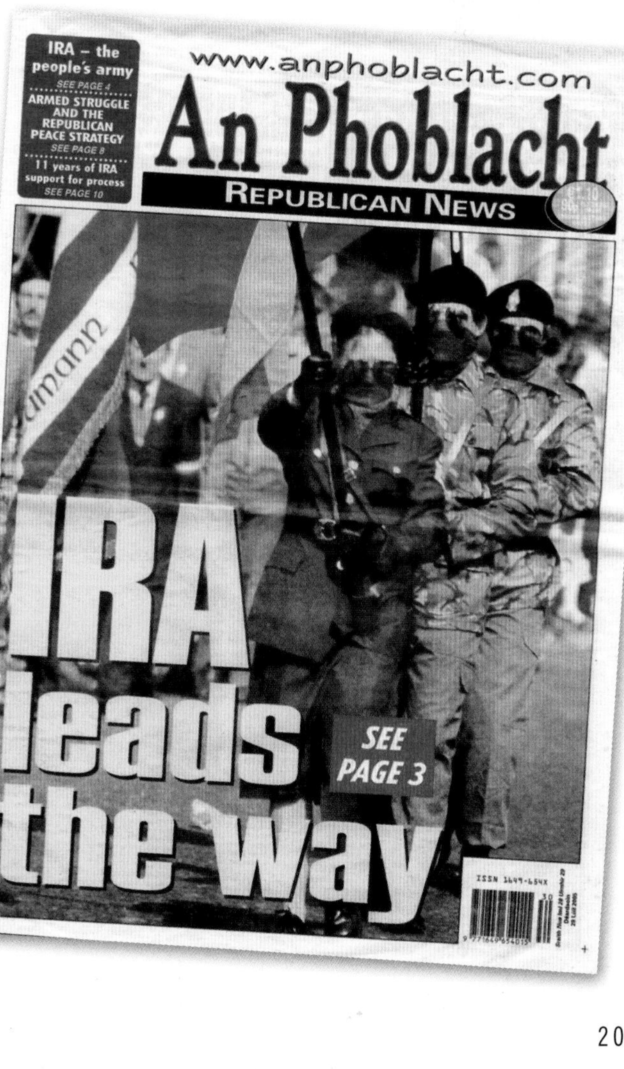
IRA – the people's army
SEE PAGE 4
ARMED STRUGGLE AND THE REPUBLICAN PEACE STRATEGY
SEE PAGE 8
11 years of IRA support for process
SEE PAGE 10

www.anphoblacht.com

An Phoblacht

REPUBLICAN NEWS

IRA leads the way

SEE PAGE 3

An Phoblacht cover, 28 July 2005
AP/RN

An Phoblacht/Republican News   Thursday 28 July 2005   LEATHANACH 3

Irish Republican Army orders an end to armed campaign

The following historic statement was issued by Óglaigh na hÉireann, the Irish Republican Army, today, Thursday 28 July 2005.

"The leadership of Óglaigh na hÉireann has formally ordered an end to the armed campaign. This will take effect from 4pm this afternoon.

All IRA units have been ordered to dump arms.

All Volunteers have been instructed to assist the development of purely political and democratic programmes through exclusively peaceful means. Volunteers must not engage in any other activities whatsoever.

The IRA is fully committed to the goals of Irish unity and independence and to building the Republic outlined in the 1916 Proclamation

The IRA leadership has also authorised our representative to engage with the IICD to complete the process to verifiably put its arms beyond use in a way which will further enhance public confidence and to conclude this as quickly as possible. We have invited two independent witnesses, from the Protestant and Catholic churches, to testify to this.

The Army Council took these decisions following an unprecedented internal discussion and consultation process with IRA units and Volunteers.

We appreciate the honest and forthright way in which the consultation process was carried out and the depth and content of the submissions. We are proud of the comradely way in which this truly historic discussion was conducted.

The outcome of our consultations show very strong support among IRA Volunteers for the Sinn Féin peace strategy. There is also widespread concern about the failure of the two governments and the unionists to fully engage in the peace process. This has created real difficulties. The overwhelming majority of people in Ireland fully support this process. They and friends of Irish unity throughout the world want to see the full implementation of the Good Friday Agreement.

Notwithstanding these difficulties our decisions have been taken to advance our republican and democratic objectives, including our goal of a united Ireland. We believe there is now an alternative way to achieve this and to end British rule in our country.

It is the responsibility of all Volunteers to show leadership, determination and courage. We are very mindful of the sacrifices of our patriot dead, those who went to jail, Volunteers, their families and the wider republican base. We reiterate our view that the armed struggle was entirely legitimate.

We are conscious that many people suffered in the conflict. There is a compelling imperative on all sides to build a just and lasting peace.

The issue of the defence of nationalist and republican communities has been raised with us. There is a responsibility on society to ensure that there is no re-occurrence of the pogroms of 1969 and the early 1970s. There is also a universal responsibility to tackle sectarianism in all its forms.

The IRA is fully committed to the goals of Irish unity and independence and to building the Republic outlined in the 1916 Proclamation.

We call for maximum unity and effort by Irish republicans everywhere. We are confident that by working together Irish republicans can achieve our objectives. Every

Our decisions have been taken to advance our republican and democratic objectives, including our goal of a united Ireland. We believe there is now an alternative way to achieve this and to end British rule in our country

Volunteer is aware of the import of the decisions we have taken and all Óglaigh are compelled to fully comply with these orders.

There is now an unprecedented opportunity to utilise the considerable energy and goodwill which there is for the peace process. This comprehensive series of unparalleled initiatives is our contribution to this and to the continued endeavours to bring about independence and unity for the people of Ireland."

HISTORIC STATEMENT READ BY SÉANNA WALSH

THE historic IRA statement was visually recorded and read by Séanna Walsh at the request of the leadership of Óglaigh na hÉireann.

Séanna served over 21 years as a Republican Prisoner of War in both the Cages and the H-Blocks of Long Kesh. He was among the first republicans 'on the blanket' after his arrest in 1976, the year the British Labour Government began its policy of attempting to criminalise IRA prisoners. Séanna was a friend and cellmate of Bobby Sands, the Officer Commanding in the H-Blocks and the first of the Hunger Strikers who died in 1981.

Since his release Séanna Breatnach has played a key role working with Sinn Féin's negotiating team and advancing the republican peace strategy.

'IRA leads the way' July 2005
AP/RN

part of the United Kingdom while a majority there desired this, accepting what was once denounced as the 'Unionist Veto'.

During the course of the conflict, the Provisional IRA was responsible for over 1,770 deaths, (over 600 of them civilian) lost over 300 of its own members and saw thousands of them jailed. Neither the suffering it inflicted, nor that which its members endured, was ever predicated on the basis that it would lead to a power-sharing settlement within Northern Ireland.

THE END?

The Provisional IRA, for most people 'the IRA' of the last 30 years, decommisioned and declared its war over in 2005. In 2010, the Irish National Liberation Army and part of the Official IRA also destroyed arms and equipment. But there remain at least three organisations, the Continuity IRA, the Real IRA and Óglaigh na hÉireann which are determined to carry on armed actions. The Continuity IRA came into being after 1986 and adhered to the politics of Republican Sinn Féin. The Real IRA emerged in the mid-1990s because of disputes over the republican leadership's support for the two ceasefires. By 1997, it had begun to carry out bombings, without claiming responsibility for them, and in August 1998, a Real IRA car bomb killed 29 people in Omagh, Co. Tyrone. The group called a ceasefire and in the aftermath of Omagh, it seemed impossible that there would be the appetite for a return to armed struggle. But by 2001, the Real IRA was carrying out attacks in Ireland and Britain.

Both the Real and Continuity IRAs suffered splits during the first decade of the new century and both were involved in killing some of their own members suspected of being informers. The Real IRA would also claim to have killed the informer Denis Donaldson, shot dead in Donegal in 2006.

Mainstream republicans sometimes ridiculed the lack of success of these groups in targeting security forces and alleged that they were directed by intelligence agents. In 2009, however, both organisations succeeded in killing two British soldiers and a policeman in separate incidents. The 'dissidents' as they were labelled, were now denounced as 'criminals', 'micro-groups' and even 'traitors to Ireland' by the Sinn Féin leadership. But as far as those still engaged in armed activity were concerned, the logic that drove the Provisional IRA's campaign remained: as long as Britain stayed in Ireland, they had a right to take up arms. The fact that a much more intense (and widely supported) armed struggle over 30 years failed to remove the British did not seem to deter them, nor did their evident lack of popular support. In 2010, there were still those willing to take up what they saw as the IRA's historic mission.

SELECT BIBLIOGRAPHY

Abbot, R., *Police Casualties in Ireland* 1919-1922 [Cork, 2000]

Adams, G., *Before the Dawn: An Autobiography* [London, 1996]
Cage Eleven [Dingle, 1990]
The Politics of Irish Freedom [Dingle, 1986]

Alonso, R., *The IRA and Armed Struggle* [London, 2006]

Ambrose, J., *Seán Treacy and the Tan War* [Cork, 2007]
Dan Breen and the IRA [Cork, 2006]

Anderson, B., Joe Cahill: *A Life in the IRA* [Dublin, 2002]

Andrews, C.S., *Dublin Made Me: an Autobiography* [Dublin, 2001]
Man of No Property [Dublin, 2001]

Anon., *Fianna Fail and the IRA* [Dublin, N/D]
Fianna Fail-The IRA Connection [Dublin, N/D]

Augusteijn, J., (Ed) *The Irish Revolution, 1913-1923* [London, 2002]
From Public Defiance to Guerrilla Warfare: the Experience of Ordinary Volunteers in the Irish War of Independence, 1916-1921 [Dublin, 1996]

Barrett, J.J., *In The Name of The Game* [Bray 1997]

Barry, T., *Guerilla Days in Ireland* [Dublin, 1981]

Bartelett, T., & Jeffrey, K., *A Military History of Ireland* [Cambridge, 1996]

Barton, B., & Foy, M., *The Easter Rising* [Sutton, 2000]

Bean, K., *The New Politics of Sinn Fein* [Liverpool, 2007]

Bean, K, & Hayes, M., *Republican Voices* [Monaghan, 2001].

Bell, J.B., *The Secret Army: The IRA 1916-1979* [Dublin, 1989].
The Gun in Politics: an Analysis of Irish Political Conflict, 1916-86 [New Brunswick, 1991]
The Irish Troubles: A Generation of Violence, 1967-92 [Dublin, 1993]
IRA Tactics and Targets [Dublin, 1990]

Beresford, P., *Ten Men Dead* [London, 1987]

Bernard, M., *Daughter of Derry: the Story of Bridget Sheils Makowski* [London, 1989]

Bishop, P., & Mallie, E., *The Provisional IRA* [London, 1988]

Borgonovo, J., Spies, *Informers, and the 'Anti-Sinn Féin Society': the Intelligence War in Cork, 1920-21* [Dublin, 2006]

Boyne, S., *Gunrunners: the Covert Arms Trail to Ireland* [Dublin, 2006]

Bourke, R., *Peace in Ireland: the War of Ideas* [London, 2003]

Breen, D., *My Fight For Irish Freedom* [Dublin, 1989]

Brennan, M., *The War in Clare 1911-1921* [Dublin, 1980]

Bryson, A., [ed] *The Insider: The Belfast Prison Diaries of Eamonn Boyce 1956-62* [Dublin, 2007]

Campbell, B., McKeown, L., & O'Hagan, F., *Nor Meekly Serve My Time: The H-Block Struggle 1976-1981* [Belfast, 1994]

Campbell, F., *Land and Revolution: Nationalist Politics in the West of Ireland 1891-1921* [Oxford, 2005]

Carey, T., *Mountjoy: The Story of a Prison* [Cork, 2000]

Carroll, A., *Seán Moylan: Rebel Leader* [Cork, 2010]

Clarke, K., *Revolutionary Woman: Kathleen Clarke 1878-1972* [Dublin, 1991]

Clarke, L., & Johnston, K., *Martin McGuinness: From Guns to Government* [Edinburgh, 2002]

Clarke, L., *Broadening the Battlefield: the H-Blocks and the Rise of Sinn Fein* [Dublin, 1987]

Clann na h-Eireann., *The Battle of Belfast* [London, 1972].
Spies in Ireland [London, 1974].

Coleman, M., *County Longford and the Irish Revolution* [Dublin, 2003]

Collins, E., *Killing Rage* [London, 1997]

Collins, M., *The Path To Freedom* [Cork, 1996]

Coogan, T.P., *The IRA* [London, 1995]
The Troubles: Ireland's Ordeal and the Search for Peace [London, 1995]
De Valera: Long Fellow, Long Shadow [Dublin, 1993]
Michael Collins: A Biography [London, 1990]

Costello, F., *The Irish Revolution and Its Aftermath* [Dublin, 2002]

Cronin, M., *The Blueshirts and Irish Politics* [Dublin, 1997]

Cronin, M., & Regan, J.M., *Ireland: The Politics of Independence, 1922-49* [London, 2000]

Cronin, S., *Frank Ryan: the Search for the Republic* [Dublin, 1980]
Irish Nationalism: A History of its Roots and Ideology [Dublin, 1980].
The McGarrity Papers [Tralee, 1972]
A Man of the People: Jemmy Hope [Dublin, 1964].

Daly, T., *The Ras: Ireland's Unique Bike Race, 1953-2003* [Dublin, 2003].

Davenport, M & Sharrock, D., *Gerry Adams: Man of War, Man of Peace* [London, 1997].

De Baroid, C., *Ballymurphy and the Irish War* [London, 1990].

Deasy, L., *Towards Ireland Free* [Cork, 1992]

Devine, F., Lane, F., & Puirséil, N., *Essays in Irish Labour History* [Dublin, 2008]

Devine, F., & O'Riordan, M., *James Connolly, Liberty Hall & The 1916 Rising* [Dublin, 2006]

Dillon, M & Lehane, D., *Political Murder in Northern Ireland* [Middlesex, 1973].

Dillon, M., *The Dirty War* [London, 1990]

Dolan, A., *Commemorating the Irish Civil War* [Cambridge, 2003]

Donnelly, D., *Prisoner 1082: Escape from Crumlin Road* [Cork, 2010]

Dooley, T., *'The Land for the People': the Land Question in Independent Ireland* [Dublin, 2004].

Douglas, R.M., *Architects of the Resurrection: Ailtirí na hAiséirghe and the fascist 'new order' in Ireland* [Manchester, 2009]

Doyle, T., *The Summer Campaign in Kerry* [Cork, 2010]
The Civil War in Kerry [Cork, 2008]

Dunne, D., *Out of the Maze* [Dublin, 1988]

Dunne, D., & Kerrigan, G., *Round Up the Usual Suspects* [Dublin, 1984]

Durney, J., *The Volunteer: Uniforms, Weapons and History of the IRA* [Kildare, 2004]

Dwyer, T.R., *The Squad and the Intelligence Operations of Michael Collins* [Cork, 2005]
Tans, Terror and Troubles: Kerry's real Fighting Story [Dublin, 2001]

English, R., *Armed Struggle-A History of the IRA* [London, 2003].
Ernie O'Malley: IRA Intellectual [Oxford, 1998]
Radicals and the Republic: Socialist Republicanism in the Irish Free State, 1925-1937 [Oxford, 1994]

English, R., & O'Malley, C., *Prisoners: the Civil War Letters of Ernie O'Malley* [Dublin, 1991].

Fallon, C.H., *Soul Of Fire: A Life of Mary McSwiney* [Cork, 1986]

Farrell, M., [Ed] *Twenty Years On* [Dingle, 1998]
Northern Ireland. The Orange State [London, 1980]

Farry, M., *The Aftermath of Revolution, Sligo, 1921-23* [Dublin, 2000]

Feeney, B., *The Insider: Gerry Bradley's Life in the IRA* [Dublin, 2009]
Sinn Féin: a Hundred Turbulent Years [Dublin, 2002]

Fisk, R., *In Time of War: Ireland, Ulster and the Price of Neutrality 1939-45* [London, 1983]

Fitzpatrick, D., *Harry Boland's Irish Revolution* [Cork, 2003]
The Two Irelands, 1912-1939 [Oxford, 1998]
Politics and Irish Life: Provincial Experience of War and Revolution [Cork, 1998]

Flynn, B., *Soldiers of Folly: the IRA Border Campaign 1956-62* [Cork, 2009]

Flynn, S., & Yeates, P., *Smack! The Criminal Drugs Racket in Ireland* [Dublin, 1985]

Foley, C., *Legion of the Rearguard: the IRA and the Modern Irish State* [London, 1992]

Foley, G., *Ireland in Rebellion* [New York, 1971]
Problems of the Irish Revolution-can the IRA meet the challenge? [New York, 1972].

Foy, M., *Michael Collins and the Intelligence War: the Struggle Between the British and the IRA 1919-21* [Sutton, 2006]

Gallagher, R., *1922: Violence And Nationalist Politics In Derry City, 1920–1923* [Dublin, 2003]

Garvin, T., *The Birth of Irish Democracy* [Dublin, 1996]

Geraghty, T., *The Irish War* [London, 1998]

Gilmore, G., *Labour and the Republican Movement* [Dublin, 1966]
The Irish Republican Congress [Cork. 1974]

Greaves, C, D., *Liam Mellows and the Irish Revolution* [London, 1971]
The Life and Times of James Connolly [London, 1961].

Hanley, B., & Millar, S., *The Lost Revolution: the Story of the Official IRA and the Workers' Party* [Dublin, 2009]

Hanley, B., *A Guide to Irish Military Heritage* [Dublin, 2004]
The IRA, 1926-1936 [Dublin, 2002]

Harnden, T., *Bandit Country: the IRA and South Armagh* [London, 1999]

Hart, P., *Mick: The Real Michael Collins* [London, 2005]
The IRA At War 1916-1923 [Oxford, 2003]
The IRA and its Enemies: Violence and Community in Co. Cork, 1916-1923 [Oxford, 1998]

Hartnett, M., *Victory and Woe* [Dublin, 2002]

Hay, M., *Bulmer Hobson and the Nationalist Movement in Twentieth Century Ireland* (Manchester, 2009)

Hayes, S., 'My Strange Story' in *The Bell* 17, 4, [1951]

Hennessey, T., *Northern Ireland: the Origins of the Troubles* [Dublin, 2005]
The Evolution of the Troubles, 1970-72 [Dublin, 2007]

Hepburn, A.C., *Catholic Belfast and Nationalist Ireland* [Oxford, 2008]

Holland, J., *Hope against History: the Ulster Conflict* [London, 1999]
Phoenix: Policing the Shadows [London, 1997]
The American Connection: US Guns, Money and Influence in Northern Ireland [Dublin, 1989]
Too Long a Sacrifice: Life and Death in Northern Ireland since 1969 [New York, 1981]

Holland, J. & McDonald, H., *INLA: Deadly Divisions* [Dublin, 1994]

Hopkinson, M., *The Irish War of Independence* [Dublin, 2002]
Green Against Green: The Irish Civil War [Dublin, 1988]

Johnston, R., *A Century of Endeavour: A Biographical and Autobiographical view of the Twentieth Century in Ireland* [Dublin, 2006]

Jordan, H., *Milestones in Murder: Defining Moments in Ulster's Terror War* [Edinburgh, 2001]

Joy, S., *The IRA in Kerry 1916-1921* [Dublin, 2006]

Kautt, W.H., *Ambushes and Armour: the Irish Rebellion 1919-1921* [Dublin, 2010]

Kelley, K., *The Longest War: Northern Ireland and the IRA* [Dingle, 1982]

Kissane, B., *The Politics of the Irish Civil War* [Oxford, 2005]

Kleinrichert, D., *Republican Internment and the Prison Ship Argenta, 1922* [Dublin, 2001]

Kostick, C., *Revolution in Ireland: Popular Militancy 1917 to 1923* [Cork, 2009]

Lane, J., *Miscellaneous Notes on Republicanism and Socialism in Cork City, 1954-69* [Cork, 2005]

Larkin, P., *A Very British Jihad: Collusion, Conspiracy and Cover Up in Northern Ireland* [Belfast, 2004]

Lawlor, D., *Na Fianna Éireann and the Irish Revolution 1909-1923* [Offaly, 2009]

Lawlor, P., *The Burnings 1920* [Cork, 2009]

Laffan, M., *The Resurrection of Ireland: Sinn Féin, 1916-23* [Oxford, 1999]

Long, D. *Awakening the Spirit of Freedom* [Limerick, 2006]

Lundy, P, & McGovern, M., *Ardoyne: the Untold Truth* [Belfast, 2002]

Lynch, R., *The Northern IRA and the Early Years of Partition 1920-1922* [Dublin, 2006]

Lyder, A., *Pushers Out – The Inside Story of Dublin's Anti-Drugs Movement* [Victoria, 2005]

Macardle, D., *The Irish Republic* [Cork, 1999]
Tragedies of Kerry 1922-23 [Dublin, 1998]

Magee, P., *Gangsters or Guerrillas?* [Belfast, 2001]

Maguire, J., *IRA Internments and the Irish Government: Subversives and the State, 1939-1962* [Dublin, 2008]

Mahon, T & Gilhooly, J.J., *Decoding the IRA* [Cork, 2008]

Malone, S., *Alias Seán Forde* [Dublin, 2001]

Manning, M., *The Blueshirts* [Dublin, 2006]

Matthews, A., *Renegades: Irish Republican Women 1900-1922* [Cork, 2010]

Mac Donncha, M., *Sinn Féin: A Century of Struggle* [Dublin, 2005]

MacEoin, U., *The IRA in the Twilight Years 1923-1948* [Dublin, 1997]
Harry: the Story of Harry White [Dublin, 1984]
Survivors [Dublin, 1980]

MacStiofáin, S., *Memoirs of a Revolutionary* [Edinburgh, 1975]

McCann, E., *Bloody Sunday in Derry: What Really Happened* [Tralee, 1992]
War and an Irish Town [London, 1979]

McCarthy, C., *Cumann na mBan and the Irish Revolution* [Cork, 2006]

McCarthy, K., *Republican Cobh and the East Cork Volunteers* [Dublin, 2008]

McConville, S., *Irish Political Prisoners 1848-1922* [London, 2002]

McCoole, S., *No Ordinary Women: Activists in the Revolutionary Years, 1900-1923* [Dublin, 2003]
Guns and Chiffon: Women Revolutionaries and Kilmainham Gaol [Dublin, 1997]

McDemott. E., *Clann na Poblachta* [Cork, 1998]

McDermott, J., *Northern Divisions: The Old IRA and the Belfast Pogroms 1920-22* [Belfast, 2001]

McElrath, K., *Unsafe Haven: The United States, the IRA and Political Prisoners* [London, 2000]

McGladdery, G., *The Provisional IRA in England: the Bombing Campaign 1973-1997* [Dublin, 2006]

McNally, J., *Morally Good-Politically Bad* [Belfast, 1989]

McGarry, F., & McConnel, J., (Eds) *The Black Hand of Republicanism* [Dublin, 2009]

McGarry, F., *The Rising: Ireland-Easter 1916* [Oxford, 2010]
Eoin O'Duffy: A Self-Made Hero [Oxford, 2005]
[Ed], *Republicanism in Modern Ireland* [Dublin, 2003]
Frank Ryan [Dundalk, 2002]
Irish Politics and the Spanish Civil War [Cork, 1999]

McGee, O., *The IRB: From the Land League to Sinn Féin* [Dublin, 2005]

McGuffin, *Internment!* [Tralee, 1973]

McGuire, M., *To Take Arms: A Year in the Provisional IRA* [London, 1973]

McIntyre, A., *Good Friday: the Death of Irish Republicanism* [New York, 2008]
'Modern Irish Republicanism and the Belfast Agreement: Chickens Coming home to Roost, or Turkeys Celebrating Christmas?' in Wilford, R., [Ed], *Aspects of the Belfast Agreement* [Oxford, 2001]

McKeown, L., *Out Of Time: Irish Republican Prisoners, Long Kesh 1972-2000* [Belfast, 2001]

McKittrick, D., Kelters, S., Feeney, B., & Thornton, C., *Lost Lives: the Stories of the Men, Women and Children who died as a result of the Northern Ireland Troubles* [Edinburgh, 1999]

McMahon, P., *British Spies & Irish Rebels: British Intelligence and Ireland 1916-1945* [Suffolk, 2008]

McVeigh, J., *Executed: Tom Williams and The IRA* [Belfast, 1999]

Meehan, M., *Finely Tempered Steel: Seán McCaughey and the IRA* [Belfast, 2006]

Milotte, M., *Communism in Modern Ireland: the Pursuit of the Workers' Republic since 1916* [Dublin, 1984]

Mitchell, A., *Revolutionary Government in Ireland, Dáil Éireann 1919-1922* [Dublin, 1995]

Moloney, E., *Voices From The Grave* [London, 2010]
A Secret History of the IRA [London, 2002]

Moroney, M., *George Plant and The Rule of Law* [Tipperary, 1989]

Morrison, D., *Then The Walls Came Down: A Prison Journal* [Cork, 1999]

Moylan, S., *In His Own Words* [Cork, 2004]

Mulcahy, R., *My Father: The General* [Dublin, 2009]

Mulholland, M., *The Longest War: Northern Ireland's Troubled History* [Oxford, 2002]

Munck, R., & Rolston, B., *Belfast in the Thirties. An Oral History* [Belfast, 1987]

Murphy, B.P., *Patrick Pearse and The Lost Republican Ideal* [Dublin, 1991]

Murphy, B. & Kelters, S., *Eyewitness: Four Decades of Northern Life* [Dublin, 2003]

Murphy, J., *When Youth Was Mine* [Dublin, 1998]

Murray, R., *The SAS in Ireland* [Dublin, 1990]

National Commemoration Committee., *Tirghra* [Dublin, 2002]

National Graves Association., *Belfast Graves* [Dublin, 1994]
The Last Post [Dublin, 1976]

Ó Brádaigh, R., *'Dílseacht'-The Story of Tom Maguire and the Second Dáil* [Dublin, 1997]

O'Brien, B., *The Long War: the IRA and Sinn Féin* [Dublin, 1999]
A Pocket History of the IRA [Dublin, 1997]

O'Brien, J., *The Arms Trial* [Dublin, 2000]

Ó Broin, E., *Sinn Fein and Left Republicanism* [London, 2009]

O'Callaghan, J., *Revolutionary Limerick: The Republican Campaign for Independence 1913-1921* [Dublin, 2010]

O'Callaghan, S., *The Easter Lily: the Story of the IRA* [London, 1956]

Ó Conchubhair, B., (Ed) *Cork's Fighting Story* [Cork, 2009]
Dublin's Fighting Story [Cork, 2009]
Kerry's Fighting Story [Cork, 2009]
Limerick's Fighting Story [Cork, 2009]

O'Connor, E., *Reds and the Green: Ireland, Russia and the Communist Internationals, 1919-43* [Dublin, 2004]
A Labour History of Ireland, 1824-1960 [Dublin, 1992]

O'Connor, F., *In Search of a State: Catholics in Northern Ireland* [Belfast, 1993]

O'Connor, P., *A Soldier of Liberty* [Dublin, 1996]

O'Donnell, P., *There Will Be Another Day* [Dublin, 1963]
The Gates Flew Open [London, 1932]

O'Donnell, R., (Ed) *The Impact of 1916: Among the Nations* [Dublin, 2008]
From Vinegar Hill to Edentubber [Wexford, 2007]

Ó Drisceoil, D., *Peadar O'Donnell* [Cork, 2001]
Censorship in Ireland 1939-45 [Cork, 1996]

Ó Dochartaigh, N., *From Civil Rights to Armalites: Derry and the Birth of the Northern Ireland Troubles* [Basingstoke, 2005]

O'Doherty, E., *The IRA at War 1916 to the present: an Illustrated History* [Cork, 1985]

O'Doherty, S., *The Volunteer* [London, 1993]

O'Donoghue, F., *No Other Law: The Story of Liam Lynch* [Dublin, 1986]

Ó Duibhir, L., *The Donegal Awakening* [Cork, 2009]

Ó h-Again, D., *Liam McMillen: Separatist, Socialist, Republican* [Belfast, 1976]

O'Halpin, E., *Spying on Ireland: British Intelligence and Irish Neutrality During the Second World War* [Oxford, 2008]
Defending Ireland. The Irish State and its Enemies Since 1922 [Oxford, 1999]

O'Hearn, D., *Bobby Sands: Nothing But An Unfinished Song* [London, 2006]

Ó hEithir, B., *The Begrudger's Guide to Irish Politics* [Dublin, 1986]

Óglaigh na h-Éireann., *Constitution and Governmental Programme* [Dublin, 1933]

Official IRA., *In the '70s: the IRA Speaks* [Dublin, 1970]

Ó Gadhra, N., *The Civil War in Connaught, 1922-1923* [Cork, 1999]

O'Kelly, J.J., *Stepping Stones* [Dublin, 1939]

O'Leary, B., 'Mission Accomplished?' Looking Back at the IRA' *in Field Day Review 1* [2005]

O'Malley, C.K.H., & Dolan, A., *'No Surrender Here!' The Civil War Papers of Ernie O'Malley 1922-1924* [Dublin, 2007]

O'Malley, E., *Rising Out: Seán Connolly of Longford* [Dublin, 2007]
Raids and Rallies [Tralee, 2001]
On Another Man's Wound [Tralee, 1979]
The Singing Flame [Tralee, 1978]

O'Malley, K., *Ireland, India and Empire* [Manchester, 2008]

O'Mahony, S., *Frongoch: University of Revolution* [Dublin, 1995]

O'Neill, J., *A Blood Dark Track* [London, 2001]

O'Rawe, R., *Blanketmen* [Dublin, 2005]

O'Riordan, M., *Connolly Column: the Irishmen Who Fought for the Spanish Republic 1936-1939* [Dublin, 1979]

Ó Ruairc, P, Óg. *The Battle for Limerick City* [Cork, 2010]
Blood on the Banner: the Republican Struggle in Co. Clare [Cork, 2009]

O'Shea, B., *Irish Volunteer Soldier 1913-1923* [London, 2003]

O'Sullivan, N., *Every Dark Hour: A History of Kilmainham Jail* [Dublin, 2008]

Openheimer, A. R., *IRA Bombs and Bullets* [Dublin, 2008]

Patterson, H., *The Politics of Illusion: a Political History of the IRA* [London, 1997]

Prince, S., *Northern Ireland's 68: Civil Rights, Global Revolt and the Origins of the Troubles* [Dublin, 2007]

Provisional IRA., *Freedom Struggle* [Dublin, 1973]

Puirseil, N., *The Irish Labour Party, 1922-1973* [Dublin, 2007]

Purdie, B., *Politics in the Streets-the Origins of the Civil Rights Movement in Northern Ireland* [Dublin, 1990].

Quinn, R., *A Rebel Voice: A History of Belfast Republicanism, 1925-1972* [Belfast, 1999]

Rafter, K., *Sinn Féin, 1905-2005: In the Shadow of Gunmen* [Dublin, 2005]

Regan, J.M., *The Irish Counter Revolution, 1921-1936* [Dublin, 1999]

Republican Clubs., *Pogrom!* [Belfast, 1975]
Ardboe Martyrs [Tyrone, 1972]

Robbins, F., *Under The Starry Plough* [Dublin, 1977]

Ryan, A., *Comrades: Inside the War of Independence* [Dublin, 2007]
Witnesses: Inside the Easter Rising [Dublin, 2005]

Ryan, M., *Tom Barry: IRA Freedom Fighter* [Cork, 2003]
The Real Chief: Liam Lynch [Dublin, 1986]
The Tom Barry Story [Cork, 1982]

Sands, B., *One Day in My Life* [Cork, 1982]
The Diary of Bobby Sands [Dublin, 1981]

Seamus Costello Commemoration Committee., *Seamus Costello: Irish Republican Socialist* [Dublin, 1978]

Sharrock, D., & Devenport, M., *Man of War, Man of Peace? The Unauthorized Biography of Gerry Adams* [London, 1997]

Sinn Féin, *The Good Old IRA* [Dublin, 1985]

Smith, M.L.R., *Fighting for Ireland? The Military Strategy of the Irish Republican Movement* [London, 1997]

Staunton, E., *The Nationalists of Northern Ireland, 1918-1973* [Dublin, 2001]

Stevenson, J., *'We Wrecked the Place' Contemplating an End to the Northern Irish Troubles* [New York, 1996]

Sunday Times Insight Team., *Ulster: A Penguin Special* [London, 1972]

Swan, S., *Official Irish Republicanism, 1962-1972* [Lulu, 2006]

Sweetman, R., *On Our Knees-Ireland 1972* [Dublin, 1972]

Taylor, P., *Provos: The IRA and Sinn Fein* [London, 1997]

Thomson, T.K., *Irish Women and Street Politics* [Dublin, 2010]

Townshend, C., *Easter 1916: The Irish Rebellion* {London, 2006]
Political Violence in Ireland [Oxford, 1983]

Treacy, M., *The IRA 1956-69: Rethinking the Republic* [Manchester, 2010]

Valiulis, M.G., *Portrait of a Revolutionary: General Richard Mulcahy and the Founding of the Irish Free State* [Dublin, 1992]

Walsh, P., *Irish Republicanism and Socialism: The Politics of the Irish Republican Movement 1905-1994* [Belfast, 1994]

Whalen, B., *Inside the IRA* [Philadelphia, 1975]

Wilson, A.J., *Irish America and the Ulster Conflict, 1968-1994* [Belfast, 1995]

Workers' Party., *Cathal Goulding, Thinker, Socialist, Republican, Revolutionary, 1923-1998* [Dublin, 1999]

Ward, M., *Hannah Sheehy Skeffington: A Life* [Cork, 1997]
Unmanageable Revolutionaries: Women and Irish Nationalism [London, 1995]

White, R.W., *Ruairí Ó Brádaigh: the Life and Times of an Irish Revolutionary* [Indiana, 2006]
Provisional Irish Republicans: an Oral and Interpretative History [Connecticut, 1993]

Yeates, P., *Lockout: Dublin 1913* [Dublin, 2000]

INDEX